The Study Skills Handbook

Study Skills

Titles in this series by Stella Cottrell
Critical Thinking Skills (3rd edn)
Dissertations and Project Reports
The Exam Skills Handbook (2nd edn)
Mindfulness for Students
The Macmillan Student Planner
Skills for Success: Personal Development and
   Employability (3rd edn)
Study Skills Connected
The Study Skills Handbook (5th edn)
Teaching Study Skills and Supporting Learning
You2Uni: Decide. Prepare. Apply

50 Ways to Boost Your Employability
50 Ways to Boost Your Grades
50 Ways to Excel at Writing
50 Ways to Manage Stress
50 Ways to Manage Time Effectively
50 Ways to Succeed as an International Student

Academic Success
Academic Writing Skills for International Students
The Business Student's Phrase Book
Cite Them Right (10th edn)
Critical Thinking and Persuasive Writing for Postgraduates
The Employability Journal
Essentials of Essay Writing
Get Sorted
Great Ways to Learn Anatomy and Physiology (2nd edn)
How to Begin Studying English Literature (4th edn)
How to Use Your Reading in Your Essays (3rd edn)
How to Write Better Essays (4th edn)
How to Write Your Undergraduate Dissertation (2nd edn)
Improve Your Grammar (2nd edn)
The Mature Student's Handbook
The Personal Tutor's Handbook
Presentation Skills for Students (3rd edn)
The Principles of Writing in Psychology
Professional Writing (3rd edn)
Stand Out from the Crowd
The Student Phrase Book
The Student's Guide to Writing (3rd edn)
Study Skills for International Postgraduates
Studying in English
Studying History (4th edn)
Studying Law (4th edn)
Studying Physics
Success in Academic Writing (2nd edn)
Smart Thinking
The Graduate Career Guidebook

The Undergraduate Research Handbook (2nd edn)
The Work-Based Learning Student Handbook (2nd edn)
Writing for Engineers (4th edn)
Writing History Essays (2nd edn)
Writing for Law
Writing for Nursing and Midwifery Students (3rd edn)
Write it Right (2nd edn)
Writing for Science Students
Writing Skills for Education Students

Pocket Study Skills

14 Days to Exam Success (2nd edn)
Analyzing a Case Study
Blogs, Wikis, Podcasts and More
Brilliant Writing Tips for Students
Completing Your PhD
Doing Research (2nd edn)
Getting Critical (2nd edn)
Managing Stress
Planning Your Dissertation (2nd edn)
Planning Your Essay (2nd edn)
Planning Your PhD
Posters and Presentations
Reading and Making Notes (2nd edn)
Referencing and Understanding Plagiarism (2nd edn)
Reflective Writing
Report Writing (2nd edn)
Science Study Skills
Studying with Dyslexia (2nd edn)
Success in Groupwork
Successful Applications
Time Management
Where's Your Argument?
Writing for University (2nd edn)

Research Skills

Authoring a PhD
The Foundations of Research (3rd edn)
Getting to Grips with Doctoral Research
Getting Published
The Good Supervisor (2nd edn)
The Lean PhD
PhD by Published Work
The PhD Viva
Planning Your Postgraduate Research
The PhD Writing Handbook
The Postgraduate Research Handbook (2nd edn)
The Professional Doctorate
Structuring Your Research Thesis

For a complete listing of all our titles in this area please visit **www.macmillanihe.com/study-skills**

The Study Skills Handbook

Fifth Edition

Stella Cottrell

 macmillan
international
HIGHER EDUCATION

 RED GLOBE
PRESS

This edition published 2019 by
RED GLOBE PRESS

Previous editions published under the imprint PALGRAVE

Red Globe Press in the UK is an imprint of Springer Nature Limited,
registered in England, company number 785998, of 4 Crinan Street,
London, N1 9XW.

Red Globe Press® is a registered trademark in the United States,
the United Kingdom, Europe and other countries.

ISBN 978–1–137–61087–4 paperback

This book is printed on paper suitable for recycling and made from fully
managed and sustained forest sources. Logging, pulping and manufacturing
processes are expected to conform to the environmental regulations of the
country of origin.

A catalogue record for this book is available from the British Library.

A catalog record for this book is available from the Library of Congress.

Contents

Acknowledgements

I would like to thank all who provided encouragement, support and comments for earlier editions of the book. That includes academics, professional support staff and students from British and international universities and colleges for their constructive feedback on the first four editions; wherever possible their suggestions have been incorporated into later editions. I owe particular thanks to Kate Williams at Oxford Brookes; Lynn Chiswick, Robert Simpson, Pam Dixon, David Gosling and lecturers across the University of East London (UEL) who used the first iterations of *The Study Skills Handbook*; Mary Drury and Karry Omer; Andy Lloyd, Patricia Owens, Wendy Trevor, Stella Butler and Julia Braham at the University of Leeds; the support tutors who piloted material with dyslexic students at UEL and elsewhere; staff at the British Council in Tashkent; the University of Almaty in Kazakhstan; the University of Liverpool; the Institute of Technology Tallaght; Durham University; and Queens University Belfast. I am immensely grateful to all for their feedback and suggestions.

Thanks also to the many reviewers and readers from around the world who have provided comments and feedback on what they have enjoyed about the book, how they used the material, and what else they would like to see developed. I hope I do justice to their inspiring thoughts.

For the production of this fifth edition, I would like to thank:

Helen Caunce, Georgia Park, Rosie Maher, Suzannah Burywood and other staff at Red Globe Press for their continued support, enthusiasm and belief in the book.

My partner, who as always kept everything going whilst I scribbled and typed away, not only feeding me at regular intervals but also contributing so much to thinking through the various updates and proofreading the drafts.

The hundreds of students who were open to discussing with me what they found difficult about studying and willing to elaborate new and individual ways of approaching their study – to them, and to all future students who may struggle for even a day, this book is dedicated.

Foreword

Welcome to this fifth edition of *The Study Skills Handbook*. So much has changed in the world of study skills since I wrote the first edition. Back then, there were hardly any study skills books at all. Many assumed that if someone hadn't learnt how to study well by the time they entered Higher Education, they never would.

I have always been interested in what promotes individual success, and what prevents any and every student from achieving at the highest level, with maximum satisfaction and minimum anxiety. I have worked with thousands of students with varied learning histories at different kinds of institution – at Oxford University and inner-city colleges, at both modern and research-intensive universities, with pre-foundation level students through to PhD. I found that whether students were achieving brilliantly or at risk of failing, they brought experiences, attitudes and habits that drained their energy and enthusiasm. If they weren't under-achieving, they were using inefficient strategies that took up too much time or left them stressed, bored or confused.

Although students worried about what seemed to be purely 'study' issues, the key to their success usually involved looking more broadly at their stories, attitudes, self-belief, ambitions and circumstances. No two students were the same so the way forward for each was personal and distinct.

Typically, it was the shifts in self-awareness, self-belief and attitude combined with greater use of study strategy that began to make a difference. I was frequently awe-struck by what students were then able to achieve, not just in raising the standard of their work, but in staying with their courses at all despite the complications and challenges of their lives.

As study skills books used to focus primarily on a narrow range of skills such as reading, writing, note-making and exams, I developed a wider range of materials with students – often just summing up what had emerged during our sessions so they could take it away with them. Over time, the themes that emerged formed the core of *The Study Skills Handbook*. That included matters not usually covered within traditional study skills – on intelligence, self-belief, memory, personal performance, barriers to success, self-sabotage, goal-setting, peer support, stress management, personalising learning, and more. This fifth edition retains these important topics which, happily, have become standard to many study skills courses and materials.

In addition, this edition considers new themes that affect today's students. Changing teaching methods and learning environments call for greater levels of active participation, individual responsibility, social learning and peer support. Universities worldwide tend to be diverse and international environments, bringing opportunities for those who can operate flexibly and sensitively across cultures. Technologies bring new ways of doing things and also add to the pressures of student life. Well-being, stress management, course completion, study satisfaction, grades and graduate employability are of concern world-wide. This edition considers all these aspects.

Finally, whatever your reasons for study, you will gain more from the experience if you find enjoyment in it. I hope that this *Study Skills Handbook* boosts your belief in your own academic potential and encourages you to enjoy your own path to success.

Stella Cottrell, 2019

Introducing *The Study Skills Handbook*

Is this book for you?

This book has been designed to help students to achieve the very best that they can, given their individual circumstances, goals and ambitions.

Whether you already excel as a student or feel you are just starting out, it is highly likely that there are approaches, strategies, techniques and ways of thinking or being that could make your study experience more fruitful, effective, efficient and enjoyable.

This *Study Skills Handbook* developed out of practical work with hundreds of staff and students over many years. It has now been used by millions of students and thousands of lecturers worldwide. Students at all levels from school-leaver to PhD have used *The Study Skills Handbook* to fine-tune their skills, understand more about their learning and build their study confidence. I hope that you, too, will find material that is of value to you.

Study skills evolve and mature through understanding, practice, reflection, trial and error, and feedback from others as you move through the different stages of your course. You may be surprised at how your thinking and language skills develop simply through continued study. However, a good study strategy can start you off on a good footing, help you cut corners and accelerate the learning process.

Quick tips or deeper learning?

A reflective, active, self-evaluating approach to learning develops deeper understanding in the long term. However, quick tips can be invaluable, too, especially in study emergencies. This *Study Skills Handbook* offers both approaches. Move flexibly between the two approaches to meet your immediate needs and improve in your academic studies for the long term.

Aims of *The Study Skills Handbook*

The key aim of *The Study Skills Handbook* is to help you to manage your own success as a student. It does this by:

★ **Promoting understanding** of how good marks and successful outcomes are possibilities for any student

★ **Clarifying expectations** of conventions, study tasks and ways of thinking typical of Higher Education

★ **Supporting you** in identifying your strengths as well as what else you can do to achieve well

★ **Developing effective strategies** – study habits, techniques and thinking that optimise learning

★ **Encouraging a personal approach** – one that works best for you

★ **Providing step-by-step guidance** in how to undertake academic tasks typical of Higher Education

★ **Using structured activities and reflections**, to engage the mind, senses, and motor memory

★ **Offering insights** on how to tackle study activities that many students find difficult

★ **Providing resources** to help you evaluate, reflect upon and manage your studies more easily.

How to use *The Study Skills Handbook*

Decide what you need

Either dip into the book as you need – or work through the chapters to build your academic confidence and abilities in depth. Use as much or little as helps you.

Each chapter focuses on a key aspect of study. In practice, these are interconnected. Developing one area of your study will also help other aspects.

Find what you need

To help you locate what you need at speed, the following are provided in addition to the Contents and Index.

★ An overview of each part (pages 7 and 169)

★ Learning outcomes at the start of each chapter

★ Individual page headers, for fast browsing

★ Visually distinct pages and cartoons, as memory triggers that help you locate and recall material more easily.

Select from the resources

Select from the wide range of reflections, self-evaluations, planners, checklists, priority-setters, organisers and activities.

Use the self-evaluations

Most chapters contain a self-evaluation. These can help you in several ways.

★ They are a useful starting point for considering what to prioritise next

★ They break major study skills into component parts, or tasks into key steps

★ They enable you to pinpoint which components or missing steps are undermining your performance so you can address these. Often, once you identify it, it is fairly straightforward to improve a particular skill

★ They enable you to monitor your progress and identify your developing strengths.

Copiable pages

Pages containing self-evaluations, checklists, planners and record sheets may be copied for personal, individual re-use. If you use such copies, keep them with your reflective journal for future reference. Templates for most of these are also available on the companion site.

The book's companion site

Visit www.studyskillshandbook.co.uk for interactive self-evaluations, study skills videos, and other useful links and resources.

This icon indicates that material such as templates of planners and checklists are available on the companion site.

Take on the challenge

You can improve your academic performance. You can do well. How much and how well depend on you and your circumstances. Good study strategies, habits and understanding of how you learn empower you as a student. Look for the enjoyment in what you do.

There are times when being a student seems tough – for everyone. Those who stick with it and work on their study strategy get through, often doing much better than they expected. Difficult material can become comprehensible if you return to it after a gap. A growing knowledge of specialised terms and underlying theories helps you to make sense of your subject, sharpen your thinking and communicate with precision. Don't let past or present study difficulties stand between you and success.

Keeping a journal

It is recommended that you maintain a log, personal blog, journal or similar record to help you think about your learning and studies and monitor your development.

 This symbol reminds you to note down your reflections in your study journal. For details, see page 99.

Where to begin?

There are many possible starting places apart from the obvious one of reading straight through. Here are a few suggestions.

➡ **Browse** through *The Study Skills Handbook* so you know roughly what is in it. Bookmark any pages you want to come back to early on. You will get a clearer idea of what you need once you start assignments.

➡ **Consider** the *Seven approaches to learning* on pages 4–5) – to understand the overall approach of *The Study Skills Handbook*.

➡ **Complete** the *What would success look like for me?* questionnaire (page 11) to help orientate yourself as a student.

➡ **Start with self-efficacy**. It underpins everything else. See Chapters 1–7 for core aspects of study success, such as time management, stress management, optimising learning and clarifying your purpose.

➡ **Prioritise**. Use the *Study skills: priorities* planner (pages 25–6) to focus your thinking.

➡ **Evaluate**. If you are unsure where to begin with a study skill, use the *Self-evaluation* questionnaire in the appropriate chapter to clarify your thinking.

Gained Advanced Level or equivalent (BTEC, Access Diploma, IB, etc.)?

You have already achieved study success. The challenge, then, can be in recognising that there is still more you can do to improve your performance. It can be hard, at times, to stay quietly confident when surrounded by many other smart people. Chapters 1, 2, 5, 6 and 7 might be especially useful for you to ensure you focus your time, attention and emotional energies well. You can also hone all your other academic skills too.

Had a study gap or lack confidence?

Work through the first few chapters. Understand as much as you can about learning and study in general, about how Higher Education works, and about what has influenced and affected your own thinking about your studies. You may also find it especially helpful to look at:

★ identifying current skills and qualities (Chapter 3)

★ understanding 'intelligence' (Chapter 4)

★ activities for getting back into reading and writing, available on the companion site at www.studyskillshandbook.co.uk.

Dyslexic students

Thousands of dyslexic students graduate successfully every year. Many aspects of this book were developed with dyslexic students over many years. That includes:

★ the contents

★ the use of visual images

★ the book's layout and colours

★ the emphasis on structure

★ the use of varied and multi-sensory approaches.

International students

Be prepared for almost any aspect of study to be different from study back home. You might find it especially helpful to read Chapter 2 on getting the most from your course, and Chapters 12–16 on academic thinking and writing. International study is challenging, so use Chapter 7 to take care of your well-being.

Pace yourself

It takes time and practice to orientate yourself to the Higher Education environment and to develop good study habits. If you have been away from study for a while or are finding study difficult, be kind to yourself.

Your first-year marks may not count towards the final grade, giving you time to practise and improve.

Choose your own route

There are many avenues to successful study. Chapters 1–4 encourage you to look at what enhances your individual study, and offer suggestions on how to experiment with your learning to find ways to take it to the next level. Experiment. Explore. Be creative. Find what suits *you* best.

Seven approaches to learning

The Study Skills Handbook is informed by seven approaches to learning.

1 Treating learning as an adventure

Small children treat life and learning as a big adventure. They are curious and learn extraordinary amounts without trying particularly hard – simply through being relaxed, observing, playing, questioning, trying things out for themselves, making mistakes, wanting to understand. They don't treat setbacks as failures nor do they worry about what others think or tell themselves they might not be able to learn. If they fall when learning to walk, they have another go, and another, until they succeed. Adults can learn in this way too – if they allow themselves.

Find a point of attraction

2 Using multiple senses and movement

The more we use our senses of sight, hearing and touch, and the more we use fine muscle movements in looking, speaking, writing, typing, drawing, checking, deciding, the more we help our brains to help us learn.

Combining the information from multiple senses and movements enables the brain to make more connections and associations. These help it to make sense of the information, lay down memories and recall it better later. This book encourages you to use your senses to the full and to incorporate movement into your study to make learning easier and more engaging.

3 Identifying the attraction

It is easier to learn if we keep desirable outcomes in mind rather than force ourselves to study out of duty. Some aspects of study may be less attractive to you, such as writing essays, meeting deadlines or sitting exams, and yet these also tend to bring the greatest satisfaction and rewards.

You do have it in your power to find in any aspect of study an angle that sparks your curiosity, drives your personal motivation, or makes it meaningful – to find the hidden gold that attracts you. For example, visualise yourself on a large cinema screen enjoying your study – or your later rewards. Hear your own voice telling you what you are achieving now. Your imagination will catch hold of these incentives and find ways of making them happen.

Visualise your success

4 Using active learning

We learn with a deeper understanding when we are actively and personally engaged:

★ juggling information

★ struggling to make sense

★ playing with different options

★ making decisions

★ looking for links, connections, meaning, significance, solutions.

For this reason, most pages of this book require you to *do* something, however small, to help focus attention and increase your active engagement with the topic.

5 Taking responsibility for your learning

In Higher Education, it is expected that you will take on increasing responsibility for your learning and that you are ready and able to study under your own direction for much of the week, as a responsible adult. This prepares you to lead and manage, whether in academic life, work or other contexts.

This means developing a range of abilities, not least in being able to evaluate and make judgements about your own work, with a fair but critical eye, prioritising what needs further work, getting on with doing so, and monitoring how well you are doing what you planned to do. This *Study Skills Handbook* helps and encourages you to do that.

6 Trusting in your intelligence

Many students worry that they are not intelligent enough to do well, especially at times when the course seems tough. If they didn't do well at school, they can doubt whether academic ability is 'in their genes'. If they excelled at school, they can worry they have 'lost it'. Worry and stress make it harder to learn.

With the right preparation, attitude and strategy, it is likely you will do fine. Trust that you can achieve well – and make it happen. See Chapter 4 to consider this in more detail, and Chapter 7 for managing stress and anxieties.

7 Personalising your learning

Each of us learns in an individual way – and our circumstances, experiences and interests vary. We each enjoy particular aspects of the course or methods of assessment more than others. We connect with some material and not others. We might prefer to learn on our own or socially, digitally or with paper and artefacts; to be on campus or at home, and so on.

You can do well without personalising your learning, but you can make study more effective, efficient and enjoyable if you adapt how and when you go about it so that it fits you best. It is worth taking time to understand and consider the many factors that contribute to optimal learning and to work out what really works best for you (see Chapters 4 and 5).

It is likely that you will find different things work better for aspects of the course you feel confident about or enjoy, and those you don't, as well as for different tasks, the mood you are in, who you are learning with, how much time you have, or the time of the day.

Experiment with strategies and skills you currently under-use. The human brain is highly adaptable: able learners move easily between different strategies and approaches, depending on the task in hand.

As you are more in charge of your learning at this level, this provides opportunities to adapt the learning experience to suit you. The book provides many suggestions about how you can do this.

Reflection

Seven Approaches to Learning

What is your initial response to these seven approaches to your learning and study?

Which do you feel characterise your own study strategy – and which are worth your considering further?

A new beginning ...

From this introduction, you will probably have gleaned that an important premise of this book is that academic success is a consequence of many factors. Intellectual ability is one factor, but not necessarily the most important. You have the power to influence many of those contributing factors.

Whatever your experience of academic study in the past, it might not be the same in Higher Education. It is a new beginning. If you don't succeed as well as you wish, at first, there will be further opportunities to do better. Each year, each term or semester, each module or unit of study, gives you a chance to start afresh in the way you approach your study.

Always been good at study?

It is likely that you have laid down some excellent foundations for higher level study. Let that boost your confidence. Nonetheless, even excellent students can find new ways of saving time, fine-tuning their study techniques, and adapting their strategy to meet the demands of higher level study.

Tend to coast along 'in the middle'?

You have the opportunity to test out how well you could do if you aim higher and adapt your strategy. How far do you want to go? What would hold you back from achieving more? Would you get more satisfaction out of your studies if you brought more to them?

Didn't achieve well in the past?

Many people thrive in the different atmosphere of Higher Education, even if they didn't at school. This can be because the teaching and curriculum suit them better or because they adopt new strategies and attitudes. If you under-achieved in the past, this might be welcome news. Your success is not determined by your past. This *Study Skills Handbook* was designed to help you challenge beliefs that have often led to students under-achieving. It provides practical steps forward.

Good strategies matter ...

Students are often pleasantly surprised to find that they can achieve well, and more easily, if they develop study strategies relevant to their own ways of thinking and working, that fit their circumstances, and draw upon their personal interests and preferences. The best strategies tend to be broad-based, taking into consideration all your needs, including health and well-being, goals and enjoyment.

This book enables you to consider your student experience in the round, and to take a holistic approach to your study, life and success.

Enjoy
the book

I hope you enjoy
***The Study Skills Handbook* –**
and your time as a student.

PART A

Self-efficacy: Managing your Success as a Student

You in the driving seat

In Higher Education, the key responsibility for academic success lies with you. You are the manager of your study. You have the prime influence over whether you do well and whether the experience is worthwhile, or not. Although there is usually a range of support and guidance available, ultimately, it comes back to you and to what you are prepared to do to ensure that you achieve the best you can with the least stress and greatest personal satisfaction.

Students who do well tend to be those who appreciate, early on, that higher level study is different from their previous experience, who grasp what this responsibility means, and who have the mindset and strategies to respond well to the challenge.

Taking on the challenge

Being in control of your own learning brings benefits in terms of increased choices, more control of your time, and for developing a range of skills and personal attributes that will serve you well in your life and career. On the other hand, it isn't always easy. It requires a range of strong personal attributes to direct your learning successfully, to use time well, to interpret sensibly what is going on when study seems more difficult or when your motivation wanes. It can take courage and imagination to adapt your strategy and attitude when your current approach doesn't seem to deliver what you want.

The importance of 'self-efficacy'

Self-efficacy or being able to 'manage yourself' can make a significant difference to your time as a student and beyond. It is one of the most important attributes to bring to study and to take into life beyond your course. It is worth spending time thinking about this and developing your self-management abilities.

Part A of this *Study Skills Handbook* provides background and approaches that help you to do this. It helps you to understand what characterises Higher Education and what self-efficacy means in that context. It encourages and assists you to think through crucial considerations such as:

★ your study purpose and longer-term goals;

★ what success would look like for you;

★ your strategies for managing time, stress, well-being, employability and career planning;

★ organising yourself ready for study and for avoiding common mistakes;

★ getting the most from your course and from your time as a student.

It provides you with structured activities and reflections to help you think through the important issues and to plan ahead for maximum success.

Success as a student
Take charge of your success

Learning outcomes

This chapter offers you opportunities to:

- ✓ gain an initial overview of how to achieve success in Higher Education
- ✓ understand what to expect and what characterises study in Higher Education
- ✓ clarify your own vision of success
- ✓ understand the study skills and attributes needed for higher level study
- ✓ consider your starting points and priorities for developing good study skills and habits
- ✓ set priorities for further developing your abilities.

A transformational experience

The experience of studying in Higher Education can be life-changing. Most graduates look back on this time with great fondness. In part, this is because of the unique opportunities it offers ...

- ★ to study interesting subjects
- ★ to feel stretched intellectually
- ★ to explore new ideas
- ★ to engage in a wide range of new activities, not easily available elsewhere
- ★ to find out about yourself and how you rise to the challenge of academic study
- ★ to consider the kind of person that you want to be in the world
- ★ to make friends that can last for life.

Higher level study is different from that at previous levels. This chapter helps you to identify how and why this is the case, and what this might mean for you as a student.

Making your success a reality

The more you engage with your course and actively hunt out the enjoyment in study and student life, the greater the likelihood that you will not only survive the experience, but thrive and excel, too.

This chapter helps you to understand what to expect, to consider what 'success' at this level of study means to you, and to decide how you will make the experience work for you.

Make the experience work for you

Be an active agent on behalf of your own success. Start by considering some ways that your own action can make a difference.

Reflection

Taking charge

How will you 'take charge' of your experience as a student? What do you need to do first?

Think through ...

★ how your studies contribute to your broader life plan and career ambitions

★ how other opportunities at college or university can forward your ambitions.

Be well informed

Investigate. Read.

Ask. Double check.

Put the hours in

Expertise is largely a factor of how many hours you spend on an activity. This applies to study as for other skills.

Using that time effectively is, of course, just as important.

Take charge

Plan how you will use your time as a student to gain your broader life and career aims.

Don't wait to be told – find out.

Don't wait to be asked – do it.

Don't wait to be inspired – inspire yourself.

Don't wait for opportunities – create them.

Don't rely only on feedback from others; learn to make sound evaluations of your work.

Don't neglect your well-being – include it in your goals.

Develop the right mindset

Intellectually curious and open to new perspectives.

Strongly motivated and determined to succeed.

Resilient, persistent and persevering.

Make wise choices that work for you

To achieve what you want, choose the right ...

★ degree subject

★ modules or topics

★ use of your time in and out of class.

Understand higher level study

How and why it is different.

What is expected.

What you need to know about the conventions and culture.

What is regarded as important in your subject and what gains the best grades.

Use the opportunities

Use resources, support and facilities on campus, online, in the local area, through student organisations.

Use feedback from tutors.

Take extra classes, learn new skills, stretch yourself.

Learn something outside of your subject area – take up a new language or complete an enterprise project.

Use chances of a work placement or year abroad.

Network with others.

Make friends for life.

Decide what you want ...

★ from your study

★ from the broader experience of being in Higher Education.

Your vision of success as a student

A return on your investment

Students invest a great deal of time, energy and money in their education, so success matters. There are many different versions of what that success would look like. Your vision won't be the same as others'.

If you can formulate a clear vision of what success as a student means to you, you are more likely to achieve it. The way you conceive of success will influence how you spend your time and direct energies which, in turn, will affect your achievement and experience.

Reflection

Think forward

Our imaginations are extremely powerful. You can use this to help direct your energies. For example, picture yourself 10 years into the future. Will you be impressed by the choices you are making now, and your use of the time and opportunities available to you? Will you wish that you had done anything differently?

Reflection

Use your vision to direct your energies

What do your choices opposite indicate about:

★ what 'success' as a student would look like for you?

★ how to direct your energies as a student?

What would success look like for me?

Use the following questions to help you to plan. Check off ✓ all items that apply to you. Then highlight those that are most important to you.

I would feel I had made a success of university/ college if:

Career

☐ I gained a qualification that enabled me to develop my career

☐ I developed skills which helped me find a good job

☐ I made full use of the opportunities available

☐ I took on positions of responsibility that helped my CV

☐ I made good contacts that helped my career.

Transformational experience

☐ I learnt more about who I am as a person

☐ I became a different person as a result of my experience

☐ I developed a range of skills and qualities that improve my life

☐ I developed in personal confidence

☐ I developed a broader understanding of the world

☐ I met and learnt from people I wouldn't have met otherwise.

Subject and qualifications

☐ I learnt a lot about a subject that really interested me

☐ I got a good class of degree

☐ I stretched myself intellectually

☐ I developed academically.

Life and personal

☐ I really enjoyed myself

☐ I made good friends

☐ I developed new interests that enrich my life

☐ I learned to manage myself as an effective adult.

Success as a student: what lecturers say

Students who do best at university are those who are very determined to succeed, plan how they will do it, and then keep their plans in perspective.

The students who stand out to me are those who don't just read what is on the reading list, but who genuinely want to know all they can about the subject – who surprise you by having read an article just published or have a good grip on the most recent debates in the subject.

Study is important – of course, I would say that. But college life is about much more than that. It can and should be a life-changing experience – a time to have your ideas challenged, to meet people from an incredibly wide range of backgrounds, to think how your education could change your own life and that of others.

I would say that the key factor is time. If students put in the hours, they tend to do well. Of course, you do need to use the time well too.

Students need to keep their eyes on their long-term goals. If they want a good job, it won't hurt to have a good degree but they also need to show they have experience of other things. They need to get out and do things for the community, get a job, have ideas and opinions, show they are their own person.

What helps students to succeed at Uni? Most students do achieve their degree and then go on to get a job, so that suggests there are many different routes to success. Mainly, it's about the basics. Find out what you have to do, do it, and stay the course. Do more, and your marks will be better.

Universities provide the opportunities. It is then up to the students to make those opportunities work for them.

The best students for me are those who really grapple with the issues, who show they have tried to think things through for themselves, even if they haven't got it all right. The worst are those that rely on Wikipedia as their main source of information – and think no-one will notice!

As a lecturer, I like the students who love their subject and want to know as much as they can about it. As the parent of a student myself, I think it important that students use their time at university wisely. If they want an academic career, then they should put the subject first. If they want a career outside of academia, then they need to think more broadly.

Reflection

Student success

What can you take away from these lecturers' observations to help you succeed?

It isn't just about how much work you put in. You can actually get away with doing much less work than others and do better than them – but you can't get away without thinking about what you are doing and learning.

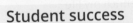

What is expected from you?

It's not like at school where you were stuck in a classroom from 9 till 4 and teachers told you what you needed to do.

– Ade, first-year student

As a student, you are expected to have the following characteristics.

Independence

You must be able to 'stand on your own two feet'. However, there is help available. The Student Union and Student Services will have details.

Self-motivation

You have to be able to work on your own a lot.

Openness to working with others

You will need to organise study sessions with friends.

Ability to work things out for yourself

'How successful was the 1944 Education Act?'

It's terrible! The lecturers expect us to tell them all the answers!

To cope at this level, you need to be reasonably good at:

★ adapting to new people and environments

★ surviving in potentially very large groups

★ being flexible in your learning style.

Ability to set goals to improve your work

Whoopee!! B+! Next time I want an A!

Ability to organise your time

You need to keep track of time. You must:

★ know when and where you should be for scheduled classes, events and exams

★ know when work has to be handed in

★ keep to deadlines for handing in work.

(See Chapter 6.)

	MONDAY	TUESDAY	WEDNESDAY
9–10	put notes in order	Ecology lecture Rm G10	prepare for botany seminar
10–11	Lecture Dr Shah Rm X22		
11–12	Do plan (Science Report)		Botany Seminar Rm R21

Ability to work out when and how you learn best

On second thoughts maybe I do work better indoors, in the daytime.

Success as a student: where am I now?

Success as a student isn't just about intellectual ability. A wide range of factors contribute, some of which are outlined here. You will probably be able to think of others. For each statement, circle or highlight the emoticon if you feel confident of that factor. Circle the arrows if you want to investigate it further.

Understanding university-level study

Clear understanding of expectations

☺ ►► I understand what is expected of me. Page 13.

☺ ►► I know what to expect from Higher Education. Pages 18–19.

Clear understanding of educational context

☺ ►► I understand how higher level study is different from previous levels. Page 16.

☺ ►► I have a good grasp of the culture and academic conventions of university level study. Pages 17, 22 and 302–3.

☺ ►► I recognise that there is specialist vocabulary I will need to learn to use.

Management of independent study

☺ ►► I understand the role of independent study for university level study. Page 19.

☺ ►► I manage independent study well. Page 124 and Chapter 6.

Management of assessment

☺ ►► I know how to use course information to help me achieve good marks/grades. Page 315.

☺ ►► I use the marking criteria to help me evaluate and improve my work. Page 315.

☺ ►► I make productive use of feedback from tutors and others. Pages 33 and 316.

☺ ►► I understand how to evaluate my own work. Page 317.

Subject knowledge and understanding

Knowledge

☺ ►► There is a good match between my own knowledge and skills and the starting points on my course. Page 69 (Butterworth, 1992).

☺ ►► I know how to research my subject in order to develop a good knowledge base. Chapters 10, 11 and 16.

Understanding

☺ ►► I appreciate the difference between information and knowledge. Page 75.

☺ ►► I recognise the importance of developing a deep understanding of the material. Pages 74–5.

☺ ►► I recognise that understanding requires me to spend time reflecting about what I have learnt.

☺ ►► I appreciate the importance of strong critical thinking abilities to success in Higher Education. Chapter 12.

☺ ►► I enjoy working on new topics and making sense of them for myself.

☺ ►► I persist with difficult material until I 'get it'. Pages 42–3.

Academic Skills

☺ ►► I understand what is meant by 'study skills' and the variety of attributes these encompass. Pages 20–8.

☺ ►► I am aware of the range of academic skills required in Higher Education. Pages 20–1.

☺ ►► I am confident that my academic skills are appropriate to this level of study. Page 22.

☺ ►► I am aware of my priorities for further developing my study skills. Pages 25–7.

Learning savvy

☺ ►► I understand the difference between intelligence and academic success. Chapter 4.

☺ ►► I know how I learn best. Chapter 4.

☺ ►► I create the optimum learning environment for myself. Chapter 4.

☺ ►► I think creatively about my study. Chapter 5.

☺ ►► I use reflection effectively to improve my academic performance. Chapter 5.

☺ ►► I have effective study strategies. Chapters 4 and 5.

☺ ►► I personalise learning so as to build on my strengths and preferences. Chapter 5.

☺ ►► I make the most of my memory. Chapter 18.

☺ ►► I am confident about participating in class. Page 36.

☺ ►► I am good at studying collaboratively with other students. Chapters 8 and 9.

☺ ►► I manage my use of technology to benefit my study. Pages 41 and 143.

Self-awareness and commitment

Clear vision, direction and motivation

☺ ►► I have a clear vision about what success as a student would mean to me. Page 11.

☺ ►► I am strongly motivated. See Chapter 5.

☺ ►► I use the opportunities open to me so as to support my career aims. Chapter 3.

☺ ►► I take the right steps to enable me to make wise choices related to my studies. Pages 10 and 47–9.

☺ ►► I use my time effectively. See Chapter 6.

High levels of personal engagement

☺ ►► I think of myself as an active agent in my own success. Page 10.

☺ ►► I understand the high level of commitment required. Pages 18 and 113.

☺ ►► I have a strong sense of purpose.

☺ ►► I recognise the importance of being intellectually curious, keen to find out more about my subject. Pages 12 and 16; Chapter 12.

☺ ►► I think about the issues for myself. Pages 12 and 17.

☺ ►► I understand the importance of reading widely in the subject. Pages 12 and 16–17.

☺ ►► I am active in finding out what I need to know for my course and as a student. Pages 29–30.

☺ ►► I am able to 'stick with it' in completing tasks and my course. Page 114.

☺ ►► I go the extra mile to do well at my studies.

Resilience, self-reliance and self-management

☺ ►► I understand what is meant by resilience. Pages 162–3.

☺ ►► I am able to identify and manage anxieties. Pages 152–3 and 164–7.

☺ ►► I keep goals and problems in perspective. Page 162.

☺ ►► I ask for help if I really need it.

☺ ►► I recognise the importance of well-being and stress management to my overall success. Chapter 7.

Reflection

Consider the thoughts that went through your mind as you worked through the list above.

★ What kind of message do you pick up about what is needed in order to do well at this level of study?

★ How ready do you think you are for engaging with your study in this way?

★ Which items stood out for you as important to act upon to help your own study?

How is higher level study different?

Study is different

As a student in Higher Education, the most noticeably different features are likely to be:

★ the teaching methods, especially the emphasis on independent study

★ the assumption that you have the maturity and intelligence to 'get on with it', managing your own study, goals and life

★ that academic work is more difficult and complex

★ the strong emphasis on 'understanding' rather than 'information'

★ learning how knowledge is created

★ that time may seem to operate differently: good time management skills are essential.

The role of the 'teacher' is different

Teachers at this level are usually known as lecturers, tutors or professors. As well as teaching, they are usually expected to engage in research and scholarship, which might feed into their teaching. When they are not involved in teaching-related tasks, they may be preparing research papers for publication and conferences, or applying research or professional skills in industry, government and elsewhere.

Creating knowledge

Higher Education is about creating knowledge as well as teaching it and learning about it. Depending on the subject, this is through:

★ thinking, discussion and writing to develop theoretical understandings

★ experimenting to test out theories

★ investigating original sources or past knowledge, finding new ways of looking at these and bringing new interpretations

★ applying knowledge and understanding to new situations.

Intellectual curiosity; learning community

Studying at this level is about being part of an adult learning community in which everyone, students and lecturers, are active in finding out new things for themselves and sharing them with others. It is assumed that you are intellectually curious, keen to find things out for yourself and to contribute to developing new understandings.

Universities play an important role in:

★ encouraging research into new areas

★ leading debate on contemporary issues

★ critiquing existing understandings

★ synthesising knowledge

★ generating new understandings of the world

★ stimulating economic development

★ … as well as teaching students.

Depending on your institution, teaching is likely to be designed in ways that encourage you to do the same. Typically, you are required to:

★ engage with debates in your subject

★ hunt out answers for yourself

★ develop your capacity to think in more creative, systematic and subtle ways

★ be open to new perspectives

★ undertake projects

★ consider the broader significance and relevance of what you find out.

Nobody knows what will happen next …

Understanding higher level study

Studying at the cutting edge of knowledge

Moving beyond generalisations

Study at previous levels often makes learning more manageable by using broader generalisations or 'brush strokes'. These are helpful when you are new to a subject. As you become more expert, you become aware of what lies behind some of the generalisations. As a result, things which had seemed straightforward become more problematic.

Journeying into the unknown

This is especially the case when you come to look at new research. Your tutors' research or scholarship may be at the 'cutting edge' of what is known, as will much of the recommended reading. As a result, course material may take you to that 'edge' too. You may study issues where:

★ the answers are not yet known

★ there may be no 'easy answers'

★ there isn't a clear 'right' or 'wrong'

★ research findings are ambiguous or contradictory

★ knowledge advances in very small steps – or may seem to be going backwards

★ there are conflicting points of view.

You may find this to be frustrating or, alternatively, you may find this to be intellectually exciting and feel driven to think about interesting possibilities.

Culture, conventions and values

Universities have a strong tradition of upholding values such as free speech, independent thinking and criticality. They strive to create objective truths, as far as this is possible, using rigorous and transparent methodologies. In general, each subject discipline has its own:

★ ways of looking at the world

★ culture, conventions and methodologies

★ specialist terminology, so that it can convey precise and specific meanings.

As a student, you are not simply learning about 'facts'. Rather, you are being trained to think in ways that will enable you, in time, to conduct your own research using secure methodologies. This means that you need to learn:

★ the specialist language of the subject

★ what is valued, and why, within the subject discipline

★ how knowledge has developed and is developing in the subject – and how to do this for yourself.

'Learning the rules of the game ...'

As with many pursuits, success is easier if you are familiar with the system. In this context, that means understanding such things as:

★ how you will be taught: pages 16–19

★ what gets good grades: page 315

★ how language is used and the right style and level of formality: Chapters 9–11

★ academic conventions: pages 22 and 302–4

★ making the best use of opportunities to develop skills and experience: Chapters 2 and 3.

Professor Smartz works at the cutting edge of knowledge

Teaching: what to expect in Higher Education

The study week

Most full-time courses are the equivalent of a working week in employment (around 35–40 hours). That is spent in a mixture of independent study at home or in a library, scheduled classes and activities and, if relevant, in labs, a studio or the workplace. See page 127.

Lectures

These vary greatly, but usually involve listening and making notes. Some expect participation or 'flipped' learning. They might be recorded for reviewing later, but it is best to still attend, too. See pages 35–7.

★ size: 50–300 people

★ length: 1–3 hours

★ weekly: 5–20 hours.

Tutorials

These are used to give feedback on your work and to guide and discuss your progress. Prepare well for them. See page 31.

★ size: small groups, pairs or individually

★ length: usually 15–60 minutes at most

★ frequency: typically 3–6 a year.

Seminars/workshops/'crits'

These involve group discussions of student presentations, set reading, guest speakers or lectures. Prepare questions and read up, so you are ready to participate. See Chapters 8 and 12.

★ size: typically 12–30 people

★ length: 1–3 hours

★ weekly: varies (perhaps 1–3 each week).

Other typical teaching methods

Independent study

This can take up most of the week. It requires good time management and strong motivation. See page 19 and Chapter 6.

Group work and collaborative learning

This could involve discussion, group tasks, projects or peer support. See Chapters 8 and 9.

Technology-enhanced learning (TEL)

Most programmes use TEL to support class-based and independent study. See pages 41 and 83–5.

Work-based learning and work placements

Some courses involve job-related learning.

Distance learning

Materials are provided, usually electronically. Contact with tutors could be by phone, email, conferencing, or in local meetings and classes.

Independent study: benefits, challenges, risks

As independent study is core to most courses, learning to do this effectively is essential. A good starting place is to consider how you will manage its challenges and risks.

Benefits	Challenges	Risks
More control over your study time	★ To manage time effectively. ★ To meet deadlines.	Wasting study time. Underestimating how long study tasks take. Forgetting things that must be done.
More control over your 'spare' time	★ To use time effectively building your CV, gaining skills and experience, to further your employability and career interests. ★ To recognise the difference between 'spare' time and independent study time. ★ To put time aside to relax, rest, socialise and enjoy yourself.	Missing opportunities to develop a wider range of attributes that will benefit you when applying for jobs or promotions. Spending all your time in study, rather than in a balanced menu of activity.
More choice about when and where to study	★ To create structures for your day. ★ To organise a place to study. ★ To work out the best places and times, for you, for diverse study activities.	Not getting down to study. Not creating a place that allows you to study without interruption. Making poor choices.
More choice about how you study	★ To identify what helps you learn best when undertaking different study tasks. ★ To take responsibility for your learning and achieving your goals.	Not bothering to explore what helps you to learn best. Getting stuck in old habits rather than developing new, more effective ones.
More responsibility for your own successes	★ To identify barriers to your learning and to address these. ★ To identify ways of improving your own performance and grades. ★ To make effective use of feedback and to learn from mistakes.	Failure to understand previous barriers to learning. Not addressing weaknesses in your performance. Giving up too easily. Ignoring feedback. Not seeing setbacks as useful guides to future improvement.
More choice about how much energy you devote to topics that interest you	★ To find the right balance between a broad set of interests at a superficial level and too much depth in a narrow range of topics. ★ To broaden your range of interests.	Devoting too much time to topics that interest you at the expense of those needed to complete the programme. Becoming specialised in too narrow a range of topics.
There isn't a teacher looking over your shoulder all the time	★ To keep on target with little guidance. ★ To keep yourself motivated. ★ To take responsibility for pursuing solutions to problems on your own. ★ To recognise when you need help and to ask for it.	Letting things slip. Falling behind in your work. Losing motivation. Losing a sense of what you are supposed to do. Not finding out what help is available, or not using it. Asking for help before trying to solve problems yourself.
More control over choice of topics	★ To make choices that contribute to a coherent programme of study that interests you and meets your goals.	Choosing topics that do not fit together well, or that do not contribute towards your goals.

Have a go at the Activity about independent study on the companion site.

© Stella Cottrell (2019) *The Study Skills Handbook*, 5th edition, Red Globe Press

What kind of study skills do you need?

What is a skill?

> *Skill*
>
> To be skilled is to be able to perform a learned activity well and at will.

A skill is a learned ability rather than an outcome achieved through luck or chance and can, therefore, be relied on reasonably securely when you perform an equivalent task again. You can fine-tune skills through practice, feedback and reflection, just as athletes improve their performance by developing underlying skills in movement, breathing and pacing.

What are study skills?

The term 'study skills' is used here to refer to abilities, habits, understandings and attitudes that enable achievement in your studies. These can be categorised into four easy-to-remember, inter-related areas:

1 **Self**
2 **Academic**
3 **People**
4 **Task**

More details of these are provided on pages 89–373.

Why are study skills important?

Study skills help you to:

1 know what you are doing
2 organise your independent study
3 build your confidence
4 reduce study stress
5 improve the quality of your work
6 enjoy study more
7 study more efficiently
8 save time
9 avoid unnecessary errors
10 gain better grades.

Reflection

Why study skills matter

Which of the 10 reasons above matter to you?

Are there other reasons why you want to develop your study skills?

You and your unique starting point

The skills you will need and develop will be a unique combination, as your experiences, aims, habits, reactions, motivations, personality and many other contributing factors make your learning distinct. That is why a personalised approach is important.

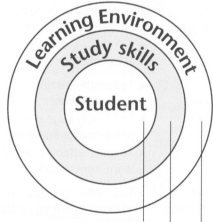

1 You, the student, with your particular circumstances, goals, educational history, current abilities and habits

2 The course and overall learning environment in their entirety, which create new learning challenges

3 The combination of skills you need, personally, to manage those challenges to best effect.

Self-efficacy skills: managing yourself for study

Good self-management is essential in higher education because of the increased expectations for autonomous learning and personal responsibility, and the level of challenge. Effective management of your time, emotions, attitudes, habits and life matter more as you progress upwards through the course. Self-efficacy is a broad concept; it involves such skills, qualities and attitudes as these 10 below.

1 **Engagement**: taking an active part in shaping your learning and success.
2 **Autonomy**: being able to think for yourself, and to make good choices to direct your own study.
3 **Managing your mindset**: adopting the right attitudes to drive your success and inspire you.
4 **Enhancing personal performance**: always looking to improve further, using feedback, data, observation and reflection.
5 **Personalising learning**: identifying and applying approaches that work best for you.
6 **Applying strategies**: creative, reflective, effective, active, well-motivated (C·R·E·A·M).
7 **Time-management**: using time to best effect; ensuring your work is submitted on time.
8 **Well-being and self-care**: balancing study, work and life; managing stress.

9 **Managing your learning environment**: coping with the broader learning context.
10 **Self-reflection:** thinking meaningfully about the consequences of your actions and thought patterns for your study, well-being and future.

Reflection

Managing your learning environment

Which of the environmental factors below might create challenges for you?

What do you need to find out or to do now in order to better manage challenges that could arise?

Who or what could help you in managing these?

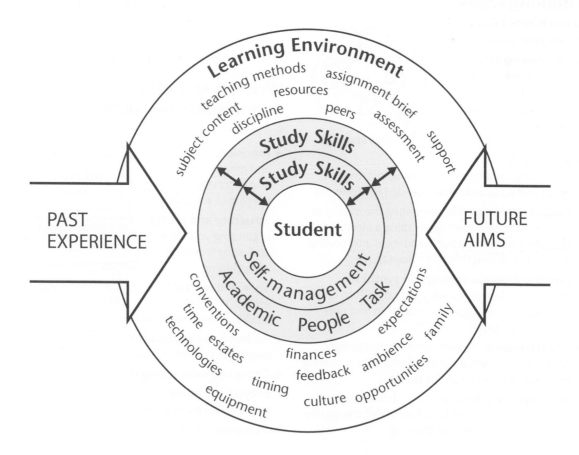

Academic Skills

Research skills

At each level of study, you will need to use increasingly sophisticated strategies for:

Investigate! Find out about it!

* **Finding information**: searching for information and knowing what is available
* **Reading** large amounts at speed
* **Using multiple sources** of information
* **Making helpful notes** of what you observe, hear, read and think – and using them well
* **Organisational skills**: sorting, storing and retrieving information for re-use; planning out tasks well (Chapter 11)
* **Using numerical data**: collecting, analysing and presenting these (Chapters 12 and 16).

Thinking skills

At this level of study, this means such skills as:

Think about it!

* **Decision making**: using sound decisions about the material to select and draw upon for your work (Chapters 10, 11, 12 and 16)
* **Memory skills**, developing strategies for recalling information easily and accurately when needed (Chapter 18)
* **Critical thinking skills**: evaluating the quality of sources of information; developing a strong line of reasoning based on sound evidence; interpreting material, data and theories (Chapter 12)
* **Creative problem-solving and synthesis**: drawing on diverse knowledge and skills to create new ways of looking at an issue or to find new solutions (Chapters 5 and 12)
* **Understanding**: making sense of increasingly complex and difficult data and concepts, including problems without clear-cut answers
* **Metacognitive skills**: 'thinking about thinking': being able to think meaningfully about the quality and effectiveness of your thinking.

Understanding academic conventions

For students, that means understanding:

Develop expertise! Know your field!

* **Higher Education** as a learning community
* **Your academic discipline**: the specialist branch of learning that underpins your course
* **Foundation concepts** in the discipline – its core theories and ideas
* **Knowledge**: how this is constructed and advanced in your subject
* **Evidence** as the basis of your argument
* **Sound methodologies**, relevant to the subject, used to establish the evidence base
* **Specialist terminology** used in the discipline
* **Academic integrity**, including the use of reputable sources, attributing these correctly, and avoiding plagiarism
* **Ethical awareness**, as relevant to context.

Written and other communication skills

For academic study, this includes:

unusual fins

Communicate! Write it up!

* **Precision**: using words and data accurately and succinctly, and keeping to word limits
* **Structure and clarity**: organising your ideas and using a clear line of reasoning
* **Style and format** for essays, reports, case studies, dissertations and other assignments
* **Audience awareness**: for written, spoken and electronic communication
* **Citing and referencing** sources correctly
* **Subject discipline**: using the style, format and conventions used in your subject.

See Chapters 13–16.

People Skills and Task Management Skills

People Skills: studying with others

Many academic tasks are undertaken in social contexts with other students, the public or clients, face to face or using technology. This calls for such skills as:

★ **Turn-taking:** taking an active part, without dominating or letting others take over

★ **Contributing constructively** in class, seminars, or in online discussions

★ **Peer feedback**: giving and receiving constructive criticism

★ **Making presentations**, to a group or as part of a group

★ **Collaborative team working and small group work**, face to face and/or using video links or social networking

★ **Cultural competence**: interacting sensitively and confidently with a diverse range of people; adapting well to new groups

★ **Supporting others**, encouraging them and sharing ideas without cheating or collusion.

See Chapters 8 and 9.

Talk it through!

Activity

Which skills?

The skills you need vary depending on your course. Take a look at the **Skills Clouds** on this book's companion site at www.studyskillshandbook.co.uk.

➡ What kind of course do you think is represented by each cloud?

➡ Which skills would stand out most on a skills cloud for your own course?

Task management skills

You will need to draw together the above skills in meaningful ways in order to complete required study tasks such as exams and assignments. Task management, in itself, requires skills in:

1) Wake at 7·00
2) Feed fish
3) Observe fish

Take charge!

★ **Producing set items** such as essays, reports, portfolios, presentations, case studies, applying methodologies, conventions and styles relevant to the discipline

★ **Managing the process** of taking a task through from start to finish

★ **Meeting given requirements** such as the assignment brief, marking criteria, ethical standards, deadlines and word limits

★ **Following the appropriate protocols** and guidance for your subject, such as for lab work, clinical practice, field work, studio, performance, practical or technical skills

★ **Using specialist equipment and resources** relevant to your course and circumstances, or using apps designed to support study

★ **Project management** of larger, more complex tasks such as research projects, dissertations, exams, field work and end of year shows.

Combining skills

The skills are outlined here, for clarity, as if they were separate categories. In practice, you would combine many skills from each category for most study tasks. For example, you cannot easily separate out basic research tasks, such as searching for information, from the process of thinking through what is relevant for a given assignment or from critical thinking. Similarly, meeting assignment briefs can mean integrating almost all of the skills outlined above.

As you develop through your course, you will integrate a wide range of skills fluidly, without noticing that you are doing so.

Developing skills: five study skills components

1 Self-awareness and self-evaluation

To develop a skill, you need first to know where you are starting from. What are your current strengths and weaknesses? What do you want to achieve? Where do you need to improve? How are you going to improve? What are your resources? What could obstruct your goals? Ways of developing such awareness include:

★ using self-evaluation questionnaires

★ monitoring your progress

★ maintaining a reflective journal or blog

★ group discussion and chat

★ feedback and criticism from other students

★ feedback and comments from tutors.

2 Task awareness: knowing what is required

To score a goal you need to know where the goalposts are. In an academic context, this means finding out what is expected of you and what your lecturers are looking for whenever you are set a new assignment.

Essential information is usually provided in course handbooks, webpages, through a virtual learning environment and in assignment briefs. See pages 32–3 and Chapter 14 for key information to find out and use.

In particular, for each subject, find out about:

★ the curriculum – the course content

★ the outcomes or objectives – what you must know or be able to do by the end of the course

★ how marks are allocated – what gets good marks? What loses marks?

★ the special preferences of each lecturer – if in doubt, ask.

3 Strategy, method and organisation

It is easier to study and saves you time if you have a method for working and are well organised. A skilled student uses strategies, and with practice these become automatic.

4 Confidence and sense of 'entitlement'

If you are to succeed as a student, you have to believe that such success is possible for you.

However, many students feel that academic success is for other people rather than for them. This may be because of their experiences at school, or because nobody from their family has a degree. Often, it is because they hold particular ideas about intelligence, especially their own academic abilities, and so do not give themselves 'permission' to do well.

For this reason, Chapter 4 focuses on what we mean by 'intelligence' and 'learning'.

5 Familiarity, practice and habit

All skills improve through practice, feedback and monitoring. The more you study and reflect on your learning, the more you become:

★ adept at finding shortcuts

★ aware of underlying skills, qualities and habits that you can improve

★ able to see patterns in what you do

★ able to focus on study for longer

★ able to perform skills automatically.

The way to study well and easily becomes a habit. If you have been away from study or are not used to managing so much unscheduled time, you may find you need to build good study habits.

You don't have to be 'clever'!

When you consider these study skills components, it is clear that good study skills have little to do with being 'naturally clever'. They owe much more to awareness, strategies, confidence and practice, leading to an overall development in your learning. Each of these aspects is covered in the various chapters of *The Study Skills Handbook*.

Study skills: priorities, stage 1

Column A **Already have the skill?** Decide ✓ whether each statement is generally true of you.
Column B **Needed?** How important is it to you? Rate from 6 to 10. (6 = not needed. 10 = essential.)
Column C **Ability?** Rate how good you are at this skill now. (Scale 1 = very weak. 5 = excellent.)
Column D **Priority:** Subtract the score in column C from that in column B (B – C). Items with the highest scores in column D are likely to be priorities. Then turn to page 26. Repeat later in the year.

Study skills statements I have effective strategies for …	A This is true ✓	B Needed? (6–10)	C Ability? (1–5)	D Priority? (B–C)
1 organising myself well for study				
2 using my time effectively (Checklist, page 124)				
3 thinking creatively				
4 solving problems				
5 reading for academic purposes				
6 searching for information for assignments (Chapter 11)				
7 making, and using, good notes (Checklist, page 184)				
8 making best use of taught sessions (Evaluation, page 39)				
9 effective group and seminar work (Checklist, page 186)				
10 working collaboratively with others				
11 making presentations (Checklist, page 195)				
12 managing writing tasks (Checklist, page 274)				
13 writing essays using academic conventions				
14 writing reports and dissertations (Checklist, page 369)				
15 undertaking a research project (Checklist, pages 352–62)				
16 avoiding cheating/plagiarism				
17 citing sources and writing references				
18 improving my concentration				
19 thinking critically and analytically				
20 critiquing my own work and others' work				
21 managing stress, anxiety and well-being				
22 preparing for exams (Checklists, pp. 380, 383 and 387)				
23 evaluating and improving my work (Checklist, page 100)				
24 developing my memory for course material				

Study skills: priorities, stage 2

Column A Using the scoring from stage 1, decide whether each item really is a priority, whether it could wait, who else could do it, or any other options you have.

Column B Number your priorities in order. Highlight in yellow the one you are going to work on next. Highlight it in red once you have worked on it.

Study skills statements I will become more effective at ...	A: Priority for action?	B	C pages
1 organising myself well for study			30–7
2 using my time effectively			123–50
3 thinking creatively			90–8
4 solving problems			93–8
5 reading for academic purposes			213–25
6 searching for information for assignments			233–44
7 making, and using, good notes			226–31
8 making best use of taught sessions			31–9
9 effective group and seminar work			175–86
10 working collaboratively with others			171–85
11 making presentations			189–95
12 managing writing tasks			273–300
13 writing essays using academic conventions			301–343
14 writing reports and dissertations			347–69
15 undertaking a research project			347–69
16 avoiding cheating/plagiarism			247–8
17 citing sources and writing references			249–51
18 improving my concentration			36; 84; 106; 141
19 thinking critically and analytically			253–72
20 critiquing my own work and others' work			266–72
21 managing stress, anxiety and well-being			151–68
22 preparing for exams			373–88
23 evaluating and improving my work			100; 315–17
24 developing my memory for course material			389–404

© Stella Cottrell (2019) *The Study Skills Handbook*, 5th edition, Red Globe Press

Study skills action plan

Bring together your thoughts about your responses to activities, reflections and self-evaluations. Use these to develop an action plan to collate your thoughts and priorities for action.

An expandable action plan and a chart to help you monitor your progress are available on the companion site at www.studyskillshandbook.co.uk.

Date:
Summary of my current strengths, skills and qualities: what I have achieved so far
Summary of what I need to work on, develop or improve
My priorities: what I am going to do, when, and how
How will I know that I have improved? (E.g. What changes would I expect in my work, in myself, or in the attitudes of others?)

Review

1 **Take charge!**
Do what you need to do to make the experience happy, useful and memorable. Use and create opportunities.

2 **Develop your vision**
Build your own sense of purpose and motivation for study. Find inspiration. Inspire yourself!

3 **Understand the context**
Recognise how Higher Education differs from your previous study and why that is so. Use that knowledge to influence how you approach your study.

4 **Get to grips with independent study**
It is a key aspect of higher level study and a sign of respect for the intelligence and potential of advanced students. It can be challenging, so think and plan carefully about how you will manage it: don't just leave it to chance.

5 **Don't take study skills for granted**
Keep updating, extending and refining your skills base. You need more sophisticated skills and better study habits as you progress to higher levels and years of study. Good skills can also free up time for other things (or for more study!)

6 **APT-S**
Give consideration to the range of Academic, People, Task- and Self-management skills that are required – and that you gain through your study.

7 **Recognise the 5 study skills components**
Use these to help you develop your skills and to feel more confident when skills don't come easily.

8 **Develop self-efficacy**
This is often overlooked and yet makes a great difference to students' success.

9 **Set priorities**
The potential skill set is vast. You can't improve in all dimensions at once. Decide which skills and study habits are of most value to you now, for your course and well-being, and for your likely future on graduation.

10 **Create an Action Plan**
Decide when and how you will take forward your study skills priorities.

11 **Believe in yourself**
You have chosen to take on the challenge. Rise to it. It won't always be easy. If you do find it easy, find ways to stretch yourself intellectually so you can look back with a sense of satisfaction and achievement.

You can do it.

12 **Take away your own messages**
The points above are key messages from this chapter, but other aspects might be more important for you. Jot down your own list of points to take away from the chapter – ones to put into action.

Chapter 2

Gaining the most from your course

Engage. Enjoy. Excel.

Learning outcomes

This chapter offers you opportunities to:

- ✓ consider the ten 'golden rules' for passing a course
- ✓ use personal tutorials and class time to best effect
- ✓ become better informed about your course and studies as a whole
- ✓ engage fully with your course, during classes and outside of taught sessions
- ✓ make effective notes of what is covered in lectures and taught sessions
- ✓ manage the more difficult aspects of your course
- ✓ get under the skin of your course, so you better understand what is important
- ✓ to make the subject your own and enjoy it.

Introduction

Whilst the benefits you gain from your course depend, in part, on the quality of the teaching and resources, much of the real value lies in what you and other students bring to the table.

★ If the course is really good, you won't be able to coast along with little effort, and you won't want to.

★ If the course is poor or dull, it is all the more important that you take charge so that you gain from the experience.

This chapter looks at some key ways of extracting the maximum value from time scheduled for study, whether in taught sessions or as independent study.

> *You invest time, money, energy and your personal reputation in your course, so it makes sense to get the most from every aspect of it.*

Reflection

10 Golden rules

Start by considering the 10 golden rules for passing a course and avoiding study problems later in your course. See page 30.

★ Which, if any, are weak points for you?

★ What will you do about that?

Ten golden rules

These 'golden rules' greatly increase your chance of passing your course and avoiding problems along the way. They might seem obvious but many students run into trouble with them. It is wise to:

★ Take them seriously

★ Commit to following them

★ Take action to address your weak or 'risky' areas.

Consider below which you follow already ✓. Highlight any areas that you need to address.

1 Turn up! You gain ... ☐

★ A better sense of the course as a whole.

★ More of a sense of 'belonging'.

★ Less stress and anxiety.

★ You don't get on the wrong side of tutors.

★ You don't miss learning that you pay for.

★ You pick up useful tutor hints and tips.

★ You meet attendance requirements.

★ You are less likely to fail.

2 Be on time; stay to the end ☐
... for every class and event.

★ It creates the right impression.

★ It is a courtesy to others, as it avoids disrupting their learning.

★ You gain important information given at the start and end of class.

★ Other people take you more seriously.

3 Focus attention during class ☐
Zone in to what is being taught and tune out everything else. Otherwise, you are wasting time you have paid for. See page 36.

4 Don't just turn up – join in! ☐

★ You learn more and develop more skills.

★ It helps you to stay focused.

★ It helps achieve sessions' study objectives.

5 Submit work/sit exams on time ☐
Handing work in late, or not at all, just makes life harder. You automatically lose marks. You probably have to do the work or sit the exam anyway, but for a capped mark and without the advantage of feedback. The likelihood is that your work is good enough to pass. If not, it is likely you can try again with the benefit of useful practice and feedback. (Your grade might be capped for a re-sit.)

6 Keep your tutors onside ☐

★ Remember, they usually want all students to succeed. (It reflects well on them too!)

★ You may need them one day as an advocate, for support, or to provide a job reference.

★ Don't lose their goodwill through making unreasonable demands, lack of courtesy, seeming not to care about your study, disrupting other students' learning, lateness, absenteeism, cheating, time-wasting, etc.

7 Avoid any kind of cheating ☐

★ Never purchase essays or assignments.

★ Don't get anyone else to do your work.

★ Don't plagiarise. See pages 247–8.

If in doubt, check with your tutors first.

8 Take the right components/credits ☐

Correct number for the year. At the right level.

In the right subjects. In the right order.

The right options to enable future choices.

9 Spread your workload ☐
As far as possible, aim to spread your workload evenly across the term or semester. Avoid carrying incomplete credit if you can, as it adds to next year's workload.

10 Use the advice and support ☐

★ Read all course handbooks and guidance.

★ Use personal tutorials effectively.

★ Use the advice and support services.

★ Take notice of all feedback – and use it!

Effective use of tutorials and personal tutors

Most courses offer personal tutoring or equivalents. As large institutions can feel impersonal, this provides a human face. The better they know you, the better placed they are to advise you, signpost help or write references for prizes, jobs or housing.

Keep personal tutors on your side

★ Don't be afraid to attend tutorial sessions. Let your tutor get to know you – you are not on trial!

★ Be realistic in what you ask for and when. Don't leave requests for help until the last minute.

★ Always be polite and courteous. Remember they have lives of their own. They are not there to fulfil your every need nor to respond to messages in the middle of the night!

★ Keep in touch so they know you are still there.

Sharing contact details

★ Keep your personal tutor's contact details close to hand, for easy access if needed.

★ Inform them of any changes to your details.

Making and keeping appointments

★ If you are asked to make appointments, do this straight away before you forget.

★ Write the details into your diary.

★ Apply common courtesies: turn up on time. Don't miss appointments. Always apologise if something goes wrong. Schedule a new appointment without being asked to do so.

Prepare well for tutorials

★ Don't just turn up – work out what you need from it. Draw up an agenda or list of questions.

★ Go over what was agreed at your previous meeting; be ready to provide an update.

★ If you have questions about feedback on your work, be prepared to discuss what you think it means or why you received it.

★ Bring a copy of a recent assignment with you – it might prove useful for clarifying concerns.

In tutorials

★ Let the tutor know your own agenda.

★ Check whether they have matters to raise; finalise the agenda together.

★ Work your way through your questions.

★ Listen to what your tutor has to say; note it down. Assume they want the best for you.

★ Agree actions to follow up before next time.

After tutorials

★ Find a quiet place and go over points raised.

★ If relevant, draw up a list of actions.

★ Follow up on actions agreed in the tutorial.

Matters to raise with tutors

★ Let them know your ideas for projects, dissertations, study abroad, careers, etc. – they might know of relevant funding or schemes or have other useful tips.

★ Let them know if you have a disability or face other difficulties that affect your completing the course or achieving as well as you could.

★ If something goes wrong, let them know.

Enjoy them!

You can enjoy good conversations with your personal tutor – about you, your course and your ambitions. Your tutor will have insights that could be valuable to you.

Reflection

★ How do you feel about personal tutorials in general? Do you look forward to them or try to avoid them?

★ What could you do to ensure that your personal tutorials are more productive and constructive?

Be well informed: find out ...

Read course material

At this level of study, it is assumed that you will:

★ find out what kind of information is available

★ read everything that has been provided, thoroughly, and in a timely manner

★ work out what it means for you

★ ask, if you don't understand its significance.

Get to know how it all works!

Don't wait to be told

Some students are caught out because they think that, at the right moment, a tutor will remind them of what they should know or do, especially if this is what happened at school or college. Although that may happen occasionally, it is not typical. It is usually up to you to make sure you are up to speed with what you need to know.

Checklist

Find out the following, as relevant to your course. Check ✓ each item once completed.

Find out what you need to know

☐ Make a list of all the information you are supposed to receive and when

☐ Clarify where information is provided

☐ Check that you receive each item

☐ Check where to find the regulations and what is in them in case you ever need them.

Find out programme details

☐ The exact name and code of your course

☐ The exact name and code of each module

☐ The names and contact details of all the tutors and lecturers teaching you this year

☐ Where to locate handbooks and guidance for the course and study units

☐ The online facilities provided for your course

☐ The content of your course (the syllabus).

Find out about levels and credit

☐ Your level of study

☐ The number of modules and credits you must take each year and/or for each level

☐ The level and credit rating of each module

☐ The right modules/credit to take for what you want to study next year or for career purposes.

Find out about attendance requirements

☐ Start and end dates for terms or semesters

☐ The minimum attendance requirements

☐ Times to log on for course-related activity

☐ Date and times of any trips or events

☐ When your classes start and end

☐ Consequences if you don't meet requirements.

Find out your time requirements

☐ The number of study hours required (page 130)

☐ The pattern of study on your course, including the amount of independent study (page 18)

☐ The weekly time commitments expected for different types of study (pages 131–2).

Find out about student representation

☐ The kind of student reps system used

☐ When and how reps are elected

☐ The training provided for reps

☐ How to become a rep

☐ How to get your voice heard as a student

☐ What your reps are doing

☐ How your course has responded to student feedback and ratings.

Find out about teaching

- [ ] The teaching methods
- [ ] What kind of participation is required
- [ ] How you will be informed about room and time changes.

Find out about assessment

- [ ] The details of how you will be assessed
- [ ] How marks/grades are allocated
- [ ] The marking criteria and what these mean
- [ ] When and how you are expected to hand in your work, such as in person or electronically
- [ ] The kind of receipt or acknowledgement provided when you hand in your work
- [ ] What is needed to pass?
- [ ] What is needed to excel?

Find out how each level of study differs

- [ ] Look at 'level descriptors' and marking criteria for each level or year of study
- [ ] Compare assignment briefs for different levels, such as for length, difficulty and complexity, and the amount of personal choice and responsibility involved.

Find out about feedback

Feedback on your work may be given in many different ways, from written responses through to informally and verbally during a clinical session.

- [ ] What kinds of feedback are offered on each module or unit of study?
- [ ] When and by whom is this given?
- [ ] With whom can you discuss this?

Find out about resources

- [ ] What kinds of learning resources are provided for you electronically or using hard copy?
- [ ] How are you informed about updates?
- [ ] Where can you find the reading lists?
- [ ] Of the items on your reading lists, which can be substituted for those not available?
- [ ] What studio/lab/practice space is provided?
- [ ] See also page 41.

Get to know your library

- [ ] Who are your library contacts this year?
- [ ] Where are course-related items located?
- [ ] If you are not a regular library user, become familiar with the space (see page 237).

Find out about support

- [ ] Who is responsible for supporting you this year, such as a personal tutor or year tutor?
- [ ] What support is available if you struggle with your coursework?
- [ ] What do you have to do to access this? Do you need to email tutors? book appointments?
- [ ] Is there a peer-support scheme?

Find out about social events

- [ ] How do course students keep in touch?
- [ ] Where do course students meet up?
- [ ] What course events are provided?
- [ ] Are trips and outings provided?
- [ ] Are there networking events?
- [ ] Is there a course-related club/society?

Organise your information

- [ ] Store all study-related information in one place.
- [ ] Book time into your planner to browse it so you know what information is provided.

Gaining from scheduled learning: purpose and value

I don't want to miss a moment!

Find out the purpose

Scheduled sessions, whether labs, lectures, seminars, placements, trips, group projects, discussion or other activity all have a purpose in the course design. Some typical reasons are listed opposite. If you aren't clear of the reason for an activity, ask the tutor.

What do you gain?

Whatever your tutors' intentions, you can decide for yourself how you will extract the most from classes. That will give you a stronger sense of purpose and help you to remain focused.

Reflection

Do you use scheduled sessions effectively, to gain all that these can offer, directly and indirectly? If not, what will you change so you benefit from their full value? What could you do to enjoy them more?

Identify the value for you

Consider which of these benefits of scheduled sessions (such as lectures, group work, etc.) are of value to you ✓.

☐ **1 A 'feel' for the subject**
To gain a broad overview or 'mental map' of the topic; to help me see how new material adds to the picture.

☐ **2 A steer on the essentials**
To find out what lecturers consider important about the topic and issues; to help me when interpreting assignment titles and anticipating potential exam questions; to gain a sense of what I am supposed to know.

☐ **3 To guide and inspire independent study**
For a steer on where to focus my reading, research, practice and thinking; for ideas to inspire my own investigations into the topic.

☐ **4 Clarifying difficult concepts**
To help me clarify complex issues, concepts, problems, etc.

☐ **5 Checking and reinforcing**
To remind me of what I have covered already, to help me understand and recall course material.

☐ **6 Reassurance of being 'up to speed'**
To be confident I am doing what is expected; to avoid the anxiety of feeling I might have missed something essential.

☐ **7 To gain different perspectives**
... from the tutor and, if there is class participation, from the questions and comments of others; these add to my understanding of how the issues can be conceptualised.

☐ **8 To develop insights, skills and behaviours**
... such as through hands-on practical work, working in groups and teams, and communicating through discussion.

☐ **9 Associating with peers before and after class**
To catch up on news, ideas, and generally gain from being part of a learning community.

☐ **10 To demonstrate and reinforce my commitment**
By giving my time and energy, I reinforce my sense of connection to the course, which helps me engage further and enjoy it more.

'Flip your learning': advance preparation for class

'Flipped classes'

'Flipping' means you don't wait to find out new material in class, you cover it beforehand so that you learn more. Whether you are required by your tutors to 'flip' your learning, or just do so for yourself, advance preparation adds value to your study.

Why prepare?

For more effective listening

★ You gain a general feel for the topic – a sense of what to expect.

★ You can then follow more easily.

★ You know what to listen out for.

★ You can bring questions and spot the answers to these more easily.

★ It is easier to take notes in class: you have a better sense of what is relevant and what not to note.

★ You have better recall of the most salient material later.

For easier participation

Many courses require active participation in taught sessions based on work prepared in advance. You are set tasks to do or it may just be assumed that you will read around the subject in advance.

★ You have greater confidence about joining in.

★ You can follow the material more easily in class.

★ You can formulate questions to guide and focus learning in class.

Reflection

'Flipping' your learning

How could you prepare better for class so that you engage more, learn more and enjoy learning more, both whilst preparing for classes and during them?

Prepare, prepare, prepare

Form an overview. Check the topics which are scheduled to come up in class over the next 2–3 weeks. Browse the topic online or in one or more key texts – just gain a feel for material that will be covered. Look at the headings within chapters to get a sense of the content, or read opening or closing paragraphs. Look for key themes, issues or debates. Jot down your own outline and any early questions that you have.

Check for specialist vocabulary. Look up specialist or technical terms you don't understand. Create a personal 'glossary' or dictionary for easy checks and to learn them.

Check for concepts and approaches. Look out for ideas, concepts, theories and approaches that are new to you. Make a note of these. Who developed these, and when and why? Why are they significant? See page 45.

Check the people. If names keep re-appearing in the literature, Google them.

Complete any set work, if your tutors have provided texts, podcasts, exercises or other activities to do in advance. Make sure you take these and the work you have done to class, or can access them there.

Consider upcoming assignments. Make a list of material to watch out for. Jot down questions about this to focus your listening. Leave space to jot down answers under each question either during or after the lecture.

Jot down your own views on issues or debates. Check whether your views change – before, during or after class.

Remind yourself of the last class: glance through notes; look for potential links with the next class. There is little value in being present in body but absent in mind during class.

Engagement during class: more than just 'turning up'

Participate in class activities

The activities are set for a reason. Don't worry about getting things wrong – that may be the point! Participating fully benefits you:

★ to focus, understand and remember

★ to develop confidence and a wider set of skills and abilities

★ to learn from mistakes

★ to get to know others better and for others to get to know you, which is useful when choosing or forming groups for classwork and projects.

50–60% of material heard in class is forgotten ...

Listen attentively

Listen out for clues the lecturer gives about the 'arc' of the lecture – its direction of travel. For example: 'I want to look at five main categories of ...' or 'So, why does this happen?' Good teachers provide an outline of key points to be covered, or flag this in their slides. Use their signalling to help structure your notes.

Maintain your focus in class

Don't miss out on important learning.

Put all distractions aside – personal messages, texts, work, thoughts, plans, etc. You may be asked to use devices or phones for class. If so, consider using an app that blocks out internet distractions.

Mentally challenge what you hear, to help you focus and to aid recall: e.g. 'Is this always the case?' 'Is it really representative?' 'But why?'

Make selective notes

Make your own notes – even if given class notes. At least 50–60% of what you hear in class is forgotten even if you pay attention. Making your notes by hand helps you remember more.

But not too many notes – as you miss points without realising. Note just enough to help you remember what to follow up after class.

In your own words. By being selective, you are less likely to end up regurgitating your lecturers' own words back to them in your assignments.

Avoid drifting off – by keeping your mind active in listening and making good notes instead.

You can copy or adapt the chart on page 37 to help structure your own lecture notes. A blank template is available on the companion site at www.studyskillshandbook.co.uk.

See also page 231.

Make effective notes during taught sessions

Notes for lectures and taught sessions	What to note
Subject (course, module or unit): **Year/Level:** **Date:** **Topic of lecture/session:** **Lecturer(s):** **Filename:**	**Good organisation**. Note information that will help you find and identify notes in future (name of course, module, lecturer, date and topic of the session, where you store these notes).
Preparation Advance work set by the lecturer. Completed ☐ To bring to the session:	**Check your prep**. Check that you have completed any set work; list anything you need to take to the lecture.
What do I want to find out from this lecture? Questions and ideas prompted by my reading, research, discussion, etc.	**Find your focus**. Jot down key questions that you want answered about the topic based on material you have read or browsed in advance. Listening out for this information will help you remain better focused whilst listening.
Opening comments by the lecturer (issues raised, reasons given for the significance of the topic, etc.)	**Note salient points in opening comments**. These often help clarify why the topic was set, its relevance to your study, etc.
Main arc and key themes of the lecture	**Spot the arc**. Note the main arc, or overarching story, of the lecture, and main themes covered.
Main points made (examples; case studies; evidence) (1) (2) (3) Etc.	**Select key points**. Don't attempt to write everything said – it is likely you will miss important information without realising and produce notes that don't make sense. Focus on listening carefully and making short accurate notes. Draw out the main issues, debates, controversies, methodologies etc. Write just enough to be able to follow these up after class.
References to books, VLE, podcasts, website etc.	**Keep together references to new sources of information** – so you can find them easily after the lecture.
Thoughts and questions raised for me by this session (1) (2) (3)	**Your own thinking**. Keep a list of thoughts, questions and other responses as they occur. Update this when you read through your notes after the session.
Any hints and tips provided, such as for assignments, exams, etc.	**Hints and tips**. Follow up on these.
To do (e.g. preparation tasks set by the lecturer for the next session; things I want to follow up from the lecture) (1) (2) (3)	**To Do**. Take careful note of any tasks set as preparation for the next session, or where to find these on the VLE. Keep a list of things you don't understand. Follow up on all of these as part of your independent study outside of class.

Gaining the most from your course

Practicals, studio and lab work

What is the purpose?

Practicals are designed to help you:

★ learn and practise techniques, procedures and equipment

★ test theory and previous research findings through your own work or empirical enquiry

★ learn how to design your own projects, enquiries, performances or experiments.

Health and safety

Find out and clarify any Health and Safety Regulations – and follow these carefully.

Learn, develop and apply skills

You gain hands-on experience. The skills you gain vary depending on your course but, typically, include such things as learning how to:

1 develop a routine for work
2 apply methods in a creative or a systematic way
3 learn and apply core methodologies
4 develop accurate observation skills
5 record observations or data precisely, using the conventions of the course
6 interpret data, situations or your creative work
7 evaluate your own and other people's work in a constructively critical way
8 report clearly on your methods, findings and conclusions or your creative process
9 clarify your thinking about how and why things are done in your subject.

You develop an understanding of such things as:

★ how and why knowledge advances in small, incremental steps, building on what is known

★ why results are often unpredictable

★ why it can be difficult to devise perfectly controlled conditions that provide straightforward, easy-to-interpret results.

Reflection

Practical work

★ What do you need to do to gain maximum benefit from any practically-based work for your course?

★ What could you do to increase your enjoyment of these?

Make these work for you

Be assertive

Get your fair share of lab or studio time. Don't be content watching others – have a go yourself.

Ask

If you are uncertain about unfamiliar techniques, processes or equipment. Check which theories, findings or approaches you are testing out.

Find out

Clarify the precise purpose of the practical work.

Discuss

Discuss your findings or work with others.

Contextualise

Read about what you are doing. Understand how it connects theoretically to the wider field or professional area: how do your findings or experiences compare with this? Consider real-life applications.

Record

Record *exactly* your methods and what happens: don't alter material to provide what you think is the 'right answer'. If you are conducting experiments, be aware that these might only work in ideal conditions. Your lecturers know this so want to see how you record and interpret your methods and results.

Write it up

Write up methods, results and conclusions neatly and clearly. Find out the required format for writing up practical work in your subject area. Are you expected to include diagrams, photos, video, artefacts?

Self-evaluation: making good use of taught sessions

Evaluate how well you make use of class time – and consider how you might do better. For each row, select a higher number if the statement on the left (☺) is most typical of you, or a lower one if the statement on the right is more typical. On this example, 4 would mean you rarely miss a class; 0 would mean you never attend.

1	I attend all scheduled classes	☺ 5 ④ 3 2 1 0 ☹	I miss lectures/classes

Typical of me	☺ 5 4 3 2 1 0 ☹	**Typical of me**
1 I attend all scheduled classes	☺ 5 4 3 2 1 0 ☹	I miss a lot of lectures/classes
2 I consider it important to use class time to learn about the subject	☺ 5 4 3 2 1 0 ☹	I feel it is a lot, already, even to turn up
3 I always arrive in good time	☺ 5 4 3 2 1 0 ☹	I am always late
4 I always stay to the end	☺ 5 4 3 2 1 0 ☹	I always leave early
5 I always check the topic in advance	☺ 5 4 3 2 1 0 ☹	I never check the topic in advance
6 I always read up on the topic before class	☺ 5 4 3 2 1 0 ☹	I never read up on the topic before class
7 If work has been set for the class, I always complete it fully and thoughtfully	☺ 5 4 3 2 1 0 ☹	If work has been set for the class, I usually turn up without having done it
8 I think about the significance of what I hear during lectures/class	☺ 5 4 3 2 1 0 ☹	I don't really think much about what is said in lectures/class
9 In advance, I make a list of points or questions to listen out for in class	☺ 5 4 3 2 1 0 ☹	I never consider in advance what I want from the lecture or class
10 I always make useful notes	☺ 5 4 3 2 1 0 ☹	I don't make any notes
11 I take my own notes even when notes are provided by tutors	☺ 5 4 3 2 1 0 ☹	I don't take notes if material is provided already
12 I never chat in class	☺ 5 4 3 2 1 0 ☹	I chat a lot in class
13 I am single-minded, and avoid 'multi-tasking' and distractions during class	☺ 5 4 3 2 1 0 ☹	I multi-task a lot in class, so I am not fully focused on the lecture
14 I never use social media or messaging during class, unless asked by the tutor	☺ 5 4 3 2 1 0 ☹	I always use class time to catch up on messages, social media, etc.
15 I never drift off or daydream in class	☺ 5 4 3 2 1 0 ☹	I drift off or daydream a lot in class
16 I take full part in class activities (such as discussion, answering questions, using voting technologies, etc.)	☺ 5 4 3 2 1 0 ☹	I try to avoid taking part in any class activities
17 I am careful to make a list of things I don't understand, to follow up later	☺ 5 4 3 2 1 0 ☹	I never note down things I don't understand to check out later
18 I am systematic in following up questions and issues after class	☺ 5 4 3 2 1 0 ☹	I don't ever follow up questions and issues after class
Total score (add your ratings for the 18 points). Then see page 407.		

Engage fully with your course outside of class time

Follow up after class

★ Read through your notes

★ Follow up on points made

★ Check out material and sources that lecturers referred to during class

★ Read more about the issues

★ Talk about it with others

★ Reflect on any issues raised by the class

★ Work on anything you didn't understand

★ Prepare for next class.

Get to know your peers

A strong, supportive cohort tends to raise everyone's performance, so you benefit.

★ Look out for others in your class – make them feel welcome and included

★ Encourage everyone to do well. Let them know what you like about their work or contributions, however small

★ Share your ambitions and remind others of their goals if their motivation drops

★ Celebrate each other's successes.

Engage your mind

★ Consider what you are learning

★ Think critically about topics you are studying

★ Reflect on what it all means

★ Think about where research into the field will lead in future.

Engage!

Engage with course events

★ Attend any trips and events

★ Attend course social events

★ Organise or help out with events

★ Plan your time so you can attend.

Engage with the debates

Find out more about the big debates, the different schools of thought, competing philosophies and theories and the burning issues in your subject. Know the players. Know the arguments. Have an informed opinion about them.

Make the material your own

★ Make your own notes in your own words and style

★ Review notes from time to time

★ Find areas that interest you

★ Become an expert in one or more aspects.

Engage with course representation

★ Attend meetings

★ Provide your opinion about the course

★ Raise points with student representatives

★ Become a representative yourself.

Engage with course feedback

Your ratings and comments make a difference to the future quality of the course.

★ Complete all the surveys

★ Provide comments

★ Consider the results of surveys

★ Ask what action is being taken.

Engage with technology-enhanced learning

Universities and colleges now routinely incorporate digital technologies into all aspects of their courses. Find out what is used on your course and how you are expected to engage with it.

Expand your digital skills

Don't restrict yourself to just a few everyday functions of your technologies: play around and see what else these can do. Explore all the features that are available.

Apply criticality and problem-solving

★ See which technologies work best, in which combinations, for tasks you have to do.

★ Consider the planet! Do you need to be using technology as much as you do? Recharging technology uses electricity – which brings environmental costs.

Observe your thinking efficiency

★ Check whether you work better when using specific technologies.

★ Check whether, for some tasks, you generate ideas more easily through talking, drawing, walking, sketching, writing out ideas on large paper drawing pads, etc.

Check whether you need to ...

☐ communicate with the course in any particular way or at specific times

☐ have a smart phone, laptop, portable device or other equipment

☐ use particular software or technology

☐ collaborate with other students online as part of your course

☐ use particular social media

☐ complete activities online between classes

☐ submit work electronically

☐ take any tests or assessments online.

Check whether your course provides:

☐ an expected means of communicating with you, such as university email, texts, etc.

☐ technology to use or loan rather than buy

☐ easy off-campus access to library and course resources

☐ a student portal to organise information, communications and administration

☐ a Virtual Learning Environment (VLE), or equivalent, for course resources

☐ free use of the internet on campus

☐ free use of the internet from home

☐ easy-to-use links to academic sources

☐ a student website or intranet

☐ course chat rooms or discussion boards

☐ online notice boards

☐ other collaborative learning tools

☐ recordings or videos of lectures/classes

☐ digitised reading lists

☐ digitised reading materials

☐ electronic journals or blogs for reflection

☐ podcasts of lectures

☐ a class wiki

☐ e-portfolios

☐ video conferencing for taught sessions

☐ assistive technologies for disabilities

☐ workshops to help you use the above.

Making sense of difficult material

Sometimes grappling course material can tie you up in knots!

Do I understand it all?

Do you:

★ understand most of the material covered on the course?

★ know how much you understand?

★ understand even when you don't find it interesting?

★ actively monitor your understanding?

★ know how to improve comprehension?

If you answered 'no' to one or more of these questions, experiment with these strategies to improve your comprehension.

Don't get discouraged

... or feel that it is 'impossible'. The more you read and work with it, the more you will chip away at the bits that don't make sense. It might all suddenly become clear or you might have to build a picture of what it means in stages.

Keep working at it

People who do well at a task tend to spend longer grappling with the difficult parts. They refuse to believe that they can't find a way – they don't let the problem beat them. Even if they get frustrated, they also find some enjoyment in the challenge. They treat it as a puzzle they have to solve.

Some people grapple with complex problems over whole life-times, determined not to be beaten by them. Even if they can't resolve the problem, they learn a lot of other things along the way.

Relax

The brain understands more when not stressed – whether from panicking about not understanding, or from hunger, dehydration, tiredness, or other stresses. Use appropriate lighting. Use music or silence as you prefer. Take care of basic needs. See Chapter 7.

Gain a broad overview first

It is easier to understand if you have a sense of the context and a general overview of the material. Watch a video, listen to some talks online, or read an introductory text. Familiarise yourself with the main issues and the vocabulary.

Guide your reading and listening

Set yourself specific questions to start off your reading. Write them down. Adapt these as your reading progresses. The clearer you are about what you are trying to discover, the quicker and easier it is to find it in the text. See Chapter 10.

Build your knowledge base

If you don't know the people, events and cultural or academic references you come across, this disrupts your attention, makes it harder to absorb information and can undermine your confidence. Follow up some or all of these first in order to make more sense of what you hear or read. See pages 67 and 69.

Avoid 'attention drift'

If your mind wanders to other things, this interrupts your flow and hinders understanding. Mindfulness practice can help to build your concentration. See page 167.

Identify the 'building blocks'

We tend to find material difficult if we don't fully grasp other sets of information that we are assumed to have learnt already.

★ Make a list of each of the components that you don't understand – whether vocabulary, concepts, formulae, or references to material that you don't know about.

★ Take your time to work through these to build a more solid knowledge base.

★ If your list is long, narrow it down by identifying the concepts that recur in lectures or your reading and start with those.

★ You will gain familiarity with specialist concepts, methods and ways of expressing ideas through exposure to these over the course: don't give up on them too early!

Sleep on it

For difficult material, work at it. Then give your brain down time to process it. Sleep helps. See page 165.

Decipher complex material

Some material is hard to understand because of the way it is written or explained verbally. Don't assume you can't ever understand it.

Separate it out. If material is presented in a dense condensed style with a great deal of information concentrated into a few sentences, draw out each point separately. List these in your own words and consider them individually before coming back to make sense of the whole.

Re-read difficult passages. Academic texts often contain difficult passages. Don't panic! You are bound to need to re-read some passages slowly, several times. See page 42.

Pose and answer 'depth questions'

★ **Purpose** Why is this included in the course?

★ **Significance** Why is it important?

★ **Focus** What do I need to learn about this?

★ **Highlights** What are the main points to take away?

★ **Connection** What else do I know that will help me understand this? How will it help me with other aspects of the course?

★ **Relevance** Why is this detail relevant?

★ **Application** 'How would this be used or applied in real life?' 'That works here, but would it work in any other situations?'

Make course material your own

Think fluidly about the material

Course material is just information until you make it your own. It doesn't have much meaning until then. It isn't enough to just collect information by noting things down, copying it, or knowing it exists somewhere in a file or on the internet. You need to get your brain around the material. That comes from thinking about it either on your own or in discussion, and from working with the material in different ways.

Don't think only about what the tutors want, although that is important. Consider, too, what the material means more broadly – to you, to people you know, to your career, to answering the big questions of our time. Find enjoyment in making the material your own, in becoming more of an expert.

Consider the diagram below and the many different ways of thinking about the material, in combination with each other. There isn't a single 'correct' sequence for thinking about material. As the connecting lines suggest, you can move fluidly from one type of thinking to another, to deepen your understanding.

Think about the material

Absorb Take in the information, at a basic level, making sure you have seen or heard correctly.

Elaborate the task Work out exactly what is required, through thought and/or investigation.

Comprehend Make sure you 'get it': understand what is said, written, signed, marked. Follow and grasp what is stated, at either superficial or deeper levels.

Select relevant information to read, note, reflect on, analyse, compare, contrast, write about, ask about, present, submit in assignments.

Analyse Investigate details in depth; identify how parts connect to the whole; scrutinise evidence to see it is all it purports to be; check the component parts for consistency, validity, etc.

Exercise criticality Scrutinise for accuracy, veracity, clarity, quality, validity, relevance, relative merits; the merits of assumptions, evidence, reasoning, conclusions, etc.

Reflect Active, structured thinking about the issues.

Compare and contrast Draw out similarities and differences relevant to the issue.

Evaluate evidence, reasoning, or solutions against criteria, or by comparing items; evaluate theory in relation to evidence or practice.

Synthesise Combine different perspectives, aspects, reasoning or solutions, to create something new.

Apply Use the information to develop your argument. Apply theory to practice.

Extrapolate Draw out deeper understandings, insights, significance, implications, applications.

Get under the skin of your subject area

It is easier to do well on your course if you understand its provenance and what matters to those who work in the academic field, such as your tutors, researchers, and professionals in related areas. Below, are some key questions to guide your initial enquiry. Jot down main points you discover.

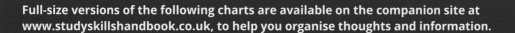

Full-size versions of the following charts are available on the companion site at www.studyskillshandbook.co.uk, to help you organise thoughts and information.

Understanding your subject area	
Aspects	**Details**
Its story and purpose When and why did it originate? Who were its first stars?	
Its distinctiveness How and why does it differ from similar subjects?	
Its focus What kinds of questions does your subject discipline look to answer?	
Values and culture What kinds of things are valued by those working in the field? What matters to them about the subject, academic thinking or the world in general?	
Main 'schools of thought' or theoretical approaches associated with the subject? (See opposite.)	
Its methodologies What is distinctive about the methods used to research issues in this discipline?	
Learning gain What kind of knowledge, understanding, skills and other attributes can you expect to develop on the course?	
Being good at it? What do you need to do in order to be good at your subject? What kinds of behaviours and ways of thinking contribute to success?	

Schools of thought	
Aspect	**Details**
Name of the 'school of thought'/ theoretical approach	
When did it originate?	For each of the key schools of thought you identify, consider and record these details.
What are the key texts or 'seminal works' associated with this approach? When were they written and by whom?	
What are the key characteristics associated with this approach? How does it differ from other approaches or perspectives?	
What did it add to study of the discipline?	These outlines are useful tools for writing assignments, reviewing course material, and revising for quizzes and exams.
What are the strong points associated with this approach?	
What are its drawbacks or limitations?	
How have later researchers and academics refined this approach? Why did they do this and what difference does this make?	

Gaining the most from your course: review

1 Ten Golden Rules!
Bear these golden rules in mind and stick to them! They will take you a long way towards completing and passing your course.

2 Make good use of personal tutorials
Recognise the potential value of this source of support. Plan for it in advance so you use the time to your advantage. Keep in touch with your tutor.

3 Be well informed
Boost your confidence by making sure you know what you need to know. Get ahead of the game by finding out in advance rather than playing 'catch-up'. Enjoy feeling in charge.

4 Find purpose and value
Identify your own purpose for course activities, including attending taught classes. Be clear why you are doing things and the benefits to your study or more generally.

5 Gain full benefit from taught sessions
Use all of this valuable time for learning – with full attention, great preparation and useful notes.

6 'Flip your learning'
Use time before and after class to make sure you really get the most from all taught time. Gain confidence from being familiar with the material before class.

7 Engage with the course and experience
Be active in participating in class, in the life of your course, and with the broader student experience. Contribute to making the experience a valuable one.

8 Value your peers
Other students can make a great difference to your experience and achievement. Get to know them – give it time. Respect their learning, too.

9 Stick with difficult bits
Don't be discouraged by material that stretches you. Work at it from different angles until you get it. Get your mind engaged.

10 Think for yourself
Don't just listen: read, note, write. Learn more and raise the quality of your work by enjoying some good thinking time about course material. Mull it over. Question it. Have ideas. Question your ideas.

11 Get below the surface
Find out what shapes and characterises your subject discipline: this helps you make sense of new material and produce better assignments. Enjoy a greater sense of mastery in the discipline.

12 Take away your own messages
Consider which messages in the chapter are most useful and relevant to you: make a list. Take a few minutes to note into your planner or journal how and when you will take action.

Chapter 3

Employability and preparing for your future

Learning outcomes

This chapter offers you opportunities to:

- ✓ integrate preparation for future employment and career progression into your time as a student
- ✓ consider how to give yourself the best chance of gaining the kind of employment you want
- ✓ identify how the skills you gain as a student are relevant to the workplace
- ✓ consider your potential 'weak' areas so that you can address these
- ✓ identify action to take now to enhance your future prospects.

Give yourself a head start

Whether or not you know which career or kinds of work you wish to pursue, you give yourself a big advantage if you start to consider and prepare for your future right from the start of your course. This gives you more time to investigate, think, and prepare, and helps with the mental and psychological journey that this often entails.

Reflection

★ Which of the 'good reasons' listed opposite are relevant to you?

★ Are there other reasons you would add, relevant to you?

10 good reasons to start early

It provides plenty of time to ...

1 become better informed of options, with an opportunity to think and plan towards these.

2 ensure you choose the right courses and extra-curricular activity all the way through your studies.

3 identify strengths and consider how to make the most of these.

4 give yourself time to identify and address any potential gaps or weaknesses that could become barriers to your preferred future.

5 build your CV and gain experience and skills.

6 test the water and see whether your initial ideas are right for you.

7 try out part-time work or placements in areas that interest you, to take reality checks (and give yourself time to change your mind!).

8 gain practice in the different stages of the job application process.

9 make applications for jobs, internships, and other opportunities at the right time – so you don't miss out.

10 build confidence that inspires you and future employers.

Planning towards your future

Personal development planning (PDP)

Study skills activities are part of a wider process of personal development. This is not something you do once and forget; rather, it is an attitude towards your future. It does not finish, as there are always changes and new opportunities to consider and prepare for.

Can you plan for the future?

Although you can't predict every eventuality, this shouldn't deter you from plans and actions that position you better for the future. You can be an active agent, creating new chances and preparing yourself to be ready to act on opportunities that arise.

Benefits of personal planning

Personal planning can give you a clearer sense of who you are in the world and what you want from life. A greater sense of purpose helps you to deploy your time and energies well, to make better choices, and gain greater control over your future. The PDP process itself develops reflective, strategic, analytical and creative thinking skills relevant to study and life. Typically, it can spur you on to gain valuable skills, habits and experience that help you to compete and cope in the world. You then gain more than just a degree from your education.

PDP: What are the benefits?

Of the benefits listed below, circle any that you value.

Deeper self-awareness	Increased motivation	Creating new opportunities
Greater clarity about the kind of life I want	Inspiration for study	Having clearer goals
Readiness to seize opportunities	A sense of direction	Awareness of my training needs
A steer on how to direct my time	Better use of work appraisals	Increased sense of purpose
A greater sense of control over my own destiny	Having a framework to help me make decisions	

What does it involve?

1 **Deep and ongoing reflection** The focus of this will change over time, but it should involve some focused thought about what kind of person you are now; who or what you want to be in future; the kind of life you want. And why.

2 **Increasing self-awareness** You are more likely to make the right choices if you are open to understanding more about what drives you; how you hold yourself back; your values, interests, strengths, habits good and bad, inspirations, preferences, qualities, and ambitions – and weaknesses and shortcomings.

3 **Being informed** It should mean you are more active in finding out about your options and opportunities and in broadening your perspective.

4 **Taking personal responsibility** You take charge of your education, training, choices and planning.

5 **Developing a strategy to get where you want to be** You set yourself goals and targets to take you further along the path towards where you want to be. You work out a strategy for keeping yourself on that path. You anticipate potential barriers and setbacks that could derail you so you are ready for them!

6 **Engaging with what is on offer** – such as the Careers Service, awards, training, speakers, portfolio-building available through your college or Uni.

Your personal development so far

Your personal development history

It is likely that you already have experience of personal planning. Draw on that to consider what worked well and lessons to apply to future planning. Use the Activity below to start your thinking.

Activity

My Personal Development Planning so far

Identify ✓ which types of personal planning you have already undertaken.

☐ Deciding on which qualifications to take at school, college, or at work

☐ Deciding and preparing for a major life event (such as the birth of a child or moving home)

☐ Planning and preparing for College/Uni

☐ Deciding on a Uni and course of study

☐ Planning and preparing to find a job

☐ Planning a study or work project

☐ Thinking through how to give bad news

☐ Working out how to balance a busy schedule

☐ Deciding and planning to develop expertise over time (e.g. driving, technical, music, sports, creative, academic)

☐ Thinking long-term when making choices

☐ Taking courses that develop self-awareness (e.g. coaching, counselling, management)

☐ Taking courses to develop personal interests

☐ Travelling in order to challenge your ideas and broaden your perspective

☐ Building a Curriculum Vitae (CV or résumé)

☐ Others?

What lessons have you learnt so far about effective forward planning?

Personal development as a student

Reflection

Personal planning now

★ How are you using personal planning now to make choices that affect your future (such as when choosing subject options, work experience, taking on responsibilities and extracurricular activities)?

★ What do you want to achieve through these choices?

★ Are you doing enough to enable future opportunities and create good foundations?

★ What is provided by your college or Uni to assist personal and professional development?

PDP skills developed through study

Skills useful to study can help PDP, such as:

1 Clarifying what you want from study, in order to increase your focus (page 11).

2 Planning towards a focus: setting goals and targets to achieve desired outcomes (pages 116–20).

3 Monitoring progress and evaluating your progress towards what you want to achieve (pages 99–100).

4 Developing a personal study strategy: based on your goals, experience and preferred ways of doing things (Chapter 4).

Developing work and career readiness

Below are key steps to take now to increase your readiness later when applying for jobs and pursuing careers that interest you.

Visit the Careers Service

It is never too early to use Careers Services: choices and decisions made in the first and second years can have long-term effects. Most Careers Advisers would prefer students used the service in their first year. An early chat about your aspirations and goals can point you in the right direction, helping you make good decisions such as about module choices and extra-curricular activity, which can save you time, money (or disappointment) later.

The Careers Services can advise on the wide range of choices open to you: around half of graduate jobs are open to graduates of any degree subject. They may have useful contacts and can advise on how to make strong job applications.

Labour market trends

Ask Careers Advisers about labour market trends and how these could affect you. What opportunities are there locally and elsewhere? Are these expected to change in the next few years?

Decide how to use Careers Services

Careers Services usually provide a range of services such as those below. Decide ✓ which could be useful, or of interest, to you.

- ☐ Ideas about possible career routes for me
- ☐ Labour market information, trends and data
- ☐ Things I can do to become more employable
- ☐ Choosing the right courses and subject options so I can follow particular career routes
- ☐ Further qualifications I might need
- ☐ What employers look for in job applicants
- ☐ Building my CV
- ☐ Experience and skills I should acquire
- ☐ Best times to apply for specific kinds of job
- ☐ Entrepreneurship
- ☐ Enterprise
- ☐ Projects for local employers
- ☐ Finding a mentor
- ☐ Self-employment
- ☐ Progressing to a further degree (e.g. Masters, Doctorate or teacher training)
- ☐ Pursuing a research career
- ☐ Practice with applying for jobs
- ☐ Feedback on practice applications
- ☐ Job interview skills
- ☐ Information about part-time work opportunities
- ☐ Internships
- ☐ Volunteering opportunities
- ☐ Networking opportunities
- ☐ Working/jobs in other countries
- ☐ Work visa information

What questions do you have?

To make the most of your visit to the Careers Service, prepare a few questions on issues that matter to you. As a starting place, consider:

★ What kinds of jobs are open to me?

★ Is there much competition for these?

★ What kinds of jobs do most students with my degree enter?

★ What further training or qualifications would I need for careers I have in mind?

★ What do employers want in job applicants?

★ What should I be doing now?

What is important to you?

Before you commit yourself to a particular career route, find out what it would entail. Beware of the apparent glamour of some jobs: search below the surface for details of what day-to-day work would be like and think through whether this suits you. For example:

★ What are typical working hours in those careers or jobs? Do these suit you?

★ Would you be willing to work for many years on a training wage until fully qualified?

★ Would you work on a voluntary basis to gain relevant experience?

★ Would you take more qualifications in order to pursue your chosen career?

★ Can you afford the further training?

★ Would you like the kind of people who are usually attracted to this kind of work?

★ Would a lot of travel be required? If so, would this be acceptable to you?

★ Would you be open to travelling a lot? Or working nationally and/or internationally?

★ How stressful is the job? How much stress would you be prepared to put up with?

★ Are there health and safety risks associated with this kind of work?

★ What would be the effects on family life? Would you be prepared to accept these?

★ Would you have to socialise outside of work with colleagues? Does that appeal to you?

Reflection

What matters most?

★ What do your reactions and responses to these questions suggest about the types of work, career and life-style that suit you?

★ Do the careers or work you are considering fit the kind of life you want or the kind of person you want to be?

The impact of study options?

Find out the potential benefits if you:

★ take a complementary subject that would give you atypical but marketable expertise

★ develop particular skills or languages

★ study, work or travel abroad

★ gain business or enterprise skills.

Stand out from the crowd

What will make you stand out as 'distinctive' when competing with others for jobs or academic places? What could you do that would help this?

Stand out from the crowd

Recognising your skills and qualities

You can develop skills from all kinds of experience; the trick is in being able to recognise these for yourself and transfer them to new contexts.

Skills audits

One way of recognising your skills is to take a periodic 'skills audit', reflecting on attributes that contributed to success. Skills audits help you …

★ **with strengths**: to become aware of your strengths, enabling you to articulate these better to others, and building pride in your achievements

★ **with self-improvement**: to develop the confidence and insight to identify areas that need further development

★ **with prioritising**: to judge which aspects to develop next

★ **with self-assessment**: to become used to forming well-founded, evidence-based judgements about your work, performance and abilities, rather than being dependent solely on other people's estimation of you.

Activity

Skills from experience

Choose one thing you do well, a difficulty you overcame, or a personal achievement, no matter how small. It might be success in arts, performance, sports, with people, coping with illness or life challenges, or being accepted for your course. Use the *beautiful garden* example for ideas. Consider the following questions in relation to whatever you chose.

How did I do it?

1 What did you do to create the conditions that led to success? Did you practise? Or urge yourself on in some way? Or find others to help? Or just believe you could do it?
2 Which skills, attitudes and qualities did you exhibit?

Example: the beautiful garden

Supposing one year your garden or window box looked absolutely beautiful. How did that happen?

Many small things might have led to a perfect outcome. You might have watered the plants very carefully, depending on the weather. If so, you used powers of *observation* and *deduction*.

You might have weeded and pruned in the rain when you wanted to stay indoors. Here you *kept in mind your long-term goal* for the garden, showing *dedication* and *perseverance*.

You might have *selected* plants from a wide range of options, to match your garden conditions.

You probably did *research,* possibly online or by reading gardening books, questioning others who had grown them or watching television programmes.

You *followed specific instructions* on how to grow them, and purchased special fertiliser, prepared the ground in a certain way or pruned at particular times: such care requires *method, attention to detail, time management* and *task management*.

All these skills can be relevant to academic study and to work contexts. Whatever your experience, you might have skills, qualities and attributes you haven't acknowledged. Take stock of these and recognise their value so that you can draw on them when needed.

Your personal skills profile

Reflection

Skills from experience

For the activity above (page 52), were you surprised to find out how many skills you have already? Do you tend to underestimate or overestimate your skills?

By doing the 'Skills from experience' activity, you probably found that you have more skills and qualities than you thought. If not, go through the activity with someone who knows you, or use the list on page 54 as a prompt. Most people already have qualities and skills that they can adapt to academic study.

★ Those entering from school have the benefit of recent study and established study habits.

★ Mature students typically bring experience of responsibility, working with others, managing time, and perseverance – all valuable assets when studying.

Evaluating skills and setting priorities

Awareness of your current skills increases your confidence, which in turn increases your chances of success. The following pages are a chance to pause and consider your skills and their relevance.

★ Identify current skills and strengths.

★ Consider how skills apply in different contexts.

Update your profile

As you progress with the course, your skills profile and self-evaluation will change. Take time to update these on a regular basis, either as you go along or at least once every few months. Schedule a time for this in your diary/planner.

Activity

Current skills and qualities

Use your notes from the 'Skills from experience' activity (page 52) and the list on page 54 for the following activity.

1 **Select ✓** On your copy, check off ✓ the items at which you are reasonably skilled already.

2 **Add** any personal skills that are missing.

3 **Rate ★★** Use one or more stars to indicate those at which you excel.

4 **Give examples** For each item you selected, starting with those you starred, jot down an occasion when you demonstrated that skill or quality. The 'prompt box' below may help you recall situations in which you might have developed these skills.

5 **Use** Display the list where you can see it. Use it for job applications, for setting priorities for personal development, and to inspire yourself too!

6 **Congratulate** yourself!

If you did not select many items, search through your past experiences for better examples – or go through the list with a friend. You may be being too modest!

Prompt box: Where did I develop/demonstrate my skills and qualities?

- ☐ School or college
- ☐ Employment
- ☐ Applying for jobs
- ☐ Family life
- ☐ Domestic responsibility
- ☐ Caring for others
- ☐ Interests and hobbies
- ☐ Independent study
- ☐ Emergency events
- ☐ Sport

- ☐ Personal development
- ☐ Saturday jobs
- ☐ Employment
- ☐ Unemployment
- ☐ Voluntary work
- ☐ Making a home
- ☐ Friendships
- ☐ Travel/holidays
- ☐ Clubs/societies
- ☐ Personal setbacks
- ☐ Ill health

Skills Audit: Current skills and qualities

People

- [ ] Ability to get on with a diversity of people
- [ ] Understanding other people's points of view
- [ ] Sensitivity to cultural differences
- [ ] Dealing with the general public
- [ ] Customer service
- [ ] Teamwork and collaboration
- [ ] Networking
- [ ] Managing or supervising others' work
- [ ] Teaching, training, coaching, mentoring
- [ ] Negotiating and persuading
- [ ] Languages
- [ ] Helping others to arrive at decisions
- [ ] Consideration of others' feelings
- [ ] Caring for others
- [ ] Supporting and motivating others
- [ ] Understanding others' body language
- [ ] Coping with 'difficult' people
- [ ] Speaking clearly and to the point
- [ ] Audience awareness
- [ ] Taking direction from others
- [ ] Giving constructive feedback
- [ ] Leadership skills

Task management

- [ ] Creativity, design and layout
- [ ] Innovation and inventiveness
- [ ] Ability to see the 'whole picture'
- [ ] Argument and debate
- [ ] Seeing patterns and connections
- [ ] Attention to detail
- [ ] Searching for information
- [ ] Classifying and organising information
- [ ] Making decisions
- [ ] Managing change and transition
- [ ] Setting priorities
- [ ] Organising events
- [ ] Organising work to meet deadlines
- [ ] Facilitating meetings
- [ ] Reading complex texts
- [ ] Digital literacy
- [ ] Picking up quickly on new technologies
- [ ] Applying technology to tasks
- [ ] Using social networking tools
- [ ] Working with numbers
- [ ] Selling
- [ ] Problem-solving
- [ ] Quick thinking
- [ ] Practical skills
- [ ] Understanding quickly how things work
- [ ] Seeing practical applications
- [ ] Writing reports or official letters
- [ ] Enterprise and entrepreneurship
- [ ] Business and financial skills
- [ ] Managing difficult situations and crises

Self-management

- [ ] Setting my own goals
- [ ] Working independently
- [ ] Maintaining a high level of motivation
- [ ] Taking responsibility for my own actions
- [ ] Learning from my mistakes
- [ ] Willingness to take risks and experiment
- [ ] Assertiveness
- [ ] Determination and perseverance
- [ ] Self-reliance
- [ ] Recognising my own needs
- [ ] Taking care of my health and well-being
- [ ] Maintaining calm in a crisis
- [ ] Coping skills and managing stress

Other:

- [ ]
- [ ]

Preparing for work with employers

Gaining the right skills and attributes

By themselves, your degree subject and grade will not usually be enough to impress employers. They want to know how far you already demonstrate attributes relevant to their business and can 'hit the ground running'. It is likely that they will consider how well you used your time as a student, such as the choices you made and extra-curricular activities.

What do employers want?

Although each employer is different, below are typical requirements for 'work-readiness'. Consider if, and how, you could demonstrate these already, and which to develop further whilst a student.

★ Highlight those you have already to some extent

★ Circle those you intend to develop further

Takes responsibility for their own work	Enables others to work effectively	Has work experience
Can plan ahead successfully	Cultural sensitivity	Commitment to diversity
Spots, creates and uses opportunities	Commitment to personal development	Reliable
Understands how to behave at work	Commitment to personal performance	Punctual
Good self-awareness	Learns from mistakes	Gets things done – and on time

Ideally, preparation should start in your first year of study, so that by the time you apply for jobs you are in a strong position and can give good examples of each.

Develop a 'rounded portfolio'

When you make job applications, you will be asking yourself a range of questions:

★ 'How have I used my time ...?'

★ 'What have I done that will make my application stand out?'

★ 'What will make this employer choose or consider me rather than others?'

★ 'What evidence have I got that I can deliver the skills they are asking for?'

★ 'What experience can I offer ...?'

Your time at college or university is an investment. Obviously, it is important to spend time gaining your degree. However, you do not have to invest *all* your time in study. There are 'smart' ways of using your time and putting a degree together, so that you leave with a rounded portfolio.

Typically a rounded student portfolio will contain 'investment' in at least three of the following:

1 the degree subject(s)
2 complementary subjects
3 skills development
4 unusual technical expertise
5 work experience
6 volunteer activity
7 contributing to the community
8 a position of responsibility
9 study, work or extended travel abroad
10 a broad set of skills that could be transferred to the workplace.

Activity

Work-readiness

➡ For each of the attributes above, what examples could you give that would convince an employer?

➡ Of those attributes you intend to develop, how will you do so? (Careers Services can advise.)

Activity

Personal portfolio

➡ In which of the ten areas listed above have you invested already?

➡ Realistically, what else could you undertake in the next six months to develop your personal portfolio?

Articulating your abilities to employers

Speaking a common language?

The Association of Graduate Employers reports that almost one-third of large employers find it difficult to find students with the right skills to fill graduate vacancies. Often, the skills they are looking for are:

★ skills that mirror skills you would use on your course, but with a different name or emphasis;

★ 'soft skills' you could acquire through extra-curricular activities and a part-time job.

It is worth thinking not just about the skills you have, but differences in the way those skills might be described and used in education and in the workplace.

Which 'soft' skills?

Employers value soft skills in the following areas:

1 Managing yourself: self-efficacy

Self-reliance; self-awareness; focus; the capacity to learn, plan action and take initiative; resilience; flexibility; resourcefulness; motivation; realism.

2 Managing people: people skills

Networking; teamworking; communication; negotiating, persuading, influencing; customer focus; leadership; ability to support and motivate others; cultural awareness; languages.

3 Managing projects: task management skills

Ability to get on with tasks without close supervision; devising and implementing an action plan; attention to detail; being logical, methodical and systematic; applying technology; numerical reasoning; problem-solving; versatility, flexibility and multi-skilling; willingness to take risks; being results-orientated and solution-focused; business awareness; work ethic.

For more about developing such skills, see:

★ Cottrell, S. (2015). *Skills for Success: Personal Development and Employability,* 3rd edn. London: Red Globe Press.

★ Free resources can be found on www.thestudyspace.com.

Activity

Which skills do employers value?

➡ Browse advertisements for graduate jobs, and websites such as www.prospects.ac.uk, noting the skills employers ask for.

➡ Which of these skills could you develop whilst a student?

Translate skills into 'employer-speak'

Consider how skills you acquire as a student could translate into the language of 'soft' skills used by employers or in career areas that interest you and could be transferable to employment. See page 57 for examples and add your own.

Then, make a chart (as below) to record work-relevant attributes you gain as a student, with examples to demonstrate your ability.

Articulate skills for employers	
Skills, qualities, attributes, experience and achievements	**Specific examples**
☐ Self-awareness and self-reliance	
☐ Verbal skills	
☐ Team working	
☐ Practical skills in managing projects	
Other transferable skills I can offer	
☐ Driving licence ☐ Technology skills ☐ Languages ☐ Other	

A template is available on the companion site.

Translating academic skills into employment skills

Area of academic activity	Examples of potential transferable and soft skills which could be developed through academic study
Personal development / personal planning	Self-management; forward planning; taking responsibility for improving performance; increasing personal effectiveness; reflective skills.
Independent study	Working without supervision; organising your own time and work; taking personal responsibility; self-reliance; knowing when to ask for help.
Lectures	Listening skills; identifying and selecting relevant points; recording salient information; preparing for meetings; using the information heard; critical thinking.
Seminars, group work, team projects, collaborative learning	Listening; teamwork; negotiating; oral communication; giving and taking directions; taking responsibility; working with people from diverse backgrounds; cultural sensitivity; dealing with differences in opinion; sharing knowledge; contributing to meetings and discussions.
Lab work	Following protocol and instructions; taking responsibility; designing tasks for particular purposes; precision and attention to detail; attention to health and safety requirements; ethical understanding; measuring change; recording results; being systematic; drawing conclusions.
Oral presentation	Speaking in public; persuading and influencing others; making a case; time management; presentation skills; using audiovisual aids; planning; sharing knowledge; adapting communication style.
Writing essays and other forms of academic writing	Task analysis; structuring writing for specific audiences using relevant style and conventions; developing an argument; making a strong case; working to word limits and deadlines; sharing knowledge; breaking tasks into component parts; attention to detail; critical thinking.
Maths and statistics	Problem-solving; presenting information; interpreting data; sharing knowledge; critical analysis.
Observations	Listening skills; working with a diverse range of people; information management; attention to detail; drawing conclusions; making precise and accurate notes and reports.
Research projects	Time management; using search tools; managing large amounts of information; working to deadlines; decision-making; project management; using technology; developing ethical understanding; taking responsibility for larger pieces of work; critical thinking.
Exams and revision	Planning; working towards deadlines; using time effectively; decision-making; managing stress; coping with challenges; resilience.

Building your CV whilst a student

When you apply for a job, you might be asked to provide a curriculum vitae (CV). On this, you list your educational and work history, your interests, and other activities you have undertaken. Your academic qualifications form only one part of a CV. If you do nothing but study, you might have little to write on your CV or discuss at interview.

Expect employers to ask you for examples of:

★ where you have demonstrated skills, qualities or competences stipulated in the job description and person specification

★ how you dealt with situations typical of the workplace (such as dealing with the public, being a good colleague, managing tight deadlines, being flexible in response to change)

★ good citizenship such as volunteering or roles with responsibilities.

Plan and prepare ahead so that you have some experience to draw upon when applying for jobs and in job interviews. This may be through work experience, but can also be through activity related to your course or interests, such as putting on an exhibition, taking part in or producing a play, clinical practice, collaborative projects or similar activities that involve multiple skills.

Keep your CV up to date

Update any changes to personal details, experience, skills, job roles and the dates and addresses of employers. Do this regularly so you can send it at short notice, if needed. Adapt it to fit the roles for which you apply.

Update your personal records

Keep good records, or a portfolio, to help you when writing your CV, personal statement and other aspects of job applications.

Every six months, update a thumbnail sketch about yourself. Include the following:

★ What inspires you most at present?

★ How have you used skills in new contexts?

★ What personal qualities have you developed out of recent experience?

★ Your long-term and short-term goals.

Gain work experience

There is no substitute for work experience; it develops skills and attributes hard to gain through study alone. It need not be in your intended career area if opportunities don't arise there. It is better to have *any* recent work experience than none, especially if you haven't had paid employment before. Consider such choices as:

★ part-time jobs, paid or voluntary

★ sandwich programmes, work-based learning modules or work placements

★ work or placements abroad

★ internships

★ mentoring-in-schools projects

★ artists in residency (for arts students)

★ Student Union work.

Broaden your life experience

Look for ways to develop a broader range of skills and experience, to enhance your CV.

★ Build your confidence in coping with a wider set of circumstances and situations.

★ Take part in competitions and projects, such as enterprise projects if offered at your institution.

★ Take on positions of responsibility such as course rep, mentor, coach or supervisor roles; gain problem-solving and leadership experience.

★ Consider the global perspective on issues you study.

★ Work or study abroad: encounter a broader range of people and situations.

★ Consider community work, Student Union work, drama, music, or political activity, such as through student societies.

Further reading and resources

See *Employability and personal development* on page 405.

Recording your achievements

Celebrate success

When you have achieved a goal or personal success, take the following steps.

1 **Acknowledge your achievement:** Give yourself credit for what you have done.

2 **Celebrate:** Give yourself a reward, appropriate to the scale of your achievement.

3 **Record it:** Note down what happened.

4 **Use it:** Use your success as an example of what you can achieve when you focus your energies. When applying for jobs, or to build personal motivation, use your records to find examples of different kinds of achievement.

Records of achievement

Records of achievement can vary from being a list of qualifications to a more detailed formal record such as the HEAR (in the UK) or a portfolio of work.

Your institution will issue a formal transcript listing subjects studied and your marks or grades. However, only *you* will know:

★ how your confidence has grown

★ how you have developed as a person

★ personal goals you have achieved

★ how you did it – the steps you took and the personal qualities you called upon

★ how you kept yourself motivated

★ what you learnt about yourself in the process.

It is useful to maintain a record of *how* you achieved your goals, for future reference and for preparation for job interviews.

Maintaining a personal portfolio

A portfolio is a folder where you bring together materials on a theme, such as art work or evidence of occupational competencies. A personal portfolio is your collation of materials about you. Keep it meaningful and easy to use.

★ Divide it into sections.

★ Label and date everything.

★ Create a contents page.

★ Refresh regularly, removing old materials.

★ Include all certificates and transcripts.

★ If you wish, include self-evaluations, action plans, reflections, photographs, examples of your work, etc.

★ Include your CV and an updated personal statement.

What is the purpose of a portfolio?

A portfolio has several uses:

★ it helps you organise key information and documents

★ it helps processes such as reflection, self-evaluation and personal development

★ for some jobs, you take it to job interviews.

Write a personal statement

Personal statements are a means of drawing together, succinctly, key details about where you are now, where you want to be, and how you will get there. Typically, they include:

★ career and life goals

★ what you have done so far towards achieving these (at school, college, university, or work)

★ personal significance of goals/achievements

★ what you learned about yourself along the way (e.g. how to stay motivated or to perform best / how you applied the lessons you learnt)

★ skills and qualities you have achieved, with the best examples to demonstrate your ability

★ what your next steps will be.

Employers might request a personal statement in support of job applications. If so, refresh yours so it focuses on the person specification for the job. Ask your careers service for feedback on your CV and personal statement.

Taking further qualifications and training

Why take more qualifications?

Whilst studying

You might be able to take modules, units or workshops alongside your main qualification or as choices integrated into it. These can be useful for:

★ **broadening your knowledge** into areas that are new, topical, enhance your CV, or just interest you

★ **a niche career**: choosing modules or short courses in sports, media, health, art or marketing, for example, could open up interesting specialist careers if your main qualifications are in law, finance, technology or data analysis

★ **generic employability skills**, such as languages, data-analysis, coaching, mentoring, leadership, communications, work-based or work-related learning, and careers or employability modules

★ **sharpening basic skills**, such as numeracy, typing and grammar. Ask support services about resources or workshops at your institution, local colleges or online.

Post-graduate study

Check whether graduate careers that interest you require a post-graduate certificate, diploma, Masters, doctorate, or updates in training as part of continuous professional development (CPD).

Activity

Identifying opportunities

➡ What opportunities are open to you for adapting your degree programme or for taking options that develop useful skills?

➡ What opportunities are there for gaining credit for work-based learning?

Preparing for post-graduate study

If you need or want to progress to higher level awards, use your course and time as a student to prepare. Such courses can be competitive so put yourself in the best possible position to gain a place.

Research your options widely: Choose a course that speaks to your aims and interests.

Check the entry requirements: Would you need a minimum degree classification or Grade Point Average (GPA)? Do you need to have studied particular subjects or gained specific experience first?

Develop your specialism: Through your course, reading and work experience, build understanding of areas in which you could specialise. This helps ensure you choose the right qualification and that your application is knowledgeable and convincing.

Build research skills: Developing these to a high standard now can boost grades as well as position you well for post-graduate study.

Dissertations and/or projects: Consider topics that prepare you for the next level qualification or future doctorate. It is a good way of testing your interest and gives you a head start on your post-graduate study.

Interested in an academic career?

★ Observe what academics do.

★ Talk to your lecturers about their experiences.

★ Consider being a peer mentor and/or work on peer support schemes, as good preparation for teaching.

★ Extend your research skills and understanding.

★ Consider your specialism: what would you be happy to research and teach for many years?

★ Gain an academic mentor if you can. Ask a tutor.

Enterprise and self-employment

Reports on student employability tend to focus mainly on the views of a relatively small number of large employers. The overwhelming majority of jobs are with small businesses that value an entrepreneurial approach. A great many are micro-businesses with just one or two employees. You might want to join one of these, or to set up your own business, or work for yourself.

One-person freelance businesses

In the last two decades, the one-person business sector has grown much more quickly than jobs in traditional paid employment (Maimon, 2016). You may be one of that growing set of people who prefer to work in the so-called 'gig economy', or whose skills are now engaged primarily through short-term contracts.

Services for freelancers

Services are developing fast to support freelance working, and include:

★ Intermediary technical 'match-maker' services that can connect freelancers with companies seeking their skills.

★ Accountancy, insurance and legal advisers who specialise with one-person and micro-businesses.

★ 'Crypto-currency' services that help with international fund-raising, financial exchanges and speedy, cheaper transactions.

Enhance your marketability

You are more likely to get work if you have skills and experience that are in demand.

★ Take care to express your skills in ways that enable search engines and bots to pick them up and match them against demand.

★ Your work as a freelancer is likely to be monitored, at least in the longer term, via the Internet of Things (IoT) – such as via GPS, smart cameras, phones, and data analytics. Consider what your selling point is – such as speed versus accuracy? Delivery time versus quality?

Understand your obligations

If you work for yourself you are responsible for such things as registering for tax and national insurance, and for personal insurance.

If you employ others

Being an employer increases the scope of your obligations, such as:

★ registering your company and ensuring it is fully insured, including for public liabilities

★ setting up your business in ways that match the legal, tax and data security requirements in the country where you live and in that of the business (if different)

★ meeting responsibilities to employees, such as for pay, tax, national insurance, pensions, holidays, parental rights, sick leave, health, safety, well-being and data protection

★ social, moral and ethical considerations, such as managing business risks to help protect employees' livelihoods; taking care of the environment.

Support for enterprise

Enquire at your Careers Service about:

★ Becoming self-employed.

★ Finance and schemes available to support new businesses, including any enterprise or live units supported through the institution or in the local area.

★ Enterprise competitions.

★ Courses, modules or workshops in enterprise or entrepreneurship, or aspects of running a business.

★ Mentorship schemes or networking opportunities arranged with business people.

Review

1   **Start early**
– on personal development, career planning and becoming 'work ready'.

2   **Develop deeper self-awareness**
... so you make the right choices and understand your strengths.

3   **Investigate your options**
Be aware of the wide range of jobs, careers and other options open to you.

4   **Identify personal development needs**
... including 'soft skills'. Maintain your personal development.

5   **Recognise your skills**
... and personal qualities and experience that could add benefit to the workplace.

6   **Build your CV**
Create a rounded portfolio of skills and experience. Tailor it to the job.

7   **Articulate your skills**
Phrase and describe your skills, abilities and learning in ways that help employers to see how these can benefit their business.

8   **Develop a distinct personal profile**
– of skills and experience that make you stand out.

9   **Consider further qualifications**
... that you might want or need.

10   **Investigate self-employment**
– understand the benefits, risks and responsibilities.

11   **Maintain good records**
... to support job applications over the longer term.

12   **Make use of services and opportunities**
... such as Careers guidance, enterprise and extra-curricular activities.

Chapter 4

Successful study

Intelligence, strategy and personalised learning

Learning outcomes

This chapter offers you opportunities to:

✓ **reflect upon your own views about intelligence, considering how these affect your confidence in your academic abilities**

✓ **understand the learning process and factors that affect optimal learning**

✓ **consider how your experiences, study habits and personal preferences impact on your study**

✓ **identify your personal learning formula and ways of customising your learning in order to optimise your academic performance**

✓ **identify the best strategies to apply to different aspects of learning.**

Three essential steps towards successful study are:

1 **self-awareness**, including insight into how your own and other people's opinions about your intelligence and academic abilities impact on your capacity to achieve at your best

2 **strategic awareness**: understanding that successful study is largely about understanding the field, developing good study habits and applying good approaches and techniques – rather than how 'bright' you are

3 **personalised approaches**: being able to adapt your study strategies to suit your strengths, interests, and circumstances.

Students do not, typically, give much time to thinking about these three aspects of study: it can seem easier to launch into learning more tangible study skills such as making good notes or writing an essay. However, it is worth putting time aside to think more strategically about what learning is, what has an impact on successful outcomes, and how, through reflection and planning, you can exert greater control over your own academic performance.

This chapter focuses on the learning process itself, looking at how intelligence develops through learning, the conditions that are necessary for learning to occur, and how you can take an active role in creating the optimum conditions for your study.

'Intelligence' – or 'intelligent study'?

It is often taken for granted that academic success is the result of 'being clever' or 'bright' and that this is something you are blessed with – or not – at birth. Such thinking creates barriers to success. It leads students to assume, falsely, that they will either:

★ continue to do well academically, on the strength of being 'clever' alone, or

★ fail to achieve the highest marks because they are inherently less intelligent than others.

'Am I intelligent enough for university?'

This question haunts many students even if their grades are excellent. They worry that 'secretly' or 'deep down' they aren't clever enough to succeed.

Your marks were OK last time – but that was a fluke. This time you might fail, and you'll be so embarrassed because now everyone expects you to do well.

64%

So far I've been lucky …

It is very common for students to underestimate their potential or to lose confidence, especially if, as happens to most students at some point, they receive lower grades than they hoped for. Many students can remember an occasion in the past when someone such as a teacher or relative undermined their confidence in their abilities. Such memories can resurface, exercising a disproportionate power to undermine self-belief.

Reflection

The impact of views of intelligence upon academic confidence

Jot down your initial thoughts about how your own views of intelligence, and those of other people, might have affected your previous academic performance – in both helpful and unhelpful ways.

One reason students can become anxious about their capabilities is that they haven't been taught to evaluate their own work or to develop criteria for doing so. As a result, they feel prey to the whims of chance: good or bad marks and grades 'just happen', or depend on the luck of the draw of how 'naturally clever' they are or which tutor they get. Such thinking leaves students feeling disempowered or adrift, even if their grades are good. They worry about their luck changing or suddenly being exposed as stupid.

Anxiety can create a vicious cycle in which students:

★ can't settle down to study

★ can't concentrate or focus their attention

★ can't take in what they read

★ can't remember what they learnt

★ are reinforced in their suspicions that they 'really' lack intelligence.

This is very common, so it is important to look at what we mean by intelligence.

Intelligent study

Intelligent study means applying good strategies to study, appropriate to the academic level and to your own ways of learning. University level study makes greater demands, so requires new approaches. The right strategies and mentality can bring success to any student, whereas failure to apply these can result in any student under-achieving.

What is intelligence?

Reflection

Thinking about intelligence

Jot down your initial responses to the views of intelligence above.

Read the pages that follow.

Then return to the notes that you jotted down above and add to them. Note in what ways, if any, your opinions about your own intelligence change as a result of reading and reflection.

Ten different views of intelligence

1 Intelligence is a general, underlying 'cleverness' which is fixed for life

Early psychologists believed each individual has a fixed, general level of intelligence, their *intelligence quotient* or IQ (Terman, 1975 [1916]; Spearman, 1927). A person who did well on one intelligence test would do well on others. If you performed poorly on one test, that suggested you were generally less 'bright'. More recently, psychologists and geneticists have used studies of identical twins to support the idea of general intelligence (Plomin and Deary, 2015).

However, other psychologists have argued against the concept of general intelligence (Thurstone, 1960) and the roles of genes (Gardner, 1993). Pairs of twins used in twin studies are often brought up in similar environments and, as they look the same, they might evoke similar responses in other people so that their experiences could be unusually similar.

Environment and culture can contribute to intellectual performance. 'IQ' and academic achievement can change for societies, groups and individuals (Armor, 2003). In high income nations, IQ scores rose across the 20th century. Known as the 'Flynn effect' this seems to be linked to increased levels of mass education (Baker et al., 2015).

The *Raven's Progressive Matrices* test was designed to measure abstract reasoning ability with people of any language, age or culture. The test requires participants to choose one visual pattern from a selection of options in order to complete a visual sequence (see below). Scores for *Raven's* correlate strongly with those of other IQ tests, including language-based tests, appearing to support the idea of a 'general' intelligence.

A Raven's-style question

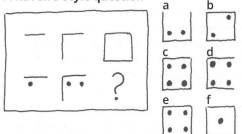

Identify which option from a–f fits the space at '?'

However, although *Raven's* is meant to be culture- and language-free, Asian children's scores, scaled according to age, rose by 15–20 points after they had lived for five years in Britain, a significant change (Mackintosh and Mascie-Taylor, 1985). This suggests that intelligence tests are just a snapshot of a person's experiences to date, within a given environment, rather than a good indicator of fixed potential.

We feel she has infinite potential for future improvement.

A snapshot of current performance

2   There are different kinds of intelligence

Gardner (1993) argues that intelligence consists of separate independent systems that interact with each other. For Gardner, there are at least seven 'intelligences': each consists of abilities in solving problems or producing objects relevant to a person's culture and environment.

Neuropsychology suggests that different cognitive abilities such as speech may be semi-separate 'domains' of ability, controlled by different circuits within the brain (Karmiloff-Smith, 1992). Some people show a weakness in one area such as a complete inability to recognise faces. Other people show poor development for most skills, but have an outstanding ability in one area such as drawing or mathematical calculation. This supports Gardner's view that intelligence is 'multiple' rather than 'general'.

Research indicates that spatial abilities involve skills that can be differentiated from performance on other kinds of 'IQ' tests. Spatial abilities can be important predictors of success in science,

technology, engineering and maths (STEM) study and other life outcomes (Rimfield et al., 2017).

It is obvious that most of the intelligences on Gardner's list can be developed. For example, people can attend workshops to develop interpersonal skills, and counselling or meditation to develop intrapersonal awareness. A scientific way of thinking is formed through practice, training and exposure to the language and conventions of scientific research (see pages 305–6). Skill in writing essays, reports or poetry can also be developed through training and practice.

Gardner's multiple intelligences

1 Linguistic
– such as reading, writing, talking, listening, or poetry

2 Logical, mathematical
– such as ability with numbers, or legal or scientific thinking

3 Spatial
– such as navigating a boat or plane, driving, or architecture

4 Musical
– such as singing, composing, playing an instrument, or appreciating music

5 Bodily–kinaesthetic
– such as sports, drama, dance, or making things

6 Interpersonal
– such as counselling and teaching skills, and understanding others

7 Intrapersonal
– such as self-efficacy, self-understanding, self-management, and reflection

Reflection

Multiple intelligences

For which of Gardner's multiple intelligences do you show most aptitude? What reasons might there be for your having developed those abilities rather than others?

3 Intelligence can be developed

In Japan, the Suzuki Violin Talent Education Programme has trained many children to play the violin to virtuoso level. The programme begins with exposure to music soon after birth and involves daily practice from an early age. Even the less remarkable students perform to a level that in other cultures would be considered that of a child prodigy (Suzuki, 1969; Gardner, 1993).

Similarly, children exposed to several languages from an early age tend to become multilingual quite naturally. People who start later in life can also develop into good violinists or linguists. The Suzuki Programme suggests the importance of the belief that *anyone* can learn to a high standard, as well as showing the role of environment and practice in developing skills. Excellence need not be the preserve of the few.

Just as we would not, in general, expect excellent violin playing from somebody who rarely played the instrument, we would not expect outstanding intellectual performances from people whose minds are not regularly challenged by ideas and problems. University provides part of that necessary stimulation. As you go through your course, the language and thinking styles of your subject will become part of your own thinking processes and linguistic expression.

4 Intelligence depends on life opportunities

As the Suzuki example illustrates, life opportunities can make a significant difference. Academic intelligence may be fostered by opportunities such as these:

★ easy access to books, equipment, and appropriate teaching

★ sufficient time to study, think or practise

★ stimulating conversations that require active engagement and reflection

★ validation by people who are important to you, of your specific learning interests, whether for geometry, philosophy or *cordon bleu* cookery

★ being part of a culture that values academic intelligence.

There are ways in which you can increase these opportunities, such as by making use of library and online resources, through courses and study, and even through your choice of newspaper, radio and other media. If you did not have ideal opportunities for learning when young, or if you were not then ready for these, it might take some time and work to catch up but it can be done. It *is* done, every year, by thousands of mature students.

Reflection

Using opportunity

In what ways could you make more of opportunities available for developing your intellect?

5 Intelligence depends on what is needed and relevant in the culture

According to this view, intelligence is not just something that individuals carry around in their heads, but depends on what a society regards as important, and the way this is made tangible through its labour requirements, social structures, technologies, education, communications, networks – everything needed for the society and culture to continue. Intelligence is not measured in isolation as individual, but is seen as a *social* phenomenon (Vygotsky, 1978; Resnick, Levine and Teasley, 1991).

For example, the intelligence needed in industrial settings is different from that required for a rural economy or life in the mountains or desert. Similarly, the education valued for girls, or for the youngest child within a family, has often varied from that valued for boys or for older siblings. Children adapt to what is expected of them.

Sternberg (1985) described intelligence as being, in part, a sensitivity to the environmental context. This can apply to learning contexts also. One learning environment might match what a person is used to, making learning easy. For another person, the same environment and teaching methods might not work. Some people learn best in quiet stillness; others find that sitting quietly is a torture. Some find it difficult to learn from books, and learn better by ear. One student learns best when the curriculum is highly structured; another when it is flexible and offers choice about what they study, when and how.

If you did not do as well at school as you might have done, it may be worth reflecting on how *you* learn best – then compare this with the way you were taught. You might also consider what you were good at when you were a child, and what you valued as important. Were your interests shared and valued by the people around you – your teachers, parents and friends? If not, this could have made learning more difficult for you.

Are the things you value *today* shared by the people around you? Do they understand and support your desire to study? If not, as an adult, you can now take responsibility for setting up the right environment for yourself as a student.

You might need to find suitable times and spaces for your study on campus or at home. You can organise information in a way that suits your learning preferences, such as by converting information to colourful charts or podcast recordings – whatever works for you. On the whole, your lecturers will not be able to create the ideal environment *for* you, as each person's needs will be different. So it's up to you to look after your own needs.

Reflection

Managing your learning environment

How could you change your total learning environment so that you don't repeat earlier learning experiences? Do you need to surround yourself with more people who support your study ambitions? (Chapters 1, 4, 17 and 18 might give you further ideas.)

6   Intelligence is about applying what you know to new contexts

Sternberg (1984) emphasised that any skill is made up of underlying processes and sub-skills; he saw intelligence as the ability to transfer those skills easily when confronted with a new task. What is important is not just that you are able to perform a given task, such as making a pancake or writing an essay, but that you are able to apply what you know to new situations, such as making a cake or writing a report.

However, it is not necessarily an easy matter to transfer a skill from one learning situation to another. Research into mathematical problem-solving suggests that for skills to be transferred from one problem to another, the student has first to be helped to identify their common features and the underlying principles in solving that kind of problem. If students can recognise that two problems have similar underlying structures, they can apply the principles for solving one problem in solving the other.

Also, unless the teacher makes the link between the old and the new learning explicit, the student may not realise that two problems are connected. Further, the new learning needs to be at around the same level of complexity as that already covered (Reed, Dempster and Ettinger 1985).

If teaching has not followed these lines, a student can feel lost and give up. In addition, students might think that the fault lies with their intelligence, rather than in the way the problem was presented. A good teacher will help students to see what they already know, and to use this as the basis for the next step in their learning.

Applying multiple intelligences to study contexts

Gardner suggests that different intelligences interact, a view also supported by genetic behaviourists (Kan et al., 2013; Plomin and Deary, 2015). Students who work in a multi-sensory or a multi-disciplinary way often find that learning in one area enhances learning in other areas. If you develop a sense of rhythm, this can improve not only music and dance, but maths and spelling. Similarly, students who are sensitive to shades of colour can use these to structure and organise information visually and spatially, which in turn can help memory and understanding.

It is important to look for connections between the intelligences you have already developed and those in which you feel you are weak. You don't need to be a genius in music or art to harness music, colour, shape, and movement as learning tools. Croaky singing of chemical formulae, imagining your relatives as courtroom personalities for law revision, or using the rainbow to sequence paragraphs from pattern notes, are ways of using multiple intelligences to make studying easier – and more interesting.

Reflection

Working from your strengths

Look back to your reflection on multiple intelligences (page 66). How could you transfer abilities from your area of strength to help your learning?

7 Intelligence is a question of how much you know

The popular view of intelligence is that it is an ability to answer the type of closed factual questions set on TV quiz shows. This does not take into consideration aspects of intelligence such as creativity or coping in real-life situations. Another view is that intelligence is a capacity for abstract reasoning such as formulating hypotheses or deriving answers from first principles: you don't need to *know* much at all to reason well.

Donaldson (1978) argued that the way we reason depends upon the particular context we are in and on what we already know. She demonstrated that both children and adults interpret what they hear by attending not just to the meaning of words, but also to their personal understanding of those words based on their own thoughts and previous knowledge. It follows that the amount and kinds of background knowledge you bring to academic study will affect the ease with which you can process new information and reason with it.

Our ability to think in abstract ways about something can depend on having already had real-life experience of similar problems. Butterworth (1992) describes how abstract notions such as 'generosity' are actually concrete social realities: real-life experience allows us to develop a mental model, and this model later provides the basis for abstract thinking. If we have gaps in concrete experience – such as with manipulating numbers – we are likely to find it harder to move on to more abstract examples until we have filled the gaps.

Butterworth suggests that when presented with a familiar problem in an unfamiliar context, we may be unable to recognise that the two are similar. This can make us look and feel like complete beginners when it is not the case. It might take somebody else to point out the similarity between what we already know and the new learning. When we see the link, we can do the problem.

'Plastic brains'

The brain has 'plasticity': it is capable of change and development. When a person takes up a new skill, millions of fresh connections are set up between different neurons in the brain to deal with the new information – rather like a set of telephone wires relaying information. The more you develop an ability, the more elaborate the neural networks or wiring system, and the faster your brain can process information related to that skill.

When you begin to study a new subject, the speed at which you will be able to take things in and make sense of them will depend on how far your brain can use past learning experiences. If you have studied something very similar in the past, you may experience the new learning as quite easy.

If a subject is very new, however, there is little foundation upon which you can build. Your brain has fewer connections it can use to make sense of the new information. If the language used is also unfamiliar to you, the brain will need to build connections for this too. You may *experience* this as finding it harder to listen or harder to read: you may get tired more quickly, or you may feel that your brain is 'dead', or that nothing makes sense. As you go over the same material from different angles, though, the new connections will get stronger and learning will become easier.

8 Intelligence can be measured

IQ tests only measure things that can be measured! Many areas of human excellence, however, cannot be measured easily – such as artistic and musical creativity, emotional maturity, sensitivity to others' needs, managing well in emergencies, being enterprising and inventive. Some people may excel in these areas and yet perform poorly in tests that are language-based. Students who struggled with language- or number-based subjects at school can excel on university courses in the arts. Similarly, people whose spoken communication skills are weak can excel on a range of university courses.

Einstein's schoolwork was not very good – yet IQ tests are said to correlate well with school performance. Einstein claimed that his initial ideas on the relativity of time and space struck him in a moment of inspiration while he was daydreaming that he was riding on a sunbeam. This kind of imaginative thinking is difficult to measure using IQ tests.

9 Intelligence is about applying effective strategies that can be learnt

This book is based on the premise that what we regard as intelligence is often a question of good study strategies and skills that you can develop. For example, research shows that students who do best at problem-solving spend longer than other students in working out exactly what the problem is before trying to solve it. Other students look at the surface of the problem and do not see the underlying structure which connects it to problems they already know how to solve. Some students fail because they don't spend enough time considering the examples and information they are given; others copy out examples without reflecting on the underlying purpose of the activity (Keane, Kahney and Brayshaw, 1989). Successful students use strategies that can be learnt.

Although the research mentioned above referred to a particular kind of problem-solving, its findings apply to study in general. Some students skim across the surface of their learning, copying a bit from one book and a line from another, without really looking at why the work was set, what the information means, its relevance to them, nor how it

might be applied to new contexts. With most university assignments you benefit from taking time to reflect, clarifying what is really being asked, the issues within the title, the reasons it was set, why it is phrased exactly as it is, and the best strategy to use. This way of thinking and working can become a habit.

10 Intelligence is a question of habit and practice

As with any skill, study skills develop through frequent use until your application of them is like a reflex and feels instinctive. Rapid and skilful reading comprehension develops through constant reading, and familiarity with specialist texts typical of your subject. The more you write, the better your writing skills are likely to be. The more you apply your mind to thinking in critical analytical ways, the more fine-tuned your thinking ability. If you want to achieve well, constant practice, coupled with critical reflection on your work, is essential.

Reflection

Views of intelligence

★ With which of these ten views of intelligence are you most familiar?

★ Which make most sense to you?

★ Which best encourage you to engage with your learning and develop your academic abilities?

What is 'learning'?

We have looked at how intelligence and achievement can be fostered through a learning process, but what is 'learning'?

Learning as process

Learning is clearly more than just intelligence or study skills. It is, rather, a multi-faceted process, involving such factors as:

★ each person as an individual learner

★ and his or her learning history, knowledge, experiences, skills, ambitions, interests, attitude, self-belief and circumstances

★ the current learning context including teaching methods, resources, materials, peer group and physical environment

★ the content and expected outcomes of the learning being undertaken

★ and the interactions between these.

We can say that learning has taken place when we both understand something and can explain, teach or demonstrate it to others.

Five learning dimensions

Many different routes can be followed to arrive at the point where learning has taken place. These vary in level of enjoyment and active engagement; we might not even be aware that learning has taken place. Below are five dimensions along which learning activity can vary. These are considered in more detail opposite.

Five dimensions of learning

1 Conscious or unconscious
2 With different levels of attention
3 Via different sense sequences
4 By detail or by the whole picture
5 By fast track or by the scenic route

1 Conscious or unconscious

Conscious learning

Learning is conscious when we are *aware* that we are learning, as when we set out to memorise a poem or an equation, or when we recognise that we have understood new material. Typical methods of learning consciously are:

★ repeating something

★ writing it out

★ checking that we have remembered it

★ telling someone else what we know.

Unconscious learning

We are aware of a small part only of information taken in by the senses, which the brain processes. Learning is unconscious when we are unaware of it happening. Occasionally, unconscious learning may emerge into consciousness later, as when we feel we 'just know' something we didn't realise we had learnt. You may have experienced suddenly recognising which way to go on an unfamiliar car journey, or surprising yourself by answering a question quickly, and then wondering, 'How did I know that?'

Conscious learning   Unconscious learning

Reflection

Unconscious learning

How could you create conditions which promote easy, unconscious learning of course material?

2 With different levels of attention

Our level of attention may vary, depending on:

★ our mental or physical state for learning

★ how focused we are on a single task

★ the way information is presented to us

★ whether the material is completely new.

As we saw from the example of Einstein and the sunbeam (page 70), learning can take place in a relaxed, aware state: it doesn't always require effort and concentration. You may recall occasions when you tried hard to remember something but forgot it quickly, while remembering easily something to which you had paid little attention, such as an advertisement or song.

3 Via different sense sequences

Each of us has our own preferred sequences for seeing, hearing, speaking, writing, and manipulating information in order to learn it.

Activity

Find your preferred sense sequences

Identify some material that you need to learn – it could be a list of words you have difficulty spelling or course work that you are revising for an exam. Experiment with different sense sequences and motor movements to see which work best for you when learning that material.

Three examples:

1 Look at it (sight); say it aloud (sound); write it (sight/motor); check what you've written (sight and/or sound).

2 Draw it; look at it; say it aloud; write it; check what you've written.

3 Say it; record it; listen to it; repeat it; write it; check what you've written.

4 By detail or by the whole picture

Some people learn best when they see the overall picture first; they are confused or overwhelmed by too much detail early on. Others learn best through building up details, allowing the whole picture to emerge. The 'whole picture' may be meaningless to them until they gain a flavour of the specific details.

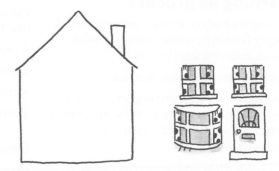

5 By fast track or by the scenic route

Some people find efficient 'motorway routes', learning exactly what they need and only that. Others take scenic routes, gathering material which, though not essential, adds to understanding, recall and interest. The scenic route can lead to deeper processing and a richer experience. However, it can generate information not relevant to the task in hand. Which way is appropriate depends on the learning task and the time available.

Learning across the dimensions

At any one time, we occupy different positions along each of these five dimensions, depending on information from the environment and according to our needs and focus. It is easier to design effective study strategies when you are conscious of these dimensions and can use them to advantage.

Six conditions for learning

For learning to occur at all, and for us then to know that the learning is complete, we need the following:

1 New experiences
2 Solid foundations
3 Rehearsal
4 Processing
5 Understanding
6 Demonstration

1 New experiences

In order to learn, we need to be exposed to novelty: to new ideas, new information, new situations, new challenges, new emotions.

Imagine, for example, discovering that when Hannah put her hand in a flame, she did not feel pain. This discovery might challenge your previous learning: that fire burns and is likely to cause pain. It might stimulate a series of questions about why and how this might *not* happen.

A new experience is an opportunity to learn – based on curiosity, a desire to know, a wish to see how everything fits together. Our brains try to fit new information into what we already know: to assimilate it. If that is not possible, the brain adapts previous knowledge to accommodate the new data.

2 Solid foundations

Learning is easier if it builds on earlier learning – if it can use similar or related experiences as a foundation to 'make sense' of new information. Thus, if we look at the object in the diagram and are asked what we know about it, we can only describe what we see.

However, if we are told it is a *fruit*, we know how to react to it, what to expect from it: it can be eaten, it will probably be sweet; it is unlikely to move, make a noise, attack us, or want to go for a walk. If, on the other hand, we are told it is an *animal* or a musical *instrument*, we will automatically call upon different sets of knowledge. Our knowledge provides models (or schemata) to help us to make sense of the world.

The same is true of academic learning. For example, it is easier to read when we have a good vocabulary. If we need to keep looking up words in the dictionary, our attention to what we are reading is continually interrupted – we lose the flow, which affects our comprehension. We also have to try to make sense of what we are reading, whilst simultaneously remembering the meaning of the new words and fitting it all together. This leads to overload, and is often the point where people feel they 'can't learn'. In reality, they are learning a great deal – but too much at once.

Your brain will take time to assimilate new information, and may need to see how it all fits together, as well as what all the parts are individually, before it feels it 'knows' what it is taking in. People who seem to learn things very quickly may simply have good foundations of information, and practice in similar problems.

3 Rehearsal

Academic learning is similar to learning physical activities such as dance, karate or football. We generally need to repeat the action or the new information several times to take it in at all, and then we need to come back to it or practise it in order to remember and master it. Otherwise, we don't learn it fully, or soon become 'rusty' and forget. This is just as true of writing essays or reading academic books as it is of athletics, drawing, playing the violin or making a chocolate soufflé.

If you think back to what you learnt at school, you will probably be aware of a vague overall knowledge of some subjects even though the details may seem hazy. You would learn these subjects more quickly a second time around. Just glancing again at some old schoolbooks may bring whole areas of knowledge flooding back.

4 Processing new information

Superficial or 'surface' processing

We may process new information at a superficial level. For example, we may just note and remember that Hannah (page 73) does not feel pain, and then think no further about this. We may learn it by heart as a fact, like learning maths tables, or record it as an entry in our notebooks.

Memory and recording are only part of learning, however. If we use only surface methods, we don't develop a sense of the underlying structure or the significance of what we learn. This makes it more difficult to apply the new knowledge in other situations.

Deep processing – making sense of what you learn

Alternatively, we may try to make sense of Hannah's experience, looking for explanations. We may ask ourselves questions to stimulate our thinking, exploring the problem from many angles. Perhaps Hannah is very good at exercising mind over matter? Maybe she has a neurological condition that prevents her from feeling pain? Maybe she *does* feel pain, but hides this?

We may also start to wonder what pain really is. How does it work – is it regulated by the brain? Or chemicals in the body? Or our attitude? Or maybe the flame was different from the flames we are used to? Possibly, they were not hot flames at all. Maybe the answer is not in Hannah but in chemistry?

As you analyse the experience from different angles, raising new questions and experimenting with potential answers, you process at a deeper level. That is how much academic work progresses.

"No, I don't need to practise – I have a natural gift"

5 Moving to another level of understanding

In order to understand a new phenomenon, such as what happens when Hannah's hand is in the fire, we may have to change our previous views of the world. We may have thought that everybody would feel pain from fire.

★ When we realise that there are situations in which people don't feel pain in quite the same way as others, we move to a different level of knowledge.

★ When we know why this occurs, we move to a deeper level of understanding.

★ When we appreciate how we came to hold our previous set of beliefs, and why we now hold a different set, we are learning at an even deeper level – understanding how knowledge is constructed, and how we come to know and understand at all.

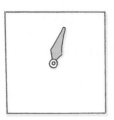 

Understanding derives from seeing things in a different way

When we learn in this way we have to be prepared to open our minds to new ways of seeing and doing things, even to new ways of thinking about ourselves, looking at how we came to believe what we believe. This makes study exciting, and is one reason why so many students return to postgraduate study.

6 Demonstrating learning

We are not really sure of our knowledge until we have put it to the test – demonstrating to ourselves and others that we really do *know* it.

One way of testing our understanding of new material is to put it to use. In some cases there may be a practical application, such as fixing a piece of machinery or producing a new design. In other cases, such as understanding how pain works, we can demonstrate learning by explaining it to other people. If we can do this:

★ in writing, speech, a diagram, or by practical demonstration

★ without checking the details as we do so

★ and in a way that is clear and makes sense to our audience,

then our thinking is also likely to be clear, and a stage in our learning is complete.

If we *cannot* demonstrate what we think we know, then our knowledge and understanding are likely to be incomplete. We may need to check back over what we have learnt. It may then help:

★ to take a different angle on the issue

★ to use a different book

★ to see whether we missed a step earlier.

See also page 395 and *The C·R·E·A·M strategy for learning* (Chapter 5).

Learning at university level

Some people think that memorising 'facts' is all there is to learning. Certainly, it *is* useful to have information readily available when you need it. For most courses, however, what counts is not how many facts you can fit into your answers, but how you *use* information. You will be expected to demonstrate different aspects of learning such as:

★ that you have made sense of course material

★ that you can evaluate and select what is relevant and important, and what can be omitted

★ that you can interpret information in a reasonable way, as relevant to the subject discipline

★ that you know how ideas are linked and interconnected

★ that you can apply knowledge, methods and algorithms to new problems and contexts

★ that you can structure and present your ideas and knowledge in a convincing argument.

Reflection

Strengthening your learning

Looking back over pages 71–5, consider what insights these give you into your own learning.

How could you flex or adapt your approach to learning to take on board those insights and strengthen your learning?

Optimal learning

Optimise your learning

This chapter emphasises that, as adults, we can play an active role in personalising our learning, manipulating those factors that make our study more enjoyable and effective.

These two pages sum up some of the key factors that have an impact on learning. Consider these and identify which you could use to better effect.

... you are in a physical state to learn

You can't learn easily if you are tired, stressed, hungry, dehydrated or on a high-sugar diet.

★ A glass of plain water several times a day helps neural activity in the brain, and releases energy. If you tire easily when studying, or if your thinking is muddled, drink some water.

★ Foods which release natural sugars slowly such as cereal-based products (rice, oats, wheat) help balance your energies.

★ Stress can put your system into 'survival mode', diverting energy away from your brain to your muscles (see page 394). We learn best when relaxed, interested and motivated.

★ Sleep helps the brain to absorb and recall information, and helps reduce stress.

Learning is easier and more effective when ...

... you *believe* you can learn

★ Believe in your intelligence (pages 64–70).

★ Allow yourself to do well.

★ Create a positive state of mind for learning.

I can do this!

... the material suits you

Take action, where possible, to ensure that:

★ you are on a course you find interesting and relevant

★ the material you use is at the right level. If you don't have background knowledge in the topic, start with basic texts and build to specialist ones.

... the time is right

★ at the right time in your life

★ at the best time of day or night to suit your learning of that material for that kind of activity

★ when you have cleared away distractions

★ when your time is planned out well to make the study session interesting

★ when you can learn at your own pace and without undue haste.

See Chapter 6.

... you use the 5 learning dimensions to best effect

Create opportunities for:

1 conscious and unconscious learning
2 varying your level of attention and for close undivided attention
3 using your senses in preferred sequences
4 learning from detail or globally
5 at different speeds and intensity.

Pages 71–2.

... you combine technologies to suit you

★ Experiment with paper-based and technology enhanced learning to find the best combination.

★ Use face-to-face methods solely, or in combination with technology, if this helps you learn best.

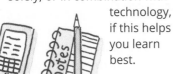

When the medium suits you

★ Rewrite, draw, act, record, photograph, video, or sculpt new information so that it is easier to absorb.

★ Experiment with different layouts, colours, fonts, etc.

When information is organised

... so that it is easier for your brain to recall it (page 401).

When you use C·R·E·A·M strategies

Be creative, reflective, effective, active and highly motivated (see Chapter 5).

When you take full advantage of your brain

★ Use multiple methods and all your senses to encode information richly in the brain (pages 396–8).

★ Space learning across several days (page 392).

★ Pause frequently to reflect and distil information so the brain can absorb and recall it.

When five key study-skills components are in place

You need:

1 self-awareness
2 awareness of what is required of you
3 methods and strategies
4 confidence and permission
5 familiarity, practice and habit (see page 24).

When you put into place the 6 conditions for learning

1 New experiences
2 Solid foundations
3 Rehearsal
4 Processing
5 Understanding
6 Demonstration

See pages 73–5.

When you enjoy it

Make learning fun. Make sure that:

★ it has meaning for you
★ you really care about the outcome, attracted to success like a honey bee to pollen

★ you are fully engaged in what you are learning
★ you create points of interest, challenge and enjoyment if these do not occur naturally for you for a given task.

When you work with others

★ for interest and enjoyment
★ for support and solidarity
★ for different viewpoints
★ to use time effectively.

See Chapters 8 and 9.

When you personalise study to suit you

★ Keep experimenting.
★ Be honest about what really works best for you.
★ See pages 78–85.

Reflection

Optimising my learning

List five things that would optimise your learning and that you are willing and able to undertake now. Write these into your planner/diary.

Recognise what kind of learner you are

Learning styles or 'types'?

There are many psychological theories that divide people into a small number of basic types. You may have come across these at school. Some students find it helpful to identify with a type and consider this offers insights into, or explanations for, how they learn. However, the evidence base for such 'typologies' has been challenged.

We bring to each learning situation different levels of knowledge, confidence and skills that impact on how we learn. It isn't necessarily helpful to reduce such individual complexity to a small range of types based on a few shared characteristics. It can limit our understanding if we look only to a given learning 'type' for explanations.

Individual learning SHAPES

In practice, we each draw on a complex and individual combination of styles, habits, attitudes, preferences, experiences and strategies. This can be referred to as our learning SHAPES (Cottrell, 2015).

★ **S**kills: aptitudes and abilities (pages 22–3)

★ **H**abits: our typical way of doing things – how we have become used to studying

★ **A**ttitudes: the mindset and beliefs we bring to study

★ **P**references: how we like to study; approaches we enjoy even if not always the most effective for us

★ **E**xperiences: the educational and life history that impacts on how we study

★ **S**trategies: the tactics, plans and approaches we deploy when studying and learning.

Awareness of these factors can help us to make conscious choices about how we study so as to use time more effectively, with more enjoyment and better results. It can help to consider the particular factors that seem to work for us – and how these might change depending on when, and what, we are learning.

Considering your learning SHAPES

The following section provides material and activities to help you reflect in a structured way about the kind of learner you are, what has shaped your learning, and how you can personalise your learning and study to better suit you.

If this aspect interests you, you might like to look further at your personal learning formula, using *Skills for Success* (Cottrell, 2015).

Learning experiences

Activity

How do you learn best?

Enjoyable learning experiences

Think back to a time when you found something very easy or enjoyable to learn. It might have been at school, home or work.

Jot down your thoughts about *why* this was the case. What made it into a good learning experience for you?

For example:

➡ Was it the teaching?

➡ Your interest in the subject?

➡ The teacher's faith in you?

➡ Because it was visual? Or practical? Or outdoors, or some other special reason?

➡ Because each step was clear?

Your notes for the activities on pages 52–3 can help with this activity.

Difficult learning experiences

Now think of a time when you found something difficult or unpleasant to learn. Jot down your thoughts about:

➡ What happened in this second example that was different from your first example?

➡ What could have made the second experience more manageable?

Learning from your experiences

➡ What do these two experiences tell you about how you learn best?

➡ What light do they throw on your learning habits and attitudes to learning?

Identify your personal learning formula

Highlight or (draw a ring) around those factors below that you consider contribute to your performing *at your best* (whether or not you always enjoy that approach to learning most). There may be many or just a few. Add in any others that you consider relevant to you.

1	**Social**	On my own. With friends. With other students. A mixture. It depends on the day or task.
2	**Input from others**	Motivating myself. Working to my own agenda. Working things out for myself. Studying collaboratively. Sharing ideas. Encouragement. Support. It depends on the day or task.
3	**External direction**	Detailed instructions. Lots of guidance. Some guidance. Instructions. Freedom to study my way. Some choice. No choice. Lots of choice. It depends on the day or task.
4	**Timing**	Start early. Well-paced. Last minute. No fixed pattern. Studying for hours uninterrupted. Studying for a set amount of time. Lots of short breaks. Studying with no fixed pattern. Breaking up time with different tasks. It depends on the day or task.
5	**Sensory**	*Visual*: Colour; Shape; Film; Layout; Seeing material on the page or screen; Observing. *Auditory*: Listening to lectures/podcasts/recordings of my own voice; Singing/rapping information. *Kinaesthetic*: Moving around; Making things; Making a diagram or model of the problem; Writing. It depends on the day or task.
6	**Planning**	Systematic. Well-planned. Clear priorities. Using lists. Scheduled. Unplanned. Studying what I feel like at the time. Going with the flow. Creative chaos. It depends on the day or task.
7	**Global: detail**	Seeing the big picture first. Sorting out the details first. Moving back and forth between the big picture and the details. It depends on the day or task.
8	**Location**	On campus. At home. In a library. In a set place. Anywhere. It depends on the day or task. It makes no difference.
9	**Noise**	In silence. With music. With the TV on. It depends on the day or task. It makes no difference.
10	**Light**	Bright light. Dim light. Average light. It depends on the day or task. It makes no difference.
11	**Medium**	Paper-based. Electronic. It depends on the day or task. It makes no difference.
12	**Other things that characterise the way I learn best:**	

What's your personal learning formula?

Student comments

Jumoke I selected 'It depends ...' for nearly every answer. For example, for new topics and problems we have to solve, I develop my ideas best when we chat about these in the library or on a discussion board. But I get to a point when I want to clear my head about what I really think. Then, it is better if I withdraw to a quiet place where I can work through my thoughts without interruption.

> She says she's experimenting with her learning style.

Milan I want to name my formula 'creative chaos' as that suits my nature. But actually, what works best for me is to plan everything phenomenally well so nothing can deflect me from what I have to do. This counteracts my natural disorganisation and tendency to drift into what entertains me.

Louis Although I think of myself as an introverted person, I am quite a social learner. If I talk about lectures or what I read, it becomes clearer to me and I remember it better. I learn a lot from sharing ideas in groups – they just need to be small, quiet groups that are focused on the task.

Adele I work best in a heightened environment – bright light, lots of space, big tables so I can spread out my books and papers and have everything opened at once, lots of stimulus to keep my ideas flowing. If I am at home, I put the TV on in the background – I don't really watch it, but it blocks out other distractions.

Reflection

Characteristics of my personal learning formula

Using the evaluation from page 79, consider the following:

★ What characterises the approaches and conditions that help you to study at your best?

★ Can you detect any patterns in the factors that help you to study best?

Activity

Name your personal formula

It is useful to name your formula for learning at your best, as:

➡ it helps you to formulate in your own mind what is distinctive about how you learn best

➡ it helps you to sum up the factors that contribute to you learning at your best

➡ when you sit down to study, this helps you to remember to apply the specific approaches that help you achieve best

Choose a word or phrase that accurately sums up those factors that help you learn best. Make this as individual and specific as you can so that you are more likely to remember it – as in the example below.

Student examples: Name your formula

Saskia: *'Ninja Learning': I think of learning as a secret mission where I have to sneak up on myself and get engaged before the boredom baddies get me.*

Mark: *I call it 'Extreme Learning' as I work best in extremes of quiet, applying all my attention.*

Abi: *'Squirrel', that's me. I squirrel away lots of details that I think nobody else will find out, little nuggets of information, and then feast on them when I have to write my assignment.*

Learning preferences and habits

The ways we prefer to learn, enjoy learning, and approach learning habitually, might coincide with what we need to produce our best work – or might not!

Etienne I prefer to learn by browsing interesting facts on the Internet, especially late at night, assembling these into some sort of order for my assignments. My formula for getting good marks I call 'Global chatter', as I do best when I get an overall sense of the subject from discussing it with others. I didn't realise this at first as I don't enjoy it as much as studying on my own.

Claire I get my best grades when I start early, am methodical, make a lot of notes, and work on a draft over several sessions. I call that my *All Method No Madness* style. In stark contrast, my learning preference is *High Pressure High Intensity*. When I studied to my preferences, I used the approach of 'get in, do it, and get out quickly'. This meant reading whatever I could get my hands on fast, ignoring any material unavailable on that day, and rushing out a rapid piece of work with no drafting or proof-reading.

Nita By preference, I am very competitive and enjoy studying on my own, using every minute effectively. I don't like group work as I don't want to share my ideas and it can feel like a waste of time, a bit slow. Overall, my learning preferences and formula are the same, as I get good grades. But, then again, even though I find collaborative work annoying, I gained my best ever grades from it: the range of ideas and perspectives stimulated my thinking and richer answers.

'Actually, I think I prefer to learn at this angle'

Activity

Identify your learning preference

Return to page 79, *Identify your personal learning formula.* This time, highlight in a bright colour those factors that you *prefer* when studying – that is, those you think help you to engage with study and enjoy it.

Harnessing your learning preferences

It makes sense to use approaches that we enjoy most – if we can make them work for us.

Reflection

Effective formula versus preference?

★ How different, if at all, are your learning preferences from what helps you produce your best work (page 79)?

★ How can you adapt your study methods so as to gain a good balance between those you enjoy (which are likely to motivate you and keep you on task), and those you enjoy less but help you achieve better outcomes?

Activity

Study habits

What study habits have you developed over the years? How far do these equate with each of the following:

1 Your personal formula for learning at your best?

2 Your learning preferences (what you like doing)?

3 Your early learning experiences rather than what you need now?

4 The attitude, or mindset you bring to your study?

Which study habits might it be useful to change for studying in higher education?

Personalise your learning

Use the insights gained from analysing your study and working out your personal learning formula, to design a strategy for study overall and/or specific study tasks. Create environments and combine approaches that enable you to:

★ engage effectively

★ enjoy your time studying

★ achieve your best possible grades.

Adapting your course to suit you

If your course is not structured in a way that already matches your learning preferences, complement its approaches with your own.

Example 1

Prefer studying with others

Organise a study group, or study alongside a friend. Work in libraries and get involved in student activities. Use your social networking tools to connect with students outside of class. Ask questions about material you are studying. Comment on ideas that others raise. Make opportunities for collaborative study, such as creating a class wiki or setting up a discussion board.

Example 2

Prefer working to own agenda

Focus on time management so that you have maximum control over where time goes. Look for articles that nobody else is likely to use; find examples and details that others may not think of. For each study brief you are set, look for your own angle. If you are required to work with others as part of your course, take charge of your own contribution: consider what kind of constructive role you could take within that group and play an active part.

Example 3

Prefer learning through listening

Use any podcasts that are provided or online. Record lectures, extracts from books, your notes, ideas, lists of key points, formulae or quotations – or make a podcast of these. Listen to them whilst studying – or whilst travelling. Look for talks and audio texts that can be downloaded to a portable device. Investigate assistive technologies such as screen readers. Consider software such as *Texthelp!* that enables you to listen to words, sentences or paragraphs of text as you type or highlights them as you listen. Form a study group – to learn via discussion (see page 183).

Gain a rounded skills portfolio

Whilst personalising your learning, take care also to vary your study choices and strategies so that you gain the widest set of perspectives and skills.

For example, if you prefer to work on your own, create opportunities to develop team working and people skills, so that you are able to draw on these when needed for assessed group projects or for future employment. Conversely, if you always work with others, make time for independent study and thinking things through on your own.

Reflection

Varying study approaches

It is important to consider approaches to study that we enjoy less or try to avoid – to see we don't lose out.

★ Which approaches do you try to avoid?

★ Which skills, experiences and insights might you miss out on as a result?

Using technology to personalise learning

Some students prefer to work completely online; others prefer to use hard copy books, artefacts, experiences or face-to-face learning; others a combination of methods. Experiment to find the best combination for you. You might prefer to search for materials online, but then read books in hard copy. You may find chat rooms useful for general discussion but prefer to meet face-to-face for particular aspects of study such as preparing for a group presentation. It's up to you.

Taking part

Make use of the opportunities that are available so that you have the widest range of methods from which to choose. For example:

★ If there is a chat room or discussion board set up for your programme, contribute to it. Once they get used to them, many students prefer to exchange ideas in this way.

★ Use the links that are built into electronic learning materials. You lose these links when you print out the materials.

★ Turn up to face-to-face study activities more than once so as to give them a chance. Get to know some of the other people. Make an active contribution before deciding whether this is the right method for you.

★ Once you have met group members and have a sense of what they are like, you may prefer to use social networking tools to maintain contact with them.

Reflection

Taking part

In general, do you have a preference for taking part in activities and discussions face-to-face, online, or a combination of these?

Planning and being organised

★ Maintain an electronic diary. Set this to give you advance reminders of appointments.

★ Maintain a paper-based planner so that you can keep track of appointments at a glance, at speed, and at times when you lack an internet connection.

★ Investigate bespoke student planners in online and paper-based form.

Reflection

Keeping organised

What kinds of planning do you prefer to undertake in paper formats, such as a student planner or address book? For which do you prefer to use electronic tools?

Using library resources

Work out the best pattern for you when working with materials in libraries and resource centres. It is useful to visit the library in person to:

★ get to know the librarians and gain a sense of who to talk to about different kinds of enquiries

★ make use of the different kinds of learning spaces provided: many libraries provide spaces where you can study quietly without disturbance, as well as places for group study

★ gain from the ambience, which can help you to remain focused on your work

★ use time well if you have occasional hours between classes

★ access services and resources not available online

★ check out social activities such as book clubs and book swaps, or offer to organise these.

Most library services are now also available online, especially for:

★ ordering books and articles

★ digital copies of texts and learning materials, including audiovisual

★ open source materials.

This means you can use the library flexibly in support of your personalised approaches.

Reading and making notes

Consider the optimum combination for you in recording, maintaining and accessing your notes from lectures, reading, writing and thinking about course material.

You may prefer to take all your notes onto a tablet device or to jot down notes by hand, especially in class. You may choose to type up highlights of handwritten notes later so they are easier to read. Alternatively, you may find it easier to use and recall material by making visual posters, charts or flash cards.

Whatever your preferred methods, it is usually worth maintaining an electronic bibliography of all the texts you read. This will save you rewriting details if you use the same resource for another piece of writing. There are apps designed to help you record material for use in references. See Chapter 11.

Reflection

Paper or electronic notes?

What kinds of material do you prefer to work with in hard copy? And which electronically? Which help you remember the material best?

What is best for learning?

Whilst working electronically is essential now on most courses for at least some of the time, it is important to be aware that some studies suggest that attention, concentration and recall are better when using paper-based resources or just listening (Wood et al., 2012; Farley et al., 2013; See Cottrell, 2018). This can make a difference to your grades.

It is worth considering how you vary your approaches so as to gain the benefits that come from working without technology as well as with it.

Capturing and developing your ideas

Experiment with using:

★ a notebook and pen or pencil

★ a flip camera, phone or tablet to video yourself or your practical work 'in progress'.

Designing your own materials

Consider working on paper, in notebooks, on large card, and using software such as Impress (which is Open Source), Publisher, PowerPoint or Adobe Illustrator for:

★ designing posters for assignments

★ making charts and posters to organise information for revision.

Use video, photography and drawing software to find alternative methods of laying out information in ways that help you to make sense of it and to recall it. For example, if you make large charts or pattern notes (page 228) to organise material visually, you could use your phone, tablet or flip camera to record this and play it back at intervals whilst on the go, to help you remember it.

Using apps for study

Experiment with different apps to see which you prefer for study. Visit app stores at:

★ https://play.google.com

★ www.itunes.apple.com

★ www.microsoft.com

★ www.android.com/apps

Alternatively, see recommendations updated annually in *The Macmillan Student Planner* (Cottrell, 2019b).

Activity

Personalised use of technology for study

Enhance your study by using varied combinations of technologies, drawing on those provided for your course and those that you enjoy using in everyday life.

Use the chart on page 85 to stimulate your thinking about what would work best for you. Indicate ✓ the technologies you would choose for each aspect of study.

Consider different ways to combine technologies and other study approaches to make aspects of your study more interesting and effective.

Personalised use of technology for study

Aspect of study/ Technology	To keep myself organised	To research and understand the subject	To get the most from taught sessions	To work on group projects / activities	To learn from practice and feedback	To produce essays, talks, reports, etc.
Videos, photos, animations						
Course-based discussion board						
Online practice tests						
Social networking e.g. Facebook						
Micro-blogging tools e.g. Twitter						
Podcasts						
Blogs						
Wikis						
Lecture chat						
Apps (e.g. referencing tools)						

How I would use the technologies in combination:

Also available on the companion site at www.studyskillshandbook.co.uk.

Study strategy – individual or social?

For each aspect of study below, jot down which combination of approaches a, b and c would work best for you and how you would combine them.

Aspect of study	Strategy	(a) Studying on my own (b) Studying with others face-to-face (c) Studying with others online
1 Preparing in advance for taught sessions		
2 Engaging and maintaining my interest in the subject		
3 Reading around the subject and researching new topics		
4 Understanding difficult concepts and making sense of material covered in taught sessions		

Aspect of study	Strategy	(a) Studying on my own (b) Studying with others face-to-face (c) Studying with others online
5 Making sense of assignment briefs		
6 Keeping motivated and staying on task		
7 Developing my ideas and gaining different perspectives		
8 Managing time and being organised for study		
9 Reviewing and revising material		

Review

1 **Develop your intelligence**
Recognise that you can build your knowledge, sharpen thinking skills and deepen your understanding. Take steps to develop your intellect.

2 **Believe in yourself**
Most students would achieve more through better study strategies, habits and self-belief. Belief and hope of academic success are good indicators of eventual success.

3 **Understand your own performance level**
Whether you do well, poorly or coast in the middle, there are many factors, past and present, that combine to affect your current level of performance. Give these thought. Get to grips with why you achieve as you do, what it is good to maintain, and what to change.

4 **Understand more about the learning process**
If you understand more about the learning process, you can apply it to the benefit of your study, gaining in confidence and a sense of control. Take an interest in what is written about learning.

5 **Take a holistic approach**
Consider the broader learning environment, the impact of those around you, and your life style. All have an effect on your time, motivation, energies, support, ability to concentrate, options and choices.

6 **Don't get discouraged**
When we don't do well, there are reasons. We can isolate specific aspects that let us down and learn to do better. Everyone struggles with some things and not others. Use the experience to gain insights into how to improve.

7 **Optimise your learning**
Consider the multiple factors that impact on learning, from food, rest and sleep through to attitude, attention, use of time and more. Identify which of these you are not using fully to optimise your learning.

8 **Consider your 'SHAPES'**
Give thought to your study Skills, Habits, Attitudes, Preferences, Experiences and Strategies. Identify your 'personal formula' for learning.

9 **Personalise and customise your learning**
The way things are, or have been, taught are not the only ways to learn. In Higher Education, much study is by independent learning, so you can experiment with different approaches and your 'personal formula' to see what works for you.

10 **Technology and 'hands-on'**
Draw creatively on the wide range of technologies available to support study. Combine these with each other and with more hands-on and varied approaches, to make study more interesting. Find what works best for you.

11 **Devise your strategy**
Draw your insights together and use them to devise the optimal strategy for you for specific aspects of study.

12 **Find out more**
For further information about using your values, inspiration and personal learning formula to enhance your personal success, see *Skills for Success* (Cottrell, 2015).

Chapter 5

The C·R·E·A·M strategy for learning

Learning outcomes

This chapter offers you opportunities to:

✓ become aware of the contribution of each aspect of the C·R·E·A·M strategy to the learning process
✓ develop ideas about how to take more creative and active approaches to your study
✓ learn to problem-solve creatively
✓ become more effective as a student, without necessarily working harder
✓ clarify your purpose and goals in order to maintain strong engagement and motivation
✓ build upon the reflective work of previous chapters.

C·R·E·A·M

C·R·E·A·M stands for:

C – Creative
Have the confidence to apply imagination to your learning and problem-solving.

R – Reflective
Be able to sit with your experience, analyse and evaluate your own performance, and draw lessons from it.

E – Effective
Organise your time, space, priorities, state of mind, resources, and use of technology to maximum benefit.

A – Active
Be personally engaged physically and mentally, in making sense of what you learn.

M – Motivated
Be clear about the outcomes you want to achieve, the steps you need to take to achieve these, and what you will do to build and maintain your engagement and enthusiasm.

Developing each of these aspects strengthens all the others. For example, being motivated involves reflection about what you really want. Active learning and creativity require motivation and also help you to stay motivated. Effective organisational strategies benefit from imagination and reflection – and so on.

Finding your creative streak

Creativity is especially important for generating ideas in the early stages of new assignments. You can use more logical approaches later, to evaluate which creative ideas to use.

Attitudes that stifle creativity

★ 'It's a waste of time.'

★ 'It's childish.'

★ 'There's a time for work and a time for play.'

★ 'There's a right way of doing things.'

★ 'It's not logical.'

★ 'I'm not creative.'

★ 'I can't.'

Reflection

Creative blocks

Do you express any of the above attitudes? Were you given any messages when you were younger which stifle your creativity now?

Approaches that foster creativity

'Play' and lateral thinking

Select any two random objects, such as a cup and a plant. Find as many connections between them as you can (e.g. by size, colour, owner, the way they break, how they spin, when they were bought). How could you apply this type of 'play' to your coursework?

You find what you are looking for

★ Find ten round things in the room.

★ Find ten things that 'open'.

Once you start to look, your attention becomes drawn to such items. If you look for new strategies or answers for coursework, you are more likely to find these too.

There's more than one right answer

Once you find one answer, look for more. These may be better – or help you fine-tune your first one.

Combine things

Take the front half of one animal and the rear of another. What new animal have you invented? The essence of invention is mixing two different ideas or contexts to create a new variety. This helps in academic thinking too – such as synthesising ideas to forge a new position on the issues.

Metaphor

Let one thing stand for, or represent, another, as a metaphor or analogy. Look at objects, or study problems, from different perspectives, making these visual or concrete in playful ways, as below. If an issue doesn't make sense to you, map it out with objects on a table – just as generals used to check out military strategies with miniature soldiers and a model terrain.

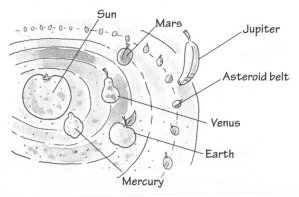

'Suppose this apple is the earth, this orange is the sun, and these other fruit are the rest of the solar system ...'

Activity

Search for connections

See how many ideas you can generate by completing the sentences below:

➡ Writing essays is like making cakes because ...

➡ Study is like a game of football because ...

➡ Being a student is like being a sandwich because ...

➡ What metaphors can you think of that best describe what study or learning is like for you?

Be a professor – and other ideas

Give yourself a new sub-personality

In our minds, we carry various sub-personalities, such as an internal *critic* who reprimands, a *playful child* who sees the funny side of things, a *hero* who wades in to save the situation, and many others.

If you pay attention to your thought processes, you can become aware of those different characters within.

Add to your dramatic cast and find a professor within yourself

Activity

Call on your 'inner expert'

Experts don't find problems easy, but they are more open to dealing with the seemingly impossible. Those working at the forefront of research cannot look up the answer in a book – it isn't there yet! Like Einstein daydreaming on a sunbeam (page 70) they may play with ideas, juggle with options that seem crazy, and go on flights of fancy, imagining 'what if …?', generating lots of possible answers, and then examining them more closely to see whether any could actually work.

You can do that too. When you cannot think of a way of doing a piece of work, imagine that you are a professor or inventor dealing with a world-important problem.

What does your internal professor look like? Sound like?

How do you move your hands and head when you are in 'professor' mode?

Let your professor come alive, and talk to you about possible approaches to study problems.

Keep an ideas notebook

Value each passing idea, as writers and artists do. Jot ideas down at once in a notebook or on sticky labels. Keep paper and pen by your bed.

Go through the ideas later to see which you can use. Many will lead nowhere – that's part of the creative process – but sometimes one will be just what you need.

Be curious about what you don't know

Creative people are curious. They want to know everything – just in case it fits together with something else one day.

It is difficult to be creative if you fear or resist what you don't know. Be open to the curious child in you who wants to have a go at everything.

Create opportunities to break a routine

When you take a different route, even if it is not the quickest way, you discover new things of interest.

Examine your routines. Ask:

★ Why am I doing it this way?

★ Have the original reasons now changed?

★ How else could I do things?

Imagine alternatives

Ask 'what if … ?' questions

What if the weekend were three days long? What if this essay had to be in tomorrow? What if I were only allowed 100 words to write up my research?

How would others do it?

Consider: 'How might people, live or historic, approach this study problem?' Picasso, for example. Or Nelson Mandela? J. K. Rowling? Mozart? Beyoncé? A current politician? Choreographer? Your mum? Your internal professor? Whose approaches can help and inspire you?

Creative learning

People devise many different strategies to help them to learn. Here are a few.
Tick ✔ the box beside any *you* could use. What other methods can you think of?

☐ **1**
We like to argue with each other.

No – we discuss things, really.

It's a sort of argument, though.

I make a big chart out of wallpaper – and link up all I learn on one subject.

☐ **2**

☐ **3**
I sort my ideas out while I vacuum – then no-one can hear me talking my ideas through.

I record my ideas and play them back to myself.

☐ **4**

I have a notebook to jot down ideas as they come to me – I take it with me everywhere.

☐ **5**

We talk a lot …

… Share ideas …

… Work things out together.

☐ **6**

☐ **7**
I like a method:
a) I work out the main ideas;
b) think of headings;
c) summarise notes;
d) summarise onto one page.

☐ **8**
I map out lots of skeleton essay plans. I fit new information into one of the plans.

☐ **9**
I try to imagine I am a lawyer – I always have to argue the other side of what I think.

'It is therefore clear, my Lord that …'

☐ **10**
Ⓢwahili Ⓘbo Ⓕarsee Ⓔsperanto Ⓒhinese

I imagine crazy pictures to help me to remember things.

I use 'look and cover': I read or try to learn something; then I cover the page. I write down what I can remember. Then I check back to see what I got right. Then I try again.

☐ **11**

☐ **12**
I scribble my ideas down as fast as I can and see where my mind takes me. I sort them out later to see which bits I can use.

Creative problem-solving

What?

Problem-solving takes different forms such as:

Real-life, everyday situations in study, personal life or work.

A 'teaser' question or activity in class or on a discussion board for a group to solve. This could be a game or puzzle.

A case study that provides a problem-based or enquiry-based, approach to a complex issue such as in health care, politics or business, and often requiring you to make recommendations.

A mathematical problem requiring an answer using specific measures (of time, distance, length, energy, etc.).

Why ...

Exercises in problem-solving train you in a range of thinking skills. They enable you:

★ to develop creativity and reasoning abilities in generating potential solutions and deciding between them

★ to research issues from different perspectives

★ to develop your understanding of theory and principles and put these to practical use

★ to practise specific procedures.

You can apply a problem-solving approach to any research or study activity.

Typical mistakes

Do any apply to you? ✓

☐ **Rushing at the problem**
... rather than taking the time needed for the early stages in defining the task. This can create difficulties later, and leads to students thinking that they can't solve problems they could manage.

☐ **Being imprecise**
... about the specific nature of the problem; not examining the details in a systematic way.

☐ **Jumping to conclusions**
... about the strategy or formula to use before thinking through all the options.

☐ **Missing out on clues**
... rather than using the initial information provided in order to work out what further information is needed to solve the problem.

☐ **Giving up too early**
... rather than keeping going, looking for new angles, or researching examples that throw new light on the set problem.

☐ **Under-use of material**
... such as course work and texts that could have thrown light on how to understand the problem and solve it.

☐ **Disorganised working**
... jumping steps in the process; misreading their own working out.

Easy problem-solving

Problem-solving is easier if you use the following approaches:

Mindset Approach it as a puzzle rather than a 'test'. As this is more enjoyable, it is more likely that you will stay on task in a relaxed, engaged mental state until you arrive at a solution.

Time Spend as much time as you need to really tease out precisely what is needed before you start to search for and apply solutions.

System Use an organised, step-by-step approach, so that you take account of all the important information and clues with which you are provided, and so that you cover all essential stages in the right order.

Knowledge Call upon what you know. As a student, it is likely that any problems that you are set will relate in some way to material covered previously in class or about which you can find essential information in the reading materials and resources provided.

Preparation Research the problem carefully before deciding on a solution. Assemble all the information and material that you need. Go through your formulae, or undertake the background reading or investigations.

Creative problem-solving: stages in problem-solving

Stages in problem-solving

1 Define the task.

2 Identify a strategy.

   ★ *Draw upon familiar problems*.

   ★ *Weigh up alternative approaches*.

   ★ *Make a decision*.

3 Work it through systematically.

4 Check your answer.

5 Write it up.

6 Evaluate.

Apply creative problem-solving

To course assignments: If you are not sure how to go about a new assignment, stand back and consider it as a candidate for creative problem-solving.

To stressful situations: It puts some distance between you and the stress of not knowing what to do, and provides a means of working towards a solution.

1 Define the task

The most important part of problem-solving is 'elaborating' what is being asked of you (see page 70). This usually provides a pointer to the kind of answer required, which in turn can prompt a means of finding the answer. Unless you recognise the nature of the task instantly, you might need to move back and forth between the following strategies until you are clear what is being asked.

(a) Put it into your own words
Reword the problem to check you understand it.

(b) What *sort* of answer will it be?
A formula? Actions? A decision? A set of conclusions? A particular unit of measurement? Recommendations?

(c) Verbal sketch
Jot down a quick outline of the problem.

What do you know? What are the key facts available in the information supplied?

What do you need to find out?

What kind of a problem is this? How does it compare with problems already covered in class?

Simplify Rewrite with less detail. If relevant, find a formula or equation to sum up the problem.

(d) Sketch it as a diagram
For mathematical problems, and others if it helps, make a rough sketch to outline the problem. Use stick people, symbols or basic shapes that help you to see at a glance how one part of the problem relates to another.

On your diagram, mark in:

★ what you already know

★ anything you can work out

★ what you need to find out.

(e) What information do you need?

★ Which of your notes, texts or other resources are relevant?

★ Which theories, case studies or formulae apply?

(f) Define it

Write it out clearly
Once you are clear in your thinking about the nature of the problem, write this out as the first part of writing up the problem.

Keep referring back to this ... remain focused on the precise task in question.

Defining the task: clarify the problem precisely

Defining the issue: the tortoise and hare

One hot day, a tortoise and a hare decided to race each other. The hare shot away quickly whilst the tortoise followed at a very slow pace. The hare was nearly at the finishing line when he decided he could afford to stop for a drink. In the heat of the day, he soon fell soundly asleep. Many hours later, the tortoise crept past the sleeping hare and crossed the finishing line first.

Before spending months resolving the problem of *how* to build a bridge, be sure the problem is not actually about *whether* to build one or not

A question of speed?

If you were set the problem of whether the hare or tortoise were faster, you would need to attend to the exact wording of the problem. A hare can run faster in general terms, and did so for the greater distance. The tortoise took less time to complete the race overall. To calculate speed, you divide the distance by the time taken:

$$\text{Speed} = \frac{\text{Distance}}{\text{Time}}$$

As the tortoise completed the whole distance in the least time, it was faster. The correct answer would depend on the exact wording of the problem set.

2   Identify a strategy

For your subject, there will be formulae, precedents or protocols that would be applied to the kind of problem you have been set. If you identify the nature of the problem correctly, this generally gives you a clear steer about the steps needed to arrive at a solution.

Draw upon familiar problems

Of problems covered previously on your course or in the recommended course materials:

★ Which are the most similar to those you have been set? How might their solutions help here?

★ In what ways does the problem you are working on differ from previous problems you have worked on? As a result, how might the solutions to this problem also be different?

Weigh up alternative approaches

Jot down a list of strategies that might, potentially, lead to a solution to the problem. Give initial thought to where each might lead.

★ What are the advantages of each solution or combination of solutions?

★ What might be the disadvantages?

Make a decision

Make a reasoned decision about the best approach for arriving at the solution. Apply this to the problem to test it out.

Difficulties finding a solution?

If the answer isn't immediately apparent, work creatively to find a different approach.

(a) Simplify

Remove unnecessary detail: Sift the essentials from the broader background information. Hone this down to get to the core of the problem.

Generalise: Find points of commonality with other material you have covered.

★ In maths and sciences, this usually means identifying the appropriate formula, as in the tortoise and hare example above

★ For other subjects, look for features or characteristics such as structure, sequence, protocols, genre or theories that enable you to make cross-comparisons with other events or situations in your discipline.

Make broad assumptions that help you generalise the problem. In the case of the tortoise and the hare, if we didn't know the hare fell asleep, we would solve the problem of relative speed by making reasonable assumptions based on the known typical average speed of hares and tortoises.

(b) Consider alternative ways of looking at it

Take a different angle

If you find it difficult to understand a problem:

★ Rephrase it.

★ Look up similar examples of the problem.

★ Use analogies to gain insights into this problem.

★ Play with the material – move it around. Imagine scenarios that would arise from varied or incorrect applications. Apply creative approaches from pages 90–3.

Make it real

It can be helpful to relate problems to parallel, concrete problems from real life: when might you or others apply this kind of problem to a real situation? Which parts of that real-life issue match parts of the problem you have been set?

Combine the possibilities

Consider combining solutions from diverse problems you have solved in the past. Could the problem have several parts to it that each need to call upon a different formula or aspect of previous course work?

3 Work it through systematically

★ Think through, step by step, the implications and potential outcomes of your preferred method or strategy.

★ For problems which require you to apply formulae, write out each step you take, so that you can see later how you arrived at each stage of your working out.

★ Consider which aspects of the solution might not work – and what might work instead.

4 Check back over your work methodically

★ Check that you interpreted the problem correctly.

★ Check each step of your working out for errors.

5 Write up the problem

★ Write out precisely and succinctly the nature of the problem and its solution.

★ Set out the steps you would take to solve the problem – your method or 'working out'.

★ Make sure that the solution, whether a number, recommendation or conclusion, is set out clearly.

6 Evaluate your work

★ Did you spend long enough considering the nature of the problem and what was required?

★ Were you able to find similar problems that might help?

★ Did you 'play' sufficiently with possible alternative solutions and combinations?

★ Did you leave enough time to work it out?

★ Do you need help understanding the coursework?

Creative problem-solving: identify the task

It can help to use a chart to map your way through the problem. The example below is available for you to use on the companion site, or you can devise your own chart.

1 Define the problem	
Put it into your own words What exactly are you being asked to do?	
Sketch it ★ How do the different parts of the problem relate to each other? ★ What information can you write in? ★ What else can you work out or add in that would help? ★ What do you need to find out?	
Similarity to other problems? Which kinds of problems have you solved before that were similar in some way to this?	
Other information? Which of your notes, texts, learning resources, websites etc. would be of most use?	

Creative problem-solving: apply strategy

2 Identify a strategy: weigh up alternative problem-solving strategies	
Strategy Option A (advantages)	*Strategy Option A* (disadvantages)
Strategy Option B (advantages)	*Strategy Option B* (disadvantages)
Strategy Option C (advantages)	*Strategy Option C* (disadvantages)
Decision: Which strategy to take (Consider combining aspects from all options.)	

Working through, checking and writing up *(Check off ✓ each stage once completed.)*

3 ☐ I have worked through the problem systematically.

4 ☐ I have checked my solution, step by step, for errors and omissions.

5 ☐ I have written out the problem succinctly and accurately, demonstrating clearly how I arrived at the solution.

6 Evaluate your work *(See step 6, page 96 above.)*	

The C·R·E·A·M strategy for learning

Reflective learning

Reflecting about learning

In effect, this just means being more thoughtful about anything that relates to your learning. Reflective thinking can be really exciting, and sometimes challenging, as you don't know quite where it will lead. If you already knew, it wouldn't be worth doing.

Why does it matter to study?

In Higher Education, and later in employment, you are responsible for your own performance and your development as an autonomous learner. You can approach your learning in superficial ways so that little changes, or aim to understand more so you increase your control over the experience and outcomes. Although you receive grades and feedback from tutors, it is important to become better at making independent, realistic, well-based evaluations of your learning and performance. You are then better placed to produce good work in advance of tutor assessments and independently of supervision.

How do I go about it?

You have already started. This book is structured to help you reflect on your study from different angles. By considering its questions, you start to develop the habit of thinking about your learning in greater depth.

1 **Create the time**. Pause what you are doing for some good thinking time.

2 **Jot down thoughts** in a journal or blog (page 101).

3 **Use prompts** to stimulate your thinking, such as this book's reflection boxes. Create your own prompts.

4 **Broaden your self-awareness**. Use self-evaluation questionnaires. Don't just tick the boxes, think about what is being asked and what you could learn from both the questions and responses.

5 **Review your progress**. Think about your development and achievements, such as when updating your CV or personal profile (pages 58 and 100).

6 **Use tutors' feedback constructively**. Think about what is behind the feedback. What good advice lies behind each correction or suggestion? (page 316).

7 **Use stimulus material**. Read, watch or listen to a piece about learning, or on how the brain or mind works. Let this prompt fresh ideas (Chapter 4).

Reflect on your performance over time

★ Reflect on your performance now and later in the year. Compare answers, looking for progress. See *How well am I doing*? (page 100).

★ Compare your earlier and later assignments.

★ Check back over your journal regularly. Notice changes; comment on your progress.

Make a fair evaluation of your progress

When making judgements about your learning, consider your *reasons* for deciding whether you are strong or weak, skilled or unskilled. What criteria are you using (see page 105)? What would excellent be like? Or wise? Or healthy? Work out what is involved in the task, breaking it into smaller tasks or sub-skills. Are you better at some parts than others? What makes some parts more difficult than others?

People can easily underestimate themselves when:

★ they have been out of education a while

★ they learn more about a subject. The more we know, the more we are aware of what we don't know, which can be unsettling.

How well am I doing?

Course, unit or module:	Date:
Level:	**Year of study:**

1a Generally, how well am I doing?

1b On what am I basing this self-evaluation – Marks/test results/grades? Tutor feedback? Monitoring personal data (see page 105)? Other ways?

2a In this module/unit, I am best at:

2b On what am I basing this self-evaluation?

What makes me better at these aspects?

3a To do better, I need to improve:

3b How will I bring about this improvement?

What prevents me from doing as well at present?

My timescale for this improvement is:

4a What have I already learnt, or improved, since starting this course, module or unit?

4b How do I know this? How do I measure or monitor what I have learnt? (How long it takes? My level of confidence? My understanding? My level of enjoyment?)

Reflective learning journals

Maintain a reflective learning journal, using either a strong notebook, electronic file or personal blog.

Why?

★ It helps clarify thoughts and emotions, work out strategies, and focus on your development

★ It helps you see progress and improvements, which you could easily overlook otherwise.

Start a reflective learning journal now!

'I used to read the hardest books first – to be a 'real' student. Now I look for a simple overview first.'

'Why am I always late? I think it's because I always try to get somewhere on time, whereas I should think about getting there 5 minutes early – then I might be on time!'

'... I can't believe the difference between my first essay (very bad!!!) and this one. Keeping an ideas book has helped.'

Who is it for?

For yourself, primarily – to help you focus on your own performance. In some instances, for tutors.

What do you write?

It is up to you – anything that helps you.

Successes – and what you learnt from these

Challenges – where the difficulty lies; how to tackle it

Feelings – about your experience, behaviours, interactions, successes, challenges and progress

Personal insights – things you discover about you, your learning process, needs, interests and ambitions

Ideas – things to try out; thoughts about things you read; ways of approaching an assignment; etc.

Opinions – about things you have read or heard

Observations – about what works for you and others

Strategy and skills – the appropriateness of your current approaches and skills to tasks you undertake

Career and employability – ideas of things to do, or how your learning will be of use to you in the future

Blocks and gaps – to your learning and creativity and how you might tackle these

Changes – in your attitude, habits or motivation

Other uses of reflective journals

As a basis for discussion

It can be helpful to discuss your journal or blog entries with other students on your course. How do their experiences of the course compare with your own? Do they use strategies which you could adopt too?

Preparing for tutorials

Go through the journal and make a list of issues that you want to discuss in your next tutorial. Put these in order of priority. If you have any problems, think through some possible options, so that the discussion with your tutor will be more focused. See page 31.

Risky writing

Keeping a private journal helps to develop your writing. It is a place to experiment with different styles, to take risks. The journal is for *your* benefit – and for your eyes only. This may make a welcome change from writing to the demands of your course or tutors!

Studying hard is not the same as working efficiently or effectively.

Reflection

Get started: Reflect on excellence

If you haven't already started a reflective journal, use these questions to get started:

★ What would 'excellence' look like for your course?

★ What would help you get closer to that?

Virtue versus effectiveness

Consider the table below, which shows the study strategies of one student, Leila. Leila feels she should get good marks because she works very hard. She studies 50 hours a week, and gets all her work done by the deadlines.

Reflection

Ineffective strategies

Can you see why Leila's marks are getting worse, even though she is working harder? Note your thoughts in your journal.

Leila's study strategies	
Leila feels virtuous because ...	**... Yet her study strategy is weak because ...**
Leila reads every book on the reading list, and searches the internet constantly.	★ The same information is repeated in several books. She does not select from one book to another.
She reads every book from cover to cover.	★ Not all of the book is equally relevant. She does not use smart reading techniques (see pages 215–17).
She writes very detailed notes.	★ She has more information than she needs. ★ Her notes are repetitive and take a long time to read. ★ She doesn't think much about what she is noting down. ★ It takes her a long time to find things in her notes. ★ She has to rewrite her notes to revise from them. ★ She copies out large sections – and then copies these into her own work – which loses her marks.
She writes her notes neatly, and in full sentences.	★ Using abbreviations would save time. ★ As long as she can read her notes and find information easily, they do not need to be neat.
She works long hours with few breaks.	★ She gets tired and cannot think as clearly. ★ She gets bored and loses interest easily. ★ Her mind wanders and she forgets what she has read. ★ Sometimes she takes notes without realising she has done so – with no idea what they say.
She locks herself away to work solidly.	★ She misses out on other people's opinions, suggestions and perspectives.
She never asks for help or attends support workshops.	★ She would benefit from guidance on how to use her study time, and the experience of being a student, more effectively.

Effective and efficient study

Activity

Virtuous or effective

Do you think the following examples are 'virtuous' or 'effective' ways of studying – or neither?

In the boxes below, write:
V for Virtuous   **E** for Effective   **N** for Neither

1 ___ Linking new information to what you already know or have studied.

2 ___ Learning difficult information 'off by heart'.

3 ___ Copying chunks from textbooks – because the writer says it better than you could.

4 ___ Questioning whether what you have heard is really true or representative.

5 ___ Writing fast so that you can take down almost everything the lecturer says.

6 ___ Reading your essays and other writing slowly and out loud before you hand it in.

7 ___ Studying when you are too tired to concentrate.

8 ___ Changing to a new topic or type of study activity if you find that your mind is wandering to other matters.

9 ___ Asking for help as soon as you find something difficult.

10 ___ Relating your studies to real life.

Answers are given on page 407.

Reflection

Effective strategies

★ Jot down any other examples of ineffective study that you have noticed either in yourself or others.

★ What strategies would be more effective in these examples?

Unhelpful thinking

Do you:

★ feel guilty if you are not working?

★ feel you are cheating if you don't read a book from cover to cover?

★ worry if you cannot remember every detail of what you have learnt?

★ worry that other people have taken far more notes than you?

Instead, work out a strategy for learning in the most effective way. See below and page 104.

Start tasks early ...

★ You only need an available device or some paper and a pen to get started. Don't wait until you have all the books or tidied your desk (excuses to delay starting).

★ If you don't feel like studying, give yourself permission to study for only ten minutes. Quickly jot down questions to focus your ideas, write a list of things you need to do, etc. Attend to the 'excuses' afterwards – if you still want to. You will probably find you are 'hooked' into the study and want to keep going.

★ Get your mind working on a problem as soon as you can. It will continue working on it even when you move on to something else. This is why it pays to start looking at new assignments as soon as you receive them.

Effective, well-organised study

Check your own effectiveness as a student. For the following items, indicate ✓ all that apply to you already. Follow up on gaps until you have completed the checklist.

1. Study strategies and mindset

- ☐ I have a strategy for approaching my course overall
- ☐ I have a strategy for doing well on the course
- ☐ I keep looking for ways to improve (see page 105)
- ☐ I devise a strategy for approaching each assignment
- ☐ I take steps to understand how to learn effectively (Chapter 4)
- ☐ I use active learning strategies so I learn more from the time I spend studying
- ☐ I check that I really understand what I am learning
- ☐ I stick with difficult material until I 'get it'
- ☐ I personalise study so it works for me (pages 79–85)
- ☐ I work at maintaining a high level of motivation
- ☐ I look for what I can learn from setbacks – and apply that learning next time.

2. Study space that invites effective work

- ☐ I have a dedicated study space, used just for study
- ☐ I keep it clean, pleasant and inviting for study
- ☐ I keep everything I need in one place
- ☐ I have a desk or surface where I can spread out
- ☐ I have a good chair that supports my back
- ☐ I work in good light, such as near a window
- ☐ I have a good reading lamp
- ☐ Surfaces are cleared and 'de-cluttered'.

3. Organised material and resources

- ☐ I organise the materials I will need for assignments as soon as I receive the brief
- ☐ I keep papers sorted, labelled and well organised, so I can find things quickly and easily

- ☐ I organise my electronic files or folders so I can find things quickly
- ☐ I have all the equipment I need (pens, pencils, paper, notebooks, technologies, apps, etc.)
- ☐ I keep all tools, equipment and technologies in good condition, ready for use
- ☐ I manage my use of technologies well
- ☐ I apply technologies effectively to study.

4. Planning and preparation

- ☐ I take the initiative: I take action to find out everything I need to know about my study (Chapters 1 and 2)
- ☐ I plan assignments well-ahead
- ☐ I start to prepare early for tests and exams
- ☐ I prepare my day in advance
- ☐ I plan my week in advance
- ☐ I use my time effectively (Chapter 6)
- ☐ I use a diary/planner effectively (pages 137–8)
- ☐ I am well informed about the 'rules of the game'
  - ☐ How Higher Education works (Chapter 1)
  - ☐ Academic conventions (Chapters 1 and 12)
  - ☐ Expectations for my course/subject (Chapter 2)
  - ☐ To avoid cheating and plagiarism (pages 247–8).

5. Holistic approach

- ☐ I spend the right amount of time on study
- ☐ I am fully engaged in what I am doing in the moment
- ☐ I put time into my broader development
- ☐ I plan towards time after my course
- ☐ I take care of my general well-being (Chapter 7).

Effective management of grades and personal performance

Performance here refers to a number of things, such as:

1. Learning and understanding course material
2. Producing a high standard of work
3. Developing the underlying habits, behaviours and attitudes that enable you to do well
4. Gaining the best possible marks or grades that you are capable of achieving
5. Developing a range of skills and attributes that help you in your work or career beyond the course.

What kind of work gets good grades?

Although study is not all about grades, for most students grades matter. For good grades you need to:

a) produce work of a high standard ...
b) that isn't just good but also performs well against specific criteria for assessed work ...
c) and also meets any other course criteria, such as attendance, learning outcomes or work placement.

Standards and criteria not effort

The standard of work required for university level study is high and is usually tied in to national benchmarks and international and/or professional standards. The *quality* and *relevance* of your work is assessed, not *effort*. It is essential to understand the standards, requirements and criteria for your course, year and level.

Managing your performance

Reflect: Effective study means thinking about what you are doing, what works, and how to do even better.

Review: From time to time, go back over your work. After a break of a few weeks, you will bring a fresh eye to it. Compare recent work with work you did some time ago. Check that you are raising the standard of your work over time. Take pride in progress you make – let that spur you on to do even better.

Use feedback: Whether it is positive or full of corrections, don't ignore feedback. Treat it as free consultancy – it can help you pin-point where you can do better. Put it aside until emotions die down if needed, but then go back over it until you understand it. Make a list of all the improvements you could make.

Use data or dashboards: Many institutions now provide students with these to help monitor study behaviours and progress much as you can for fitness or games. Alternatively, you can devise your own dataset and charts to monitor performance. Consider including:

1. Your % attendance in class
2. Your % punctuality/lateness
3. Number of hours spent reading in the library, working in the studio or lab, training or rehearsing
4. Hours spent in independent study
5. The % of study time spent on study/wasted
6. Scores for class tests or tests you set yourself
7. Consecutive days spent forming a new study habit
8. The number of sources used for assignments
9. The number of academic articles read
10. Time taken to complete certain tasks.

Choose whatever gives you insights into how you are doing.

Reflection

Managing performance

★ How do you, or could you, take charge of managing and improving your performance?

★ What kinds of study behaviours would it be most useful for you to monitor?

Use technologies effectively

1 Save time and add interest ...

Use your phone or device to add variety and interest to study: listen to podcasts, watch TED talks, take free online courses such as 'MOOCs', share interesting sites, argue your point of view using course discussion boards, forums or chat rooms, etc.

2 Use referencing tools

Tools such as Zotero or Monterey are great for ensuring you take details down in full and accurately for referencing sources used in assignments.

3 Be selective!

There are tens of thousands of apps and sites created to support study. You don't need them all! Watch out for new ideas but beware of time-wasting: they don't make much difference and you can achieve well without them.

4 Build concentration

As you progress to higher levels of both study and paid employment you need greater levels of concentration to deal with more difficult and complex issues. Multi-tasking, such as checking messages, using social media or being diverted by multi-media, are all associated with reducing levels of attention. Bad habits can limit your brain! Train yourself to focus attention and work towards longer periods of sustained concentration (Cottrell, 2018).

5 Know when to log on – and log off!

The art of using technology effectively includes knowing when to use it and when not to. For example, making your own notes by hand is most effective for engaging the brain and laying down memories of what you study. Typing ideas saves time if you plan to incorporate these into assignments.

6 Keep files and folders organised

Label everything as soon as you create it. Group together files on the same topic, and keep an active contents list or key, all so you can find everything at speed when needed. Choose filenames that will help you recall the contents. Number each main draft of assignments separately, so you don't confuse versions.

7 Avoid preventable disasters!

Save your work every few minutes so that if there is a computer glitch or loss of power, you don't lose much work. Make sure you have a back-up copy, by using cloud storage or a memory stick. Don't leave printing or electronic submission until the last minute – in case something goes wrong then. Tutors expect you to plan for such hitches and do not usually accept them as reasons for late work.

8 Choose the right technology

Make sure your own software is compatible with that of your course and that you install antivirus software.

9 Support your group

Use your technologies to offer support to others. Send a motivating message when you know someone else is working late. Stay in touch over vacations and encourage each other to get on with reading, assignments, revision or other course tasks.

Combining work and study effectively

Students may combine work and study in various ways and circumstances, such as:

★ studying and working part-time

★ undertaking occasional work

★ starting their own business whilst studying

★ home-based work, including family and care commitments

★ full-time work or helping the family business

★ studying on programmes or options that include work placements or work practice

★ studying on programmes that are primarily work-based, such as for health- and medicine-related professions, Foundation Degrees and higher-level apprenticeships.

Benefits

Which of the following potential benefits of combining work and study are relevant to you?

☐ A broader range of experience and skills

☐ Greater confidence in adult work settings

☐ Increased maturity and self-reliance

☐ Professional and/or business awareness

☐ Understanding how academic theory relates to professional practice

☐ Income from work

☐ Networks and work contacts

☐ Developing my own business.

Reflection

Working whilst studying

★ What other benefits would work/study combinations bring for you?

★ What arrangements would you need to make?

Before you start

If you want to combine study and employment, it is worth investigating, early on, potential obstacles and ways of managing these. For example:

☐ Check you can meet attendance requirements.

☐ Find out if there are tutorials, trips and other non-timetabled events to attend.

☐ Plan out typical weeks to see whether your intentions are manageable.

☐ Check whether, and how, your timetable might change from one term or year to the next.

☐ Sort out your finances – study costs, loans and financial support can vary depending on what you earn and your mode of study.

Look for creative and efficient work/study synergies

If you are already in employment and have sympathetic employers, talk to them about how best to manage your work alongside study:

★ Are there ways your study could be counted as professional development as part of a work-related appraisal scheme?

★ Can you undertake relevant work-based projects that could count towards your qualification?

★ Would your employer be willing to provide study leave, quiet space and time to study at work, or help with meeting costs?

★ Some jobs lend themselves less easily to work–study combinations than others, but appropriate projects may still be possible.

Some jobs lend themselves more easily to work/study combinations ...

Effective management of work-based projects

Most academic aspects of work-based projects use skills that are outlined elsewhere in this book. Such projects have specific logistical issues you must also learn to manage. Some key issues are identified on this page and the next.

Do you need your employer's agreement?

Before undertaking a work-related project, check whether you need your employer's agreement. For assignments that are more theoretical in content, or that call upon informal observations and your own experiences, you will often not need permission. On the other hand, you *will* need your employer's permission, for example:

★ if you would be using work time or your employer's resources in carrying out an assignment

★ if you would be making use of certain types of information acquired in the workplace (such as confidential or commercially sensitive information)

★ if the nature of your assignment is such that you might lose the trust of your employer or your colleagues if they were unaware of it in advance

★ if you are likely to produce work that could be published or stored, and in which your employer or clients might be identifiable.

Before giving you permission to carry out a work-based project, your employer may wish to impose conditions: if so, put these in writing so that you are both clear about what has been agreed.

Organise yourself for the project

★ Check legal 'data protection' requirements and consider how you will meet these.

★ Gain permission for use of workplace data and information.

★ If you are using observations, photographs, client material, or the like, obtain written agreements from those concerned.

★ Schedule interviews and observations early on to be sure that colleagues will be available when needed.

★ Find out whether you yourself need to undergo any formal checks, such as clearance from the Disclosure and Barring Service if children or vulnerable people are involved (or the equivalent, depending on which country you are studying or working in). Arrange such checks well in advance.

Workplace mentors

It is helpful to have a workplace mentor to provide support. Ideally, this will be someone who:

★ knows the pressures a student faces

★ can help to negotiate access to data, relevant work tasks, study time or other resources

★ can be a sounding board for ideas about what is feasible in the workplace

★ can provide current professional and practical perspectives on issues.

Effective use of workplace mentors

★ Build your relationship with your mentor. Show your appreciation for her or his time.

★ Clarify what you need from your mentor, and when. Check that the mentor is able to provide these before starting the mentoring arrangement.

★ To help mentors support you effectively, identify what they will need from you for meetings, observations and at other times.

★ Arrange dates and outline agendas in advance for a series of meetings.

★ Respect your mentor. Arrive prepared for each session. Ensure that you have completed whatever is asked of you. Respond quickly to their messages.

Project-related skills: Sections in *The Study Skills Handbook*

★ *Working with others.* Chapters 8 and 9.

★ *Research skills.* Chapters 10 and 11.

★ *Managing projects.* Chapter 16.

Effective management of study leave

Employers may offer study-leave time at work or off-site. If managed well, this is a valuable resource.

Student comments

> Half a day a week study leave made all the difference to me. It meant I could get onto campus to sort out administrative bits and pieces, meet tutors and so on, that would have been hard to do outside college hours.

> For me, an afternoon a week was OK. I went to the library to read things that weren't online.

> I didn't get much out of study leave. By the time I did the shopping and got home, the day was almost over and I had to start the family's dinner.

> I tended to use the time to catch up on other things – not much on study.

> I meant to take the half day but something always came up at work so it didn't happen.

> I preferred taking a whole study day once a fortnight rather than a half day each week.

Reflection

Study leave

★ What do the experiences of these students suggest to you about how best to approach and plan any time you have as study leave?

★ What kinds of circumstances might prevent you from making best use of study leave time and what would you do to manage these?

Half-day or full-day study release?

Half-day study leave can be the more difficult to manage effectively. It can mean time is wasted in travel, and it provides less opportunity for consolidated study. It tends to suit people who:

★ prefer short bouts of academic study

★ like to study 'little and often'

★ have little travel to undertake

★ manage study time well.

Reflection

Making best use of time

★ If you prefer more concentrated bursts of study time, see whether you can consolidate weekly study leave into longer, less frequent periods of study leave.

Making effective use of study leave

★ Plan ahead so that you make the most of the time available. For example, identify tasks that could be completed during study leave, so you gain a sense of achievement by the end of it.

★ Check whether there is a quiet room at work that could be used for study, to save travel time.

★ If you have negotiated study time in the workplace, see whether you can connect to appropriate online study resources from there. If not, would you study more effectively on campus or elsewhere?

★ Plan use of a half-day study leave allocation within the context of your overall working week. Check whether you can use the time flexibly – such as by consolidating it into a day per fortnight to cut back on travel time in to work.

★ If you find it better to use study leave for non-study purposes, ensure that you do put aside equivalent study time elsewhere in your schedule.

Active learning

Why does this matter?

Consider the characteristics of passive and active learning below and in the illustration opposite.

From these, you should be able to see for yourself why developing and using active learning strategies makes success more likely.

Reflection

Active or passive?

★ What initial reflections and ideas do you have about whether your study habits are passive or active?

Characteristics of passive learning	Characteristics of active learning
1 You wait for directions and information to be fed to you.	1 You take the initiative, find things out, and become involved in what you are learning.
2 Information is delivered to you – you just follow what is said or written, and do as you are told.	2 You are engaged in the whole learning process (and in a position to see why information has been selected).
3 Different pieces of information are treated as separate units.	3 You look for links between different things that you discover.
4 You repeat information without understanding it.	4 You make a conscious effort to make sense of, and find meaning in, what you learn. Understanding is usually deeper.
5 You don't reflect upon what you have learnt.	5 You reflect on, and evaluate, your learning, to drive understanding and improvement.
6 You may become bored and tired easily.	6 Your attention span is longer because your mind is more fully engaged.
7 You use surface processing (page 74), in which case you are less likely to understand or remember.	7 When working with new material, you relate it to what you already know as this means you are more likely to understand and remember it.
8 You are less likely to be able to use what you learn.	8 Linking information helps you to see how you can apply it to different situations.
9 What you study may seem irrelevant.	9 Learning is personalised and more interesting.
10 You expect others to prompt you or to remind you of steps, stages and deadlines, so you often feel uncertain about what to do next.	10 You take charge of your learning and manage it like a project, so you feel confident that you know what to do, when, and why.

Emphasis on action!

Active learning strategies

Consider the illustrations below and the ideas on page 112. Jot down any ideas you have about making yourself a more active learner.

(A) Inactive learning strategies

A1

A2

A3

A4

A5

(B) Active learning strategies

B1 Prepare for lectures

B2 Set yourself questions

B3 Rework your notes

B4 Link ideas and information

B5 Discuss with others

B6 Mull things over

B7 Organise information

B8 Draft and redraft work

B9 Evaluate your own work

B10 Use feedback constructively

Active learning strategies

1 Decide ✓ which of these active learning strategies to try out.
2 Select *two* to try this week.
3 Select *two more* to try later this month.

☐ Summarise a passage in 8–12 words. This makes you think about what you have read.

☐ Make spider diagrams – or other patterned notes (page 228).

☐ Think of 3–5 real-life examples of what you have learned, to help you apply what you learn.

☐ Work out which is the ONE best example, and why. This will help you to prioritise and evaluate.

☐ List 50 mini-questions about one aspect of the subject ('what, why, who, where, when, how did *x* happen?'). This helps you to explore the subject.

☐ Answer your own mini-questions – to help you research in an organised and focused way.

☐ Draw a diagram or a cartoon to illustrate a theory or concept.

☐ Use smart reading strategies (pages 215–17).

☐ Write action plans – and carry them out!

☐ 'Teach' what you have learned to a real or an imaginary person. Imagine you are giving a lecture or instructions.

☐ Keep a reflective study journal.

☐ Sum up the three most important points of a lecture. Which is the *one* most important point? This helps you to evaluate and select salient points.

☐ With other students, start a course wiki.

☐ Make a wallchart or a large plan, linking all you have learned about an aspect of your studies.

☐ On your wallchart, in a different coloured ink, link information from another area of your studies.

☐ Decide which book(s) you would recommend as best for the topic you are studying.

☐ Which section of the book you are reading is the most interesting or useful?

☐ Play 'devil's advocate': pretend you disagree with everything you read – how would you argue your case? What examples and evidence would you use?

☐ How does what you have learned link with your work or your everyday life?

☐ Make your own e-book, to support revision.

☐ Invent titles for essays or reports. Give yourself 5 minutes to write a quick outline plan for one of these.

☐ List all the key points for one aspect of study. Draw a simple picture or symbol to remind you of each aspect.

☐ Discuss your ideas – or your difficulties – with other students, your tutor or support staff.

☐ Contribute to your course chat room or discussion board, or start one.

☐ Write key points on index cards or sticky labels. Juggle these around to see how many ways you could organise the same information.

What other active learning techniques could you devise?

The C·R·E·A·M strategy for learning

Motivation

Your level of motivation will affect your success. No matter how much you love your subject or want to gain a good degree, there may be times when you don't feel like studying or wonder whether you would be better off doing something else. You need strong motivation to keep yourself going at such times.

What affects motivation?

Motivation is affected by all kinds of things, from changing your mind about your career or course, to doing less well than expected, feeling overwhelmed by study difficulty, or friends dropping out. Most students work through some periods of low motivation – you can get through it.

Key influences on motivation

Motivation to study is affected by such things as:

★ clarity of purpose
★ being on the right course
★ managing the 'boring bits'
★ confidence of the outcome
★ using time well.

Reasons for weak motivation

★ loss of direction
★ boredom, resulting from poor study strategies
★ too much or too little challenge
★ crises of confidence.

Signs of weak motivation

★ finding excuses not to study
★ not being able to settle down to study
★ losing interest
★ becoming easily distracted
★ giving up quickly.

How strong is your motivation? Make a frank evaluation of your own motivation. Rating: 1 = low; 5 = high.	Rating
1 I have a strong sense of purpose	1 2 3 4 5
2 I know my reasons for study	1 2 3 4 5
3 I am clear how my study will benefit my life	1 2 3 4 5
4 I set myself clear targets for completing tasks	1 2 3 4 5
5 I am driven to achieve well	1 2 3 4 5
6 I can get going quickly when I sit down to study	1 2 3 4 5
7 I have strategies for getting myself down to work	1 2 3 4 5
8 I stay focused once I sit down to study	1 2 3 4 5
9 I always complete work by the deadline	1 2 3 4 5
10 I create the time I need to complete tasks well	1 2 3 4 5
11 I set personal challenges that inspire me	1 2 3 4 5
12 I take pleasure in achieving milestones/goals	1 2 3 4 5
13 I study well even when I don't feel like it	1 2 3 4 5
14 I keep going even when things get tough	1 2 3 4 5
15 I give thought to how to keep myself inspired	1 2 3 4 5
16 I find ways of making study sessions enjoyable	1 2 3 4 5
17 I make the subjects I study interesting to me	1 2 3 4 5
18 I avoid actions that might sabotage my study	1 2 3 4 5
19 I use criticism as a spur to doing better	1 2 3 4 5
20 I manage anxieties and crises of confidence	1 2 3 4 5
Total score out of 100	

 What do you think your overall score and your rating of individual items tell you about your motivation?

Keeping motivated

Below are some strategies that can help to raise and then maintain your motivation. Identify ✓ which ones would work best for you.

☐ **Clarity of purpose**
Be clear about your reasons for studying this course, and how you will benefit. If you are excited about your course now, you may not feel this is necessary. However, it is well worth spending time doing this.

☐ **What I want from my study**
Use the reflective self-evaluation *What I want from my study* on page 116 to focus your thinking.

☐ **'I am doing this because ...'**
Jot down your response to this prompt, drawing on your ratings for the self-evaluation above. List as many reasons as you can. Underline those that are most important to you.

☐ **Link to longer-term goals**
Make a list of all the ways, directly and indirectly, that your studies will be of benefit to your life, personal and professional, over the longer term. Use your reflective journal to think this through.

☐ **Motivational chart: sticking with it**
Using your responses to the activities above and to that on page 11, write out your reasons for sticking with your studies. Inspire yourself! Add photos, newspaper clippings or other material that reinforces your sense of purpose. Update this as relevant.

☐ **Make a screensaver of your motivational chart**, so that you are continually inspired.

☐ **Make good choices**
★ Find out as much as you can about your course and options, so that these support your overall objectives.

★ Be active in finding points of interest and relevance.

★ If necessary, speak to financial and careers advisers at your institution about either (a) changing course, or (b) how your current course can help meet your objectives.

☐ **Seeing results: short-term goals**

The end of your course may seem a long way off. It is natural to want to see results. You can gain a better sense of this by setting short-term goals, milestones, targets or challenges that are:

★ meaningful to you, and

★ can be achieved in small steps in the near future.

See *Managing the challenge*, page 119.

☐ **Give yourself a precise focus**

If you are easily distracted from study, start each session by jotting down a quick list of the things to complete in that session. Check these off as you complete them.

Make Mum & Dad proud   I want a degree   Work overseas

REWARD SYSTEM
study
1hr = 15mins surfing
4hrs = go for swim
8hrs = watch DVD

EMERGENCY MEASURES
RING JOHN TO TELL ME TO KEEP GOING

Develop a routine

If you find it difficult to put time aside for study, take a more structured approach. Write specific times for study into your diary and keep these as appointments. Where possible, study at the same time and place each day. See Chapter 6 on *time management*.

Manage boredom

★ Clarify exactly why the task is relevant and what you will gain by completing it.

★ Be active in searching for points of interest, either in the material or in the way you design the study session for yourself.

★ Use active learning strategies to break up time and focus the attention (page 112).

★ Set yourself short-term goals and mini-challenges (page 119).

Awareness of positive triggers

Take note of the conditions that encourage you to get down to study, and then create these around you. So, if you work best with others, set up a study group. If you work best under pressure, set yourself demanding challenges to complete during a study session rather than leaving work to the last minute.

Awareness of negative triggers

★ Become aware of the circumstances that demotivate you; plan how you will avoid these.

★ Take note of the people around you who have a demotivating impact on you.

★ Notice those aspects of your own thinking or behaviour that demotivate you. Devise a strategy for using your positive triggers instead.

Manage anxieties and confidence

Academic study is demanding, which can sap confidence at times.

★ Note and respect your feelings but don't dwell on them. Speak to a counsellor to clarify your thoughts and devise a way forward.

★ Set yourself short-term goals to provide focus and a sense of achievement.

Use a 'supporter'

Ask a friend for motivational support, such as:

★ to check in with you occasionally to see that you are on task

★ to remind you of your goals and ambitions

★ to help you clarify a strategy.

Meaningful reward

Give yourself treats for undertaking the aspects of study you find least motivating. Make these proportionate to the time or emotional effort.

Have a 'Motivation Plan'

Feelings of low motivation may just pass, but it is wise to plan for such occasions.

★ Decide which strategies you are going to use for various kinds of circumstance.

★ Put them where you can see them.

★ Put the necessary resources into place (such as putting money aside for rewards, or time to spend with a mentor).

★ In your diary or planner, write in times when you will check whether your plan is working. If it isn't, revise it so that it does.

Reflection

Of the items you identified above, what do you need to do first? When will you do that?

Clarity of purpose: what I want from my study

What are the outcomes you wish to achieve from your studies. (Circle) the number that indicates how important each potential outcome is to you.

Outcome	Less important					Very important			
Personal development									
To prove to myself I can do it	1	2	3	4	5	6	7	8	9
To feel better educated generally	1	2	3	4	5	6	7	8	9
To develop higher level skills	1	2	3	4	5	6	7	8	9
Course-related									
To find out more about a subject that interests me	1	2	3	4	5	6	7	8	9
To develop an area of personal expertise	1	2	3	4	5	6	7	8	9
To have the opportunity to study	1	2	3	4	5	6	7	8	9
To get a good grade	1	2	3	4	5	6	7	8	9
To gain the qualification	1	2	3	4	5	6	7	8	9
I just want to get through	1	2	3	4	5	6	7	8	9
Life- and work-related									
To get my life out of a rut	1	2	3	4	5	6	7	8	9
To improve my career opportunities	1	2	3	4	5	6	7	8	9
To be better at my current job/employment	1	2	3	4	5	6	7	8	9
To improve my chance of promotion / higher salary	1	2	3	4	5	6	7	8	9
Other outcomes									
To show my family/friends that I can do it	1	2	3	4	5	6	7	8	9
To make up for missing out on education earlier	1	2	3	4	5	6	7	8	9
To be a role model for my children	1	2	3	4	5	6	7	8	9
Other reasons									

Reflection

Motivation for study

Select two outcomes you have decided are important to you. Write in more detail about what you aim to achieve.

Look back at this from time to time to see if your aims, and motivation for studying, are changing. Use pages 117–20 to explore your goals further.

Using your goals to guide your study strategy

Your reasons for studying and your goals can guide the way you proceed with your study, as in the following examples.

Goal A: to learn about the subject

If learning about the subject is the most important outcome for you, then reading around the subject and doing what interests you may be more important than following the curriculum.

Goal B: to have a good grade

If your chief priority is getting a good grade, then it is likely to be important that you 'play the game' and find out exactly what is required.

Goal C: just to get through

If you have many other demands on your time, or gaps in your education, you may have to limit yourself to covering essentials. What is important is that you know how to find and use information to get you through – you can fill gaps in your knowledge later in life.

Stating your goals

Goals are most motivating when stated in the present:

> I am able to achieve a 2:1!

It is also best to state them as positive objectives:

> I am able to gain a good job.

Negatively worded goals, such as 'A degree will help me to escape from my current employment', are less effective in providing motivation.

The effect of thinking negatively

Having a negative outcome is like going shopping with a list of what you are not going to buy.

O'Connor and McDermott (1996)

Analyse goals in detail

The following questions are based on an approach known as Neuro-Linguistic Programming (NLP). For each goal, go through the following questions and the resource sheet on page 120.

Are your goals 'well-formed'?

★ Are the goals clear and specific?
★ Are they at all limiting?
★ Do they help you?
★ Are they realistic?
★ Are they sufficiently motivating?
★ Are the outcomes worth it?
★ Are they really desirable?
★ How will you know you have achieved the outcomes – what will be different?

What are the implications of having these goals?

★ Will you need to put everything else on hold?
★ Will you have to change your study options?
★ Who else will be affected?
★ Are there other implications?

What are the potential gains?

★ Will you feel more in control of your life?
★ Will you have more respect for yourself?
★ Are there other potential gains?

What are the potential losses?

★ Will you see less of family and friends?
★ What sacrifices are involved?
★ Are there other potential losses?

Visualise yourself in the future, having achieved your goals

★ Where are you as a result of your achievement?
★ Are there any good or bad consequences?
★ What has changed for you?
★ Are you as happy as you thought you would be?

Using your goals to guide your study strategy

What exactly will you do?

Think through exactly what you will do and when, with as much vivid detail as you can, so that your mind can grasp your plan as 'real'. For working on an assignment, look at the time laid out in your planner. Visualise yourself busy at that time, focused on the study task. Ask yourself:

★ Where am I sitting?

★ What can I see around me?

★ Is it bright or dark?

★ Where are my books and notes laid out?

What setbacks could you face?

Think through potential problems and setbacks in advance so you are better prepared for what arises.

★ What (or who) could stop you achieving your goals?

★ Have you set yourself too much to do?

★ Are there concerns you have already?

★ How will you overcome each obstacle? What kind of precautionary steps could you set in train now to pre-empt difficulties later on?

Visualise yourself in rich detail, taking steps to deal with each potential obstacle. Conjure up sights and sounds, so your mind forms a strong image of you taking action.

Fine-tune your goals and objectives

Keep modifying your goals and objectives until they feel, sound and look right for you.

★ Use the chart on page 120 to clarify and focus your thinking about each of your goals.

★ Do you need to revise or reword your goals so that they are more realistic and motivating?

Make a clear mental plan

Create in advance a rich mental plan of activities you are going to undertake, whether working on your assignment, making a presentation, sitting an exam or going for a job interview. The better the detail, the easier it is for your mind to orientate you towards achieving it.

Self-sabotage

It can sometimes be hard to accept that we may *achieve* our goals. Many people have set patterns that they use in their daily life to sabotage their own best-laid plans.

It is not clear exactly why this happens. Sometimes it is simply hard to accept that we can be successful where once we struggled. If we do succeed, we may start to feel that we should have tried harder in the past. If we fail now, however, this will 'prove' that we were 'right all along'. At other times, we may fear failure so much that we just want it to happen quickly so that it is over: waiting to see whether we succeed can feel painful.

Kinds of self-sabotage

Students sabotage their studies in all kinds of ways. Examples include:

★ not turning up to lectures and classes, or not maintaining concentration once there

★ leaving work until the last minute and then missing deadlines

★ not turning up for exams because they feel they will fail them

★ filling their time with any activity *except* study

★ not thinking about life after the course

★ spending too much time socialising.

There are many more to choose from!

Reflection

Self-sabotage

★ What kinds of self-sabotage are you most likely to engage in?

★ What is most likely to trigger you into self-sabotage?

★ How could you recognise that you had started to sabotage your studies?

★ Who do you trust to point this out to you?

★ What would you do to prevent this and/or turn this around?

Motivation: managing the challenge

Setting goals

Devising clear, realistic goals can give you a sense of momentum and early success.

Give yourself manageable short-term goals

Set yourself mini-goals as milestones, so that you have a sense of achievement. In time these add up to greater achievements.

★ Break larger assignments, such as writing a report, into smaller tasks: 'Read course notes', 'Find resource materials', etc.

★ Break each of *these tasks* into smaller ones: 'Make notes of pp. 20–40 *Media Now*.'

★ Set a realistic time allowance for each mini-goal: 'Make notes on pages 31–70: 20 mins.'

★ Give yourself a start time – and stick to it!

★ Set a target end-time and work to that. The key aim isn't to keep to time but to *complete* the goal, so keep going until you do.

Effective mini-goals or milestones are:

★ *integrated*: clearly linked to a larger plan, such as your essay, project, or your overall motivation for the course

★ *manageable and realistic*: set goals you could actually achieve, even if there is some stretch

★ *specific*: decide precisely what you are going to tackle

★ *measurable*: such as a set number of pages to read, or a report section to write

★ *flexible*: plan time in for emergencies; be ready to change things round if necessary.

Celebrate successes

Increase your chances of early success by setting targets and deadlines you know you can meet.

When you achieve a target (such as two hours' reading), reward yourself (such as by taking a half-hour's break). Give yourself bigger rewards for completing whole tasks, to encourage yourself next time.

Mark success

Note down your achievements and successes in your journal or personal blog. It is important to note what you do well, so that you can do it again! After a few months, look back on your early work. Give yourself credit for any progress you have made (pages 99–100).

Aim for higher peaks

When you achieve one set of goals, set new ones, making these a little more challenging. Add further 'stretch' so that you keep developing academically and personally. Keep surprising yourself with what you can achieve!

Keep setting yourself new goals and challenges

Achieving my goals

Goal *State this here with positive wording, in the present tense*	
Potential gains	
Potential losses	
How I'll recognise when the goal has been achieved	
Targets (short-term goals and milestones)	
Possible obstacles	
Steps to overcoming obstacles	
How I'll celebrate success	

Integrating C·R·E·A·M strategies into my study

C·R·E·A·M strategy	How I will incorporate this strategy into my study
Giving more freedom to my imagination and playfulness	
Finding ways to increase my enjoyment in study	
Taking creative and systematic ways of resolving problems that emerge	
Being flexible in study strategies and having plenty of variety	
Reflecting on my learning and evaluating my progress	
Organising time and space, and being in the right state of mind for study	
Seeing where I waste effort by being over-virtuous	
Linking learning in one subject to other subjects and to real-life issues	
Increasing my motivation	
Formulating clear outcomes and milestones	

Review

1 **Trust and enjoy your creativity**

Apply your imagination and self-awareness to finding ways of making your study more dynamic, useful and fun. Create the physical and mental space that enables you to learn at your best.

2 **Use creative problem-solving**

Apply both imagination and systematic approaches to resolving problems you encounter as part of your study or student life.

3 **Reflect on your performance**

Pause at frequent intervals to bring thoughtfulness to what you are doing and to reflect on your progress. Check whether your studies are working out as you would wish. If not, adapt your study strategies accordingly.

4 **Keep a reflective journal, log or blog**

Get your thoughts down. It helps you think things through. Look back at these later to notice changes in your thinking and to monitor progress.

5 **Make your study effective**

Make your efforts count – so you learn well and achieve your best for your circumstances. Don't mistake effort and hours studied for quality and standards, nor virtue for effectiveness.

6 **Make your study efficient**

Optimise your use of all available study resources: your time, energy, tutors, classes, support and opportunities. Focus your energies rather than wasting them.

7 **Plan, plan, plan!**

Great organisation and planning can make a huge difference to every aspect of study, giving you more control, confidence and time. Chapter 6 enables you to look at time management in more depth.

8 **Engage actively with your studies**

Work course material in ways that engage your brain and stretch you intellectually. Personalise your study strategy so that you maintain a lively interest, avoiding boredom and passive regurgitation of information.

9 **Set motivating goals**

Clarify your study purpose: decide what you really want from your experience as a student. Use your goals to guide your study strategy and to sustain motivation, especially on days when study feels tough.

10 **Beware of self-sabotage**

Be alert to ways that you could undermine your own goals and best intentions. Be active in checking whether your plans and behaviours are delivering what you really want for your future. If not, take steps to get back on track. Ask for help where needed.

11 **Maintain your motivation**

Monitor and review your study in such a way that you gain and build a sense of progress and achievement. Use this to spur you on to greater things.

12 **Apply C·R·E·A·M strategy to life and work**

It is a 'meta-strategy' applicable to any area of life or work. Creativity, professional reflection, self-reliance, self-motivation and personal effectiveness are valued and rewarded by employers.

Chapter 6

Time management as a student

Learning outcomes

This chapter gives you opportunities to:

✓ understand the importance of effective time management to successful study

✓ consider the time requirements of your own programme of study

✓ gain a clear sense of how you spend your time now and plan out how you want to spend it in future

✓ apply time management strategies to help you save time and make best use of study time

✓ organise your independent study in ways that make the best use of your time.

Introduction

As a student, only part of your week and year will be formally timetabled. You are responsible for organising most of your study time for yourself. This can be challenging. It is likely that you will:

★ experience many demands on your time: from study, jobs, family, social life, sports, music, personal interests, shopping, eating, travel, moving across campus, and managing other basics of day-to-day living

★ have to manage competing deadlines, with several assignments to turn around in quick succession or for the same hand-in date

★ spend much of your time in independent study and online, both of which can lead to interesting but time-consuming diversions.

If you feel that your time is under pressure, or you suspect that you waste time that could be better spent on other things, then it is worth developing your time-awareness and time management skills.

This chapter provides strategies, approaches and tools to help you to:

★ evaluate how you use your time currently

★ decide how you want to use it

★ organise your time so that you feel that you are more in control of it

★ save time for the things you really want to do.

Oh my days! I thought the ark was leaving next week.

How well do I manage my time now?

For each of the items below, (circle) the response which best fits you. Then follow up the 'Next step' to check for strategies that could help you fine-tune any areas in which you want to improve.

Item	Do I ...	Response			Next step See page(s)
1	have a good sense of why time management is important for students?	Yes	No	Don't know	125–6; 129
2	usually *know* where I should be and at what time?	Yes	No	Don't know	137–8
3	usually *turn up on time* to where I need to be?	Yes	No	Don't know	137–8
4	keep good track of all the things I need to do?	Yes	No	Don't know	131; 137; 139
5	have an accurate sense of where my time goes?	Yes	No	Don't know	130–6
6	use breaks and blocks of study time creatively, to help me study effectively?	Yes	No	Don't know	141; 148
7	know how many study hours are expected for my course?	Yes	No	Don't know	131
8	know how many hours I am expected to spend across the year in different kinds of study?	Yes	No	Don't know	129
9	prioritise effectively the things I most need to do?	Yes	No	Don't know	25–6; 136
10	use a planner or diary effectively?	Yes	No	Don't know	137–8; 140
11	know when all assignment deadlines and/or exams fall?	Yes	No	Don't know	140
12	map out in my planner how I will organise my work so as to meet all deadlines?	Yes	No	Don't know	137–8
13	use my time online effectively?	Yes	No	Don't know	106; 143; 147
14	know how to manage distractions?	Yes	No	Don't know	141; 143; 145–7
15	use time management strategies effectively?	Yes	No	Don't know	127–8; 143; 144; 149
16	have time for myself and to relax?	Yes	No	Don't know	133

Reflection

Evaluating my own time management skills

★ What do your answers to these questions suggest about how well you manage your time now?

★ Do you need to change any of your attitudes to time in order to manage your studies well?

Why time management matters

Time management = study success

Your success as a student will be strongly affected by the combination of two time-related factors:

★ **How much** time you spend in study

★ **How well** you use that time.

The more time you put into the various tasks of reading and thinking about your subject, preparing for exams or fine-tuning your assignments, the more likely it is that you will do well.

If you both spend more time in study AND manage that time effectively, you are much more likely to achieve well and have a great time as a student.

You feel more confident that you are in charge and can cope – and that you don't forget or miss out on things that are important.

You make sure you have time for 'basics', such as eating and sleeping properly and making friends.

You learn to juggle the various demands of study, social life, employment, family, and personal interests and commitments.

You learn where you can take short cuts that save you time – and where not to.

Time = choice

If you use time effectively, this gives you choice in how you spend the time saved, such as in ...

★ pursuing some topics in more depth, so that you are more expert in these and so that your work stands out

★ reinforcing what you have learnt, so that it makes more sense to you

★ preparing better for exams and assignments so as to achieve better grades

★ working and earning, being with your family, or enjoying more leisure and social life.

What students say

Social media is my downfall! I can't help feeling I am missing something important if I don't keep checking. On good days, I set myself times to check, and I get so much done!

Sorting out how you use time – that is the one big thing to get right about study – especially if you go online a lot. In my first year, time just disappeared before I knew it and everything was rushed! My grades were OK but not great. This year, I am the other extreme. I am constantly thinking about how I am using the time I have.

I am very selective about which search engines I use – there isn't much point using lots of search tools when a really good one gives you as much as you are likely to need.

I thought time management was just a catchphrase, not something I should actually think about. I had no idea how much time I wasted until I actually started to take note of it. It made me realise all the things I could actually do if I was more disciplined in how I use time – so now I am!

I just don't waste time reading material on sites where I can't validate the source or the reliability of the information.

The thing about studying so much on your own is that you realise how you rely on other people, teachers or just others working around you, to help stay concentrated yourself. When it is just you and the screen, you drift off more easily, so you need to give yourself ways of staying focused. I always start out by making a list of things I have to do – there's always more to add than I imagine, and that usually shocks me into getting down to it.

My advice to other students would be 'Don't have your treats before you get down to work. Do the study first or else it's much harder to make yourself do it!'

When you are researching online there is always the temptation to look up just one more thing or to see what one more search engine turns up. You have to know when enough is enough.

Know your weak points and don't pretend they don't matter! Mine is Twitter. I want to tweet all the time and I'm useless at doing bits of study between tweets so basically it is no tweeting for me when I am studying. It's just easier. I know I can send some smug tweets at the end of the day about how much work I have done!

I make myself study for 45 minutes and then I let myself 'play' – play is looking at football scores, music videos, emails, games, anything I want. I am someone who needs constant rewards, so that is how I do it.

Reflection

Learning from others

Are any of these students' experiences similar to your own? What could you learn from their experiences and strategies?

10 steps to effective time management

10 steps to good time management

1 **Be systematic** in your time management
2 **Find out** your time requirements
3 **Clarify** how you use your time currently
4 **Decide** how you want to spend your time
5 **Prioritise** what is most important
6 **Plan** what you will do when
7 **Do it**, keeping to your plan
8 **Apply** time management techniques
9 **Manage distractions** and procrastination
10 **Monitor** Keep checking it is all working.

1 Be systematic ...

★ in thinking about time management

★ in developing an understanding of how you use your time

★ in working out how best to manage your time to achieve your priorities

★ in planning your time.

How and when am I going to handle time management?

2 Find out your time requirements

★ Find out the pattern of study required for your programme – and how much time you will need to spend in independent study (page 129).

How much time am I expected to spend on study as a minimum? How long does it take me to travel from A to B? How many hours do I need to work a week?

3 Clarify how you use your time now

Be aware of how much time it takes you, personally, to do things. Use or adapt the resource on page 132 to check:

★ where you *think* your time goes

★ where it *really* goes.

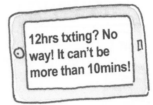

12hrs txting? No way! It can't be more than 10mins!

4 Decide how you want to use your time

★ Use the resources on pages 131–2 to work out how you will spend your study time.

★ Use time circles to decide how much time you want to give to different activities. Compare this with the way you actually spend your time (pages 133–5).

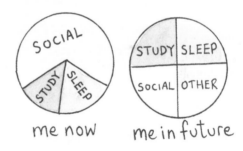

me now   me in future

5 Prioritise

You may find it hard to fit in everything you would like to do and some things will be more urgent than others. Identify your priorities; set times to start and complete these (pages 135–6).

Which is more important for me to do first? Buy socks or hand in these equations?

6 Plan

Be very specific and comprehensive in your time-planning.

★ Keep a detailed diary/planner (see pages 137–8).

★ Work backwards from deadlines such as assignment hand-in dates (page 140).

7 Do it

★ Put your plan where you will be reminded of it easily.

★ Implement your plan to schedule.

★ Work out what might sabotage your plans (page 118).

8 Apply time management techniques

Experiment with ways of saving and managing time, so that you find out what works for you and have more time for things you really want to do.

Essay done! Time for a nice lie in!

9 Manage distractions and procrastination

Build your understanding of when and how you become distracted from using time effectively, despite your best intentions.
Plan strategies to manage this (pages 145–8).

Yes – I will manage procrastination and distraction but ... um ... later.

10 Monitor

Check that you are sticking to your plan. If not,

★ either update your planning to make it more realistic, OR

★ work out what you need to do to stay on target.

(Page 130.)

It's taking all my time to manage my time management.

Working through the 10 steps to effective time management

The following pages provide strategies and resources for each of these ten steps.

★ Browse through these resources.

★ Work through the 10 steps, focusing especially on those which will most improve your own time management.

How much study time is required?

How many hours must I study?

Hours per year

Each year of successful full-time study on a degree programme is assumed to be the equivalent of 1200 hours. For work-based courses, those hours may include clinical practice or workplace activity.

Hours per week

The number of hours of study per week will vary depending on how many weeks off you take.

★ 1200 hours = 23 hours a week for 52 weeks.
★ 1200 hours = 27 hours a week for 45 weeks, if you take 7 weeks of breaks.
★ You could distribute your time in different patterns for term-time and holidays.

Nominal hours vs. actual hours

The figures above are a nominal requirement – that is, a general assumption of how long it takes to cover the work for that level of study. In practice, the time required varies from student to student, depending on such factors as:

★ how much additional work they undertake out of interest or to gain higher marks
★ how quickly they get through the work
★ the care they take in fine-tuning their work
★ whether they find study hard or easy
★ the demands of work-based practice.

Part-time study

The number of hours depends on the proportion of the qualification you study each year.

If you study the equivalent of 50% of a full-time degree, that would amount to around 600 hours a year or an average of 12 hours a week.

If you study 80%, that would mean around 960 hours a year or an average of 18 hours a week.

> ### How many hours for your programme?
> Total study hours expected per year ....
>
> Average hours per week ....
>
> Average hours per week during breaks ....

> ### How much compulsory attendance?
> Approx. hours required on campus ....
>
> Hours of compulsory attendance ....
>
> Approx. number of hours expected for independent study (including online study) ....

Where study time is spent

In practice, 1200 hours can mean very different things depending on your programme.

I spend 20 hours a week in laboratories and the rest studying online.

I spend 4 days a week at work – and it counts towards my degree. I have classes two evenings a week.

I spend 6 hours a week in lectures, seminars and tutorials, and the rest of the time in the library or online.

All of my programme is provided online.

> ### How are you expected to spend those hours?
> Within the overall number of study hours, there will be broad expectations of how those hours will be used for study. These may be detailed in your course handbook.
>
> You can use the chart on page 131 to map out roughly how much time you are expected to spend on different kinds of activity.

Monitor use of independent study time

Use a copy of this sheet for each study period until you are happy with how you use your time.

Column 1 (fill out during study)	Column 2 (fill out after study)
Date: Where: Time I am starting: Study conditions:	Were the conditions, time and place the best possible? Could I improve anything?
How long am I going to study for altogether?	How long did I study for?
How many breaks do I intend to take? Times of breaks (approx.)? Length of breaks?	When did I take breaks? Did I stick to the break time? If not, what do I need to do to get back to study?

Interruptions that occurred			
Type of interruption	Length	Time finished	Total time worked

Thoughts and observations about my study habits and time management

© Stella Cottrell (2019) *The Study Skills Handbook*, 5th edition, Red Globe Press

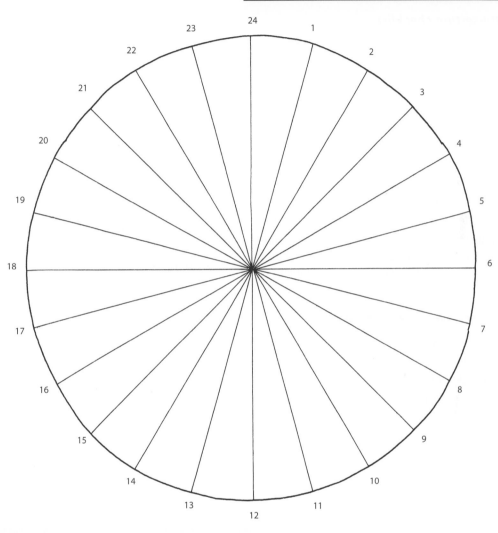

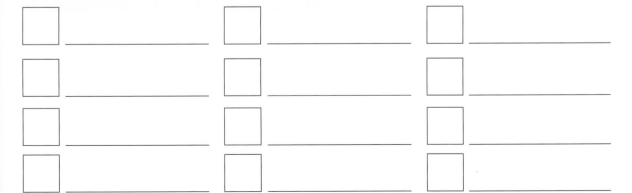

Acknowledging your anxieties

It is easier to avoid excess stress if you deal with anxieties and difficulties at an early stage. Ignoring them won't make them go away and makes them more complicated to resolve later.

It is easier to manage anxieties if you:

★ acknowledge what you are feeling

★ sort out in your own mind what is really worrying you the most

★ recognise that you are not alone in such feelings (and sharing them can help).

Identifying your anxieties

On the right are listed some anxieties which are typical of student life. Identify ✓ those that concern you the most. Add any others that affect you, using the spaces provided.

Beside each of the items you identify, write the number of the statement below that most closely corresponds with how you feel. Then read the comments on the next page.

1 I expect this to be a minor difficulty: I will get round it easily and in time.
2 I expect this to be potentially serious but manageable: I will work on a solution.
3 I expect this to be a major difficulty: I might need to ask for help.
4 I don't think I can cope with this without support: I will ask for this straight away.
5 I know I need help so I will ask for it.

Reflection

Managing anxieties

★ What initial ideas do you have about how you could manage some of these anxieties?

★ What strategies have you used in the past to deal with a new or difficult situation? Which of these strategies could be helpful now?

Study and learning

☐ Getting used to university life
☐ Believing in myself
☐ Avoiding failure
☐ Getting good grades
☐ Exams
☐ Finding the time to do everything
☐ Keeping up with other people
☐ Understanding academic language
☐ Having the confidence to speak
☐ Writing essays and assignments
☐ Submitting my work on time.

Personal, family and work commitments

☐ Homesickness
☐ Loneliness
☐ Making friends with other students
☐ Coping with travel
☐ People treating me differently/'fitting in'
☐ Coping with job requirements
☐ Family responsibilities
☐ Organising child care.

Others

☐ Money
☐ Safety and security
☐ Health
☐
☐

Where does all my time go?

As a student, there are many demands which eat up your time apart from study. Clarify where time really goes by jotting down everything you do for a few days – exercise, lectures, travel, etc. Note this roughly every hour. Then, chart it onto a *Time circle*. Use a second *Time circle* to chart how you would *want* to use your time each day. Compare the two.

Circle 1: How I use time now

Use colours or graphics to map your typical time use.
Treat each segment as roughly one hour.
Which activities don't get enough of your time?
Which take up too much time?

Example

★ sleep – 10 hr

★ eating and socialising – 2 hr

★ social media/games/TV – 3 hr

★ personal/home – 3 hr

★ travel – 1 hr

★ lectures, seminars, tutorials – 2 hr

★ reading – 1 hr

★ writing – 2 hr

★ thinking – 0 hr

★ exercise/relaxation – 0 hr

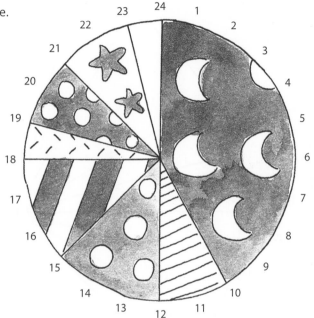

Circle 2: How I want to use my time

Divide the day into how you would *prefer* to use your time. This is your goal.

Example

★ sleep – 7½ hr

★ eating and socialising – 2 hr

★ social media – 1 hr

★ personal/home – 1½ hr

★ travel – 1 hr

★ lectures, seminars, tutorials – 2 hr

★ reading – 3 hr

★ writing – 2 hr

★ thinking – 1 hr

★ volunteering/clubs/societies 1 hour

★ part-time job 1 hr

★ exercise/relaxation – 1 hr

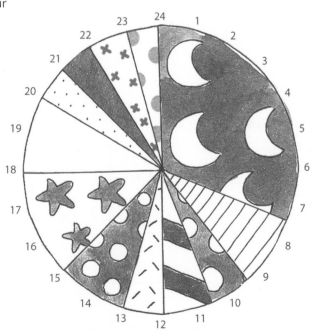

Time circle: How I use my time now

Date:

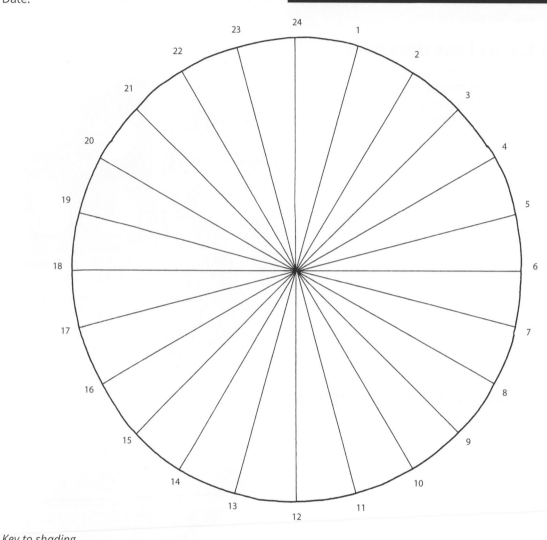

Key to shading

Time management as a student

Time circle: How I want to use my time

Date:

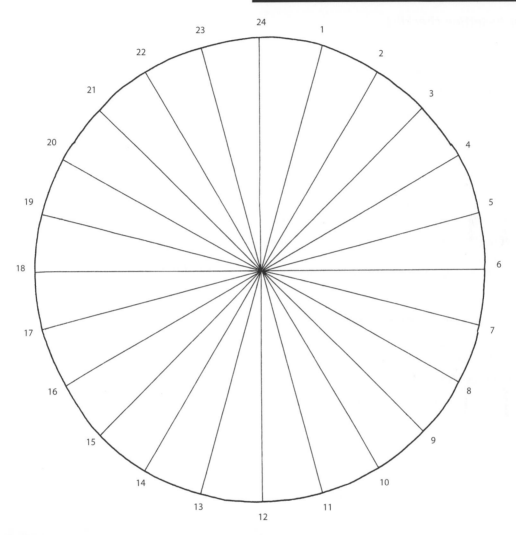

Key to shading

Time management as a student

Set your priorities

If you don't have enough time, set priorities. This checklist can help clarify what to do and when.

Priority-setting checklist

Done ✓

- [ ] **1** Write a full 'To do' list.
- [ ] **2** Highlight the essential tasks.
- [ ] **3** Identify anything urgent.
- [ ] **4** Identify the most important items (those with the most serious consequences if not completed).
- [ ] **5** Number the items in the best order to do them.
- [ ] **6** Work out how long I can spend on each.
- [ ] **7** Decide what might have to be missed out.
- [ ] **8** Enter into my timetable or planner the times put aside for each stage of all essential tasks, with both start and end times (or dates).

Work out the best order

Decide the best order for completing tasks depending on such considerations as:

★ the most urgent or important

★ the most logical order (consider tasks that precede others, or could be grouped by location, travel routes or people involved)

★ whether you prefer to do easy items first or last

★ if you find it hard to prioritise, use a rating system. Weigh up importance against urgency.

Using the Priority Organiser

You can use or adapt the chart below to help you work out your priorities.

The rating system

Column A: Importance. Rate how important it is for you to do this task at all. (6 = not important; 10 = essential.)

Column B: Urgency. If this is to be done at all, how essential is it that you do it soon? (1 = must be done at once; 5 = it can wait.)

Column C: Balance the scores. Subtract the score in column B from that in column A. The highest scores in column C are the most likely to be priorities. However, double check to see if that is really the case.

Decide on the order

★ *Column D*   Number tasks in the order that you will complete them, using your rating as a guide.

★ *Columns E and F*   Write down the date (or time) to start and complete each. Put them in your diary.

Monitor completion

★ Highlight your next task in yellow so that it stands out for your attention.

★ When you complete it, highlight it in green to show it no longer needs your attention.

Priority organiser

Full chart available on the companion site.

List of things to do	A importance? (scale 6–10)	B Urgency? (scale 1–5)	C (A–B)	D Order of priority	E Start by ...	F End by ...

Effective planning and diary-keeping

A good student planner or diary is invaluable for managing time. A 'week to view' academic diary/planner is ideal.

What to put in about your study

A comprehensive record

To be effective, your diary or planner needs to be a *complete* record of what you have to do. Write in:

★ all classes, exams, field trips, work placements, deadlines for submitting assignments, etc.

★ all non-study activities, such as family holidays, medical appointments, work hours, birthdays, volunteering, travel, etc.

★ exact location for each item, and with whom

★ specific independent study tasks, such as 'Read Chapters 2–4 of *Urban Ecology*'

★ dates and times to log-on for specific activities or when course resources are available online

★ free time, for catch up, emergencies, unforeseen events, rest, and enjoyment.

A plan for completing assignments

Map into the diary the times when you will:

★ think about the subject

★ prepare for lectures and seminars

★ prepare for other formal sessions

★ plan your work

★ research each subject, including conducting searches, reading and making notes

★ organise and condense your notes

★ reflect on your learning

★ discuss work with others

★ write early drafts, and edit and redraft these

★ check your work.

A strategy for managing deadlines

Use the **Plan backwards from deadlines** sheet (page 140) to work out the time you will need for each stage of your assignments, before entering these into your planner. Organise everything else around your deadlines.

Colour codes and symbols

Use colours and symbols to indicate different activities and subjects in your diary. If you use these consistently, you will find that after a while you don't need to 'read' the entries: you can check at a glance. Use positive or energising symbols for activities you dislike.

Examples of symbols you could devise

Diary entries

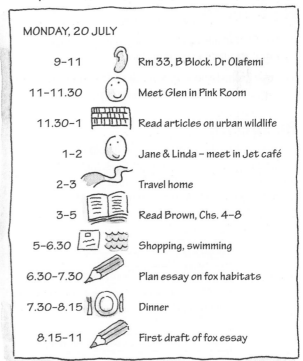

Make your planning work for you

Using your planner

Your diary or planner will be effective only if you keep it up to date and *use* it.

★ Carry it with you at all times.

★ Add all commitments straight into it so you cannot forget them.

★ Write essential appointments in pencil, so you can make changes easily.

★ Organise entries so you can see at a glance which time is filled: don't double-book.

★ Be rigorous in rescheduling appointments straightaway if there is a clash. It is easy to forget to reschedule later on.

★ Check it several times a day, especially at night and first thing in the morning.

Write 'To do' lists in your planner and update these every day. Look ahead to the end of the week in case future activities require you to add anything to today's 'To do' list. See page 139.

High visibility

★ Highlight all key dates so they stand out from other activities in your planner.

★ Enter items legibly and in full so that, later in the year, you know what each refers to.

Be specific

Enter brief but clear details that will help ensure you are in the right place at the right time. Include start times, people's names, locations and room numbers as in the example below, taken from *The Macmillan Student Planner* (Cottrell, 2019b and updated annually).

Plan short- and long-term

★ Put time aside each day to plan ahead. Check what you need to organise for the next 24–48 hours.

★ Put aside time each week to plan the week ahead.

★ Scan your planner several months ahead so you know what is coming up.

★ Consider using a year-to-view planner or wall-chart to see at a glance how your year pans out.

Keep it real

★ Don't plan actions you know you can't complete.

★ Put realistic amounts of time aside for whatever you have to do – don't try to fit an hour's journey into 45 minutes, or assignment reading into an hour!

★ Don't say 'yes' to new plans if you can't create space in your diary. Work out what can wait.

★ Review your plans and checklists. Remove items that have become unrealistic, at least for now.

Reflection

Using your planner

★ What are your current strengths in maintaining a diary or planner?

★ What improvements could you make to organise your time and life more effectively?

23 TUESDAY			
Time	Activity	Where	To do today
9	Anatomy (lect.) (leave before 8.15!)	LB 204	To buy: soap, coffee, rice
10.30	Personal tutor (bring list of questions)	R 11	
12.00	Lunch w/Maya & Tom	Green Café	Reserve books for
			Anatomy essay
1 pm	Practice run with JK for this pm	WS library	Birthday card for Kim
3–5	Seminar: Physiol. JK & me presenting	LB 202b	
			Phone home
7.45	Film at Phoenix. Book seat. Meet in foyer		

Make great checklists and 'To do' lists

Why use checklists?

Checklists provide a simple but effective way of drawing together, and keeping track of, everything you need to do. Use checklists in your student planner to save time re-thinking the basics – such as your standard shopping list, things you take back and forth each term or tips from tutors you want to draw on for assignments. You can even use checklists to keep track daily of all your good intentions for establishing new habits and behaviours.

The more precise the actions, times and details on your list, the less you need to remember – less 'mental clutter'. The more your brain feels you are in charge of completing a task, the less it gives you a nagging sense of things yet to do, and the happier you feel.

Diary 'To do' lists

★ Write a fresh list of things to do on a piece of paper or sticky note.

★ Divide the list into 'Today' and 'Soon' (so you are aware of what you need to do longer term).

★ Write items under headings so that they are easy to see: 'Study', 'Home', 'Other' (or whatever headings suit you).

★ Be as precise as possible about what exactly you are going to do.

★ Star or highlight the essential items.

★ Attach or paperclip the list to the page opposite the current page of the diary.

★ Cross out all completed items so that you are clear what is left to do.

Map out the time for 'To do' lists

★ Organise your list into a sensible running order: Which are most important? Which are best clustered together?

★ Jot down the maximum time to spend on each item or cluster of items.

★ Jot into your planner the start and end times for the most important items on the list.

★ Take note of things that take longer than planned. Take account of this in future planning.

'Next step'

For larger items on the 'To do' list, jot down what you will do next. This will help you to:

★ get started on doing it

★ reduce distracting thoughts about unfinished tasks.

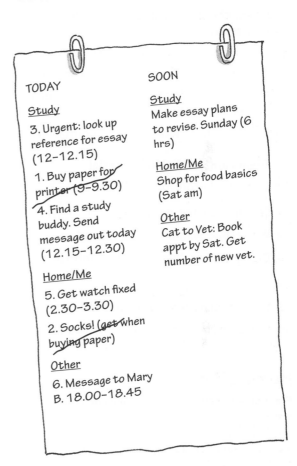

TODAY

Study
3. Urgent: look up reference for essay (12–12.15)
1. Buy paper for printer (9–9.30)
4. Find a study buddy. Send message out today (12.15–12.30)

Home/Me
5. Get watch fixed (2.30–3.30)
2. Socks! (get when buying paper)

Other
6. Message to Mary
B. 18.00–18.45

SOON

Study
Make essay plans to revise. Sunday (6 hrs)

Home/Me
Shop for food basics (Sat am)

Other
Cat to Vet: Book appt by Sat. Get number of new vet.

Making new lists

At a certain point, you are likely to have a list with many items crossed off, and others still remaining to do. Once your list starts to feel old, cluttered or confusing, start a new one, transferring over any unfinished items.

Note whether there are items that you put off continually. Decide whether you really are going to get round to them. If so, put a precise time into your diary and stick to it, so you can clear it off your list.

Plan backwards from deadlines

Aspect	How long will it take?	When will I do it?	How long it took
1 Clarifying and planning the task			
★ Early brainstorming, reflection and discussion			
★ Making an initial outline plan and schedule			
2 Researching (collecting and recording information)			
★ Working out which research methods to use			
★ Working out what information/data I need			
★ Assembling information (to read, gather data, experiment, etc.)			
★ Digesting and reflecting on the information collected			
3 Organising and linking material			
★ Grouping and organising information			
★ Selecting what to include			
4 Reflecting, evaluating and critiquing			
★ Digesting and reflecting on the information			
★ Thinking through what I will say			
5 Writing an outline and first draft			
★ Grouping and organising information			
★ Get some ideas written down			
6 Writing draft versions			
★ Thinking about and improving each draft			
★ Writing each draft			
★ Likely number of drafts	____ *expected*		____ *actual*
7 Completing the task / final checks			
★ Writing up the references			
★ Checking for sense, accuracy and completeness			
★ Proof-reading the final draft			
★ Final deadline for submission			
Use this information in planning your next assignment. Write the time for each stage into your planner.			

Use study blocks and breaks effectively

Select ✓ those techniques that you think would be most effective for you to use.

☐ Choose the right time

Some people study best at night when all is quiet; others think more clearly first thing in the morning; others study 9–5, following a working day.

★ Choose the time when you are most alert mentally and best able to remain focused.

★ Avoid times when you may be interrupted.

★ Match the study task to the time available.

☐ Use workable blocks of time

Some students study best for bursts of 30 minutes, separated by 5-minute breaks. Others find it hard to settle after breaks and work better in longer study sessions. Organise blocks of study time that:

★ help you stay focused and interested

★ enable you to do a significant piece of work

★ avoid time-wasting.

☐ Mix it up

If you get bored with routine, then divide your time into blocks of different lengths, allocating these to activities that either lend themselves well to shorter bursts or need sustained application.

★ Follow longer blocks of study with short ones.

★ Build-in breaks of different lengths too, so that your use of time feels less regimented.

★ Move frequently between tasks such as reading, noting, writing, thinking, calculations and so on, to keep your mind alert.

★ Intersperse online study with other activities.

☐ Plan efficient breaks in study

Longer breaks are important for rest and for enabling the brain to absorb information. Too many breaks can disrupt concentration, making it harder to refocus on the material. Taking no breaks at all suits some people, but tends to lead to tiredness, boredom or taking ill-advised short-cuts.

☐ Build in some longer breaks

Time these so that you can:

★ clear your head and keep your thinking fresh

★ rest your eyes and check your position if you have been on-screen for some time

★ check that you are spending time as planned.

☐ Take micro-breaks

★ Take micro-breaks of 2–10 minutes.

★ Whatever the length of the break, give yourself a set time by which you must return to study.

★ Move right away from your books or screen – get a change of scene to let your mind refresh.

★ Get a drink or snack if needed. Move about (good for your health!); stretch your limbs and unwind.

Reflection

What breaks and blocks make your study more effective?

1 At what times of day (or night) are you at your best for different kinds of study activity?

2 What kinds of study block suit you best?

3 Do these vary depending on the study task?

4 Is your study more effective with frequent breaks? Or does that disrupt your concentration?

5 How long does it take you to settle down to study when you take a 3-minute break? A 20-minute break? A break of an hour or more?

6 How could you plan out a session of independent study time to best maintain your concentration and interest whilst using all the time effectively?

Apply varied time management techniques

☐ Work to your rhythm

Take note of how you respond to different kinds of study task. For example, if you are slow to warm up to study, schedule short activities such as brainstorming ideas early in the day. You may find you are increasingly engrossed by study as the day progresses and can settle down to complex reading or to writing tasks once you have 'warmed up' with shorter or simpler tasks. Look for ways of scheduling activities to suit your study rhythms.

☐ Get focused first

Take a few quiet moments to focus the mind before starting a new task. Let your mind clear of distractions and direct your full attention to the task before you (see Cottrell, 2018).

☐ Set early deadlines

Set yourself deadlines for completing assignments earlier than the official submission time. Leave time to fine-tune your work and manage unforeseen events.

☐ Keep track of time

★ Jot down as a list your start times for each new activity.

★ Put this where you can see it easily, such as on a sticky note on your diary or computer.

★ Check it frequently as you study. Adapt your times sensibly if you start to fall behind.

☐ Use a timer

★ Use a timer on your phone or use an alarm clock. Set it to go off a few minutes before the time you wish to start on your next activity so you can finish up the task you are on.

★ When the timer sounds, finish your current activity promptly so you don't fall behind on the next.

★ It may take some experimentation to work out realistic amounts of time to set for each type of activity.

Stop the Tweets! Time for Keats!

☐ Use support networks

If you have demanding commitments outside of study, it helps to build the kind of support networks that fit your life style. For example, if you volunteer or work part-time, there may be ways of sharing shifts with others so that there is cover available when you need to be in class. If you have children, you may be able to organise childcare with other students who are parents.

☐ Organisation = time-saving

Good organisation helps time management.

★ **Manage your files**, so that you don't keep more material than you need.

★ **Organise space**, including your online space, so that you can find everything quickly.

★ **Name it and label it**, so you can find things easily (page 106).

★ **Plan your day** so that you can use pockets of time well.

> See also: *50 Ways to Manage Time Effectively.* Stella Cottrell, 2019.

Apply time management techniques: online study

☐ Beware the addiction ...

Surfing, browsing and communicating online make study more interesting but can be more addictive and time-consuming than we realise. Listen to those who say they never see you! Be rigorous in monitoring how long you spend in online activities.

Time online

Just 5 minutes looking at this website ...
+ 2 minutes on this one ...
+ 1 minute just quickly doing ...
+ 3 minutes for a quick catch-up with ...
+ 2 minutes looking for ...
+ 2 minutes ...
+ more time ...
Total time online today = 23 hrs

☐ Monitor time used for online study

You are likely to engage in online activities to support your study, such as:

★ browsing for material for an assignment

★ watching online videos

★ watching or listening to recorded lectures

★ sending messages to students on matters related to your study.

As these activities are study-related, it is easy to persuade yourself that it is all beneficial for your study, even if you spend more time on them than is helpful. You might then have too little time for other important aspects of your study, such as reading, analysing material or proof-reading assignments.

★ Check out exactly how much time you spend on each type of online study activity.

★ Consider whether that time allocation is working well for your study.

★ If not, decide on the times you want to spend on those activities – and stick to these.

☐ Monitor online distractions

When timing your online activities, be scrupulous in timing how much time you spend on things that distract you from your main study plan.

1 Include distractions that take 'just a minute'.
2 Note how much time it takes you to settle down to study after each break or distraction.
3 Note whether the occasional minutes are really just that or whether they add up to significant distractions.
4 Add up the total study time lost to these distractions over an hour, day, week and year.
5 Consider whether that is how you still want to spend your time online.
6 There are apps you can use to monitor time use and block access to online distractions.

See the companion site for details.

Time online spent in study

2 hours for study ...
minus 2 minutes logging on
minus 10 minutes trying to find where I put the file
minus 3 minutes answering a message from Sam
minus 2 minutes on a quick email
minus 10 minutes ordering a book
minus 5 minutes online shopping ...
minus ...
Total time spent studying: 17 minutes

☐ Plan-in response times

If you will need to await responses from others, including tutors or people you are asking to take part in projects, work on the assumption that they may take 24 hours or even several days to get back to you. It isn't realistic to expect everyone to get back to you immediately.

Ten time-saving strategies

1 Save time when making notes

★ Don't obsess about notes looking tidy, as long as they are legible and useful.

★ Avoid writing notes in full sentences – use headings and keywords (Chapter 10).

2 Save time copying between files

★ Use Dropbox, Google Docs, or similar software to access the same documents from any computer or device that you use, rather than copying across from one to the other.

★ If you use a tablet, email documents to yourself in Word format so that you can save them into Dropbox.

3 Make the most of spare moments

Make a list of tasks that you could complete in spare moments such as when queuing, or that you can combine with other activities that require little mental input. Ideal study tasks include listening to podcasts of lectures or revision points, memorising flash cards, or reading short sections from books.

4 Save time looking for notes

★ When making notes, write each major point under a different heading. Use a large bold font for headers so you can find points quickly when browsing your notes for specific items.

★ Name and date your notes clearly.

★ Maintain an updated contents guide to folders of notes, so you know exactly where to search in them for what you need.

★ Keep detailed records of source materials and page numbers in your notes, so you can find them again easily if needed to check details.

5 Save time reading

★ Use 'smart reading' strategies (see **Am I a smart reader?** on pages 215–17).

★ Read only what is relevant to this essay or assignment. If something looks interesting for the future but is not relevant, make a note of it rather than becoming distracted by it now.

6 Save time in writing references

For every book, article, etc. that you read, keep a full record of the details required for your references (pages 249–51). Do this electronically for ease in pasting into your assignment or use electronic referencing tools. For online articles, check whether they provide a ready-to-use citation. If so, download that and adapt it to suit the course style (page 251).

7 Use word limits to focus your energies

Usually, you won't need to read and note as much for a 1000-word essay as for a 2000-word one. Map out how much to read, note and write to match the word limit (pages 322–3).

8 Save time thinking

★ Carry a small note-book to capture ideas as they occur: don't waste time trying to recapture them.

★ Use 'brainstorming' and pattern notes to generate ideas quickly (pages 275 and 228).

9 Save time organising information

★ Use a folder or a resource such as *The Macmillan Student Planner* (Cottrell, 2019b and updated annually) to draw together your study-related information in one place (page 405).

★ Don't note down the same information twice. If two writers make the same point, note a reference to the second source in the margin where you first noted that point.

★ Use shading or highlighter pens to indicate information relevant to each section of your assignment.

★ Cut and paste together items shaded the same colour. Read these again once regrouped.

★ If you have the option, read your shaded notes on a page or in a window alongside the one in which you are writing your assignment.

10 Avoid duplicating effort

Find a study partner to bounce ideas, exchange study strategies and share permitted study tasks.

Manage procrastination and distraction

Effective study depends on having your state of mind, space, time and materials organised in the ways that best suit your learning.

Creating a state of mind for study

Many students find it difficult to get into the right mood for study. They put it off to another day. Everyone has their own particular distractions: endless cups of coffee, texting and tweeting, phone calls, TV, browsing online, housework, anything rather than settling down to study.

Give yourself study triggers

Many people need a 'trigger' to start a study session. One student clears his desk each time he finishes studying: his study trigger is a clear, inviting surface. Another has a 'ritual' of logging on, getting a glass of water and then opening her books at the appropriate pages so she is ready to begin. One makes a coffee while standing in the kitchen, brainstorming ideas onto paper; he feels he has already started to study before he sits down. Some spend a few minutes in 'Mindfulness of Breathing' exercises to focus the mind for study.

Reflection

Study triggers

What actions or thoughts can trigger you into 'study mode'? If you don't know, experiment until you find triggers that work for you.

Create the right environment

Make a conscious note of the kind of environment that suits you best for different study tasks. Do you need quiet, music, background noise? Is study better at home or in a library? Alone or with friends? In clear space or chaos? What else do you need?

Reflection

Study environment

What kind of study environment works best for you?

Does this change for different aspects of study?

Use your distractions to help you study

Study on the move

If your distractions involve movement (such as sport, shopping or housework), spend ten minutes first browsing a chapter or going over notes. Then give in to your distraction if you still want to – but go over what you have just read as you do it. If you are an active person, combine sport or movement with study tasks such as thinking through how you will approach an assignment, or rehearsing material covered in class to see how much you remember. Some people learn better 'on the move'.

'Stealth study'

If you find it off-putting to be 'obliged' to study, begin by allowing yourself a limited time to study initially – maybe just 5–10 minutes. Ease yourself gradually into increasingly longer spells.

Alternatively, after ten minutes, move away from your study, changing activity, but doing something that enables you to continue thinking about what you have just studied. Set yourself questions to answer if that helps you to remain focused. For example, consider whether you agree with what you have just read, or decide how you would use it in under 30 words in an assignment. Jot down any ideas or phrasing that occurs to you.

If you feel compelled to sit down to check a point or write something up, then do so. You may find you become engaged in your study at that point.

Use distractions as resources

If you tend to phone or text friends as a distraction, ask them to help you focus on your work. Tell them to ask you about the assignment or use them as a sounding board, but be considerate – your friends will probably be delighted to hear from you, but may also be trying to concentrate on their own study. Set time limits for calls.

Connect to your motivation

See pages 113–20.

Getting down to study

Settling down to study is a common difficulty for students, even those who enjoy study once they get going. If this is true of you, it might be because you have not established the right conditions for you for that aspect of study. Check your own effectiveness for diverse tasks to see what you do best, and most easily, early in the day, in the afternoon or at night. Identify your best time and place for diverse tasks, such as when to redraft a piece of writing, read difficult texts, or calculate numbers.

Why can't I get going?

When you are struggling to get down to study, it is worth checking your responses to the questions opposite.

Organise your time, space and mind for study

Reflection

Getting down to study

For each of the five areas opposite, write at least one suggestion of a change you could make now to improve your studying.

---

1   Am I doing this for myself?
- [ ] Am I clear of the purpose of this?
- [ ] Could I make this more interesting?
- [ ] Could I make this more enjoyable?

2   Are my expectations realistic?
- [ ] Am I taking it one step at a time?
- [ ] Do I need to set smaller milestones?
- [ ] Do I need a better reward system?
- [ ] Am I taking the right kinds of breaks?
- [ ] Have I worked too long without rest/sleep?
- [ ] Have I had enough to eat and drink?
- [ ] Have I set myself the right level of challenge?

3   Am I set up effectively for the task?
- [ ] Am I in the right place to do this?
- [ ] Am I likely to be uninterrupted?
- [ ] Do I have a good surface to write on?
- [ ] Do I feel comfortable?
- [ ] Do I have good light and ventilation?
- [ ] Do I have the right equipment/materials?

4   Am I working at the right time?
- [ ] Do I work productively at this time of day?
- [ ] Is this the best time for this activity?
- [ ] Am I completing tasks in order of priority?

5   What are my excuses for procrastinating?

What kinds of excuses do I use for putting off getting started ('First, I just need to …')?

1 _____

2 _____

3 _____

I will manage these excuses by:

Identifying and managing distractions

Time-eating 'danger zones' online

As time spent online often creates the greatest challenges to students' time management, it can help to identify your personal 'danger zones'. These are the websites and e-resources that take up a disproportionate amount of your time. They could be useful sites that you over-use, that distract you too easily from your main purpose or serve too easily as launch pads to other sites.

★ Note which sites, apps and tools you use most.

★ Decide how much time you really want to spend on these.

★ Decide how you will build a reasonable use of your favourite sites or resources into your day.

★ Consider how you will keep yourself to that amount: how will you monitor how long you are using each? How will you motivate yourself to close the site or app?

My 'danger zone' websites and tools

The main websites and resources that take up too much of my time or distract me from study are:

1

2

3

4

5

6

7

8

I'll manage my time using these by:

My 'danger' apps

The apps that take up a disproportionate amount of my time or distract me from study are:

1

2

3

4

5

I'll manage my time using these by:

Other distractions

You may find that you are also easily distracted by friends, family, personal interests, games, day dreaming, or a host of other things.

Other key personal distractions

The other main distractions that prevent me from settling down to study or draw me away from study once started are:

1

2

3

4

5

I'll manage these distractions by:

Staying on task

Once you get started on a task, the next time management challenge is staying with it. This is sometimes referred to as 'stick-with-it-ness'.

Start off well

It can help to stick with a task if you feel you have made a good start. To achieve this, set yourself a timed challenge to complete in the first 10–15 minutes of each period of independent study.

Reflection

The first 10–15 minutes

★ How effectively do you use the first 10–15 minutes of study?

★ What kinds of challenges could you set for yourself to use those initial few minutes in effective and motivating ways?

Remaining focused

Some reasons that students give for not staying on task are listed below. Which, if any, apply to you?

- ☐ not having a clear purpose
- ☐ continuing with the same activity for too long
- ☐ getting bored
- ☐ finding the material too difficult
- ☐ not seeing the relevance
- ☐ getting tired
- ☐ getting distracted

Strategies for remaining focused

1 Take a few moments to focus the mind if you start to drift off task. Doing this before you start helps maintain concentration for longer (page 142).

2 Clarify your purpose: what do you want to achieve today, this session, or in the next hour?

3 Block your time: break longer sessions into blocks of different lengths (page 141).

4 Set yourself specific challenges for each block – with just enough time to complete them, so you know there isn't time to waste.

5 Set a schedule of tasks for the time allocated. Alternate tasks of reading, noting, writing, listening to podcasts, thinking, searching, etc. to maintain your interest through variety.

6 Set short questions relevant to your assignment to focus your attention for that study session.

7 Look for the debates and controversy in the topic: these add interest. Consider how these will impact on your own perspectives on the issues, and on your assignment and revision.

8 Consider spending some time working with others – agree a time schedule together for staying on task.

Reflection

Remaining focused

What could you change about the way you study to help you to remain focused on the task?

Life–study balance

It can be hard to stay on task if your life and study are not in balance; other needs intrude to distract you or to make it harder to concentrate. Organise your time so that you take care of yourself generally and can replenish your energies. It is better to plan these into your week along with time to deal with unforeseen circumstances. See Chapter 7.

Reflection

Life–study balance

★ To which aspects of life, work and study do you pay most attention?

★ How effective are you at replenishing your energies? What could you plan differently to help you concentrate better and stay on task?

Activate your time management strategies

Reflection

Which strategies?

Which of the strategies from pages 127–48 could you adopt or adapt to manage your time?

1

2

3

4

5

6

7

What other strategies, if any, could you devise for yourself to improve your time management?

1

2

3

4

5

6

7

Activity

Next steps for putting time management strategies into action

For the strategies that you identified as right for you, decide how you will plan these into your daily routine. Start the ball rolling by identifying the next set of steps you need to take in order to effect a change in your time management.

For example, if you need to use a planner, your first step might be to find a website or shop to purchase one. If you need to manage your online time better, then identifying your personal online 'danger zones' (see page 147) may be your next step. Jot down your 'next steps' as a 'To do' list.

To do: (what and when)

1

2

3

4

5

6

7

Review

1 **Take charge!**
Increase your control over where your time goes and how well you use it. Make it work for what you want to achieve.

2 **Be more time-aware**
Be active in considering your use of time, and what you could do in order to make best use of this to serve your study, career aims and well-being.

3 **Apply the 10 steps**
Don't just hope that time issues will sort themselves out. Consider the 10 steps. Decide which ones would make a difference to your study, life, happiness and stress levels. Follow through on what you decide.

4 **Be aware of course expectations about time**
Check whether you meet these. If not, decide whether this makes a significant difference to your study (for better or worse?).

5 **Schedule and plan**
Be clear how you will spend your time and for what purpose. Know when important dates and deadlines lie. Plan systematically towards these.

6 **Be systematic in using a diary/planner**
Keep your life organised. Be clear about what you are doing and when. Take the effort out of having to remember.

7 **Monitor your time use**
Don't assume you know where your time goes – check this out. Be aware of what distracts you and leads to time-wasting. Use your insights to change your 'time habits'.

8 **Prioritise**
You can't do everything so make decisions about what is essential and what fits best alongside other tasks.

9 **Focus on the task**
Find ways of maintaining attention on whatever you are doing. Tune in to the task calmly. Set triggers. Organise your time and space so you can maintain concentration.

10 **Use time-saving strategies**
Use small pockets of spare time for reviewing work or short study tasks. It can add up to many hours freed for other things – and make a great difference to your success.

11 **Enjoy your time**
Time is a precious resource but it is easy to forget this when it feels pressurised. Take time to pause, reflect, breathe. Consider where the enjoyment lies.

12 **Maintain perspective**
Balance study with other life essentials, including friendships, preparing ahead for life after study, and staying fit, healthy and happy.

Chapter 7

Managing stress and well-being

Learning outcomes

This chapter offers you opportunities to:

- ✓ acknowledge and manage your anxieties as a student
- ✓ build your resilience in coping with the challenges of Higher Education
- ✓ take on key milestones for completing a course successfully – in manageable steps
- ✓ take action to enhance well-being, for benefits to study and more generally
- ✓ harness positive aspects of stress and prevent or reduce excess stress.

Studying in higher education is meant to be challenging. Whilst that is great for stretching and developing you, it can also be daunting. At times, the pressure can feel too much.

When you first start at university or college, it is natural to feel some anxieties about what you might be taking on and how you will cope. Similar feelings can arise at the start of a new year or level of study, when joining new groups, or doing study tasks for the first time.

It is important to keep thoughts about stress in perspective. Stress isn't all bad. It is a natural part of life, essential to our survival. Those survival mechanisms help us to stay alert and focused when dealing with challenges such as exams, speeches, presentations and performances, as well as external dangers. Harnessing the energy that comes from stress can be helpful to your studies.

On the other hand, too much stress, or poor stress management, can affect your learning, health and well-being. It can be tough to acknowledge that you are feeling anxious, nervous or stressed, but it

is wise to do so. Whilst it isn't good to dwell on anxieties, it isn't useful to pretend that they aren't there either. Denial is likely to result in anxiety finding unhelpful ways of expressing itself. Once you acknowledge what you are feeling, thinking and doing when over-stressed, then you can start to put your anxieties into perspective. That helps you to think more clearly about what to do. It is better to take action to manage stress early.

Taking care of your well-being makes a difference to how you cope with stressful situations when these arise. Factors that contribute to well-being also enhance brain function, concentration and your general ability to study effectively.

Acknowledging your anxieties

It is easier to avoid excess stress if you deal with anxieties and difficulties at an early stage. Ignoring them won't make them go away and makes them more complicated to resolve later.

It is easier to manage anxieties if you:

★ acknowledge what you are feeling

★ sort out in your own mind what is really worrying you the most

★ recognise that you are not alone in such feelings (and sharing them can help).

Identifying your anxieties

On the right are listed some anxieties which are typical of student life. Identify ✓ those that concern you the most. Add any others that affect you, using the spaces provided.

Beside each of the items you identify, write the number of the statement below that most closely corresponds with how you feel. Then read the comments on the next page.

1 I expect this to be a minor difficulty: I will get round it easily and in time.

2 I expect this to be potentially serious but manageable: I will work on a solution.

3 I expect this to be a major difficulty: I might need to ask for help.

4 I don't think I can cope with this without support: I will ask for this straight away.

5 I know I need help so I will ask for it.

Reflection

Managing anxieties

★ What initial ideas do you have about how you could manage some of these anxieties?

★ What strategies have you used in the past to deal with a new or difficult situation? Which of these strategies could be helpful now?

Study and learning

- ☐ Getting used to university life
- ☐ Believing in myself
- ☐ Avoiding failure
- ☐ Getting good grades
- ☐ Exams
- ☐ Finding the time to do everything
- ☐ Keeping up with other people
- ☐ Understanding academic language
- ☐ Having the confidence to speak
- ☐ Writing essays and assignments
- ☐ Submitting my work on time.

Personal, family and work commitments

- ☐ Homesickness
- ☐ Loneliness
- ☐ Making friends with other students
- ☐ Coping with travel
- ☐ People treating me differently/'fitting in'
- ☐ Coping with job requirements
- ☐ Family responsibilities
- ☐ Organising child care.

Others

- ☐ Money
- ☐ Safety and security
- ☐ Health
- ☐
- ☐

Manage anxiety

Study and learning anxieties

Give yourself time to settle in. Many institutions pace the first year to let you find your feet. See pages 155–7.

Believe you can. Expect it to be tough at times. It is meant to be. Use this *Handbook* to find strategies for getting through typical study challenges, such as speaking, essay writing, meeting deadlines, getting through exams and generally setting yourself up to succeed.

Find the enjoyment. It is harder to feel anxious when you are curious, fascinated, enjoying yourself and having fun. Focus on your motivation for study and be determined to enjoy it. Think of yourself as being on an adventure – not on trial.

Be your own person. Focus on what works for you and planning your own study rather than worrying about how well others are doing. Some people play psychological games, claiming that they do no work or can write essays overnight. Ignore them. Very few can really do this; it is not expected and it is not a sensible way to study.

Don't do it alone. Most students are anxious about some aspect of their study or life, or are lonely, homesick or feel left out. It helps to share concerns. Make time to talk to students outside of class. Once you form bonds with others, you will gain confidence and a sense of belonging.

Managing other anxieties

There is pressure on students to juggle careers, CVs, employability, jobs, family, social life and other commitments. This requires creative problem-solving and developing time management skills Chapters 3 to 6 can help with these.

Student support services usually offer guidance about money, jobs, stress, disability and help work out solutions to whatever arises. Advisers can help you more successfully if you approach them before problems turn into emergencies.

Plan a course of action

For the anxieties you identified on page 152, follow the steps below.

Identify priorities

★ What needs to be done immediately?

★ Which things can wait?

★ In which order do you need to deal with these anxieties? (See **Set your priorities** on page 136.)

Find support and identify resources

★ Find out about support services, groups and online guidance where you study.

★ Talk about it. Form a study, discussion or support group (page 183).

Identify your personal resources (such as friends, family, contacts). You might like to use *What are my personal resources* on the companion site at www.studyskillshandbook.co.uk.

Reflection
Thinking things through

It helps if you write down and explore your anxieties and options.

★ Jot down some thoughts about how you are feeling.

★ List your options and decide between them.

★ Record how you dealt with each problem so that you can evaluate your progress later.

Staying the course: commit to completing

Many students worry about whether they will get through their course and gain good grades. It is important to remember that millions graduate every year worldwide, most with good degrees. One of your key objectives is to ensure you are one of these success stories. A first priority is to ensure that, at the least, you complete and pass your course. A good starting place is to consider why some people complete and others don't.

Why don't all students complete?

Non-completion isn't usually about failing exams or lack of ability.

Typically, it is about such things as:

★ Mindset: Letting self-doubt creep in

★ Well-being: Ill-health or excess stress

★ Choices: Being on the wrong course

★ Pacing: Studying too much or too little over too short or long a time

★ Personal life: Unexpected life challenges that come as a shock

★ Strategy: Poor study habits and planning.

Usually, these can be managed successfully, with support and guidance if needed.

Difficult life circumstances don't have to be a barrier to success

Students who complete are not necessarily any cleverer, nor are their lives free of challenge. Almost all students struggle at some point, and those with extreme and multiple challenges find ways to complete their degrees. The details of how individuals do this vary widely, but the following are some common themes.

Ten characteristics of completers

1   **They commit to completing**. They are determined not to let anything prevent this. When they encounter challenges, they search out ways to deal with them. Once you decide to commit to your course, you don't need to worry about whether you should.

2   **They meet the 'golden rules'**. These take you a long way towards passing a course (page 30).

3   **They adopt a 'learning mindset'**. They take setbacks in their stride, using them to learn, rather than sinking into self-doubt or a sense of failure.

4   **They manage key milestones**. Once these are achieved, success is increasingly more likely. They get a boost from surviving the first year (page 155).

5   **They are realistic about what to expect**. See page 13.

6   **They ask for help in a timely way**. They recognise that it is fine to ask student services for support and do so early on so solutions can be found.

7   **They regard feedback as helpful**, rather than as criticism that knocks their confidence.

8   **They are well-organised**, planning time and study.

9   **They pace study well for their circumstances**. It can be useful to extend study, or to study part-time, rather than leave. On the other hand, the longer the time taken, the less likely you are to complete.

10 **They take reasonable care of general well-being**, such as health, sleep, food, stress, etc. (pages 165–7).

Reflection

Committing to complete

How far do these ten characteristics apply to you? Which do you need to work on further?

Have you made the mental commitment, yet, to complete your course? If so, how are you going to make this a reality? Page 113 may help.

Achieving key 'milestones'

Key milestones

Certain stages in the student journey are more challenging: more students leave at these points. These milestones are not things to be afraid of: there is no reason why you can't get through them and enjoy the process too. Being aware of them means you can be prepared for them and manage them better, mentally and emotionally.

Take it day by day

One more day ...

Survivors of severely challenging life circumstances, when asked how they survived, tend to say that, after the first shock, they settled into a routine of telling themselves each day that they can survive just one more day. Then one more.

It is natural for there to be days when being a student seems just too much. At such times, reduce your time horizon – just get through the day. Then do the same the next day.

Every milestone makes it easier

Each milestone you get past makes it more likely you will survive the next. If you get through the first day, week, six weeks, you are well on your way. Completing the first year tends to give a big boost to confidence and completion.

Reflection

Manage the milestones

★ Which of the milestones below are potential trigger points for you, and likely to affect your mood or commitment to the course?

★ What will you do to make sure that you are not thrown off track at these times?

★ Are there any other milestones that would have significance for you?

Milestone	Passed it! Yay! ☺
1 First day	
2 First week	
3 First 6 weeks	
4 First classes	
5 First assignment	
6 First exam	
7 First 'break'	
8 First vacation	
9 New tutor or group	
10 Schedule changes	
11 First year/ level	
12 New study levels	

Mark off above each milestone you complete. Each is a key stage – worth a celebration!

Surviving the first day and first week

First day

Enjoy it! Set out with the right attitude.

Attend welcome and induction events. As well as covering essential administration, they play an important psychological role in helping you to settle in and gain control over your study.

Put time into first day events. Don't rush off when essential tasks are complete. Walk around; have a coffee or a meal; visit the library, check resources and facilities. Go to student events. Try things out.

Use the queues. These are great opportunities to start a chat with other students and get to know a few faces. It makes the place feel more friendly.

Be friendly, smile, say hello. Even if others seem confident, they might feel disorientated and anxious. They could be hoping someone will speak to them. Even if they know other students from school or college, they probably want to meet new people, too.

Go with the flow. Don't get anxious if most of the information goes over your head or the day seems overwhelming! It will all become familiar soon.

Use your diary/planner. Carry it everywhere. Write everything down!

First week

Be present on campus, or log on if studying online, as much as you can. Build your familiarity with the course, its people, buildings, technologies, services and facilities. It will make a difference.

Ask questions. There will be lots to take in and much may not make immediate sense. It is OK to ask questions to check things out.

Daily sort, browse, store. You will receive a mountain of information. Put time aside each evening to browse through this. Sort out what you need and want and devise a system for labelling, storing and finding it when needed. You will forget you have much of it, otherwise. Throw away the rest.

Take stock. Put time in your diary to go through essential information at the weekend.

On the right course?

You are much more likely to complete if you are on the right course – and more likely to get stressed and/or leave early if the course is not what you expected. Usually, there are a few days when you can change course; after that, you might need to wait until next year, which could cost more. If the course really isn't for you – act quickly. Check the following.

> ### Quick checklist: Right course?
> 1 In principle, is it possible to change course? If so, how and by when?
> 2 Check the course is right for your career aims.
> 3 Check the course details. Be clear what it entails from start to finish.
> 4 Use the 'Find out ...' pages (32–3) to check your assumptions are correct (such as for attendance, exams, placements, etc.).
> 5 Attend all early sessions, so you get a feel for the course in time to change it if needed.
> 6 Check whether you can change route later in the course if you want. Are there conditions?
> 7 What are the consequences of changing course or leaving, such as costs and lost opportunities?
>
> Arrange to speak to your personal tutor or course tutor if you are unsure – don't just disappear!

Reflection

The first week

★ How do you feel about the experience so far?

★ Are you keeping information well organised?

★ Are you joining in?

What do you need to sort out now so that you avoid unnecessary stress and problems later?

Managing the first few weeks

Seven things to do in the first weeks

1 Investigate and check out everything.
2 Make the place your own.
3 Get to know as many people as you can.
4 Plan your time in fine detail (Chapter 6).
5 Keep organising your material.
6 Build your relationship with your personal tutor (page 31).
7 Create a study space (pages 104 and 146).

Managing tough first reactions

Are you experiencing any of the following ✓?

☐ **The shock of the new?** Struggling to settle into new unfamiliar routines, culture, locations, travel, schedules, ways of talking and thinking?

☐ **Homesick? Lonely?** Home, family and former friends seem more attractive? It seems hard to make new friends?

☐ **Don't feel like you belong?** Everybody else seems to know each other, or to have things in common or to be better at coping? They seem to have more fun, more to say, more confidence with each other? You feel left out and isolated?

☐ **Unexpected demands on time?** The total amount of time needed for travel, study, co-curricular activity is greater than anticipated?

☐ **The academic challenges seem too great?** Study demands are more than you expected?

☐ **Self doubt?** You wonder if you are up to this and whether to escape before you set yourself up to fail?

These are typical responses at the start of a new course. If you experience these, don't assume that it means you can't fit in, make friends and feel at home. Most students come to work them out. The probability is that you will too!

Start problem-solving!

Anticipate the kinds of difficulties and problems that could emerge.

Don't wait for them to happen: think through how you would address them if they occurred. Gain the confidence of being mentally prepared for most eventualities.

Get a head start on assignments

Get a sense of what you will need to do across the year. Look for potential clashes with holidays or for dates when several assignments have to be submitted at once. Schedule tasks early to reduce the chance of crises later on.

Start work on the first assignment straight away. Don't wait until the last minute nor for everything to be covered in class. Think how you will approach it. Start reading and making your own notes (pages 213–33).

Deal with unexpected life issues

Many early-leavers do so for 'personal reasons' such as family demands, changes at work, moving home, illness, bereavement, financial issues, pregnancy, losing confidence and so on. If your circumstances change, or start to feel unmanageable, here are some important steps to take.

Don't panic – Almost every student is affected by personal issues at some point and does get through. That is likely to be true for you, too. If not, there may still be ways of reducing the study load or withdrawing temporarily to keep your future options open.

Keep key people informed, such as the course leader, your personal tutor/adviser, and work-placement supervisor if relevant. They will be more sympathetic if you keep them in the picture.

Talk it through. Even if your circumstances seem impossible, student services may be able to suggest options you hadn't thought of, either for staying on course, or leaving the door open to return later.

Nurture your well-being

Getting to know people

Student life provides great opportunities for meeting new people, but can also be lonely or isolating. To get through such times:

★ Get to know people one by one rather than only through large groups.

★ Study on campus when you can.

★ Get out of your room: use the Student Union and campus facilities.

★ Join in: use clubs, societies, sports. Start your own!

★ Ask people to go for a coffee, a walk, a meal or to see a film, etc.

★ Remember that people who end up as your closest friends might not be those you meet in your first few months.

Using the experience

★ Get to know the campus, online resources, library, and facilities. Tour these, use them and make them feel like your own.

★ Make time to take part in academic and social activities, especially if you study part-time, by distance learning, or live away from campus.

Reflection

Taking care of yourself

★ Which, if any, of the issues identified in the box opposite are ones that you tend to neglect?

★ Make a 'to do' list of things that you could do differently in order to take better care of yourself.

★ Which of the items on your list are priorities – to do now?

Take good care of yourself

Don't assume that your well-being will take care of itself. With all the things there are to do as a student, this is often put on hold, with unwanted consequences at just the wrong time. Take sensible steps to look after yourself. Give thought to the following.

Safety   Consider this from many perspectives: accommodation, travel, activities, privacy settings online, who you spend time with.

Sleep   You might find that your sleep patterns change whilst you are a student. Getting sufficient sleep is important to keeping healthy and maintaining your immune system so you don't catch infections. It affects your ability to take in information when studying, to recall what you learn, and for being alert generally. Stress and lack of sleep are also strongly associated.

Health   Register with a doctor or health centre once you arrive at university. Take note of any health warnings and immunisation programmes that are advised. Take symptoms of ill health or mental ill health seriously and, at the very least, have a check up if you have concerns. Get an annual eye-test. Visit the dentist!

Food   Eat proper food. Use the college refectory or canteen. Find out where you can get different kinds of meal for the lowest prices or learn to cook if you don't already. Get a good cookbook – there are lots designed especially for students (such as *Student Brain Food* by Lauren Lucien).

Money   Keep track of your spending from Day One. Use financial planning. Make sure you are aware of all the sources of support available to you: speak to a financial adviser at the university or college if you are unsure.

See the companion site at www.studyskillshandbook.co.uk for information about useful sources of support for student well-being.

Digital you: safety, security and well-being

A high proportion of stress-related student enquiries relate to digital issues, from cyber-bullying to social anxiety, compulsive use of media, stolen items, lost data, copying, and other poor use of technologies. Learn to use and apply your technologies wisely, to avoid unnecessary problems and stress.

Your online presence

Whatever you or others write or post online may be there forever. Consider carefully the trail you leave. Ask your friends to do the same.

Consider your career. Bear in mind that potential employers are likely to look you up online. Don't let comments or photos you post come back to haunt you at job interviews.

Build a positive online identity. Post items that showcase your work, responsibilities and achievements well. These also will be seen by future employers.

Use different online identities for personal life, student life and work. Consider different identities for all your accounts, whether Twitter, LinkedIn, Instagram, Snapchat, Whatsapp, etc.

Security: Take care not to put yourself, other people or your files at risk in any way. Take care of your identity and data and use software to protect against viruses. Your university can offer guidance.

Respect for others: Consider whether any of your posts could cause distress to others. Avoid any that might be considered offensive, insensitive or bullying.

For collaborative learning

Many courses encourage social and group learning as a means of developing teamwork, communication skills and intercultural awareness, to enhance future employability.

Avoid allegations of cheating: Do not share your written work electronically before it is marked as, if other students make use of your academic work in their own assignments, you could be held jointly responsible. Do not cut and paste from electronic material – this too can be detected electronically when you submit work.

Maintain control of your information: Be careful to whom you give access to your details through social media, blogs, etc.

Tools and apps

There is a growing range of tools and apps that help save time when studying or support well-being. You can use these to research topics, for citations and references, and for collaborative study. Details of these are provided in the relevant chapters below.

Annual updates on useful apps and websites can be found in *The Macmillan Student Planner* (Cottrell, 2019b and updated annually; see page 413).

How do other students manage?

Consider these students' experiences of their first months of study. You might notice that their time seemed very pressurised: being organised is a recurring theme. However, they made time to relax, meet others, use the opportunities for sports, drama and social life which are also important to the overall student experience.

The first few weeks

I thought I had a pretty good idea of what to expect as I had family at Uni and I had been on a university summer school. These did help but it was very different once I got here … more people, more reading, more things to do, and everything seemed to sort of 'swim around' – there was so much information and so much to think about. I have become very good at writing lists!

Meenaxi

A typical day

On Tuesdays I have a lecture from 10 a.m. to 12 noon. This lecturer does not just talk at us: she breaks the time up into short tasks, discussions, videos, etc. When all 90 of us are discussing something in groups, it can be noisy, but you get used to it. The rest of the day is 'free' but as I am already on the site, I go to the library and prepare for the next day's lectures, or do some reading for seminars I have every second Wednesday. Some Tuesday afternoons, I go to the gym, and study in the evening instead.

Krishna

'The mystery of time ...'

Time moves in weird ways – you seem to have loads of time on your hands – empty timetables compared to school, and all those empty evenings in the diary. And then not enough time to fit everything in. It took me a while to realise that I need to be the one who organises things, to see I get everything done if several assignments have to be handed in at around the same time, and just getting out there and mixing so I have a social life.

Olivia

Making it as a student

I nearly left after the first few weeks. I had already left one uni and I was about to give up on this one as well. I had been studying really hard, so I felt I deserved high marks but that wasn't happening. I was very angry. I felt the tutors didn't like me and were being unfair. At the same time, I realised that I couldn't do more work and I thought I just wasn't up to university.

I told my tutor I was leaving and I am so glad that I did. That was the beginning of really getting to grips with where I had been going wrong. It wasn't that I couldn't do the work, which is what I had thought. I was spending my time doing the wrong things. I wasted a lot of time online and taking copious notes about everything. I didn't have a systematic approach to doing the essays and I didn't believe in my own ideas so these didn't come across in my work. Mainly, I wasn't thinking enough, neither about what I was studying nor about how to go about studying.

I am still building my skills in reading and writing – these underlie everything, really, but my marks are now good and getting better. The main thing is that I can see how having a strategy can make a difference to your study. There is always a way to get things done. Knowing this keeps me looking for ways of doing things, rather than giving up. If I can succeed this far, anybody can.

David

My first term

After the terrible time I had in school, I was very worried about what I might be putting myself through coming back to study as an adult. I was sure I wouldn't be able to keep up. When I got my first few pieces of work back, the marks were not very good, and I felt I ought to leave.

Luckily, I was talked out of leaving. I made an effort to meet other mature students and found many had similar experiences to me. One of them encouraged me to ask my tutors for more detailed feedback on my work. I had not wanted to ask for any help in case the lecturers thought I was not good enough for the course. Bit by bit my marks started to get better, and some were very good. This boosted my confidence.

I had expected study to be difficult. What I had not expected was that other aspects of being a student could be just as hard. It took me ages to build up the confidence to eat in the canteen – it seemed so enormous and bustling. I used to rush away after lectures rather than talking to strangers. My train service is very erratic and I kept arriving late. My sister, who was going to look after my children, moved house. Sorting out all these things has made me very skilled at problem-solving!

I have to say that there are many things I love about being a student. Now that I know other people here, I look forward to coming in to study. I feel like I am escaping into time which is just for me. I like having the library to work in – and not being disturbed while I just get on with it.

I would recommend to new students that they give themselves a chance to settle in, and not panic if anything seems to be going wrong. If they have children, I cannot over-emphasise how important it has been to me to have plans to cover every eventuality. I wish I had had reserve plans for child care right from the beginning because that, more than anything else, had an effect on my studies. I also recommend that they find

other people with similar experiences to themselves – talking to each other you can come up with good ideas about how to tackle problems and boost each other's morale.

You are bound to find you think differently about many things by the time you finish your course. For me, discussing things with other people has become a very exciting activity.

Above all, I think students have to consider: 'I might never get this chance again – how am I going to get the most out of it?' There are many facilities and you can try out all sorts of new things. I would never have imagined I would take up karate, go on an expedition and help local children to read. It is a wonderful opportunity, but you have to make it work for you.

Sasha

My Thursday as a student

Dash the kids to the nursery. Dash into the labs for 10. Suddenly time changes. I am caught up in what I am doing – the project I am working on with two other people. I can spend hours mixing and measuring, comparing my findings with others'. We talk a lot about what we are doing, and why, and make suggestions on why our results are different. I always ask my lecturers if I am unsure – some are very helpful, but some are not. In the afternoon, I have one lecture. Recently, I have arranged it so I can go to drama club on Thursday nights.

Charlie

Reflection

Learning from others

★ What lessons can you take away from the experiences of these students?

★ What advice would you give to students who are anxious or struggling? Do you follow that advice yourself?

Resilience as a student

What is resilience?

Resilience is the quality of being able to withstand times of difficulty or change in such ways that you can either cope reasonably at the time or bounce back afterwards. It isn't that you never feel stressed, disappointed or out of your depth: it is about developing sufficient inner resources to get through and to keep going. There will be times as a student when resilience will be of real benefit.

How resilience contributes to success

★ It helps you manage when things get tough.

★ It gives you the experience of recovering from setbacks and of coping.

★ It builds your confidence that you can cope, even if everything seems to be going wrong.

★ It gives you confidence to take risks, take part, and to take on new challenges.

Resilience helps you as a student when ...

★ you are experiencing a lot of change: new environments, people, expectations, ways of thinking

★ there are challenges and pressures: emotional, financial, academic

★ there are many demands to juggle at once: work, study, family, friends

★ things don't go as planned: grades lower than you expected; not getting a job you wanted; relationships ending

★ you feel down or want to give up on your studies.

Rate your resilience

Below is a list of behaviours associated with resilience. Consider your own resilience by rating yourself for each. Use a 5 point scale, where 5 is a high level of resilience.

Reflection

Resilience as a student

What kinds of situations or issues arise for you as a student where you feel it would help to develop greater resilience?

How resilient am I?

1   I can bounce back from knocks.

☹ 1 2 3 4 5 ☺

2   I look for solutions that help me to solve problems.

☹ 1 2 3 4 5 ☺

3   I can keep a sense of perspective or can bring things back into perspective.

☹ 1 2 3 4 5 ☺

4   I can manage stress and keep myself calm.

☹ 1 2 3 4 5 ☺

5 I use the support and guidance available.

☹ 1 2 3 4 5 ☺

6 I use my time effectively ... to help me stay on top of all I have to do.

☹ 1 2 3 4 5 ☺

7 I use a routine ... to keep myself on track even when I don't feel like it.

☹ 1 2 3 4 5 ☺

8 I keep myself motivated and am effective in encouraging myself to study.

☹ 1 2 3 4 5 ☺

9 I persevere, even when I don't feel like studying or staying on the course.

☹ 1 2 3 4 5 ☺

10 I build and maintain relationships with others, for mutual support and to enrich my life.

☹ 1 2 3 4 5 ☺

Reflection

Personal resilience

★ When am I at my most resilient in life?

★ What enables me to be resilient in those contexts?

★ How can I draw on those qualities and factors to help me as a student?

Other relevant sections of this book

★ *Creative problem solving*: Chapter 5.

★ *Staying motivated*: Chapter 5.

★ *Time management*: Chapter 6.

Dealing with stress

A moderate degree of stress can be helpful, bringing focus, stimulation and even excitement. Some people even search it out for the thrill.

However, excess stress can severely affect physical and emotional health, concentration and memory. Be aware of the signs of these. If several of those below are typical of you, especially when under pressure, take note of that. You can take steps to prevent and reduce excess stress.

Spot the signs

Do you ...

- ☐ sleep poorly /lie awake worrying?
- ☐ feel tired all the time
- ☐ get headaches or muscle aches?
- ☐ feel anxious when you aren't studying?
- ☐ get easily irritated or frustrated?
- ☐ get a dry mouth, rapid, heavy or irregular heart beat, dizziness, shaky legs, nausea, sweating or trembling when anxious?
- ☐ get 'upset stomachs' from worry?
- ☐ grind your teeth at night?
- ☐ flare up easily at other people?
- ☐ regularly eat in a hurry, or go on 'binges'?
- ☐ smoke or drink 'to unwind'?
- ☐ drop or break things frequently?
- ☐ have a general sense of panic, anxiety or of being overwhelmed?

See also www.nhs/uk/conditions.

Know your own triggers

When do you start to feel the pressure?

- ☐ When things don't go your way?
- ☐ When work mounts up?
- ☐ When trying to please others?
- ☐ When other people irritate you?
- ☐ When you set unrealistic goals?
- ☐ When working on assignments?
- ☐ When you miss meals?
- ☐ In traffic jams/on public transport?
- ☐ Other triggers?

Reflection

Stressful situations

In your journal, list the times when you get most stressed – or what makes you feel tense. Describe what happens. What do you do to handle the situation? What else *could* you do?

Reflection

Managing stress

Consider ways of managing stress on pages 165–7. Identify ✓ those you neglect and/or could help you prevent and reduce stress. Decide at least *one* to start now.

Strategies for managing stress and well-being

1 Get enough good sleep

- ☐ Aim to sleep for 7-8 hours each day. Much more or less than this can tire you
- ☐ Follow your own sleep clock
- ☐ Stick to the same hours for sleep
- ☐ Use the same routine before sleep
- ☐ Power down for an hour before bed, switching off back-lit devices.

2 Eat for health

Check what you are putting into your body.

- ☐ Could you fill it with less coffee, smoke, alcohol, unhelpful chemicals, fast food?
- ☐ Does it need larger helpings of substances that help it renew itself – fruit, vegetables, protein, cereals and grains?
- ☐ Do you need more water? De-hydration stresses the body and brain.

3 Create 'breathing spaces'

If every day is packed with activity and you are forever rushing, it can be hard to maintain a good sense of your well-being. Stress can start to mount without your having time to realise until you start to feel burnt out or overwhelmed.

Plan 'down-time' into your day

- ☐ Set aside times for rest, relaxing, fun, socialising, eating, quiet time. Give your body and mind time to refresh themselves. Return to tasks energised and ready to enjoy them.

Take breaks

- ☐ Give yourself regular breaks in whatever you are doing. Watch for signs of tiredness.

4 Treat yourself

- ☐ Take a relaxing bath. Don't rush it. Light a candle, or treat yourself to aromatherapy oils.
- ☐ Put some time aside every day for activities you enjoy or in time that is just for you.

5 Get enough exercise

- ☐ Build at least 20 minutes of exercise or strenuous activity into each day
- ☐ Do something energetic – walk, swim, run, play a game, clean the room, do some gardening. Get rid of pent-up energy and excess adrenalin (page 394).

6 Manage your mindset

Stress is affected by attitude towards challenge. What excites one person can panic another.

Check your 'inner chatter'

If you tend to think, 'I can't ...', 'Other people can ...' or 'I'm useless at ...', change the record!

Turn the message round: 'I can ...', 'I have already ...', 'I am able to ...', 'I am going to ...'

Use the STOP! Exercise

☐ If you notice that your mind is racing or keeps going over the same worries, let yourself stop everything for a moment and take stock.

★ Repeat 'Stop' to yourself until you actually register that you are going to stop the anxious train of thought.

★ Breathe slowly or count slowly to 100.

★ Let yourself smile – even if this is difficult. It encourages the brain to release 'happy chemicals'.

★ Spread out your hands and relax your fingers.

★ Hold your hands and feet still and relaxed.

Question your way of thinking

Ask yourself questions such as:

☐ Is there another way of thinking about this?

☐ Am I being a perfectionist?

☐ Am I expecting too much of myself (or others) in the current circumstances?

☐ Am I getting things out of proportion?

☐ What is the effect on me of having this attitude?

☐ Am I blaming myself for things that can't be helped?

☐ What can I do to improve matters?

7 Avert 'crises'

Be organised

☐ Being in control helps avoid stress. Make lists, timetables and action plans to avoid predictable crises and panics. Take charge of your time (Chapter 6).

Set priorities

☐ Work out your priorities – don't try to do more than is feasible for you (see page 136).

8 Notice your successes

It is easy to spend so much time racing on to the next thing, or worrying about things we haven't done, that we don't acknowledge what we have achieved. When we do notice that we complete a task, our minds reward us with 'happy chemicals' that give our mood a boost.

☐ Take stock of what you achieve each day.

☐ Take a moment to feel satisfaction when you complete a stage in a task.

☐ Reflect on your achievements over the week. Note them down.

☐ Give yourself credit for what you achieve.

Further resources

★ www.nhs.uk/conditions/stress-anxiety-depression/understanding-stress/

★ Cottrell, S. (2018). *Mindfulness for Students*.

★ Cottrell, S. (2019a). *50 Ways to Manage Stress*.

Enjoying some calm time

Experience quiet time

Spend at least 20 minutes on your own in quiet each day to refresh your mind, re-charge your batteries, and restore your sense of well-being.

★ Make a list of places where you can go to enjoy some quiet time.

★ Don't skip this time as unimportant.

★ Really take in the quietness and enjoy it.

Daydream to relax

★ Imagine your mattress is a cloud or a large ball of cotton wool. Sink into the softness.

★ Imagine being on a magic carpet, watching the view below. Where would you like to visit?

★ Imagine yourself on a mountaintop, enjoying the view.

Be fully in the moment

At different moments in the day, slow down for a few minutes and be fully present in that moment.

★ Take in your surroundings. Let yourself enjoy noticing the details.

★ Notice how are you feeling – your mood.

★ Whether you are eating, walking, taking a shower, washing the dishes – or studying, consider whether you are doing so in ways that allow you to focus on it fully, to enjoy it to the full.

Take up a meditative practice

Consider taking classes in a meditative practice such as yoga, mindfulness, or other meditations. These can be useful for sharpening the mind whilst calming your responses to stress.

Use a body scan relaxation

1 Lie on the floor or sit in a comfortable chair.
2 Close your eyes and breathe out slowly several times. Don't force the breathing.
3 Notice where your body feels tense. Then do each of the following several times.
4 Clench your toes tightly, count to three, then 'let go'. Repeat this several times.
5 Repeat this with all the muscles you can, working from your toes up to your neck.
6 Tuck your elbows in close to your body and draw your shoulders right up to your ears – then let them drop. Repeat several times.
7 Tense your facial muscles. Then relax them. Open your mouth into big slow yawns.
8 Imagine yourself in a peaceful, beautiful, safe place, real or imaginary. Listen for sounds; look at the colours there. Build the detail and your sense of the space. This can be a safe 'retreat' in the mind for you to go when stressed.

Breathe calmly

After relaxation, sit or lie comfortably. Close your eyes. Put on relaxing music if you wish. Imagine that you are breathing in calm and tranquillity with each in-breath, and letting go of stress with each out-breath.

Review

1 **Respect your feelings**
Acknowledge what you feel. Don't drive anxiety underground where it can kick back at your health, mood, relationships or sense of well-being.

2 **Address anxieties**
Don't let your worries fester away. Take action to prevent, reduce or manage stress. Look to resolve difficulties early – before they become more complicated to address.

3 **Commit to complete**
Don't waste time worrying about whether you *can* complete the course – decide you *will*. Then focus your energies on finding the strategies, help and resources that will make this happen.

4 **Take things in stages**
Identify the key milestones for your course and ambitions. Direct your attention towards achieving the next ones. Steps which seem daunting early on will feel less so later, when you have studied more at this level.

5 **First day, first weeks**
Don't judge your course, abilities or stress from the experience of the first few days. They are not typical. Give yourself time to adapt to change.

6 **Nurture well-being**
Don't underestimate the importance of basic human functions such as sleep, rest, relaxation, nutrition, hydration, social life and a sense of safety and security to your mood and stress level. Take good care of yourself in all aspects.

7 **Reduce digital stress**
Be aware of how your use of technologies and social media can contribute to stress. Take care of your online identity, security and digital life to avoid unnecessary problems for your course.

8 **Build resilience**
Use challenges to build (and recognise) your resilience. 'Sticking with it' and taking care of yourself will develop your coping strategies and confidence. Believe in yourself.

9 **Be kind to yourself**
Being considerate of your needs and feelings doesn't have to impede your ambitions – and can even give you the edge to succeed. Give yourself a break.

10 **Regulate stress**
Apply a range of relaxation techniques and stress-busting approaches to help avoid excess stress and to keep this at a manageable level. Use stress to address challenges.

11 **Find calm**
Appreciate the value of calm. Create a few oases of calm in your day. Learn techniques such as mindfulness meditation and breathing exercises to restore a sense of equilibrium when needed.

12 **Don't be a super-hero! (yet)**
You don't have to struggle on alone. Help and support will be available and is there for a reason. Don't be afraid to acknowledge that you need a helping hand sometimes.

PART B

Academic, People and Task Management Skills

Study Skills comprise many elements, as was outlined in Chapter 1. Those related to self-efficacy were considered in Part A. This part of *The Study Skills Handbook* looks at three other core, inter-related sets of abilities essential to study and student life.

Academic skills

Being a student in higher education is rather like being an apprentice academic or professor. You develop skills that enable you to conduct enquiry and build knowledge within the spirit and culture that characterises academic endeavour.

Academic skills encompass the kinds of thinking, behaviours and methods typical of academic work and of study in higher education. These can sharpen your thought processes in ways useful to most aspects of life – should you choose to apply them. They help you interpret the world and present your insights to others.

Just as, if you were learning a martial art, you would practise core moves, building in difficulty, so academic study requires you to build on skills that should be familiar to you: reading, writing, investigating, problem-solving, discussing. Increasingly, you become more expert at methods of researching a topic and expressing yourself so that you can convey advanced concepts with precision and accuracy. This can also increase your ability to discern when others are vague or evasive and whether you have sufficient information for arriving at wise decisions and useful solutions.

People Skills

Academic work takes place within a learning community, typically a diverse and international one. Good people skills and inter-cultural understanding enhance the experience for everyone, facilitating the interchange of ideas and mutual support. As a student, you benefit if you can collaborate with others, giving and receiving support and exchanging ideas whilst maintaining the academic integrity of your own work.

Task-management

Task-management is essential to academic success. You need to be able to complete increasingly complex tasks in a planned and organised way within a set time. It helps if you are clear about how to execute tasks from start to finish, independently and where appropriate, with others. Part B provides step-by-step guidance on managing tasks typical of higher level study, such as essays, reports, case studies, dissertations, group projects, presentations and exams.

Integrating your skills

Part B considers specific study skills separately, so that you can focus on each in detail. It looks at the routine skills you are likely to draw upon, such as reading and note-making for higher level study, working with others, developing your powers of recall and critical analysis, writing essays and other assignments, and tackling exams. In practice, you will benefit from drawing flexibly on skills from across all chapters, including those in Part A. In time, with practice, you will come to integrate such skills automatically and with ease.

Chapter 8

Working with others: Collaborative study

Academic study at university level generally focuses on the achievements of individuals. In part, this is to ensure that everyone is awarded a qualification on the strength of their own work.

Increasingly, courses also require collaborative working in groups or teams. Typically, this involves such activities as group work in class or between classes, contributing to group discussions, undertaking group projects, making presentations in seminars or group tutorials, providing constructive feedback to others, and peer support.

There are a number of reasons for encouraging students to undertake collaborative working.

★ *Learning community*: to enable students to learn from each other, sharing knowledge as active members of a learning community and for mutual support.

★ *Diverse viewpoints*: to promote an appreciation of what can be gained from drawing on multiple perspectives.

★ *Learning strengths*: to provide diverse ways to learn and excel, given that some students prefer social learning, group work and discussion.

★ *Cohort effect*: students in strongly bonded groups tend to do better, spurring each other on to complete the course and achieve well.

★ *Graduate skills*: to enhance skills important later in employment or in research teams. Good interpersonal skills are essential to many graduate jobs and prized by employers.

This chapter looks at skills and principles for working well with others, whether face to face or online. It considers behaviours that can help you with collaborative tasks, such as:

★ being open to what others have to offer

★ getting your own message across clearly

★ giving and receiving constructive criticism

★ giving and receiving peer support, whilst retaining your own academic integrity

★ playing a useful role as a group member, contributing to group effectiveness.

Studying collaboratively

Contexts

Find out which of the following contexts for collaborative study are likely to arise on your course.

- [ ] seminars
- [ ] chat rooms
- [ ] group projects
- [ ] class wiki
- [ ] lab groups
- [ ] discussion groups
- [ ] work placements
- [ ] support groups
- [ ] mentor schemes
- [ ] art 'crit' groups

Others:

Challenges

In collaborative study tasks, you gain a chance to hone skills and abilities valuable to work and life. These include such things as awareness and understanding of group dynamics, of how others think and feel, of what motivates others, and of how to deploy a team's skills and time to best effect. It means thinking about how you can help others to contribute well, whilst taking on board what others say about your own role.

Developing such attributes can be challenging as it requires greater self-awareness and owning new responsibilities, which can be uncomfortable at first. It can also mean putting group interests before your own.

Reflection

Skilful collaborative work

Identify one occasion when you were in a group that worked particularly well.

- ★ What made the group successful?
- ★ How did that group differ from others?
- ★ What skills and qualities do you think are important to effective collaborative working?

  Do you need to develop any of these further?

The value of collaborative working

Which of the following aspects of collaborative working do you value? Select ✓ all that apply.

- [ ] Enjoying a sense of group solidarity
- [ ] Sharing ideas and stimulating each other's thinking, so everyone gains more ideas
- [ ] Gaining new and diverse perspectives
- [ ] Tapping into a wider pool of experience, background knowledge and styles of working
- [ ] Developing skills relevant to employment
- [ ] Learning to stay focused on tasks even when enjoying the company of others
- [ ] Achieving greater outcomes than I could alone
- [ ] Having a chance to take on responsibility
- [ ] Opportunities to try out varied team roles
- [ ] Learning to 'give and take', rather than dominating a group or being dominated by others in it
- [ ] Clarifying my thoughts through discussion
- [ ] Gaining confidence in asserting my viewpoint
- [ ] Learning to work with people I find difficult
- [ ] Learning to deal with challenge and criticism from others
- [ ] Picking up general tips, such as hearing about useful new study apps
- [ ] Giving and receiving support.

Reflection

The value of collaborative study

Which of the above do you value most, and why?

How could skills in these areas help your future career or life ambitions?

Collaborative working: what students say

Studying can be quite a solitary activity – you are on your own with your thoughts or books or your essay a lot of the time, so it was actually a really nice change working in a group.

My group bonded very well. We got very close and had a laugh. I worked so hard on that project because I knew others were relying on me and I didn't want to let them down. I even worked harder on my other assignments because the group members kept asking how they were going and texting me with encouraging comments.

The most useful part was getting feedback on my ideas. I often make judgements very quickly about where I think an idea is leading. The others saw things that I hadn't spotted. I recognise now that there is value in not rushing to the first solution … . I am also a bit less impatient now, which helps me get on with people at work.

Our project group is brilliant. We all have a lot going on in our lives so we just keep each other going. I was going to leave the course at one point and everyone just got me to think about ways of staying.

I really don't like discussion groups much but we had to be in one. I am very focused and I hate it when groups wander off point. The turning point for me was when some of these meanders went in directions I wouldn't have thought of. Some were really unexpected, really good. This made me a bit less vain about my own thinking, which was probably a good thing. And less shy.

I can't say I enjoyed group work. It wasn't my thing. I found it slow and I hated wasting time. I am competitive and didn't like sharing my ideas. That said, I came to terms with it because I can see how the skills you use help my CV. I wouldn't have thought I could be a good leader as I am not a very sociable type. But I like to get things done and found out I am good at seeing what a group needs to do, explaining this to others, and seeing everything gets organised. I am interested in developing leadership skills further, so I look on group work differently.

Doing group evaluation was a bit of a shock to me as I think of myself as a people person. I am very chatty so it was quite hard to hear that the group felt I should, basically, talk less and listen to others. I thought I was listening, but the group said I didn't actually take on board what people were saying and act on it. I can't say it was easy to hear this but it was something I needed to know. It was one of the most useful parts of the course.

The thing that used to annoy me about collaborative working was people not pulling their weight. I have learned that, right at the start, you need to spell out the ground rules, who is doing what, and what will happen if someone doesn't do what is agreed. If you do that, then you can get a really good group going.

Self-evaluation: studying with other people

Rate your skills

First make an honest critical evaluation of these aspects of studying with others, using a 1–4 rating scale

4 = excellent; 1 = weak.

Interpret your ratings

Use your ratings to consider your skill and comfort levels in working with others for varied tasks and contexts.

★ How strong is your overall rating?

★ Where are your relative strengths?

★ Which areas are 'ok' but could be strengthened?

★ Which were your lowest ratings? Do these have anything in common?

Reflection

People skills

Which skills would it be helpful for you to develop further?

Want to know more?

Follow up on aspects you want to check out further, using this chapter or, for cultural competence, Chapter 9.

How good are my collaborative skills?	Rating
1 Considering what a group needs for it to work	1 2 3 4
2 Helping others stay focused on tasks	1 2 3 4
3 Giving full attention to what is said and done	1 2 3 4
4 Creating a supportive environment for group work	1 2 3 4
5 Setting good ground rules for groups	1 2 3 4
6 Sharing out roles and responsibilities well	1 2 3 4
7 Contributing well to discussions	1 2 3 4
8 Undertaking agreed tasks for the group	1 2 3 4
9 Dealing with difficulties in a group	1 2 3 4
10 Listening carefully to what other people say	1 2 3 4
11 Building effectively on what others contribute	1 2 3 4
12 Getting my point across clearly	1 2 3 4
13 Taking a fair share of time and decision-making	1 2 3 4
14 Dealing well with difficult moments in groups	1 2 3 4
15 Offering constructive criticism effectively	1 2 3 4
16 Receiving criticism effectively	1 2 3 4
17 Dealing with unfairness in groups	1 2 3 4
18 Setting up study groups/peer support groups	1 2 3 4
19 Knowing how to share study without cheating	1 2 3 4
20 Managing group projects effectively	1 2 3 4
21 Making an effective presentation to others	1 2 3 4
22 Making an effective group presentation	1 2 3 4
23 Contributing to seminars/taught sessions	1 2 3 4
24 Being aware of the needs of an audience	1 2 3 4
25 Working effectively with people of diverse cultures, countries and backgrounds	1 2 3 4
Total Score (out of 100)	

Making a group work

Although there are many benefits to working in groups, it isn't always easy. Dealing with the challenges, though, helps develop skill and awareness. The following guidelines can help with most group work, whether in class, seminars, workplaces, for projects, support or discussion.

Create a supportive group atmosphere

Be aware of people's feelings

People are often more anxious than they seem, and worry about being criticised or found wanting. Be constructive in your comments. Aim to be kind and helpful rather than score points.

Address anxieties directly

Groups work best when members bond. In the first session, give time to checking how everybody feels about the group or the course. What were their concerns before arriving? Did others feel the same way? It helps to know that you are not the only person who has concerns. Discuss how the group could turn anxieties into opportunities.

Make ground rules

This is especially important if you are forming a study or project group. Ground-rules should address directly the anxieties raised by the group. Also include:

★ expected attendance, punctuality and commitments

★ behaviour or comments that would be unacceptable

★ what the group will do if someone dominates, does not pull their weight or ignores the ground rules. See page 180.

Set clear boundaries

Clarify what the group will or won't do to support each other. Be supportive and encouraging, but avoid being drawn too deeply into others' personal difficulties or trying to 'rescue' them. Help them find the appropriate support services.

Plan – to prevent problems

If you are going to work collaboratively with one or more people over a period of time, think through what you hope to gain from working together and what might go wrong. Write down your considerations under three sets of headings:

★ 'Advantages'

★ 'Potential difficulties'

★ 'Ways we could deal with these difficulties'

Go through all the advantages together. Consider each potential difficulty and brainstorm ways of dealing with it. Be creative in looking for strategies. If you are truly stuck, speak to a tutor.

Create an effective group environment

Clarify the group's purpose

Keep the group focused on its purpose and on what it was set up to achieve. This might be:

★ a particular task, product or outcome such as a report, wiki, project, discussion?

★ to develop interpersonal skills?

★ to gain personal insights?

★ for peer support and solidarity?

★ social interaction?

Set clear agendas

★ Be clear about the purpose of each meeting.

★ Set an agenda for meetings, decide how long to spend on each item, and stick to this.

★ Meet in a suitable venue. If it isn't a social group, avoid social venues.

★ Arrange meeting times and venues well in advance, so that everyone can attend.

Check progress

If the group does not seem to be working well, address this directly. Each person in turn should say what they think could be done to improve matters including what they, personally, could do differently. Consider such aspects as:

★ Does the group need to bond through a social activity, or meet earlier to socialise?

★ Are tasks shared fairly?

★ Is somebody dominating?

★ Are you considerate enough about each other's feelings and ideas?

Aim to avoid negative criticism or allocating blame.

Making a group work

Taking responsibility

The responsibility for the group lies with each member. Everyone needs to play an active part. If a problem arises, even if it seems to be the fault of one person, everyone has responsibility for sorting it out so that the group can function.

Investigate group strengths

Find out the range of skills and experience in the group. Who prefers to organise, run meetings, write? State clearly what *you* would like to do. If several people want to do the same thing, rotate roles or share tasks out. Ensure everyone has a role.

Task allocation and group roles

For each session, decide who will take which role.

★ Be clear who will do what.

★ Set clear deadlines for completion.

Chairperson

Although everybody should help, the chair helps the group to draw up an agenda and keep to it, ensures that everyone gets to speak and that their views are heard, keeps the group focused on the point being discussed and sums up the main points.

Timekeeper

The timekeeper ensures the group keeps to time schedules. Sometimes, in meetings, they allocate each person a set time for contributions.

Record-keeper or secretary

The record-keeper notes who is going to do what and when, and any other decisions made.

Task or project manager

The task manager checks, between meetings, that everyone is doing what was agreed.

Sharing group work fairly

Consider what is fair in the circumstances, and what to do if someone really cannot do what was agreed. Be clear what the group will do if someone doesn't pull their weight. Talk through whether, for this group, it is better to assign tasks according to individual strengths – useful if the group needs to produce an outcome at speed or in a competitive context. Alternatively, if a key aim is to learn to work collaboratively, consider rotating roles so that everyone has a chance to develop a range of skills and experience.

Manage potential 'saboteurs'

Be alert to individuals or groups that seem to want to divert time and attention by complaining about the nature of the group or shortcomings of the task set. Avoid being drawn into this. Keep bringing the group back to task. Consider what next step the group can take towards achieving its purpose. Focus on potential solutions rather than problems.

Sabotaging your group

It is quite easy to sabotage a group. Often this happens unintentionally, because people are nervous or worry about being judged by others, so they act as if they don't care.

Reflection

Sabotage

In which ways are you, personally, most likely to sabotage a group unintentionally (such as by being late, not preparing, chatting)? What could you do differently?

Being effective in group discussion

Getting the most out of discussion

Before

★ Ensure you have done any tasks agreed for the group.

★ Read around the subject. Think about it.

★ What questions do you want answered?

During

★ Check that everyone can see and hear everyone else.

★ Be open to hearing something new.

★ Jot down useful information.

★ Jot down questions to ask.

★ If you don't understand something, ask.

★ Link what you hear to what you already know.

★ Make contributions – for example, raise points that interest you.

After

★ Go over your notes and summarise them. Add any new details and thoughts.

★ Check that you know exactly when you will do activities arising out of the group. Are they in your diary?

Enabling good discussion

Be encouraging
Encourage others. For instance, you might say, 'I found it interesting that ...'.

Include everyone
Speak to everyone in the group, not just particular individuals. Make sure that everybody has a chance to speak.

Use 'body language'
As you listen, show your attention by smiling, by nodding agreement, and so on. If you want to speak, make clear signals.

Listen to other students
Your fellow students deserve your respectful attention as much as does your tutor – just as you deserve theirs.

Indicate when you agree
Express your agreement: 'So do I ...'; 'Yes, that's true ...'

If you disagree
Instead of just rejecting the other person's ideas, explore them: 'What makes you think that?' 'Have you thought about ...?'

Admit mistakes
Acknowledge your errors, and apologise: 'Sorry, my mistake'; 'Oh, I see! I misunderstood ...'

Make suggestions
Share your ideas: 'Why don't we ...?'

Help the flow
★ Contribute to the discussion – but don't dominate it.
★ Ask questions – but not too many.
★ Take responsibility: don't leave everything to one person.
★ Encourage the group to keep to the subject.

Offer information
Share your knowledge: 'There's some useful information on that in ...'

Sum up for the group
'Well, have we agreed on these two points so far? First, ...? And second, ...?'

Build on other people's ideas
'That's an important point you made, for several reasons ...'

Be willing to share ideas
Let others know if you have found a good source or if you have a different perspective on the issue. Have the courage to ask the group for their input on ideas that you are working on.

Speaking and listening skills

Good communication is a two-way process. It requires both good listening skills and participation in the discussion.

Do you talk *to* people, or *at* people, or *with* people?

★ People who talk *at* you are listening to themselves. They leave no space for a response.

★ People who talk *with* you are keen for you to join in.

★ People who talk *to* you consider you, and your response, carefully.

Non-verbal communication

We indicate to other people how well we are listening through our verbal responses, and also through non-verbal communication, such as:

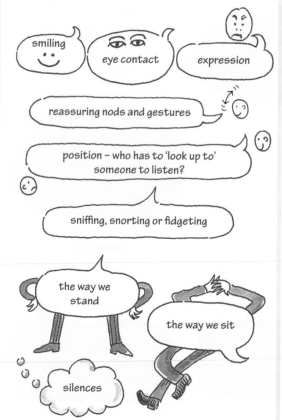

smiling

eye contact

expression

reassuring nods and gestures

position – who has to 'look up to' someone to listen?

sniffing, snorting or fidgeting

the way we stand

the way we sit

silences

How well do you listen?

★ Ask someone to watch you while you are listening in a group.

★ Ask for feedback about your non-verbal signals to various group members.

★ Does any of the feedback surprise you?

★ Do you come across to others in the way you imagined?

★ If not, what would you like to change?

Reflection

Listening skills

In your journal, consider how well you listen to others. Do you:

★ take in what other people say?

★ give other people room to speak?

★ let other people finish before you start to speak?

★ use encouraging non-verbal signals?

★ 'switch off' when bored or if you dislike the person?

Could you do anything differently to put others more at ease when they are speaking?

Which non-verbal communication are you sensitive to? What do *you* find encouraging? What do you find *discouraging*?

 ## Better listening

Make a conscious effort to tune in to speakers. Some of these techniques may help:

★ Give them your full attention: don't be screen-watching, distracted or impatient.

★ Consider the speakers' feelings.

★ Find ways of encouraging them.

★ Focus on the content – think of some way this could be of value to you.

★ Listen for key words and jot them down.

★ Think of a question you could ask (when they have finished speaking).

★ Link what they are saying to something you already know.

★ Find one positive comment to contribute.

Speaking up

Playing your part

Discussion sessions in class or within groups are most effective when everyone makes a contribution. This requires each student to take personal responsibility for:

★ creating the kind of environment where everyone has the chance to contribute

★ having the courage and making the effort to contribute.

Professor Locke's discussion group wasn't an instant success

Reflection

Taking your space

Are you someone who needs to focus more on:

★ creating space for yourself to speak, and making more of a contribution in class/groups?

★ leaving more space for others to speak?

Speaking out in a group

If you are anxious at the idea of speaking out in a group, the following can help.

Before the group

★ Make a decision to speak at least once during the group – even if it is only to hear yourself say 'yes' out loud. Build up from a small base.

★ Get to know other group members, if possible, so that you feel more at ease.

During the group

1 Sit next to somebody you find reassuring.
2 Jot down what you want to say. If it helps, read it out.
3 Give an example to illustrate your point.
4 If you are nervous, breathe out slightly more slowly than usual.
5 Take your time when speaking – aim to speak more slowly than usual.
6 Make eye contact with at least one person.
7 Be brief. When you have made your point – *stop*. Don't go back over it again.
8 If something you say does sound confused, say 'I'll make that clearer', and clarify what you meant.
9 Speak up so everyone can hear. If people have to strain to hear you, they will be less sympathetic to what you are saying – and you may have to say it all over again.
10 Act confident, even if you don't feel it. Don't apologise – smile!

After the group

★ Congratulate yourself on any progress.

★ Keep any mistakes or stumbling in proportion – it is not the end of the world.

★ Decide what you will do next time.

Lead – but don't dominate

★ Be aware of how long you speak and the proportion of group time you take up with your own questions, comments, etc. If this is disproportionate, say less.

★ Remember you don't have to comment on every issue that arises – leave room for others.

★ Be aware of whether you are always taking the lead – if so, stand back and encourage others occasionally.

Individual voices and accents

Many people feel self-conscious about the way they speak, even though clever and successful people have all kinds of accents. Don't worry about your own accent nor judge others by theirs. Focus on content.

Dealing with difficult moments in the group

Strong emotions in a group

It is usually helpful for the group to understand why strong feelings arise in groups and to think through together how to respond. See also Chapter 9.

Emotions arising from strong opinions

A strong attack on somebody's views can be distressing; people often identify themselves with their own opinions. If you reject the *opinion*, the *person* may feel rejected. The group may need a ground rule that *opinions* can be challenged, but not the person who holds them.

Emotions arising from group problems

If emotion arises from the group not working effectively, then talk through how to improve the way the group operates. For example, if some people feel their views are ignored, check:

★ What would make them feel heard?

★ Is what they want realistic?

★ Does that affect anyone else?

★ Can a compromise be found?

Emotions arising from outside the group

People bring into any group events or emotions from everyday life. It can be disrupting if it is unclear where sudden strong outbursts are coming from. Consider:

1 Each time the group meets, everyone taking 1–2 minutes to report on what is going on for them.

2 Deciding together on how the group will manage unacceptable expressions of emotion, such as, 'If one person is aggressive towards another, the rest of the group will intervene.'

Tears

If people are distressed for whatever reason, let them have a few minutes' quiet or some space to express their emotions. Don't worry about tears – crying can release pent-up stress. Distressed people may need to be alone, or to speak with just one other person quietly. Show kindness. Ask the person what he or she needs.

Silences

Silences often seem longer than they really are. This is because we so rarely experience them. They can be very productive, however. Sit with silence and value it, especially if the group is discussing a weighty issue. Don't feel obliged to fill silences with questions or jokes.

Dead-ends

If silences suggest stagnation or stalemate, take a new approach. Consider:

★ breaking the task into smaller parts

★ splitting into pairs for 15–20 minutes to work on different angles; share these as a full group

★ charting or drawing the issues visually as a group

★ brainstorming ideas – might one work?

Imbalances in group interaction

Group discussions can easily become unbalanced if:

★ one or two people dominate

★ two people are locked into an exchange

★ there are no spaces in which quieter people can get into the discussion.

The chairperson or group members can address these imbalances directly by:

★ thanking dominant members and indicating it would also be good to hear others' views

★ asking anyone who hasn't spoken whether they wish to

★ pointing out any imbalances so that the group can discuss ways to deal with them.

Some contributions – such as updating the group at the start of a session about your day or week – are important, but can drift on too long. Set time limits in such cases.

Giving and receiving feedback and criticism

One of the most difficult aspects of working collaboratively is offering constructive feedback or criticism on other people's work or contributions to the group. You may be asked to do this either formally or informally on your course.

What is meant by 'constructive'?

Constructive criticism is feedback to others that:

★ provides insights or suggestions that benefit them, encourage them in the right direction and that they can apply to improve their work or achieve their goals

★ is offered in such a way that it does not belittle or undermine the recipients.

Reflection

Giving criticism

How skilled are you at giving criticism in this way? What, if anything, could you do better?

Receive criticism in a constructive way

It can be hard to hear any criticism, whether positive, in the form of compliments, or as areas for improvement. However, we can learn a great deal if we are prepared to listen to feedback. This is now a requirement of many courses and in the workplace.

1 **Be open** to hearing what people say, even if you find it difficult to do so. Be ready to learn from it.

2 **Be positive**. Assume that the person giving feedback wants to be constructive and is on your side, even if it doesn't always feel like it.

3 **Listen attentively.** Take time to think about what has been said. Look for the truth in it.

4 **Hear the main message**, rather than questioning whether the speaker has understood everything about your intentions or has all the facts right.

5 **Ask** questions, or for a concrete example, to clarify anything you do not understand.

6 **Show gratitude**. Always thank people for their feedback: it takes time and effort to give this.

Offer constructive criticism
When to offer constructive criticism:

★ if you are asked to do so by the recipient

★ if it is a requirement of your course

★ if it is a ground rule set by the group

★ if you have something worthwhile to offer that you consider that the recipient is willing and able to hear.

How to offer constructive criticism:

1 **Be sensitive**: comment on behaviour, actions, products or outcomes, not on people.

2 **Be current**: refer to what is going on now, rather than the past.

3 **Be balanced:** point out what is good and what could be improved. It is important that the recipient knows strengths to build on and how to do better.

4 **Be honest**: don't say things you do not believe. When listening, jot down a list of positive points and ways of making improvements, so you have something concrete to refer to.

5 **Be productive**: start with positive points and praise. This helps recipients to be open to more negative comments later.

6 **Be selective**: choose just one or two areas for improvement that would make a real difference.

7 **Be helpful**: phrase your suggestions in ways that can lead to practical outcomes. Suggest ways forward, rather than just stating what is wrong.

8 **Be realistic**: only suggest changes that can be achieved.

9 **Be precise**: give a clear example of what you mean.

10 **Be kind**: use a voice and a manner that help others accept your criticism.

Being fair to everyone in the group

When groups don't act fairly towards all members, everyone loses out. The group isn't working to the best potential of the whole team. Individuals may experience stress, or ill health, and be unable to contribute to the best of their abilities. It can also produce tensions and anger, which affect the study of everybody in a group or on a course.

Avoiding unintentional unfairness

Some people set out to hurt others deliberately, but a great deal of unfairness and discrimination is unintentional, caused by thoughtlessness, awkwardness or not being aware of the issues. Many people are concerned to find out they have unintentionally caused distress to somebody else.

The atmosphere may become very tense

Unfair treatment

This may take the form of:

★ not being given the chance to undertake certain group roles

★ not being listened to

★ contributions being ignored or not heard – especially if another person makes that point a few minutes later and gains the credit for it

★ being overlooked or left out of activities

★ experiencing discrimination on the grounds of colour, ethnicity, appearance, disability, age or other such reasons.

Reflection

Experience of unfair treatment

Think about an occasion when *you* were treated unfairly, because of somebody else's attitudes. This could be a time you felt left out, overlooked, blamed for things you didn't do, called hurtful names, or when others tried to embarrass you.

What were your feelings and attitudes then?

Did the incident have any longer-term effects, such as on your trust and confidence?

What can you learn from this that could be helpful to others?

Activity

Awareness of fair play

➡ There are dozens of ways in which members of a group could be unfair to its members, maybe without anybody realising. Jot down as many such situations as you can think of, drawing on experiences of previous groups or issues you have come across in the media.

➡ What questions could you ask yourself to help you monitor whether everybody in your group is being included, or whether anyone is being left out?

When you have completed this exercise, compare your ideas with suggestions on page 408.

➡ What could you do to involve everyone in a fair way?

See also Chapter 9 about *Cultural competence*.

Study groups

Types of study group/support network

Some courses organise a study group or network. It could be led by a 'mentor' – a student from the year above. If not, you could set one up yourself. It could communicate by telephone or online, or meet after class in a study area, café or library chat space. Follow the principles outlined above, as for other groups.

What a support group can do

The work of the support group is limited only by your imagination, but the following activities are generally helpful to most students.

Select ✓ aspects that interest you. Decide when and how you could arrange these activities with others.

Encourage each other

- [ ] Arrange to phone, text or Skype each other to encourage work on a particular activity.
- [ ] Talk through your difficulties and concerns – others may feel the same way. Help each other to find solutions.
- [ ] Comment on each other's blogs.
- [ ] Let others know what they do well. If you appreciate a particular contribution, say so!

Befriend each other

Simply listening to each other is helpful – don't underestimate its value.

- [ ] Meet up for coffee, suggest a group goes out for a meal, or organise a social event such as a trip.
- [ ] Befriend each other on social networking sites. Send supportive texts or tweets. Leave comments in group members' social networking accounts.
- [ ] Set up a support group, chat room, or discussion board for students in your subject, year, college or club, or for mature students, work-based students, or for those studying on a particular project.

Review lectures

- [ ] Go through your lecture notes together. See if you picked out different points. Each person notes different things, so by sharing information you each gain a fuller set of lecture notes.

Share ideas and study tasks

- [ ] Share ideas about how to tackle assignments and strategies for coping with work, study and life.
- [ ] Divide different aspects of your study between you: for example, you could each check a different library or organisation for information, or act as guinea pigs for each other's project questionnaires.
- [ ] Share background reading. Read different texts and summarise verbally the main points.
- [ ] Discuss your ideas about what you read.
- [ ] Help each other to revise material for exams.

Signpost each other to good resources

- [ ] Let each other know about helpful learning resources, apps, workshops, services, places to study, discounted products, and local events.

Learn from each other's marked work

- [ ] Share essays once these have all been returned and graded. Notice how these differ.

Action Learning approaches to study

★ Give one person, 'person A', 5 minutes to describe a current study problem while the rest of the group listen without interrupting.

★ As a group, spend ten minutes clarifying the issues. Brainstorm ideas for dealing with the problem, whilst A listens without interrupting.

★ Person A has 5 minutes to draw on the suggestions to identify action to take, to set a timescale for doing this, and negotiate support from the group.

★ Repeat the process for each group member. At the next meeting, check that you all carried out your actions, and set new ones.

See Beaty and McGill (2001).

Sharing work without cheating

Tasks that can be shared

Tasks that *can* be shared out include:

1 deciding on the group project title

2 clarifying each other's understanding of course material, by discussing lectures, notes, texts, case studies, experiences and ideas

3 discussing publications, trends, artefacts, government policies etc. related to the course

4 sharing administrative tasks, such as booking rooms, keeping agendas of meetings, or writing for permission to interview people

5 undertaking a literature search; identifying texts or sections for you all to read

6 discussing and deciding on a methodology

7 checking out useful websites

8 collecting, discussing and interpreting data

9 helping one another to use software packages

10 encouraging each other to succeed.

Some kinds of work can be shared with other people, whereas sharing other activities would be considered cheating. Below are some guidelines. If you are in any doubt, however, always check with your tutors.

Accidental cheating?

Tutors are usually adept at finding identical and near-identical sections in students' work. Software is available that helps them to find work copied from the internet or other students. If they find similar wording in more than one assignment, they might investigate for cheating. It could mean that you are asked to leave your course or retake parts of it. Cheating is considered a serious academic offence.

All in your own words ...

Usually, all writing you submit should either be in your own words or referenced as on pages 249–51.

When making notes ... of ideas discussed with others, write these in bullets and avoid noting phrases used by others. If they use the same phrases in assignments, you could both be regarded as cheating.

When recording discussions, do not write out phrases word for word from the recording. If you do, you may accidentally copy someone else's words into an assignment – this too would be cheating.

When writing up group assignments, always make your own notes about the design, methods, data collection, results, discussion, and conclusions. Write the final account from your own notes – not from anyone else's.

Don't share out writing tasks between group members unless it is a requirement to do so.

Don't copy and paste from group members. If you used that in an assignment, it would be cheating. The person who sent it might also use it in an assignment, and that is likely to be noticed.

Don't share ungraded work. Wait until the tutor has marked and returned the whole group's assignments. If someone copies your work and hands it in as their own, you may also be held responsible.

Write your own references. Errors creep easily into references, and tutors are usually good at detecting copied mistakes.

Communicating as a group

Negotiate as a group

Good communication is essential to effective group working. For some group work, you will need to negotiate the following factors.

Access: How long will it take for members to travel to face-to-face meetings? Which forms of communication can all group members access? Do they all have home internet connections?

Group knowledge and skills: Do some students need more encouragement to speak than others? Does everyone know how to use the preferred apps? Do they all use Dropbox or Google Docs? Can you share these skills within the group?

Shared interests and understandings: Do members have the same attitude towards meeting up or using social networking sites? Do they share the same values for privacy, use of texting or Skype, or speed of responding to messages?

Using a group moderator

Page 176 looked at the roles typical of face-to-face groups. For online discussion groups, it can also be useful for a group member to act as a 'moderator' to facilitate interactions, such as the following.

To set up the group

★ Set up the chat room or discussion board.

★ Let group members know that it is there.

★ Invite the group to set ground rules and to decide actions to take if these are not followed.

To help generate discussion

★ Stimulate debate by asking key questions, making comments or offering useful prompts.

★ Summarise the discussion so far.

★ Respond to comments.

★ Bring out links between contributions.

★ Encourage new discussion threads.

To keep it live

★ Archive material that is not in use.

★ Allocate tasks to group members.

★ Check that ground rules are being followed.

Setting ground rules

For all kinds of group interactions, it is worth setting ground rules for a group's communications, and renegotiating these as the group takes shape. Be clear for yourself what you would want addressed as ground rules. Select ✓ any that apply.

- [ ] 1 The group's staying focused on its core purpose and/or on the subject of the discussion/chat room
- [ ] 2 Use of the group's meeting time to arrange outside meetings or to discuss other items
- [ ] 3 Punctuality for logging in or arriving at meetings
- [ ] 4 Attendance, including leaving or logging off early
- [ ] 5 Contributing fairly to activities and discussion
- [ ] 6 'Lurking' (reading messages but not contributing)
- [ ] 7 'Small talk' and socialising
- [ ] 8 Making personal comments
- [ ] 9 Showing respect towards other participants
- [ ] 10 Unacceptable behaviours such as aggression, belittling, flaming, trolling and cyber bullying
- [ ] 11 Managing disagreements
- [ ] 12 Spelling, grammar and use of 'text-speak'
- [ ] 13 Other netiquette and security (e.g. protecting each others' online identities; agreeing who has access to the group's personal information and project materials; using anti-virus software if sharing files).
- [ ] 14 Other:

See also Chapter 9.

How well do I contribute to seminars and groups?

Unit/module:	Seminar:
Aim of this evaluation	**Strategy**
★ To make seminars and groups work more effectively, both for me and for others.	★ To evaluate my contributions using this evaluation, discussion and reflection.
★ To ensure that everybody feels included and safe in contributing.	★ To compare my self-evaluation with a colleague's evaluation of me.
★ To ensure that, as a group, we cover the material we need to cover.	★ To use our evaluations to develop a joint strategy for better seminars.

Self-evaluation: How well do I contribute to seminars and groups?

Rating: Use a scale of 1–4 (1 = considerable room for improvement. 4 = excellent)

Aspect	Rating	What could I do better?
1 I had prepared well beforehand so knew about the subject	1 2 3 4	
2 I was encouraging to the speaker (such as through my body language)	1 2 3 4	
3 I demonstrated interest in what the speaker had to say	1 2 3 4	
4 I participated fully and/or made contributions during the session	1 2 3 4	
5 I spoke a fair share of the time (neither dominating nor being too quiet)	1 2 3 4	
6 I asked at least one question	1 2 3 4	
7 All my questions and comments were relevant to the discussion	1 2 3 4	
8 I listened to, and considered, points raised by other people	1 2 3 4	
9 I was encouraging to other people in the group	1 2 3 4	
10 I paid full attention (I didn't check messages, surf the web, etc.)	1 2 3 4	
11 All my contributions were to the full group (none just to those near me)	1 2 3 4	
12 I made positive comments to the speaker afterwards	1 2 3 4	

Group projects

Student projects

You may be asked to undertake different kinds of group project throughout your course. These can vary in size and length but, typically, you need to:

★ investigate a topic, for which you might have a choice of the topic and title

★ decide a methodology for your investigation

★ gather and collate information and data

★ share your findings with each other as a group

★ report as a group, such as through a presentation in class or a seminar session, or through a group report, wiki, blog or poster

★ write up the details of your project either as an individual or as a group.

Managing your project

Effective project management draws on the skills covered throughout the book, and especially:

★ the collaborative working skills referred to in this chapter and Chapter 9, and

★ research project skills covered in Chapter 16.

Group project 'To do' List

1 **Communication, tools and approaches**: Decide how you will communicate as a group (page 185). Decide whether to use a wiki, blog, shared space, social media, apps, etc.

2 **The project brief**: What learning do you have to demonstrate? Does this relate only to subject content or are you required to demonstrate how effectively you functioned as a group?

3 **Roles**: Decide the range of roles needed, how these will be allocated, and who will fill each (and for how long, if relevant). See pages 176 and 188.

4 **Planning a timetable**: Make a detailed list of all the things to do. Draw up a project plan detailing what will be completed by when and by whom (page 188).

5 **Reporting**: Be clear how you are intended to report on the group project. Leave plenty of time to write up your report and/or prepare and rehearse the group presentation.

Using a group wiki

A wiki is a website containing information that multiple users can edit. You can add your own contributions to other people's ideas, and they can add theirs to yours. Using wikis can develop useful collaborative working and team skills in researching, negotiating, and co-writing.

Your group may wish to create a wiki:

★ to draw together information on the topic

★ as a resource for students on your course

★ to build knowledge of a topic that group members find challenging

★ to build understanding and critiques of a difficult text or theory

★ to develop the group report together

★ to publish the results of a project or to communicate this to others in the class.

For more information, see:

http://en.wikipedia.org/wiki

Using a group blog

A blog is a web-based log or electronic journal written by an individual or a group, which others can read online. You might opt to use this:

★ to maintain a research diary, recording group methods and findings as these arise

★ to keep team members up to date about the progress of those aspects of the project for which you each have responsibility

★ for mutual support, to share experiences with other group members, especially if the assignment brief encourages reflective analysis of your project work

★ as a group, to communicate with others about your project.

Managing group projects: Record and share information

Make and record group decisions

★ Take a systematic approach to making decisions as a group on each aspect of your group process.

★ Keep good records: devise a record sheet such as this, or adapt this for your own purposes.

★ Share this electronically with all group members so that everyone can refer to the same information.

> A more detailed sheet for recording details of your project from start to finish is available on the companion site for you to use. Adapt it to suit your project, if needed.

1   Communications

Agree ✓ the combination of communication methods that best suits your group. Before finalising this, check whether anyone has a disability or other difficulty that prevents them from making full use of these.

- ☐ Face to face
- ☐ Email
- ☐ Blog
- ☐ Chat room
- ☐ Other:
- ☐ By phone
- ☐ E-messaging
- ☐ Shared electronic space

2   Ground rules and processes

Discuss the following. Indicate ✓ when completed.

- ☐ Setting ground rules (see page 185)
- ☐ How you will allocate roles
- ☐ What you expect from one another
- ☐ Any concerns group members have about working together on the project – and how to resolve these
- ☐ Decisions about communications; how often members should log in/meet
- ☐ Whether you all wish to assign someone to manage communications for the group.

3   The project brief

Check the project brief carefully. Discuss the following. Indicate ✓ once agreed.

- ☐ What are you required to do as a group?
- ☐ What will be assessed, and how?
- ☐ What are the marking criteria?
- ☐ What must be produced collectively?
- ☐ What must be contributed individually?

Outputs

Select ✓ the required outputs from your project.

- ☐ Report
- ☐ Database
- ☐ Blog
- ☐ Wiki
- ☐ Website
- ☐ Newsletter
- ☐ Group presentation
- ☐ Poster
- ☐ Other:

4   Roles and responsibilities

Decide which roles are needed and who will fill them. Some possibilities are listed below. Select ✓ those that apply for your project.

- ☐ Project leader
- ☐ Secretary
- ☐ Chair
- ☐ Timekeeper
- ☐ Record keeper
- ☐ Design aspects
- ☐ Moderator
- ☐ Research manager
- ☐ Data manager
- ☐ Communications manager
- ☐ Fundraiser/treasurer
- ☐ Deadlines manager
- ☐ Website manager
- ☐ Blog manager
- ☐ Wiki manager
- ☐ Technical aspects
- ☐ Other:

Making presentations and giving talks

What is the purpose of presentations?

Students are often asked to give presentations, either alone or in groups, in order to:

★ provide a focus for class discussion

★ enable different groups to explore various aspects of a topic or course material in detail

★ share the results of group projects

★ gain practice in speaking in front of others, useful for viva exams, job interviews, workplace presentations, and life generally.

How are presentations assessed?

Find out from your tutors the criteria used to evaluate group presentations and where to find these. Use them to help you shape your presentation as a group and to evaluate it before and after. See page 190.

Reflection

Excellent presentations

After you have been in the audience for a talk or presentation, jot down your observations of what worked and didn't work. Use this to make yourself a list of things to do/not do in your own presentations. You can draw on the items listed opposite to help you observe talks and formulate your list.

Jim knew someone would overpack their slides

What makes a great presentation?

Strong content. The knowledge base is relevant, accurate, pitched at the right level for the course and the audience.

Direction. The talk leads the audience towards a point, such as to understand the reasons behind your position, conclusions or recommendations.

Clarity. The audience can follow the argument easily because of the way it is organised and presented: well structured, logically sequenced. Its key points stand out.

Persuasiveness. It provides a strong case.

Points of interest. This could be a topical issue, a compelling argument, new data, visual material, good examples to illustrate the points.

Well-paced. It moves at a speed that maintains attention, neither tediously slow nor gabbled. The speaker doesn't 'go faster' in order to cover more material than there is time for.

Selective. What is omitted can be as important as what is included, for clarity, relevance and pacing.

Researched. Your advance research should be evident in the talk and also in the way you answer reasonable questions put to you by the audience: you should know your material well.

Enjoyable. Aim to help the audience enjoy the talk through the content and style of presentation. It helps if you are confident and enjoy what you are saying (or appear to be). A little humour can help (but is not essential so don't force it).

Audience awareness. This needs to be evident from the way the talk is both designed, prepared and presented. (Page 191.)

Technical proficiency. Materials and slides are ready. You can use the technology fluidly.

Preparation and practice. Presenters put time into thinking through exactly how it will work, and practise until they are confident everything will work and fit into the time available.

Preparing your talk

Good preparation makes all the difference. It clarifies your thinking and, if you know your material and practise well, it builds your confidence.

Deciding on the content

Decide your topic and position. To clarify your thinking and provide a focus, sum these up in one sentence. If you can't, pause and think this through, to avoid a confusing presentation.

Research the topic well. Know more about the topic than you can present – you will feel more confident about handling the talk and answering questions on the day.

Relevance. Make sure all material fits the brief, your course, the audience, your title and argument.

Select carefully. Choose material that lends itself well to the format of a presentation, such as key data, core points, images, short video clips.

Less is more. Whittle material down. If you researched well, you will have more material than you need. Remember that, typically, it takes longer to *say it* than to *read* it, and also that you should speak more slowly to an audience, so they can absorb what they hear.

Preparing your material

★ **Divide** your material into the *essential* points that you definitely want to make, and a little *extra* material you can use if there is time.

★ **Organise** the material so that it flows logically – help the audience follow your line of reasoning.

★ **Ending**. Prepare a strong closing summary that sums up your argument or recommendations.

★ **Introducing**. Prepare your introduction, including a brief overview.

★ **Include a 'Hook'**. Consider including a brief statement, image, quotation or similar – to hook your audience in at the start.

The card technique

Preparing cards to speak from can aid confidence, giving you a concrete object to hold onto. Also, using these will create natural pauses as you move from one to the next, slowing you down and pacing your talk. That gives you and the audience some breathing space.

★ Break your talk into sections. Give each a heading.

★ Write one heading, and a few easily-read prompt words, onto each card.

★ Number the cards in the order that you want to introduce those points (in case you drop them!).

Slide presentations

If using PowerPoint, Prezi, or similar software:

1. Aim at a few lines of text per slide (1–7 lines).
2. Keep font sizes, images and data large and easy to read even from the back of the room.
3. Use relevant images to add interest.
4. Introduce new slides from the same direction.
5. Keep video clips short (1–2 minutes).
6. Time yourself speaking to each slide – the number doesn't matter as much as how long you spend on each. Don't include material you can't really use.
7. Avoid animations and effects unless essential.
8. Avoid waving laser beams at the screen.

Poster presentations

1. Make posters large, visually appealing and informative: use images, colour and a strong structure.
2. Don't neglect academic content.
3. Use 4–10 blocks of text beneath numbered headings.
4. Use a simple, clear structure so that it is obvious which order to read the information. Provide arrows if needed.
5. Ensure the title and headings stand out.
6. Avoid overloading the poster – leave spaces.
7. Adapt the poster to your audience, especially if targeted at the public or children.
8. Aim for a professional finish. Use PowerPoint or suitable software, unless an informal look is required.

Be aware of your audience

Know your audience

Be clear who is in your audience (students, tutors, children, members of the public?). Think through what will help them to make sense of your talk and stay interested. Adapt it so everyone can feel included and follow the argument.

'I'm running out of time so I'll just speed up…!'

Prepare for your audience

People listen differently to talks than they do in general conversation, especially if they have to sit still for more than a few minutes. You might have noticed this in lectures or seminars. When preparing your own presentation or talk, it can be useful to consider the following.

1   As an audience's attention tends to drift in and out, your key points could be missed. Repeat key messages or essential points, using slightly different words.

2   An audience's attention span is usually short. Divide your talk into a few sections, with a planned brief pause between each.

3   Focus on your key points. Avoid unnecessary details. Don't break off into unplanned tangents – you may confuse your audience and throw out your timing.

4   It can be challenging for an audience to follow a complex argument or a sequence of points when listening rather than looking. Slides, posters, charts or a handout help.

5   Audiences usually like 'stories'. Use a strong structure and relevant examples, images and case studies to engage their attention.

6   If you run short of time, don't speed up to fit in more material or rush through slides at a great pace just to show them. Your purpose is to engage and inform, not 'cover the material'. Instead, edit the talk to fit the available time. Check this when you practise your talk.

Seminars and class-based audiences

The most typical audiences you face as a student consist of other students, such as in seminars, workshops or other class-based groups. Bear in mind that when you speak in such contexts, you have an 'audience'. Speaking and contributing in class provides practice in:

★ speaking to different kinds of audience

★ making both formal and informal contributions

★ using feedback from people who may observe you in action over several weeks, months or years

★ observing group dynamics, so you can gain insights from how other people interact with an audience and then apply these to your own group contributions.

Reflection

Speaking to an audience

How do I use audience-awareness when:

★ making a presentation or giving a formal talk?

★ making informal contributions in class?

Which of the techniques suggested in this chapter could I use to improve my contributions in taught sessions?

If you haven't done so already, complete the self-evaluations on pages 186 and 195.

Practising and evaluating your presentation

Practise! Practise! Practise!

Practise your talk several times: note and amend anything that doesn't seem to flow well.

Time yourself speaking at a reasonable, calm speed. If the talk is too long, edit it down until you are confident that you can deliver it comfortably in the time available.

Don't assume things will sort themselves on the day. Make the process easier on yourself by taking control of the talk from start to finish. Reduce the chances of unwanted surprises.

For group presentations

Group presentations should be well coordinated with everyone contributing. Practise it all (including entering and leaving) until all runs smoothly and you look like a great team.

Play to individual strengths. Use practice to identify who is best for each section of the talk. Some are better at introducing a talk with the right tone for the audience, others are better at talking through data or answering questions.

Allocate tasks. Decide exactly who is presenting which points, for how long, and in which order.

Trouble shoot. Plan what you will do if someone forgets key information or runs over their time. Other people might need to adapt their talk subtly to cope with this. Practise covering potential problems and tricky questions so they are manageable if they occur on the day.

Listen carefully during practice runs: know what everyone else will cover. It will help if you have to cover team absences later, and avoids repetition. It reflects poorly on the group if members don't seem to know what each other will say or can't cover for each other.

Practise transitions from one person to the next. Agree your cues.

Practise opening and closing the talk: these contribute to the impression you make.

Have a 'dress rehearsal'

Ask 2 or 3 friends from a different course to observe your presentation when it is ready to test out on a 'mock' audience. They don't need to be experts in the subject. Decide in advance which kinds of specific feedback from them would help you most. Ask for an honest opinion. Run through the talk or presentation exactly as you intend to on the day.

The following key questions can help you in gaining useful feedback from your mock audience. Alternatively, use some or all of the questions on the more detailed checklist provided for your own assessment of whether the talk is ready (page 193).

'Mock audience' evaluation: key questions

1. What worked best? What did they enjoy, find interesting or engaging? (Aim to retain those aspects.)
2. Did the main message come across clearly? (Check that they can tell you what it was. If they can't, that is a priority to clarify for your next audience.)
3. Did anything sound confused or hard to follow or understand? What would have helped them make more sense of what was being said?
4. Was anything annoying or irritating for the audience?
5. Was the material presented at about the right pace?
6. What, if anything, could be better about the style of presenting (such as how you greeted the audience)? Did the talk fizzle away at the end or finish on a strong note?
7. Could any slides or materials be improved?

For group presentations
8. Did the talk come across as well-coordinated?
9. Did it flow well when one person took over from another?
10. Did you all come across as an effective team?

Assessing whether your presentation is ready

Use (or adapt) the following checklist to help ensure a strong preparation. Use the evaluation on page 195 to evaluate your own performance. Both of these are available on the companion site at www.studyskillshandbook.co.uk.

Aspect	Rating		Where are the gaps? How could it be improved?
	low	high	
Strong content. The knowledge base is relevant, accurate, pitched at the right level.	1 2 3 4 5		
Direction. The talk is structured so that it leads the audience in the direction we want.	1 2 3 4 5		
Clarity. It is obvious what we want to convey. Key points stand out and are well-sequenced.	1 2 3 4 5		
Persuasiveness. It makes a strong case to support its arguments, recommendations, etc.	1 2 3 4 5		
Points of interest. It is a topical issue and/or contains interesting data, visuals, examples.	1 2 3 4 5		
Well-paced. It can be delivered at a reasonable speed that maintains attention: neither fast nor slow.	1 2 3 4 5		
Selective. The talk presents the best and most relevant information for the time available.	1 2 3 4 5		
Researched. The talk is well-researched, including answers to the most likely questions.	1 2 3 4 5		
Enjoyable. There are aspects that both speaker(s) and audience will find enjoyable.	1 2 3 4 5		
Audience awareness. The talk is shaped to fit the needs of the audience.	1 2 3 4 5		
Technical proficiency. Materials and slides are ready and use of technology runs smoothly.	1 2 3 4 5		
Preparation and practice. The talk has been practised until it is evident it can work.	1 2 3 4 5		

Giving your talk

Build up your confidence

Many people worry about talks, but you can manage the process and build your confidence. Some stress or nervousness can be helpful as it releases chemicals in the brain that help you perform better. Reduce nervousness in the following ways.

★ Prepare and practise: be confident you are ready.

★ Use techniques to relax beforehand (page 167).

★ Arrive early: cut the stress of being late.

★ Be in the room first. Instead of suddenly being confronted by a sea of faces, make it your space.

★ Smile at your audience as they arrive. Make human contact. They are just people.

★ Have water to hand so you don't worry about your throat drying from nerves.

★ Aim to enjoy it: talk yourself into doing so.

Delivering the talk

Take charge

Wait until everybody is settled before you start.

Greet the audience. Tell them the title of the talk.

Say when you will take questions (at the end?).

Don't sound apologetic. Act quietly confident that your talk is great, and you start to win your audience.

Be a team

For group presentations, leave any disagreements outside the door. Don't try to outshine others at the expense of the team performance. Pull together so the team as a whole performs well.

Speak up

Speak from your cards, a poster or from memory so the talk is easier to listen to. If you are reading your talk out in full, use a conversational style, looking up frequently.

Remind yourself to speak more slowly and loudly than you would usually. Don't mumble or rush.

Read the section on **Speaking up** (page 179).

Stick to the plan

Avoid last minute changes – these disrupt the rhythm developed in your practice sessions.

Use a clock. Jot down your end time: it can be easy to forget this and lose track of time once speaking.

Go through your cards or overheads in turn. Make each point clearly. Avoid tangents that throw out the timings.

Remember your audience

Make eye contact with at least two people in your audience. Look up from time to time, such as when changing slides or between sections.

Direct your talk towards friendly faces such as friends or those who smile or nod at what you say.

Pause and take a breath after each point, to check your pace, keep calm, and help the audience absorb it.

Ignore rudeness such as people texting whilst you are speaking. Don't worry whether people are listening – some people listen best when they look half asleep!

End well

Briefly sum up what you have said, emphasising your main argument or recommendations.

Prepare a good line to end with.

With eye contact, smile and say 'Thank you'.

How effective am I at talks/presentations?

Aspect	Rating					What could I improve?
	low				high	
1 How well did it go, overall?	1	2	3	4	5	
2 How good was my preparation?	1	2	3	4	5	
3 Had I practised enough?	1	2	3	4	5	
4 How good was my opening?	1	2	3	4	5	
5 Did I begin with a brief outline?	1	2	3	4	5	
6 Did I stick to my plan?	1	2	3	4	5	
7 Was my main argument strong enough?	1	2	3	4	5	
8 Did I give good examples to help the audience grasp my points?	1	2	3	4	5	
9 Did the talk move logically from one point to the next?	1	2	3	4	5	
10 How good were my handouts, slides, etc. (if relevant)?	1	2	3	4	5	
11 How well did I use my handouts, slides, etc.?	1	2	3	4	5	
12 Did I sum up my argument well at the end?	1	2	3	4	5	
13 How well did I bring it to a close?	1	2	3	4	5	**What did I learn from preparing and delivering this talk?**
14 Did I answer questions well?	1	2	3	4	5	
15 Did I demonstrate respect for the different viewpoints and opinions of those present?	1	2	3	4	5	
16 Did I make eye contact with most of those present?	1	2	3	4	5	
17 Did I include everybody?	1	2	3	4	5	**What would I do differently next time?**
18 Was audience feedback positive?	1	2	3	4	5	
Other aspects relevant to my talk: 1 2 3						

Review

1 **Be self-aware**

Know your strengths – and where to make the most of these. Consider ways of strengthening skills and confidence in areas where you feel less strong. Use evaluations to pinpoint where to focus next.

2 **Build awareness of others**

Become more sensitive to the reasons for people acting as they do in groups. Learn to work around difficult situations in order to help the group move on.

3 **Clarify boundaries, roles and responsibilities**

Help the group decide what the boundaries are, what is expected, who is doing what, and when.

4 **Don't be daunted**

It is quite natural for group working to present challenges. It can bring out others' anxieties, which might appear as aggressive or as a refusal to contribute. In dealing with such issues, you develop broader interpersonal and problem-solving skills.

5 **Gain the benefits**

If the groups you are in work well, you gain. You benefit from different perspectives and views. Your thinking is stretched, your ideas refined, and you gain sources of support. You develop skills essential in the workplace once you graduate. Whatever groups you are in, it's in your interest to help them function at their best.

6 **Take responsibility**

Be active in looking for ways to make the group work. Take care to listen. Contribute time and ideas.

7 **Learn to listen well**

Give others your full attention. It makes them feel valued if you do, and under-valued if you don't. You also learn more from hearing what others have to say: you already know your own thoughts.

8 **Speak up!**

If you tend to let others do the talking, take up your space. If you lack confidence, plan what to say and build up to longer contributions.

9 **Share and support**

Help yourself to succeed through helping others. Be clear what kinds of tasks you are allowed to share, and which would be considered cheating.

10 **Manage group projects**

Be organised in coordinating tasks and communicating so that the group runs effectively.

11 **Present with confidence**

If giving a talk, preparation and practice are key. Use a dry run to test it out. Be specific in gaining feedback that helps you put the finishing touches to the presentation.

12 **Be a good team member**

Work for the benefit of your group. Support each other – be a team. Look like a team to others. Do your part to make your group as effective, friendly and enjoyable as possible.

Chapter 9

Developing cultural competence

Learning in diverse and international contexts

Learning outcomes

This chapter offers you opportunities to:

✓ consider the benefits to you of developing an international and global outlook
✓ build confidence in interacting with a diverse range of people
✓ develop cross-cultural awareness and sensitivity
✓ understand how customs and expectations can differ – or be unexpectedly similar
✓ consider your own role as a member of a diverse and international student community
✓ develop insights into how the world is experienced differently by others.

What is cultural competence?

Cultural competence is the ability to work with people from other cultures in an effective and sensitive way. It combines:

★ knowledge of other cultures

★ experience of mixing with others

★ attitudes that drive towards inter-cultural understanding

★ behaviours that enable good interactions.

It involves a strong awareness of our own cultural expectations, values and beliefs, so that we are confident in our cultural identity and clear when we are drawing on our own particular cultural norms (Kohlbry and Daugherty, 2015). Building cultural competence is an ongoing process of learning to work through barriers and challenges, becoming more aware of needs and sensitivities so everyone benefits and feels more comfortable (Campinha-Bacote, 2002).

Studying in a diverse community

Higher Education is highly international, with a dynamic exchange of knowledge, ideas and people. As students and staff are drawn from many countries and backgrounds, it is likely you will meet people

with experiences, customs, accents, appearances, abilities and disabilities that you haven't encountered or fully understood before (Complete University Guide, 2018). You may gain the opportunity to study and work with those from educational, social and cultural backgrounds different from your own, coming from your own country and from abroad.

This chapter helps you to think through what it means for you and others to be part of such a diverse and international learning environment. It looks at the potential benefits to your study, career and well-being and to the student community. It provides material to help you think through differences and potential situations that you might encounter on your course, so that you and others gain from the opportunities.

Challenges and opportunities for study, work, life

A diverse and international student world

As a student, you are a member of an international, multi-cultural diverse community. Millions of students are studying abroad at any one time. Increasing numbers opt to study, work or travel overseas for part, or all, of their course. It is likely that, at some point, you will study or live with students from other countries, either at your university or through studying abroad yourself.

For confidence and well-being

You may be unsure, at times, how to react when people express views or behave in ways that are unfamiliar to you – and they may feel the same about you. Such uncertainty can be uncomfortable and stressful. Having greater cultural sensitivity and awareness helps you to identify and manage such situations better, with more confidence and interest. This can open you to new experiences, benefiting your life, study and career.

For study benefits

If students on your course feel more comfortable about expressing themselves, and space is created for all to contribute, then everyone wins – from learning things they didn't know before about the world, exposure to multiple perspectives and gaining new ideas. For example, the personal experience of students with disabilities, from other countries or from specific backgrounds might differ from the findings of research studies in your books. This can stimulate ideas for student research projects. Sharing cultural experiences and perspectives provides information on alternative ways of resolving scientific and cultural problems, opening up new ideas for business or for viewing ethical issues.

For work, study or visits abroad

Cultural awareness is important in any context where there are people from different backgrounds. It is essential when abroad, for making others comfortable around you, for effective communication, and for your enjoyment and security.

For useful employability skills

As the global workforce becomes more diverse, employers are more interested in job applicants who can demonstrate experience and understanding of cross-cultural interactions and communications. They may need you to travel, live, work or communicate trans-nationally, or to work sensitively with customers, clients or patients whose lives and opinions are different from yours.

At interview, they might check such things as:

★ how you would respond in a scenario they set to check your inter-cultural competence and alertness to cultural sensitivities

★ your suitability for working with their diverse customers or international business partners.

For the student community

Students tend to do better when the whole group supports and encourages each other. That is more likely if everyone feels seen, heard and included. Otherwise, if people feel excluded, they tend to be unhappy and withdraw, so divisions emerge within the group. This, in turn, can lead to blame, recriminations and suspicion. All this can dissipate the energy and resources of the group and undermine students' happiness, well-being and success. It also raises ethical issues, such as fairness, inclusion and social justice: some people are affected more than others when a group has poor cultural awareness.

Use page 201 to consider which of the potential benefits of cultural awareness are relevant to you.

Personal benefits of inter-cultural awareness

As with any aspect of study, it is useful to identify why inter-cultural awareness is of benefit to you, directly or indirectly, now or for the future. Select ✓ any of the following that apply.

For personal development

- [ ] For greater self-awareness
- [ ] To understand what is distinct about my own culture – and why
- [ ] To understand how my culture has shaped me
- [ ] To be more aware of my cultural assumptions and of how these might affect others
- [ ] To be more open to other people's views.

For study benefits

- [ ] To get on better with students on my course
- [ ] To gain more from others' contributions to class
- [ ] For more effective classes and/or group work
- [ ] To enhance my critical thinking skills.

For social life and community

- [ ] To connect better with others
- [ ] To be more comfortable around others
- [ ] To help others feel comfortable around me
- [ ] To make more varied and deeper friendships
- [ ] To help include students who get left out.

For work and career

- [ ] To understand group dynamics better
- [ ] To deal better with people/situations at work
- [ ] For more effective team working
- [ ] To help me develop wider networks
- [ ] To help me as a future employer/leader.

For gaining empathy

- [ ] For people who are in a minority of some kind
- [ ] For those encountering a new culture
- [ ] For people whose experiences differ from mine.

For insights on the world ...

- [ ] Into how things can be different elsewhere
- [ ] Into what is considered important elsewhere
- [ ] Into how and why perspectives vary
- [ ] Into how languages vary in what they express
- [ ] Into how cultural misunderstandings can arise, be avoided and resolved.

For interest and new horizons

- [ ] To help me when travelling abroad
- [ ] To help me in living, working or communicating across national boundaries.

For global citizenship

- [ ] To be a responsible global citizen
- [ ] To help communication in diverse groups
- [ ] To help make the world a better place
- [ ] To help other people deal with trans-cultural or trans-national issues.

For ethical reasons

- [ ] To help ensure everyone is heard
- [ ] To help ensure others achieve their potential
- [ ] To help greater social and cultural inclusion
- [ ] To help increase social harmony.

Other reasons that matter to me:

Making, and not making, cultural assumptions

Assumptions

Cultural misunderstandings can arise because individuals, or sets of people, have different experiences. These provide varied starting points for forming assumptions about the world: on what is ethical or unethical, healthy or unhealthy, commonplace or unusual, natural or unnatural, self-evident or illogical, reasonable or unreasonable and so on.

In diverse groups, there will be multiple sets of cultural assumptions competing for space, both consciously and unconsciously, aloud or silently, as the 'right' view. We tend to assume we are right (some cultures more than others).

Awareness of diverse assumptions

Members of a group may be completely unaware that assumptions shared by the majority are not shared by everyone, and that this could be causing difficulty, isolation, hurt or offence. Spending time together, getting to know each other, building familiarity and trust, showing mutual interest, talking things through, all help in bringing underlying differences to light – an important step to resolving misunderstandings.

'Don't make assumptions'?

It is easy to say that people 'shouldn't make assumptions' but that is difficult in practice. It is integral to our cognitive functioning to make rapid assumptions throughout the day based on what we have learnt and experienced so far. We can expect that people with different experiences will, inadvertently, say or do things we don't fully understand and might not agree with. The challenge is in deciding what to do about it so that everyone gains an opportunity to learn and grow.

Learning from mistaken assumptions

A group's effectiveness can depend on how well it manages differences and incorrect assumptions.

It helps if a class or group agree:

1. To create an environment of mutual goodwill
2. To recognise that anyone might make incorrect assumptions about others
3. To make an effort to check whether everyone is thinking about things in the same way before proceeding on a joint course of action
4. To notice whose voice is not getting heard, to find out why, and to find ways of including everyone
5. To speak out about differing views and incorrect assumptions, as useful to everyone's cultural learning
6. To be open to being corrected, politely, if making incorrect assumptions about others
7. To agree protocols to deal with assumptions that create unintended offence or negative consequences for others.

Thinking about culture

When thinking about cultural assumptions, it is useful to bear in mind these basic considerations.

Cultures are not homogeneous Just because some people you have met or read about from a specific country, religion, nation, ethnicity or other cultural group hold a particular view or behave in a certain way, this does not mean that others from those groups think or act the same. (Consider the diversity of views amongst your own friends and family.)

Cultures are 'dynamic' They change all the time. What was true of a set of people yesterday will usually change, either radically or in subtle ways. Few British people wear bowler hats or cloth caps any more!

Dimensions of difference – and similarity

When a new group forms, including if one person joins a pre-formed group or community, nobody really knows which experiences and assumptions are shared by all or differ significantly. It is useful to create space to get to know each other. Find out what helps or prevents each person from joining in and feeling they belong.

Look for common ground

There may be more shared experiences, values and understandings than is immediately apparent. Finding common ground helps the group. It provides a good basis for building bridges.

Check for potential differences

The more diverse the group, the more likely it is that there will be varied perspectives on almost any issue. This is an advantage for an effective and dynamic learning community, although it might be challenging at times. An important starting point is to find out what kinds of difference are felt to be significant to everyone concerned.

Key dimensions of cultural diversity

When exploring similarities and differences, some generic areas to consider are listed below. These are just to get you started: feel free to add others.

Cultural icons

★ What are the things that individuals miss most if they are studying away from home?

★ Which aspects of their own cultures are valued most by group members?

★ What are favourite foods, sports, music? Are any shared by the group?

Values and ethics

★ Are any values shared by everyone in the group?

★ What are the values that matter most to you?

★ What matters most to others?

Rights and responsibilities

★ Are there any that everyone agrees on?

★ Has everyone experienced such rights so far?

Educational experience

★ What was everyone's experience of study and assessment before this course?

★ How might any key differences make it easier or more difficult for some students to take part or to undertake certain study tasks at first?

★ Use pages 206–7 to help stimulate areas for discussion.

Experience of current study

★ What does each person enjoy about the course and/or being a student – and why?

★ What do they find challenging – and why?

★ What kind of mutual support would people in the group value – and why?

Same or different?

Be aware that something that seems obvious to one set of people, is not to others. It is worth checking out attitudes about what is considered to be …

★ good or bad

★ the right body language

★ the polite form of address

★ constructive or rude

★ wise or foolish

★ commonplace or odd

★ straightforward or puzzling

★ affordable or expensive

★ individualistic or social

★ moral or of dubious morality

★ feasible or impossible

★ something you talk about in public – or not.

Appreciating different cultures and languages

Appreciating your own culture

1 What do you think of as core to your culture?
2 How different is this from other cultures? How do you know?
3 Of which aspects of your culture are you most proud?
4 Are there things you wish were not part of your culture or that you disagree with?

Heroes and heroines?

1 Who are the heroes and heroines revered in your country or community?
2 What values do such heroes and heroines represent?
3 Are these values that are important to you?

National stereotypes

1 How are people from your own background conveyed in stereotypes such as in the media, other countries or other groups?
2 How does that stereotype differ from the realities of people you know?
3 How do you feel about such stereotypes?
4 Do others in your group know you feel that?

The power of history, time and place

How have history, personal experience, time and place shaped your own everyday assumptions?

Reflection

Being known

What might students not know about you that could affect:

★ Their ability to understand you?
★ Their ability to avoid offending you?
★ Their ability to include and support you?

Same words, different nuances

English is used as the medium of communication in many places where it isn't the first language. Spending time with people from other cultures helps you discover rich associations that an English word might have in particular countries and communities. For example, 'lucky money' has specific connotations in China that it doesn't elsewhere. Even within a country such as the UK, local expressions vary (such as 'go the messages' in Scotland refers to doing your shopping).

Activity

Find out differences

Are there ways that English words or expressions are used differently in the regions, cultures or countries of people in your group?

Language challenge

Learn to communicate a few core phrases in several languages, verbally and in writing.

Find out how to say the following in the languages of people in your group. Jot them down (with tips on how to pronounce them and when to use them – or not).

Hello	Goodbye
Yes	No
Welcome	Join us
Please	Thank you
Okay	What do *you* think?
That's great!	Sorry
Are you hungry?	Are you thirsty?
Are you tired?	Are you OK?
Can I help you?	Can you help me?

Being part of a welcoming, inclusive group

In others' shoes

Whether you are a home or international student, consider what it might be like to study on your course for students from a different country from yourself.

Reflection

Studying with students from other nations

Be aware of challenges facing international students. Highlight any of the following that are typical experiences for students on your course.

1 Getting used to everything being different
2 Missing family and friends
3 Homesickness
4 Social isolation and loneliness
5 Not knowing 'how things are done here'
6 Not knowing what is expected of them
7 Finding the right words in a foreign language
8 Not understanding conversations
9 Food is unfamiliar
10 Nothing looks the same in the shops
11 Missing important communications
12 Financial difficulties when far from home
13 Not being eligible for some kinds of support
14 May not be able to work (for visa reasons)
15 Everyday life or study tasks take much longer because they are unfamiliar
16 Things take longer because of having to translate information from English first.

★ What other challenges are you aware of?
★ How do you think these challenges have an impact on international students?

How can I help?

Many of the ways of supporting international students are those you would use to get to know and include any other student. A generally welcoming approach, interest in others, awareness that everyone has a different story and needs support or understanding about something – these take you a long way.

Be welcoming

★ A smile or wave – a small gesture that eases anxieties and helps someone feel they belong
★ A simple greeting, such as hi, hello, how are you? etc. can help people feel noticed
★ A short chat can help overcome a sense of isolation and may open up a new friendship
★ An invitation to a coffee with the rest of the group can help ease homesickness
★ Being asked for help can make others feel valued
★ A few interested questions can make people feel they count.

Just ask ...

★ Ask if other students are settling in OK
★ Ask if there are things you can explain
★ Ask if there are things you can do to help
★ Ask if they know many people yet
★ Ask about their interests
★ Ask them for help – so they feel useful too.

Planning to study abroad?

If you are planning to study or work abroad, find out about any significant differences in teaching, learning, assessment, support and cultural life before deciding where to study.

Reflect and discuss

Use the reflective activities on pages 206–7 to help you think through some typical areas where students' experiences differ.

How different are the ways we do things?

For each of the statements below, consider whether A or B better represents your experience. Indicate this ✓ on the dotted line, nearest the statement which you find most true of your culture or country. If it is only 'sort of true', make your X nearer to the centre of the box ...X... There aren't 'right' answers.

(A)	Rating A B	(B)
1 It is not polite to talk about yourself	. . . .	**1** It is OK to talk a lot about yourself
2 People don't usually talk about emotions	. . . .	**2** People talk a lot about emotions
3 Sport is not important to student life	. . . .	**3** Sport is a large part of student life
4 Alcohol isn't allowed / I can't drink alcohol	. . . .	**4** Alcohol is a big feature of student life
5 I spend time regularly in quiet, meditation, prayer or contemplation	. . . .	**5** I never take time for quiet, meditation, prayer or contemplation
6 You should usually do as your community decides is best	. . . .	**6** You should usually make your own decisions, as an individual
7 Social media are irrelevant	. . . .	**7** Social media are essential
8 You should try to help others	. . . .	**8** You should focus on yourself
9 People are expected to talk quietly	. . . .	**9** It is OK to talk as loudly as you like
10 It is expected that you mainly create space for *others* to speak in conversations	. . . .	**10** It is expected that you mainly create space for *yourself* to speak in conversations
11 Socialising with other students is not considered particularly important	. . . .	**11** Socialising with other students is considered an important part of student life
12 I rarely meet people from other countries or cultures	. . . .	**12** I am used to living with people from diverse cultural and international heritages
How many of my ratings are nearer to A? _____	**A or B**	*How many of my ratings are nearer to B?* ____

Reflection

How different or similar are our lives?

★ Notice whether your ratings are strongly A or B for any *items*. Then consider for a moment what it would be like to be a student at your Uni or college for whom the opposite is the case for those items.

★ Consider whether your overall experience is more like A or B, and whether that is strongly, moderately or mildly so. Or maybe your experience is more mixed or somewhere in the middle? Does anyone else in your group share a similar ratings profile to yours?

★ Consider how different ratings across your course might affect inter-cultural understandings.

How different are our experiences of study?

For each of the statements below, consider whether A or B better represents your experience of study up to now. Indicate this ✓ on the dotted line . . . **X** . . . If your experience isn't strongly of either A or B, your X will be nearer to the centre of the line. There isn't a 'right' answer, just your experience.

(A)	Rating A B	(B)
1 Students speak a lot in class	. . . .	1 Students never speak in class
2 Students should challenge the views of tutors and experts	. . . .	2 Students shouldn't challenge the views of teachers or experts
3 Students are expected to raise positive and negative aspects of a theory or idea	. . . .	3 Students are expected to identify only what is positive in a theory or idea
4 Assessment involves a lot of writing of essays, papers or reports	. . . .	4 Assessment does not involve writing essays, papers or reports
5 Exam answers focus on reasoning	. . . .	5 Exam answers focus on memory
6 It is typical to express what you mean explicitly, with quite a lot of detail	. . . .	6 It is typical to share implicit understandings rather than state things explicitly
7 Study involves a lot of group work	. . . .	7 Study doesn't include any group work
8 It is acceptable to ask for help	. . . .	8 Students don't usually ask for help
9 Assessment is infrequent	. . . .	9 Students do several tests a week
10 Each exam or assessment carries a high weighting towards final grades	. . . .	10 Each exam or assessment carries a low weighting towards final grades
11 It is important to cite sources as soon as you mention them in your work	. . . .	11 It isn't considered important to cite your sources
12 It is OK to ask any question in class	. . . .	12 You shouldn't waste class time on frivolous questions
How many of my ratings are nearer to A? _____	**A or B**	*How many of my ratings are nearer to B?* _____

Reflection

Adapting to different study conditions

★ Notice whether your ratings are strongly A or B for any *items*. Then consider for a moment what it would be like to be a student at your Uni or college for whom the opposite is the case for those items.

★ Consider whether the expectations for your current course are more like A or B. Does anyone else in your group share a similar profile of expectations to yours?

★ How might you, or other students, need to adapt if you changed from a course that had expectations from the opposite column?

© Stella Cottrell (2019) *The Study Skills Handbook*, 5th edition, Red Globe Press

Developing cultural competence

Effective inter-cultural group work

Gain the full group potential

Everyone should gain from the collective wisdom of the group. The group misses out if someone isn't contributing to their best.

★ Find out the expertise in the group.

★ Find out the best way of getting everyone to shine so you benefit from their being in your group.

★ Don't assume someone who says little, or says too much, hasn't a different side to them. Make the group a place where everyone can relax into their best side, rather than putting up protective shields of silence or noise.

Working together on a task

If group work is used on your course, start by checking each person's experience and understanding of this way of studying. Some people in your group may be used to it; others might find it alien. In either case, there will be some who enjoy it and others who don't; some who are confident and others who find it stressful.

1 What experience has everyone had of this activity/issue/problem/way of working before?

2 What does everyone think they can gain from the study activity?

3 Are there things people are anxious about – either for the task or for doing it as a group? How can you address these as a group?

4 For each person, what are 'pet hates' and 'big likes'? Take these on board when deciding how to do things and who does what.

5 What will help each person to contribute and participate most easily and with least stress?

Ask about non-participation

If someone isn't contributing, find out what is going on for them.

★ Show kind interest. Let them know you have noticed that they are not taking part.

★ Ask if the group is difficult for them and why? Is there anything that would make it easier for them to contribute?

Be language-sensitive

In groups with mixed languages, be sensitive to …

★ How fast people are speaking: check whether you should slow down.

★ Whether the group is using expressions or cultural references (such as TV programmes, festivals, celebrities) that need explaining.

★ Whether all group members understand the task or instructions. If not, clarify this: it helps your own understanding to explain to others.

★ Be patient and supportive in helping students note down new phrases.

★ Ask and learn how key subject-related concepts are expressed in other languages.

Group bonding

★ Make opportunities to chat outside of study sessions, so you get to know each other better. This allows for more difficult issues to emerge more naturally.

★ Do things together, so you create shared experiences you can chat about as a group.

Capture the inter-cultural learning

Groups as learning 'labs'

Many student groups are like cross-cultural learning labs – great for getting to understand how and why people think and do things differently.

It can also be surprising to discover how similar people's starting places are in terms of expectations, assumptions and problem-solving, as well as how and why they differ. This is useful for the group, and opens up interesting areas for you to explore and reflect upon to make sense of other inter-cultural contexts.

Capture the inter-cultural learning

The inter-personal and inter-cultural learning you gain from being in mixed groups is invaluable. It is likely that it will be more useful to you in life, over the longer term, than whatever it is you are working on as a study task.

1 Recognise and use the opportunity.

2 Don't be so focused on the immediate study task that you miss out on developing new inter-personal skills and cultural insights.

3 Observe and ask how others think about the task and the way the group is working.

4 Check out what is a personal difference and what is 'cultural'.

5 Capture it: jot down your observations. You never know when it might be useful.

Find an inter-cultural angle

... when working on a group project, seminar presentation or other assignment.

★ Use examples or case studies from different cultures or from around the world.

★ Make sure sample groups are representative of people from different backgrounds.

★ Ask group members to provide examples relevant to their own backgrounds.

Test out research findings

Studying in a diverse group provides a great opportunity for sounding out the results of research studies related to your course. Typically, studies are based on relatively narrow samples; this means that there is a good chance that they might not include the experiences or circumstances represented by people in your group.

★ Check details of the sample used in studies that are recommended as reading for your course or that your group is using as background material. How representative is it of people in your group – or of their communities and countries?

★ Check whether those in your group consider that the findings in a given study are likely to hold true for them or their communities or home countries. If not, explore the reasons why this might be the case.

★ Consider whether you could replicate the research as a student project, drawing on a different sample group. Your group's findings could raise interesting points for discussion in class or in your project report.

Even if it is not possible to replicate the results, you might be able to draw on insights from your group's cross-cultural experience when making a critique of research studies, theories or professional practice based on these. You could make suggestions about areas where future research using a different sample might reasonably be expected to modify current understandings. If your arguments and reasoning are strong and well-presented, this could add value to your assignments.

Different styles of communicating

It can be useful to be aware of key cultural differences in communicating. Some were raised on pages 206–7. Here are some others to consider.

Respect and politeness

Across cultures, people want others to show them respect and to save face in front of others. Nobody wants to feel shamed, uncomfortable or ignorant in front of others (Scudamore, 2013). The ways that different cultures demonstrate respect or respond to disrespect can be diametrically opposed, such as *either* ...

★ saying things directly – *or* – indirectly

★ avoiding eye contact – *or* – valuing being looked in the eye when talking

★ showing enthusiasm for something even when you don't feel it – *or* – giving an honest opinion even if it is negative

★ expecting accurate and constructive feedback – *or* – finding it rude to receive feedback

★ asking if you don't know or don't understand – *or* – concealing when you don't understand

★ offering food or gifts to others – *or* – this isn't usually done

★ making physical contact such as through shaking hands, kissing cheeks, etc. – *or* – not making physical contact

★ valuing informality – *or* – valuing formality.

Responding to requests

In some cultures, you only agree to do something if you can do what is needed; if you can't, you say so and/or apologise. That is polite in that culture but considered shocking in others.

For people from other cultures it is rude to refuse a request so that, when abroad, they are constantly being asked to do things (because they always say 'yes'!) As a result, they struggle to find the time, money or expertise to do what they agreed.

Either way, misunderstandings can cause difficulties and bad feelings unless the difference is recognised and understood.

Reflection
Communication styles

For people in groups that you are in, what are the different ways that respect and politeness are demonstrated in their cultures?

Silence across cultures

Silence can mean different things depending on the culture or the individual. It might mean ...

★ A sign of paying close attention

★ Courtesy: leaving space for others to think

★ Courtesy: leaving space for others to speak

★ A sign of respect for what has just been said

★ A sign of respect for the issue being discussed

★ A sign of respect for the previous speaker

★ A sign of distress

★ A sign of shock

★ General respect for quiet or silence

★ Confidence in leaving silences

★ A way of avoiding conflict

★ Taking time to formulate thoughts clearly

★ Waiting for inspiration

★ Lack of confidence in speaking

★ Lack of trust that others will want to understand

★ Needing time to find the right words in a foreign language.

Reflection
Understanding silence

★ How do communication styles vary in group(s) that you are in?

★ Are some people 'too quiet' or 'too loud'?

★ If so, how effective is the group in making sure everyone gets a chance to contribute?

Case studies

Consider these case studies. Form your own opinion of the different perspectives and what could be done in such circumstances. If possible, discuss these with others from your course or study group.

Case A: The quiet student

Towards the end of her course, Student A, an international student from North Asia, made a presentation as part of her dissertation. She spoke confidently and knowledgeably. Several students commented later how much they enjoyed her talk and her responses to questions from the student audience. Student A was delighted about this but felt uncomfortable by some comments that accompanied this praise, such as: 'I didn't know you could speak!' and 'Imagine how much you could have gained from the course if you had spoken out before now!'

The perspectives of students in the class were that:

★ if students didn't join in or speak up, nobody knew what they were really like, so they missed out on social events and study groups

★ you learn less if you are quiet in class

★ it was up to quiet students to find a voice and make space to speak, as a useful skill

★ that it wasn't fair on the rest of the class if some people didn't participate fully.

Student A's perspective was that:

★ the whole group should have prevented some students from dominating discussions, question times and decision-making

★ the individuals who took up a lot of class time should have learnt to take turns better, as a useful skill, leaving space for others to speak

★ by being quiet, she heard what others had to say, so gained rather than missing out

★ the class culture meant that everyone missed out on what quieter students had to offer

★ it was contrary to her culture to speak out or complain. It wasn't something she could do.

Case B: Outside the group

By the time Student B was offered a place on his course, term was about to begin. Because of problems arranging accommodation, he joined his classes over a week late. He missed events for new students such as campus tours, introduction to the course, social events, trips, talks by student services and last year's students. He also missed notices about changes to the timetable.

Student B worked hard to catch up but annoyed others by arriving late for classes at first and asking questions about things already covered. Other students complained that he wasn't 'serious' about study.

Each week, after seminars, the class met in the campus café for lunch. Nobody mentioned this to Student B so he didn't realise. He noticed that others seemed to be getting to know each other well and invited each other to join them for small group activities. He felt embarrassed having to ask to join groups and sometimes just left the room instead.

He noticed that Student C, who had also arrived late, now seemed to be included. Apparently, that student had brought in food to celebrate a religious festival. Student B felt ashamed that nobody seemed to like him or want to know him. Sometimes, he wondered if it was because of his accent, ethnicity, background or appearance, and felt angry and confused. As a result, he didn't say much in class and left campus once each class finished.

Reflection

Case studies

★ What are your thoughts about these scenarios?

★ If similar things were happening on your course, how would you know?

★ What would you consider to be the best, practical ways forward?

Review

1 **Be open and curious**
Be active in thinking through what you can do to enhance your cultural awareness and understanding.

2 **Learn more about your own culture**
Take pride in its achievements. Be confident enough about your cultural identity to be able to praise, question and critique it.

3 **Recognise benefits**
Build your motivation for developing cultural competence by identifying ways that this benefits you and people you know, as well as the broader benefits for others.

4 **Clarify cultural assumptions**
Understand how and why these arise. Become better informed so that you can avoid making incorrect assumptions that others find annoying, offensive or undermining.

5 **Appreciate difference**
Become more familiar with the variety of ways that people live, think, interact and study depending on where they are from and what they have been used to. Take an interest and search out the positive benefits and opportunities that arise from cultural diversity.

6 **Identify similarities**
Find points of shared interest and experience to build bridges across cultures and as a starting point for conversations and friendships.

7 **Welcome and include**
Take responsibility for helping everyone on your course, or in your groups, to feel welcome and comfortable. Watch out for those who might be especially vulnerable to getting left out.

8 **Extend your communication**
Learn to communicate better across cultural groups. Learn useful phrases and starting places for conversations.

9 **Check starting points**
When starting out in a new group, share starting points, skills and experiences so that any gaps or differences can be addressed.

10 **Respect sensitivities**
Be aware of areas of potential sensitivity to individuals and groups and respect that these can be deep-rooted and important to those concerned. Help others understand things that matter to you.

11 **Capture the inter-cultural learning**
Take advantage of the opportunities for gaining insights about diversity. Use the diversity of the group to benefit your study and assignments.

12 **Take away your own messages**
Consider what is most important to you about inter-cultural competence. What will be challenging? How will you cope with the challenges?

Chapter 10

Effective reading and note-making

Learning outcomes

This chapter offers you opportunities to:

✓ **fine-tune your skills in reading and note-making suitable for higher levels of study**

✓ **develop approaches that will help you manage heavy reading loads typical at this level**

✓ **consider how to adapt your reading and note-making for different types of study task**

✓ **develop effective reading and note-making strategies that save time and aid recall.**

Traditionally, studying at university is referred to as 'reading for a degree', a testament to the centrality of reading to building knowledge and understanding. For almost any subject studied in Higher Education, reading and making notes are essential tasks. They usually take up a great proportion of independent study time.

Although most students have been reading since childhood, reading at such an advanced level still brings great challenges. Typically, these include:

★ Coping with the volume of reading

★ Selecting what to read

★ Deciding what to use from what they read

★ Getting reading done in time

★ Making sense of difficult material

★ Becoming familiar with the style and vocabulary of specialist academic texts – these can disrupt established reading patterns

★ Concerns about reading speed

★ Interpreting texts with sufficient criticality

★ Remembering or being able to find again the material they have read.

Similarly, most students are familiar with making notes. However, if they don't make their own notes, using effective strategies, they waste time, can't find material they have covered, and don't understand and remember well the material covered on the course. The way that you make notes can have a significant effect on your ability to find, recall and apply information in practical contexts, such as in exams, the workplace, the lab or studio.

This chapter considers these two essential skills of reading and note-making from the perspective of university-level study.

Take your reading to a higher level

Identifying and selecting relevant material when reading

Read selectively

Use the reading list

Some courses provide long reading lists, and expect you to select items from these. Others provide a short list, expecting you to read everything on it and to supplement this through your own searches. If in doubt, ask what is expected.

Select the latest information

★ To keep up to date, google your subject to check for new titles or watch out for these in bookshops, the library and reviews in journal articles.

★ Check whether statistics and data in texts you are using are the latest – or whether more recent figures are available.

See pages 242–3.

Select the most relevant information

★ Look for the information that relates most exactly to your assignment.

★ Draw up an initial essay plan to help identify the information you need. Draw on themes covered in lectures and taught sessions.

★ Check the back cover of printed books that seem relevant, the contents list and the index to see what it covers. Alternatively, read the summaries provided by online suppliers.

★ Quickly scan the introduction or conclusion of the book: these may indicate whether the book is useful, and might provide all the information you need.

★ Browse through the headings to gain a feel for the book and where to find what you need.

Select by reliability

★ Is the source a well-known one in the field, such as a recommended academic journal?

★ Is the source likely to be biased? If so, does that affect the way you would use it?

★ Does the text have a good bibliography? Is it clear what evidence it uses?

★ Is the source from a publisher respected in your subject area? (Information in newspapers or from friends is not usually considered reliable.)

See also **Critical analytical thinking**, Chapter 12, page 263.

Select by amount

★ Use your essay plan to work out a word limit for each major theme, and then for each topic or example that you will include in your assignment. You will find that you can allocate only a few words to write about any one item.

★ Use your word limits to guide you on how much to read and note. If you can only write a line or paragraph about something, you probably don't need to read or note much.

★ Consider whether an article goes into too much depth for your purposes: you may only need to read the abstract or a section.

★ Keep questioning whether material is relevant given the title of the project, essay or report and your assignment brief.

What do I actually need to read?

If you usually read books from cover to cover, have a go at the following exercise to see how little you could read and still find what you need.

Activity

How much do I need to read?

★ Read the back cover. Browse the contents page, section headings, and the last chapter. Make a few quick notes on what appear to be the main points of the book. Record just the gist, or key points, of what you read.

★ Read the introductory and concluding paragraphs of each chapter. When you finish reading, note any extra important information.

★ Read the first line of each paragraph of one chapter. Note any additional important information.

★ Now, read the whole book. How much really important *additional* information did you gain by reading the whole book? Which parts of the book were essential? How little could you have read to grasp the essentials?

Am I a smart reader?

Do you use effective reading strategies? Which of the following do you use?

Know exactly what you are looking for

☐ Do I consider the questions I'm trying to answer?

☐ Do I consider what information I need?

Use reading lists selectively

☐ Do I use the recommended reading list?

☐ Do I know what I *need* to read?

Examine sources for suitability

For each source, do I consider whether:

☐ it's on the reading list?

☐ it's up to date or fairly recent?

☐ it looks readable and manageable?

☐ it has the information I want?

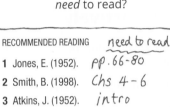

RECOMMENDED READING — *need to read*

1 Jones, E. (1952). *pp. 66–80*
2 Smith, B. (1998). *Chs 4–6*
3 Atkins, J. (1952). *intro*

Activity

Practise finding information quickly

Using an index (at the back of the book):

★ Select an item to look up.

★ Note the page numbers given.

★ Using these, find the item in the book as quickly as you can.

Index
eggs 6, 19
Elba 114
elk 1, 94
ewes 37

How long did this take you? Could you get faster? Did you notice that when you know what you're looking for, your eyes can pick out information on the page more quickly?

Select relevant parts of the book

☐ Do I browse the book quickly?

☐ Do I use the contents page, the headings and the sub-headings for guidance?

☐ Do I flag, bookmark and/ or highlight the sections I really need, for speed in locating this later?

Select relevant parts of the page

☐ Do I read the chapter heading?

☐ Do I read any sub-headings?

☐ Do I read the first sentence of each paragraph (which should introduce the topic or idea)?

☐ Do I look at any diagrams, graphs or charts?

☐ Do I read any summaries or conclusions?

Find information quickly

☐ Do I make good use of the index?

☐ Have I got faster with practice?

Using my own copy

- ☐ Do I get my own copies of the most important texts (or pages within these)?

- ☐ Do I colour-code material on the same theme to help me find it again later?

- ☐ Do I restrict highlighting just to key words and phrases?

- ☐ Do I jot ideas and thoughts in the margins? (see page 221).

- ☐ Do I make notes about the points I highlighted, to help myself remember them?

Chart the main ideas

- ☐ Do I map out ideas so that I can see how everything fits together?

Practise prediction

- ☐ Am I active in anticipating what is coming next, or what the conclusions will be? This can speed reading and help understanding and recall.

Read interactively

- ☐ Do I think about what I'm reading?

- ☐ Do I question what I'm reading?

- ☐ Do I set questions to focus and guide my reading?

- ☐ Do I make notes of the important points and ideas triggered by what I read?

- ☐ Do I challenge the assumptions of the writer, the logic of the arguments, and the validity of the conclusions?

Vary reading speed and method

- ☐ Do I keep changing my pace, according to the needs of the text? (see page 214).

- ☐ Do I scan rapidly for specific information?

- ☐ Do I read quickly to get the general sense of a passage, and then read difficult or dense parts slowly?

Make posters to link information

- ★ As you read, make reduced copies of short key passages, maps and diagrams. Organise these out onto a poster or chart for your wall or workspace.

- ★ Link ideas using colour and arrows.

- ★ Annotate with your own notes.

- ★ These posters are very useful for revision.

What is the main point or basic idea I have just read?

Can I sum it up in 10 words?

Do I agree?

Engage with your reading

Be active in your reading. As you read, always have writing tools to hand.

Using two recorders

If you have two recording devices, record your ideas into one as you listen to material on the other.

Use markers

- ☐ Do I label a corner of my own texts with a keyword summary?

- ☐ Do I insert labelled bookmarks so that I can find details easily, and need fewer notes?

- ☐ Do I use tabs and give star ratings to useful pages, to help me select material later?

Listen to yourself read

- ☐ Do I record myself reading important passages – so I hear material in my own voice?

- ☐ Do I listen to material as I travel, or work around the house?

There are three major conclusions…

Maintain your attention

I read that three times and I don't remember a word…

- ☐ Do I take in what I read?

- ☐ Do I make sure I'm doing so, by:

  - * summing up each section?

  - * taking regular breaks?

  - * reading interactively?

  - * moving on when material isn't relevant?

Create ideal conditions

- ☐ Do I read with the light from behind, sufficient to light the page but without glare?

- ☐ Do I sit with a relaxed, upright posture?

- ☐ I get my eyes tested regularly!

Reading off the computer screen

- ☐ Do I know whether I read best from screen or from paper?

- ☐ Do I re-format text on-screen to make it easier to read?

Consider time and place

- ☐ Do I read when I am sufficiently awake and alert?

- ☐ Is my study environment conducive to reading in a focused way?

I prefer Arial font 16 blue

Increase your understanding of what you read

Check your understanding

Don't assume you understand just because you can follow the text when reading: check it out.

Could you also ...

- [ ] Remember it, broadly, without looking?
- [ ] State it in a few sentences, without looking?
- [ ] Explain it aloud (to real or imaginary persons)?
- [ ] Turn it into questions and answers? (You can then use these for flashcards for revision.)
- [ ] Reproduce it as a diagram or infographic (or through a demonstration if relevant to the material).

Aim to grasp the ideas

Read reasonably quickly so you can pick up the main ideas. Reading too slowly or pausing often to look up the meaning of new words can make it difficult to grasp the main message. If there are things you don't understand at first, flag these and return to them later. They may make more sense when you have read on. If not, you can then work through relevant sections more slowly, looking up words and concepts you aren't sure about.

Look for clues

Introductions and conclusions to texts, chapters or sections help in setting the scene. Headings and sub-headings can throw light on which are the key learning blocks and main ideas in the text.

Check its context

Material can make more sense if you know why it was written. Who wrote it? What was their intention in writing it? What argument were they trying to prove or which problems were they trying to resolve? Did they have particular objectives in mind?

Highlight selectively

If you underline or highlight everything, *nothing* will stand out as important. Identify a few key words or headings. Annotate with stars or comments to indicate just the most important points.

Colour-code information

Use different colours for different kinds of information – for example, one colour for reference names and dates, and one for each school of thought or major theory. That colour combination on the page can refresh recall later.

Look for published reviews of it

Check journals around the time the text was published to see if it was reviewed. If so, the review might summarise or clarify key points.

Apply the C·R·E·A·M learning strategy

Consider how you can apply the C·R·E·A·M strategy (Chapter 5) to your reading.

Don't ...

Don't pause at every difficult section at first view. Skim these and come back to them.

Don't just keep re-reading a passage in the same way. Vary your reading strategy.

Don't copy it out. It takes too long, exposes you to cheating, and doesn't help understanding.

Reflection

Reading with understanding

How do I approach reading tasks now?

How could I spend my reading time more effectively?

Is it worth re-reading material you don't understand?

It may seem that if you can't understand material when you first read it, you never will – and then there would be no point in re-reading it. That isn't necessarily the case. Test that out for yourself.

It can be useful to re-read the same information because ...

1 You may have missed information the first time round, especially if the subject is new to you.
2 Complex material can be hard to grasp in one go. Sometimes it helps to go over small sections, thinking about them and working out what they mean.
3 Consider *why* you didn't understand and address that cause. You might need to learn some specialist terms or check details first.
4 Sometimes, sleeping on it can help.
5 Going over material, rehearsing it mentally, can help you make sense of it.
6 Repeated exposure to facts, formulae or processes helps reinforce these in memory.
7 Make a list of anything you didn't understand. Re-formulate this as a series of questions. See if you can answer these by re-reading, further thinking, or drawing on other materials. If not, ask for help.

Just re-reading many times isn't usually helpful because ...

1 The brain is conditioned to 'zone out' when it encounters situations or material it recognises as familiar. It switches off to information it finds less stimulating, or 'redundant'. Feed it a new angle.
2 You may get bored and find your attention wanders, which wastes your time and reduces your motivation, interest and mood.
3 It is easier to waste time when your attention drifts – you may not notice that you have lost concentration and focus.
4 When you read only one source, you have only a single point of reference. That makes it more difficult to find natural points of curiosity, such as why two texts seem to differ on key facts or statistics. You have to work harder to exercise critical thinking.

When re-reading, vary your reading strategy to avoid such problems.

Reading similar material in other texts can help because ...

1 Similar is not the same as 'identical'. Focus your attention to identify where differences lie. Draw out, clarify and note similarities, differences and inconsistencies in a chart or as lists.
2 Contrasting two or more texts draws attention to details you might miss otherwise. It helps you to notice subtle differences in interpretations, opinions, data or perspectives.
3 It shows you how various writers conceptualise and express the same issue in different ways. Your brain can draw upon, and synthesise, these variants to devise its own informed perspective.
4 You develop a richer mental schema of the topic or issues, building expertise and assisting recall.

Reading books of different levels of difficulty can help because ...

1 A basic text, such as one designed for younger students or the general public, provides a quick initial overview; it helps you see, later, where details fit into the big picture.
2 Advanced texts provide mental 'stretch'. Over time, you become familiar with greater levels of difficulty, raising your level of expertise.
3 Specialist texts can inspire new ideas.
4 Experts can benefit by seeing how complex issues are communicated to novices; this can help you clarify or simplify your thinking if it has become over complicated.
5 It is easy to forget the basics when operating at a high level: it is good to review them.

Develop your expert 'reader voice'

What is the 'reader voice'

Students who do well tend to maintain a lively inner commentary on tasks they undertake and with texts they read. This can involve questions, re-questioning, suggestions, criticism, querying the wisdom of doing something, reasoning about what to do or not to do, humour, releasing frustration, instructions to the self and more.

How does this help?

A focused inner commentary helps maintain attention. It also helps you to direct your attention to finer points of an argument, to pursue an idea, or decide you have pursued an avenue as far as you need to take it.

Reflection

Inner commentary

Notice your own running commentary as you work and read. Is it broadly similar to that below?

Does it remain focused on the task or does it drift onto other tasks?

Does it help you to go deeper into the topic and organise your thoughts and work? If not, re-train your commentary by devising a set of prompts to follow for a while and/or annotate texts as you read (page 221).

Annotating texts when reading

What is 'annotation'?

Annotation is a form of note-making. It involves making comments and marks on the page of a text or document as you read it or work with it. What you note depends on what emerges in your thoughts as you work with the text – which you consider worth marking on it. You can annotate written material, diagrams, formulae, calculations, photographs, and drafts of your assignments – for any subject.

Why annotate?

If you own the text, this is a great way of engaging with it.

Maintaining attention Annotation helps you stay focused, so that you are more likely to take in what you read. You are less likely to drift off or copy out chunks mindlessly.

Capturing a thought It can provide a near complete record of your thought process, so you don't lose it.

Creating memory-joggers When you flick back over a text, annotations can remind you quickly of what you read.

Making sense Interacting with the text can help you work out what it means – and aids recall.

Inspiring your creative interest It generates further thoughts and ideas.

Hooking yourself in It can help you engage emotionally with the material, making it meaningful and memorable.

Finding answers Jotting down questions can, in itself, stimulate your brain to find answers. If not, you have a reminder of things to look up later.

Appreciating, paraphrasing, summarising, reworking, questioning, challenging, checking, emoting ...

Annotation is like a 'conversation' with the text

How to annotate

Keep your thoughts 'live'. As you read, jot down your ideas and responses in the margins, header or footer.

Make material your own. Sum up sections in your own words; combine this with your thoughts, questions, reminders, etc. Highlight, colour code, number, or label sections to make the text work better for you.

Engage emotionally. Use exclamation marks, drawings, emoticons and notes to express your responses.

Stimulate your thinking. Jot down questions prompted by what you read, or connections to other aspects of your course. Write reminders of anything you want to check out further. Jot down why something you read inspired you or could be used in an assignment.

Say why. The 'why' is important if your annotation is to be useful. Otherwise, you may waste time later trying to work out why you marked the text.

Be selective. Some pages are worth annotating; others not. If you annotate and highlight everything, nothing will stand out.

Use your annotations. Return to them and think about those that look useful. Draw out relevant points into your main set of notes. Follow up your ideas, questions, queries, etc.

Example of an annotated text

Page 32

③ *Benefits of mindfulness* ←

1 **Academic and work performance**
There is a great deal of research that indicates that mindfulness <u>improves abilities associated with good performance, such as attention and concentration.</u> Continued (practice) changes the structure of the brain, helping to cement this advantage. It has been found that practised meditators have thicker cortical regions of the brain: these regions are associated with attention and intelligence (Lazar, 2005). See page 27.

2 **Empathy** Metta-style meditation (Chapter 21) increases neural activation in parts of the brain that pick up on emotional cues. This suggests a capacity for greater empathy and interpersonal skills (Lutz et al., 2008).

3 **Creativity and 'whole person' development** A report on the findings of over 40 years of research found that, as well as cognitive benefits, mindfulness practice enhanced a wide range of abilities and personal attributes, from increased creativity and self-compassion to empathy and interpersonal skills (Shapiro, 2008).

could benefit students! See pp34-5 ←

do you really need practice? Check p? ←

Can anyone achieve this? With time? ←

☺ ←

Metta: focuses on compassion (see Ch 21.) ←

meditation stimulates parts of brain assoc. w/ empathy ←

<u>*Read this*</u> *report for essay!* ←

Useful for my clinical practice !? ←

Examples of types of annotations

Your own headings and numbers, to help you draw out, list, label and organise the material you find most relevant, so it stands out from the rest

Comments: about why something is interesting/inspiring

Challenges: if something seems to you to warrant further checking out, or looks incorrect, contradictory, untrue, etc.

Questions that occur to you – and any answers these then prompt

Highlights, underlining and symbols linked to your written notes, to help relevant material stand out

Definitions and clarifications: of specialist terms or jargon that you may not have come across before

Summaries – paraphrase complex material, using your own words, to help tease out, and record its meaning

Flags to material you know you need – if particularly relevant to a work project or assignment title

Meaningful connections – draw out links to your experience in life or work, or to other reading

Source: Cottrell, S. (2018). *Mindfulness for Students*. London: Red Globe Press; p. 32.

Good annotating

Annotation is most useful when ...	Not so useful when ...
✓ **... you capture your thoughts in writing** as you go, so you have a good record	✗ ... you are just highlighting or underlining, ☺ drawing emoticons, making !!! – i.e. with less thoughtful interaction, less impression on the mind
✓ **... you engage your mind with the material** – interacting with it through questioning, challenging, appreciating, paraphrasing, interpreting, reflecting meaningfully, etc.	
✓ **... you link and connect ideas** on the page with each other, with other course materials, with your experience, etc.	✗ ... you highlight or flag or annotate everything – as nothing then stands out as important. Be selective!
✓ **... you clarify 'why'** you think something is interesting, useful, inspiring, questionable or incorrect, explaining your thoughts	✗ ... you don't make further use of your annotations
✓ **... you identify what is significant**: pick out the most significant material to highlight and annotate, so your thoughts about the issue stand out.	

Self-evaluation

Rate yourself for each of the following statements using a scale of 0–5, where 5 is very useful, and 0 not useful at all.

How useful is the way I annotate now?	Useful ... Not useful < - - - - - - - - - - - - - - >					
1 It helps me to capture my thoughts when reading	5	4	3	2	1	0
2 It helps me think more carefully about what I read	5	4	3	2	1	0
3 It encourages me to ask questions about what I read	5	4	3	2	1	0
4 It helps me think more critically about what I read	5	4	3	2	1	0
5 It helps me to make sense of what I am reading	5	4	3	2	1	0
6 It helps me to recall the material later	5	4	3	2	1	0
7 My annotations are helpful in flagging the most significant material	5	4	3	2	1	0
8 It helps me find connections in the material	5	4	3	2	1	0
9 My annotations help me to make better course notes	5	4	3	2	1	0
10 My annotations encourage/remind me to check out further details	5	4	3	2	1	0
11 When I look back at my annotations, they still make sense to me	5	4	3	2	1	0
12 I annotate drafts of my assignments, to help me rework the next draft	5	4	3	2	1	0

Reflection

Annotation

If your ratings for any items are lower than you would like, consider how to improve those facets in the next few weeks.

© Stella Cottrell (2019) *The Study Skills Handbook*, 5th edition, Red Globe Press

Increasing your reading speed

Understanding is the most important aspect of reading, but you may wish to improve your reading *speed* too.

Check your reading speed

★ Find something familiar to read.

★ Set the alarm for ten minutes' time.

★ Read for ten minutes at a speed that allows you to understand what you read.

★ Count how many words you read.

★ Divide this number by ten, to find out how many words you read in one minute.

★ Do this using different texts. If you average fewer than 200–250 words per minute, even with material that is clear and interesting, it is worth trying to increase your speed.

Vary your reading strategies

Inspect for usefulness

Check the title, the contents page, the index, the writing style, and the details on the back cover. Flick through to get the feel of the book. Do you *want* to read it? What exactly do you *need* to read in it?

Scan rapidly to locate

Scan the page. Which key words leap out at you? You may sense the 'pattern' of the argument or the general subject matter. This can help you locate what to read. Similarly, see what you can pick up from section headings, diagrams, the first lines of paragraphs, and conclusions to chapters.

Steer attention

Frame questions to help you identify exactly what you need from chapters or sections and to direct your attention to finding it. Keep asking: What am I trying to find out? What do I need to know? Exactly which parts do I need to read?

Use the tools

To find a specific piece of information quickly, don't forget to check the contents page and/or index.

Read at the right speed for the task

This may be rapidly for case studies, novels, familiar information and well-developed arguments, and slowly for material that is complex, unfamiliar, written in a condensed style or with specialist vocabulary. As you become more familiar with the ideas and vocabulary used, your speed will increase.

Recall and review

Pause to check that you understand what you read. What is the basic argument or idea? Does the text answer questions you have? Are you convinced by the evidence and the arguments offered? How does what you have read relate to what you already knew? Does it confirm or challenge your views? What else do you need to find out?

What is slowing down your reading?

Below are factors that slow reading. Do any apply to you? If so, apply relevant strategies from page 225.

☐ 1 Do you read advanced texts only rarely?

☐ 2 Do you track with your finger along the line?

☐ 3 Do you read aloud under your breath, or mouth the words?

☐ 4 Do you read books cover to cover?

☐ 5 Do you start reading before you have worked out what you need to know, or what you are looking for?

☐ 6 Do you read word by word?

☐ 7 Do you keep re-reading the line you have just read?

☐ 8 Do you get distracted a lot whilst reading?

☐ 9 Do you read difficult sections before you have worked out the general gist?

☐ 10 Do you find that the words seem to jump up off the page or that text moves or glares?

Strategies for increasing your reading speed

For each of the problems noted on page 224, there is something you can do to improve matters.

1 Read more advanced texts

Let your brain get used to unfamiliar vocabulary and dealing with complex material. Also, look out for subjects that interest you and read more about these for pleasure.

2 Finger-tracking

Move your finger down the page from top to bottom, to train your eye to move more quickly down the text. (See page 215.)

3 Know when to read aloud

Some people read out loud from habit. Reading silently can speed up reading. If you read aloud because it helps you focus, understand or remember better, then have a go at recording yourself so you can re-read 'by ear'.

4, 5 and 10 Read selectively and actively

Use the active reading strategies suggested on pages 215–17. This saves time as you don't read unnecessary material. It also engages your mind better and provides breaks to rest the eyes.

6 Read larger chunks

Allow your eyes to take in larger chunks, either by resting them less frequently along a line, or by taking in larger sections of text as you browse. Experiment with holding the book further away, so that your eyes can take in more at once. This is also less tiring for the eyes, which allows you to read for longer periods.

7 Build up to difficult material

Background knowledge of a subject can increase reading speed. If a text looks difficult, start with easier sections or read something simpler first. Return to difficult material later. (See page 219.)

8 For distractibility

Remove whatever items most distract you and set a reading goal or challenge before starting to read. A few minutes of mindfulness meditation can help settle you to productive reading (Cottrell, 2018).

9 Keep your eyes moving forward

Which of these sentences is easier to read?

A Checking back over back over what what you have read makes understanding checking back makes understanding checking back over makes understanding difficult.

B Checking back over what you have read makes understanding more difficult.

Most people find **B** easier to read because they can take in a larger chunk of memorable 'sense'. Encourage your eyes to keep reading forward to the end of a sentence (to the next full stop). You will then be reading larger units of sense rather than just words and phrases. You can read the whole sentence again if necessary.

10 Jumping and glaring text

★ Coloured filters or plastic folders placed over the page can reduce or stop this. Experiment to find the colour that suits you best.

★ Consult an optometrist – you may benefit from spectacles with coloured lenses.

★ In your word-processing package, use the line-spacing function to double space text. This, enlarged font or altering the colour of the work-space can all ease reading.

★ If the problem is serious and you prefer to 'read by ear', text-to-speech software or audio material may suit you better: consult the disability adviser.

Put understanding first

In some cases, slow reading is preferable:

★ for texts with condensed information, such as many science and medical texts

★ for detailed instructions

★ for formulae and equations

★ for close analysis of texts, such as for law, literature and history.

Making notes

Why make notes?

How many reasons can you find for making notes? After you have noted some, check the diagram on page 227. Are your reasons the same? Which of these reasons matter most to you?

> **Activity**
>
> ### Note-making
>
> Select a passage from a book and make notes on the main points of what you read – or find some notes you have already made.
>
> Compare your notes with the suggestions made below. Consider whether you could improve your note-making strategies.

Making notes for higher level study

* ★ Put writing materials aside – so you won't be tempted to copy out of the book.
* ★ If you are typing your notes, don't type as you read.
* ★ Jot down questions – then note the answers to these as you read.
* ★ Identify and sum up the main ideas of the passage. (Hear them in your own words.)
* ★ Jot down a summary or explanation of what you read in your own words. Write notes that help you understand and remember – rather than worrying about how well you have expressed the point compared with the original.
* ★ Write in brief. Keep summarising – either the whole book, a chapter, a page or a paragraph – all in just a few words. This helps you take in the information and helps prevent you copying out chunks from books to your notes and then into assignments.
* ★ Note *exactly* where information comes from – the source and the page number.
* ★ Note real names and quotations *exactly* as they are written.
* ★ If you do note anything directly from the text, use a different colour so you don't forget that it isn't your own work.
* ★ Leave space to add details later.

How to make notes

There is no one 'best method', but it is worth considering the following points.

What do you need to note?

Be selective: write just what you need. Consider:

* ★ Do I really need this information? If so, which bits exactly?
* ★ Will I really use it? When, and how?
* ★ Have I noted similar information already?
* ★ What questions do I want to answer with this information?

Organise your notes

* ★ See **Reading, recording and using information** (page 245).
* ★ See **Organising information: planning your writing** (page 287).
* ★ Use a separate folder for each subject.
* ★ Arrange points under headings or questions. (Notice how information is organised in this *Study Skills Handbook* to help you find topics quickly.)
* ★ Number and label pages so you can find them easily.
* ★ Keep an updated contents page at the front of each file or folder.

Note-making styles

Nuclear note-taking style: why take notes?

Is making notes a useful activity? Why make notes at all?

A. Useful record
1 of important points for future use
2 of where information comes from.

C. Helps understanding if you:
1 focus on selecting info. to note
2 think through where everything fits
3 build levels of detail outwards from core concepts and information.

WHY TAKE NOTES?

B. Helps completing assignments
1 Helps ideas flow.
2 Helps planning – you can see what info. you have.
3 Assists organisation – you can rearrange and renumber notes in a different order.
4 Helps you get started.

D. Helps memory
1 Summarising material helps you remember it.
2 The physical act of writing helps memory – especially writing by hand rather than typing notes.
3 Pattern notes can be more memorable visually.

E. Helps exam revision
1 Material is well organised.
2 More info. is already in memory. (See page 392.)

Linear notes: strategies for making notes

1 Good note-making: general
1.1 Think before you write
1.2 Keep notes brief
1.3 Keep notes organised
1.4 Use your own words
1.5 Leave spaces – to add notes later

2 Useful strategies
2.1 Note keywords and main ideas
2.2 Write phrases – not sentences
2.3 Use abbreviations
2.4 Use headings
2.5 Number points
2.6 Make the page memorable – with colour, illustrations, and so on
2.7 Link up points – using arrows, dotted lines, colour, numbers, boxes
2.8 Note sources of info. exactly
2.9 Write quotations in a different colour

3 Unhelpful strategies
3.1 Copying chunks and phrases
3.2 Writing more notes than you can use again
3.3 Writing out notes several times to make them neater

4 Tidying messy notes
4.1 Shade, or draw a 'square' around, sections of notes in different colours to make them stand out
4.2 Use shading, changes of colour and headings to divide pages up into clearer sections and to make each page more memorable for revision
4.3 Link stray pieces of information by arrows or colour. Number the sequence in which to read them.

Pattern notes: an example

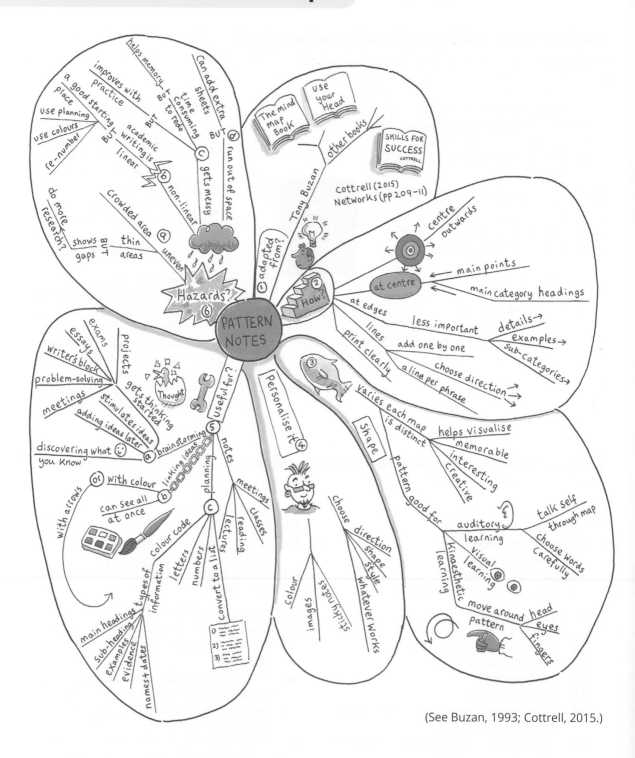

(See Buzan, 1993; Cottrell, 2015.)

Shortcuts in note-making

Plan for amendments

If writing notes by hand, leave space in your notes, and a wide margin, so that you can add new information and ideas later. (This is quicker than *rewriting* your notes to incorporate the new information.) If you type your notes, summarise, edit, highlight and rearrange them from time to time, to help your brain recall them.

Make just one set of notes

Aim to have just one set of notes. Visual familiarity will make it easier to find information later, and to recall information during exams.

Use sticky notes

Carry these with you and use to jot down ideas as they occur. Stick them into a plastic folder. You can add these to charts or posters, moving them around to organise ideas for assignments.

Number the pages

Label and number pages of handwritten notes. Cross-refer to information already noted elsewhere – for instance, 'see red file, page 24, Amphibians'. For electronic notes, number pages and keep a record of where to locate information (page 106).

Use abbreviations

Abbreviations save time. Use them in your notes, but not in assignments.

★ Work out a system you'll remember.

★ Stick to your system.

★ Introduce a few at a time, so that your notes make sense.

★ Keep a 'key' to your abbreviations to hand.

Useful common symbols

& (+)	and
+	plus, in addition to
>	greater/more than/better than
<	smaller/less than
=	is the same as/equal to
≠	is not the same as
\	therefore
[\]	because
w/	with
♀	woman/female
♂	man/male
→	this leads to/produces/causes

Useful common abbreviations

e.g.	for example
i.e.	that is, that means
etc.	and the rest
NB	important, notice this
p.	page (pp. = pages)
para.	paragraph
Ch.	chapter (Chs. = chapters)
edn.	edition
info.	information
cd	could
wd	would
Govt	Government
Educ.	Education
impt	important
devt	development
C19	nineteenth century

Which abbreviations are used in *your* subject areas?

Making notes with confidence

Students' solutions

Sonja and Charlie are two students who used to have great difficulties making notes. Here are their accounts of how they tackled their difficulties, with help from a study-skills tutor.

Sonja

There are two things which I find difficult about making notes.

Firstly, I am not very confident about using my own words – the book always seems to say things better. It is very tempting to use nearly the same words as the book. I imagine that I will rewrite them in my own words later – but then I don't have the time, or I forget which bits are taken from the book, and end up with the words of the book in my essay without even realising.

The second thing I find difficult is working out what to take notes about, especially keeping to essentials. I worry in case I miss out information I will need in the future. I can end up with 10 sides of notes from reading only a few pages. It takes ages and there is too much to even look at a second time. When I came to revise for my first exams, I had too many notes to revise – there were simply too many to read, never mind learn.

Now I spend more time thinking and planning before I even touch a book. I try to work out what information I want. I draw a mind-map with everything I already know, and what I need to find out. If I have an essay title I do a rough plan really early, even before I start reading – just to get the shape in my head.

I always start with the easiest book – just to get a picture of what it is all about. With other books, I use the contents page and headings to work out where information is. At this stage I don't write much except something like 'gold – producer countries: p. 248 and pp. 265–9' – or I annotate the book.

When I have more idea of what I am looking for, and where that information is, I take more detailed notes. Sometimes, I do this by writing a question and putting the information as an answer. When I am not sure if I want some information, I just write a few lines onto an index card, saying where I can find that information later if I really need it.

Charlie

It's taking notes in lectures that I find hardest as I either day drift off and forget to note anything, or I type notes up as I go and make far more notes than I need. It's hard to keep track of what is being said and to select out important points at the same time.

I find it helps if I prepare before the lecture. I browse the topic online and look over the chapters quickly. If something looks complicated, I work out, if I can, what it is about before the lecture. I make notes in advance, or just make a list of the things I have information on already. I make a list of the questions I still need answers to. I don't need to make loads of notes in class then.

We sometimes get podcasts of lectures and I listen to the bits of these that I think will be most useful.

Reflection

Note-making strategy

These are just two approaches to dealing with note-making. Do any of their ideas appeal to you? Or do you have a better system?

Self-evaluation How useful are your notes?

For each of these set of statements, indicate your rating along the line (..✓.......), depending on how far each is a good description of your own notes. You might find it helpful to have a folder of your notes to hand to check. Use this self-evaluation to consider ways you might improve your notes in future.

Strengths	Rating	Weaknesses
1 Easy to take in at a glance	....	Not easy to use at speed
2 Contain the information I need	....	Don't contain what I need
3 Make sense when I come back to them after a few days/weeks	....	Don't make much sense to me when I come back to them
4 Most of the information is relevant	....	Contain lots of irrelevant material
5 All points are completed and followed up if needed	....	Lots of points incomplete or not followed up
6 Everything is clear	....	Notes are jumbled/confused
7 Inviting to look at and read again	....	Messy or uninviting
8 Laid out in ways that assist recall	....	No features to help recall
9 Selective, drawing out only key points, themes, issues, debates	....	Not selective; I include material I don't need and won't use
10 Well-structured	....	No apparent structure
11 Significant points stand out	....	Not easy to spot important points
12 Succinct/concise	....	Too wordy
13 Well-abbreviated	....	Poor use of abbreviations
14 All written in my own words (apart from quotations/references)	....	Chunks copied from books, articles, internet, class, etc.
15 My own words are clearly set apart from quotations	....	Easy to confuse my words with quotations or copied text
16 Sources of information are given clearly, accurately, precisely	....	Vague about where exactly I got the information
17 All pages are numbered or labelled systematically and helpfully	....	Pages are not numbered systematically and helpfully
18 Sets of notes are labelled and stored so they are easy to find in future	....	Sets of notes are poorly organised and labelled; hard to find
19 Good contents list or index helps me find information speedily	....	I don't have a good contents list or index to help me
20 Easy for me to use them and learn from them	....	Difficult for me to use them and learn from them

Reflection

Improving your notes

★ How you might improve your notes and your use of them?

★ What is the priority?

Review

1 Read selectively
Scale the amount of reading you undertake to fit the size of your assignment.

2 Be a smart reader
Use effective, interactive strategies that help you to find relevant information more quickly and absorb it more easily, with enhanced recall.

3 Check your understanding
Pause frequently to check what you are absorbing and what you really understand. Engage your brain rather than just get through the pages.

4 Build reading speed
Build speed if your reading is slow. Consider the task as a whole, not just how quickly you can get through it. Focus on understanding rather than speed.

5 Read widely
Don't just read one book on a topic. Reading a variety of sources will help build your expertise in the subject. It will also improve your vocabulary.

6 Vary the reading level
Draw on books that are below your current level of study, to gain a rapid overview and clarity. Use more advanced texts to gain familiarity with cutting edge research and ideas, and enhance comprehension of complex material.

7 Develop an 'expert reader' voice
Maintain a running commentary that helps you focus attention and go deeper into the material. Enter into a lively dialogue with the material and the task. Talk yourself through it.

8 Annotate texts
If you own the text, make the material your own, too, by interacting with it in ways that give it more meaning for you.

9 Make selective notes
Don't waste time on notes that you don't need and won't use. Sometimes less is more.

10 Write notes by hand
For information you want to remember or understand better, writing your own selective notes by hand is more effective than typing them.

11 Write notes that are really useful
Check over your notes as you write them to make sure they are laid out and organised in ways that will enable you to use them easily.

12 Choose your own style
Your notes are for you. Don't worry if recommended styles don't suit you. Go with what works for you, not for other people.

Chapter 11

Researching and managing information for study

Learning outcomes

This chapter offers you opportunities to:

✓ understand the overall, inter-related sets of processes involved in managing information for academic tasks

✓ define research tasks well in order to facilitate searches and decision-making

✓ fine-tune your abilities in finding, organising and coping with information for higher level study

✓ understand the importance of using appropriate, 'good quality' sources

✓ find out what is meant by 'plagiarism' – and how to avoid it

✓ understand why and how to cite sources and reference your work.

The nature of research

Research is something we all do. It starts with a 'spirit of enquiry', whether this is investigating 'best buys', sports results, new music or finding a cure for diseases. In everyday life, how we go about our research will vary depending on the topic, our purpose in investigating, how much we want to know, and the availability of information. Likewise, for academic study, there are distinct research methods depending on the subject discipline, level of study, source materials or assignment.

Using research rather than opinion

At this level, you are expected to use more than just opinion, common sense or spur-of-the-moment responses. For your course, you will need to demonstrate a deeper understanding and draw on more reliable and expert sources than the average person in the street. In practice, this means you engage in tasks such as searches, reading, experimentation and critical reflection. You draw on these to contribute to class, projects and discussions at an appropriate level and produce assignments of a high standard.

Developing research skills

As you progress through your course, you build on your existing research skills so you can undertake more advanced searches, read greater amounts of specialist material with increasing ease, create your own information sets, and collect your own raw data using specialist methods used in your subject area. You learn to work with information to make it meaningful in the context of your course and assignments.

Managing information

You find, generate and use a vast amount of information whilst studying. That can be daunting at times, not least in selecting what is really useful to your purpose. It helps to step back and gain an overview of the processes involved and consider how you will manage each. Finding, organising, evaluating and citing information are essential skills for students, and the focus of this chapter.

Other skills essential to effective student research, such as reading, note-making, critical analysis and writing up are covered in separate chapters.

Managing information for academic study

Start by using and adapting the overview below to chart your own bird's eye view of processes involved.

2 Using material of suitable quality and content

Recognising what you need when you see it …

(a) being able to identify material of good quality for academic purposes

(b) identifying material that is directly relevant to the purpose, such as your assignment or research project (page 214)

(c) being able to tell quickly what to reject, so that you don't waste time on material you are not going to use (pages 242–3).

1 Defining the task, identifying precisely what you need

Working out what you really need …

Use assignment titles and the background information provided about the assignment in order to identify key words, dates and places that will help you focus your search. Be as clear and precise as possible in your own mind about the kind of information that you are looking for so that you can define your searches closely, saving time and effort. (Pages 236 and 346.)

Managing information for study

Managing information for study means:

1 defining the task, identifying precisely what you need

2 using material of suitable quality and content

3 knowing where to look for it

4 using the right tools

5 using search methodologies that offer the most direct route

6 applying effective reading and note-making strategies to extract and record the information you need

7 organising and storing information for quick and easy use

8 sharing information appropriately for group assignments

9 applying information in a way that is fit for purpose, using appropriate conventions, citations and attributions

10 moving back and forth flexibly and easily between the above stages – with the least time and effort.

3 Knowing where to look

Knowing where to start searching for particular kinds of information …

★ library catalogues
★ Google Scholar
★ Shibboleth
★ bibliographic databases
★ gateway services
★ digital repositories.

(Page 238.)

4 Using the right tools

Knowing which tools are available to help you to conduct …

★ searches
★ storage
★ referencing
★ sharing.

(Page 238.)

9 Applying information and attributing sources

Knowing how to use the information in your assignments ...

(a) selecting the best material for your purpose
(b) using information to stimulate your own ideas
(c) combining and synthesising material from many sources
(d) drawing on sources for evidence to support your reasoning
(e) giving due recognition to those whose work or information you use.

That includes ...

★ knowing what is meant by plagiarism and cheating
★ understanding how to cite your sources and provide appropriate references (pages 249–51).

8 Sharing information for group assignments

Knowing about tools and methods that can help you to study collaboratively with others online or in study groups ...

★ taking care to avoid accidental copying or plagiarism
★ sharing bookmarks
★ using Google Tools.
   (Page 246.)

7 Organising and storing for quick and easy use

Knowing how to ...

★ whittle down information to avoid overload (page 244)
★ store and tag it so you can find it again quickly if needed for assignments (page 246)
★ organise and back up files (page 106)
★ cite and reference appropriately/use reference management tools (page 249).

6 Applying effective reading and note-making strategies

(a) read at the right speed for the task
(b) read with awareness and focus
(c) adapt your reading strategy to the task
(d) make useful notes when reading, listening and using audiovisual material.
   (Chapter 10.)

5 Using the most appropriate search methods

Knowing the search methods to use to:

(a) limit your search to find just what you need
(b) extend your search if you haven't found what you want
(c) make advanced searches, including use of Boolean operators.
   (Pages 239–41.)

Reflection

Overview of processes for managing information for study

★ Do you have a set of processes in place for managing study information systematically from start to finish? (See also page 245.)
★ How, if at all, do the processes required for your subject discipline vary from those above?

Defining your research task

The nature of the task

We saw above (page 70) that successful students tend to spend more time at the start of an assignment, working out exactly what is required. Before launching into any piece of work, take time to clarify exactly what is required and plan your approach. Being clearly focused from the outset will save you time later.

1 ***Analyse the assignment brief.***
   How many parts are there to the question? What is really being asked? (Pages 284–5.)

2 ***Consider the purpose of the task or assignment.***
   Why this particular topic? Why this particular wording? Is the assignment one that is always set on your course because it covers essential background? If so, what do you really need to know? Or is it topical, related to recent research or an issue in the news? If so, what is the issue?

3 ***Consider your end-point.***
   What should your work look or sound like when it is finished? (Chapters 13–16.)

4 ***Use marking/grading criteria.***
   Display them where you can see them; use them to guide your work.

5 ***Plan and scale your research to fit your time and the word limits.***
   Consider what is expected, given the length of the assignment. Be realistic in how much you plan to read, note and write.

Start by surveying the field

What do I need to find out?

You undertake research of some kind for every piece of academic work. This might include:

★ background reading to explore the subject

★ identifying the leading experts in this topic – those whose primary research, theories or writings are regarded by academics as essential background knowledge – even if you do not read their work in detail

★ some investigation into the variety of views held on the subject: what has been written on the core issues? Do the experts agree or disagree, and in what ways and why?

★ some specialist reading, such as a recent or important journal article, or an essential text or set of texts on a given topic.

In other words, start by surveying the area. As an undergraduate you may not need to read a great deal on any one topic, but you do need to be aware of your field of study – what is important, what stands out, and why. Develop a feel for which topics are worth focusing on, and which are peripheral.

Managing the peripherals

As you carry out your research, you will come across all kinds of information that will intrigue or fascinate you and that you may want to pursue. You will not have enough time to follow up everything that catches your attention, so you will need to:

★ decide what is essential

★ decide what you have time to pursue now

★ make a list of topics to follow up later and put these aside for now.

Making the most of the library

Library services

The starting place for most research is the library. Your institution's library is likely to offer a wide range of services. Find out whether these are available:

- [ ] subject specialist librarians
- [ ] support and resources for using the library and for finding material online
- [ ] silent areas, study rooms, group work spaces, reference sections, chat areas
- [ ] books, papers and academic journals, in print and/or electronically
- [ ] specialist collections (if so, which ones?)
- [ ] printers, copiers, laminators, binding facilities
- [ ] DVDs, film, tape, slide, microfilm and digitised materials from your reading list
- [ ] specialist resources for disabled students
- [ ] facilities for making audiovisual aids such as posters for your presentations
- [ ] access to resources and help off-campus.

You did say to make myself at home in the library.

The library catalogues

Most catalogues are now electronic. Your library may also have specialist collections in your subject, or the index for a national collection. If you are not sure how to use these, don't be afraid to ask.

Make the library your own

Walk around the library and become familiar with different sections. Try out different areas to find which suit you best for working, with least disturbance. Look up books from your reading list, using the technology, checking what is available electronically, or in hard copy on the open shelves or that you can call up from stores or on loan from elsewhere.

Find out the basics

- [ ] Where are books in my subject located in the library? How are they classified?
- [ ] How many items can I take out at once?
- [ ] How many items can I take home on loan – and for how long?
- [ ] How long does it take for books to arrive once ordered?
- [ ] Can I reserve books?
- [ ] How do I reserve or renew by phone or online?
- [ ] Are there fines?
- [ ] How do I request inter-library loans? Is there a cost?

Activity

Classification system

Check the classification system (or systems) used to group books in your library – Dewey Decimal Classification (DDC), Library of Congress (LC), etc. Which number range applies to your subject for each system?

Finding information: getting started

The reading list

The most important tools for getting started are usually those provided through your course. Typically, these are:

★ reading lists

★ course handbooks

★ resources mentioned by teaching staff, provided as handouts or in the course's virtual learning environment

★ references made within set texts or course materials to other materials.

Use these to build up a sense of the academic community in the discipline, to identify respected authors and publishers and the kinds of sources regarded as useful and reliable.

Build your own trail

★ Note who you are asked to read.

★ Find out more about the other works they have written.

★ Check the references at the end of the item. Call up some of these for yourself and then check their references in turn, to call up further items.

★ Look for patterns in who writes about which kinds of topic and whose work is discussed, respected and cited in references.

★ Decide which sources you find most useful and interesting.

Indices and abstracts

Indices and abstracts are separate publications which give brief details of journal articles, including who wrote what and where to find it. In an index, you can search by subject heading and by keywords for all the articles on a given subject. They are updated regularly and are well worth using.

Finding academic sources online

Google Scholar search engine

Google Scholar is the main search engine to use for your work as a student. It is:

★ extensive: it draws on a very wide range of subject databases relevant to students

★ based on a keyword search

★ predictive: it brings up results based on the individual user's pattern of searching

★ personalised: it draws on your previous searches, so you gain unique search results.

Research tools

You can find additional research facilities online, such as those available at www.iTools.com/research. With these, you can access definitions, maps, quotations, language translations, synonyms, and much more.

Shibboleth and OpenAthens

These both manage access to sites of interest to researchers. As a student, this usually gives you free access to many electronic journals and databases if your institution subscribes to them.

Bibliographic databases / gateway services

These are maintained by professional academics, which helps to quality assure the materials. You can search by keyword, author or journal to help you find books, articles, reports, papers and documents in your subject. Your library website will have details for each subject.

Digital repositories

Banks of digital materials with millions of resources suitable for academic study are being grown by HEIs and other bodies. These are usually free to search but you may need to enter a repository to search it.

Useful resources

See pages 405–6 for useful databases, services, repositories and tools.

Conducting effective online searches for study

Starting your online search

★ Consider starting your search using Google Scholar or a specialist search engine for your subject (page 238).

★ Decide which keywords are best for starting your search (pages 240–1).

★ Browse quickly through the options presented; these are usually summary descriptions or partial quotations from websites, with web addresses. Browse entries that look promising before deciding on a few items to read.

'What exactly am I looking for?'

If you enter a general keyword, such as 'well-being', you will be offered *millions* of options – on subjective well-being, indicators, happiness, child poverty, technology, personality, cultural and national differences and so on. Precise wording narrows the range of results. For examples, a search on Google Scholar (17 April 2018) gave the following results:

Search string	Number of entries
Well-being	3,930,000
Student-wellbeing	2,480,000
Well-being Mindfulness UK students	25,700
Well-Being Mindfulness meditation effective student stress (since 2018)	1,480
Wellbeing Mindfulness meditation Freshers Wales	213

Narrow your search

To narrow your search to more relevant items, play with the keywords in your 'search string'.

★ Which keywords best describe what you are looking for? Which are most likely to be used as keywords for making electronic links?

★ Consider synonyms (words with the same meaning such as 'city', 'town', 'urban' and 'metropolitan').

★ Might unrelated subjects share keywords with your topic? If so, use at least one keyword that applies *only* to your topic.

★ Which *specific areas* of your topic do you need to focus on? Which keywords identify these?

★ To find additional material, use new keywords.

★ If a search string proves particularly useful, note it down for future use.

Searching for journal articles online

Electronic versions of journals may be free to students and available through a 'host' such as:

★ ABI Inform

★ ProQuest

★ Ingenta Connect

★ Shibboleth.

When looking for journal entries, search first for the name of the *journal*, not the name of the article.

You can search journal databases for authors, journal titles, article titles or keywords, and call up short abstracts to see what an article is about.

For speed, type in words such as 'research', 'journal', the names of leading theorists or schools of thought as well as the topic.

Saving web addresses

For useful sources, save their web addresses as a 'favourite', 'bookmark' or 'mark' it. Set up folders to group your most used addresses. Name these clearly, just as you would with your files. If you use a free social bookmarking tool such as Evernote, you can save your bookmarks online and access them from anywhere with online access.

Automated searches using eTOC

Some bibliographic databases let you save searches and return to them later. For many, you can request to be emailed details of all publications that meet your search criteria. For journals that you find especially useful, request an eTOC – the electronic copy of its contents. You can receive these by email, with direct links to the articles.

Narrowing or extending your online search

In many search tools, you can vary your search by using OR, AND and NOT (known in this context as 'Boolean operators'), and truncation symbols or wildcards. These allow you to broaden or narrow your search in order to find the most relevant pages.

Too many items? Limit your search

AND

If you type **AND** between two keywords, the search will produce only those pages that include *both* of the keywords. For example, **field AND mice** would find only pages that contain both **field** and **mice**, not those containing only one of these keywords.

Inverted commas (" ")

In many situations you can use double inverted commas to specify a phrase rather than a single word. This will narrow down the search and reduce the number of items you find, but must be used with care. For example, **"electronic mouse"** would yield references to computer mice, excluding those that mention rodents, but equally it would only list pages where those two words appeared together in exactly that form.

NOT

Use **NOT** to *exclude* items from your search. For example, to find references to mice but not to pest control, you could enter: **mice NOT extermination**.

More keywords

The more keywords you use, the fewer pages are listed. For example, a library database search may allow you to specify the author's name, words in the title, the publication date, and so on. The more of these you provide, the more precise your search will be.

Too few items? Extend your search

OR

Use **OR** to search for pages that contain *one* or *more* of two or more words. For example, a search for **car OR bicycle** would list pages that include **car** but not **bicycle**, pages that include **bicycle** but not **car**, and pages that include both **car** and **bicycle**. This kind of search is useful when authors may use different terms for the same topic (often synonyms or abbreviations), **"vitamin C" OR "ascorbic acid"**.

Truncation symbol (*)

The truncation symbol can be used to find variations of a keyword that begin with the same set of letters (the 'stem'). For example, **crit*** would find **critic**, **critical**, **critique** and **criticism**.

Wildcards (?)

Wildcards find variations of a keyword, such as alternative words in a phrase or alternative letters in a word. The exact operation of **?** varies between search engines: check the help system.

★ Alternative words: **car ?** would search for **car** plus any other word, and might find **used cars**, **sports cars**, **car insurance**, **car hire**, and so on. Beware: this may yield a long list. In a publications database, for example, **Smith ?** would list publications by *any* author named **Smith**; it would be better to include a specific initial to limit the list (**Smith W**).

★ Alternative characters: **wom?n** might find **woman** and **women**; **organi?e** might find **organise** and **organize**.

Advanced online searches

Advanced searches

With some databases you can use a more sophisticated search string that uses parentheses ( ) to link operations and to specify their order of precedence. You can continue to use operators, truncations and wildcards (page 240), within and between the groups of keywords.

You need to put some thought into what you are including and excluding. However, experiment and you will soon get a feel for whether your search strategy is finding the kinds of items you need.

Example 1

Suppose you wished to find articles about mice in cities. You might try this search string:

(mice NOT rat) AND (urban OR city OR metropolitan NOT field)

The search engine would list items in the database that:

★ include the keyword **mice** but do not include the keyword **rat**

and also

★ include any combination (one or more) of the keywords **urban**, **city** or **metropolitan**, but *not* the keyword **field**.

However, this search might exclude some useful articles that mentioned 'rat' or 'field' even once.

Example 2

"global warming" AND (glaciers NOT North)

The search would look for items that:

★ include **global warming** as a phrase (excluding items that contain the words **global** and **warming**, but not together)

and also

★ include the word **glaciers**, but do *not* include the word **North**.

Again, this would exclude any articles that mentioned the word **North** even once.

Efficient search strategies

An efficient search strategy is one that:

★ finds the most relevant items

★ does not exclude relevant items

★ does exclude irrelevant items

★ is successful in the fewest attempts.

Activity

Advanced searches

1 If you use AND in a search, you are likely to find additional references. True or false?

2 If you use OR in a search, you are likely to find additional references. True or false?

3 Which search string would find most items?

   A   global OR world
   B   global AND world
   C   global NOT world

4 Which search strategy would find the fewest items?

   A   graphic OR design
   B   (graphic OR design)
   C   "graphic design"

5 How could you enter the keyword 'design' to find references to 'designs' and 'designers' also?

6 For the following topics, how could you search for references to items using alternative versions of the keywords?

   A   A compendium of nursing methods
   B   Monopoly as a trend in world trade

7 Which search string is likely to be most efficient in finding references to the impact of global design trends on designers?

   A   global AND design AND trend
   B   global? AND (design* AND trend?)
   C   global* OR (design AND trend)

Answers are given on page 408.

Using material of suitable quality and content

Use 'authoritative sources'

Being able to identify good quality material is essential at this level of study. Only a small portion of printed and online material is suitable for assignments. In general, aim to use items produced through the academic community, professional area and official international or national bodies, rather than general media, opinion or non-expert sources.

Become familiar with your field

New research and theory are developed as part of an international academic community. As you read and develop expertise in your subject, you will come to know the experts in your field and to recognise reliable information quickly. You also become familiar with institutions, organisations and centres associated with excellent work in specific areas.

How 'old' can it be?

Data Check the latest data if relevant to your argument. Use reputable, reliable sources. If you need to compare data over time, you might need to look at older sources.

Interpretations and concept development Typically, you need to demonstrate awareness of how thinking about given issues has changed over time, drawing on both old and new material. Know where ideas originated and what has been written in recent years.

Seminal works Most branches of knowledge are associated with a few leading thinkers or works; these could be of any date. Know what these are. At the least, browse them and get a sense of what they say, their style and evidence base. It is a good idea to refer to these in assignments.

Usefulness Your litmus test should be whether the material is relevant to your argument, inspires your thinking, assists your understanding and/or is still current and helpful in some way, rather than its age, even if thousands of years old.

Who is who?

★ Look out for the names that appear in research papers, book reviews and on the editorial boards of journals.

★ Google authors – find out their latest work.

★ Check citations: is the author or work cited, how often and by whom (use Google Scholar)?

★ Check whether their work is reviewed in journals.

★ Check the qualifications, experience and occupation of the authors: are they academics such as doctors or professors at an HEI, or otherwise leading experts in the field?

Characteristics of good quality sources

Typically, you would look for:

★ where items appear, such as in a reputable series or peer-reviewed journal

★ clear references and details of source materials, so readers could check these themselves

★ the number and quality of the references they make to other experts in the field

★ use of original source material and data.

Using peer-reviewed items

'Peer-review' means that experts have scrutinised material from an academic perspective prior to publication. They consider such matters as:

★ the appropriateness of the methods used to gather, analyse and present information

★ ethical concerns

★ whether sufficient use had been made of previously published research findings

★ whether data were interpreted correctly

★ whether evidence supports conclusions

★ whether anything is misleading in the way the material is presented.

Peer-review does not mean inconsistencies and errors are eliminated or that you should accept findings in an uncritical way. You should still consider the points listed above for yourself (Chapter 12).

Journals or periodicals

These are usually good quality sources; most are available online. The articles and book reviews they contain are written by experts for experts, so they assume some background knowledge.

Journals are published at regular intervals during the year. They are collected into numbered volumes, usually one for each year. To find a journal article, browse using keywords; you might need to use a specialised database to find it. It helps if you know:

★ the title of the journal, the year it was published and its volume number

★ the name and initials of the author

★ the title of the article.

Use abstracts and book reviews in journals

Most articles open with a short 'abstract' or summary. Browsing through abstracts and reviews is a good way to stay up to date with research and publications in your subject, and to identify items to read in full for your assignments. Often, the abstract provides sufficient information for undergraduate assignments.

Podcasts

★ Good sources for students are: iTunes Podcasts, Spotify and Google Play Music.

★ Lecturers may make some or all of a lecture available as a podcast.

★ Study resources may be available as podcasts: e.g. www.thestudyspace.com.

★ Check details of the speaker in order to find out whether the material is likely to be reliable.

★ Check the date to see if it is recent.

MOOCS and short online courses

You might like to take part in a MOOC (mass online open course) or other short courses online. These are available on a wide range of topics over a few hours, days or weeks. Typically, MOOCs provide high quality material designed by experts from leading universities. Because of the large number of participants, you don't usually get personal attention from tutors. Nonetheless, you can gain a great deal from the free aspects of these courses, especially if you engage with activities, automated feedback and peer interaction. High quality providers include:

★ EdX   ★ Coursera
★ FutureLearn ★ Udacity

Note that there might also be optional paid aspects to the course, such as certification.

Wikis and Wikipedia

A wiki is a website to which many people can contribute by editing or adding to existing items or creating new pages. There are many kinds of wiki, from corporate and student-created wikis through to large free online resources. The best known are:

★ Wikimedia Commons: a large free repository of materials

★ Wiktionary: a large, free, online dictionary and thesaurus

★ Wikipedia: a free encyclopaedia that aims to provide a neutral viewpoint.

Using Wikipedia selectively in your work

Wikipedia can be a useful starting place when researching a topic. However, it is advisable to use it with caution for assignments. (Tutors don't like it!)

★ Look up and read its references, and then refer to these rather than to Wikipedia in your work.

★ For academic work, use specialist texts rather than Wikipedia or another encyclopaedia.

★ Use your course reading list and the references in academic texts to develop your information trail, rather than relying on any one source.

How I love to see so many references to Wikipedia in a student's work.

Whittling down information

Managing vast amounts of information is a perennial challenge in most academic disciplines. So much is written, and so much data available, you can only cover a small amount. You are likely to gather so much information that you cannot include most of it in your work. Most scholars feel overwhelmed, at times, by the sheer quantity of information. How can you manage this?

Prepare psychologically! You are not a failure because you can't read everything! It would be impossible to do so for most topics.

Constantly consciously choosing. Be actively selective – all the time:

★ choosing where to search

★ choosing what to browse and read

★ choosing what data to gather yourself

★ choose what to note and which notes to keep

★ choosing what to include in your work

★ choosing what to review or commit to memory.

Start in the right way. Use smart reading and note-making strategies (Chapter 10).

Keep whittling down as you go. Don't amass a mountain of items that then seems overwhelming and wastes your time to sort through.

Decide on a number. Decide roughly how many sources you are going to use, or how much data to collect, depending on custom and practice in your subject area for your level of study. Typically, this might be 2–5 journal articles, 3–5 chapters, each from a

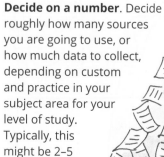

different book, 2–10 references to concepts or pages in other sources, 20–40 participants in a survey. Use your number to provide focus.

Focus on quality. Don't waste time on poor resources (pages 242–3).

Develop good search techniques. Use advanced searches. For your subject, learn short cuts such as which search words and phrases extend or reduce your list of relevant, good quality material. Use specialist repositories. Develop your own search strategies (pages 238–42).

Don't settle for the first items that you come across on the shelf or that appear in searches. They tend to reflect other people's search habits or commercial interests. It is unlikely that these will be the best sources and they could waste your time. Look to see what appears in deeper searches before spending time on a source.

Keep refining your search questions: 'What exactly do I need about this aspect? Where would I use this?'

Eliminate the tangents: 'This is really interesting – but can I really use it?'

Eliminate duplication. Don't note the same details twice.

Colour code topics – so you can find and collate information on the same topic quickly in your stores or on the page.

Review: rewrite older notes removing material you are not likely to use, or flag details so they stand out.

Reading, recording and using information

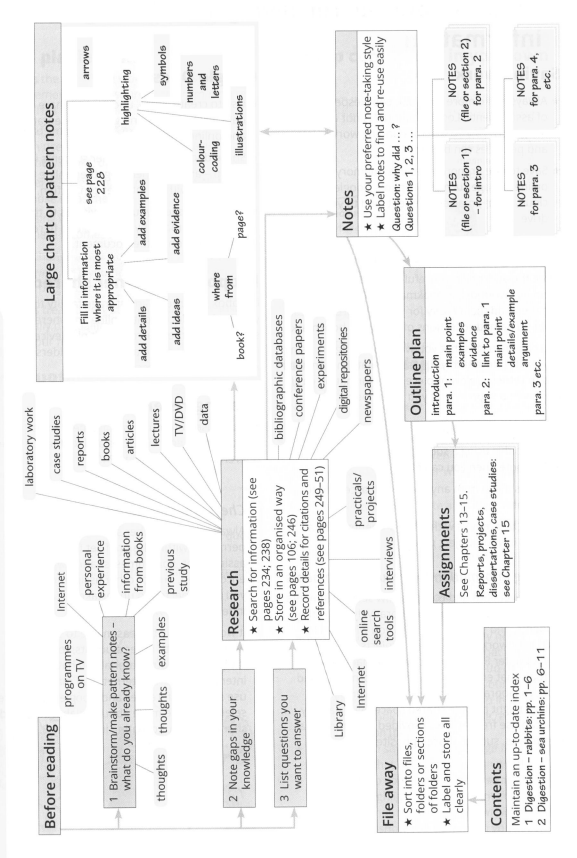

Recognising plagiarism and copying

Read each of the texts below; decide whether each is an example of plagiarism and the reason for your decision. The original text on which these are based is on pages 65–70.

1

Research shows that students who do best at problem-solving spend longer than other students at working out exactly what a problem is before they try to solve it. Weaker students look at the surface of the problem and do not see the underlying structure that makes it similar to problems they already know.

2

Many people undervalue their own intelligence because they hold mistaken views about what constitutes 'intelligence'. This is partly because too much emphasis has been placed upon the idea of 'IQ'. In addition, early educational experiences can damage self-esteem or be demotivating, undermining a natural interest in learning. There is a body of research that argues that outstanding performance in almost any field of human activity can be fostered if the right conditions are in place. Those conditions include finding the right learning strategy for each person.

3

There is strong evidence to suggest that environment plays a great part in intellectual performance. In Japan, the Suzuki Violin Education Programme has trained many children to play the violin to virtuoso level. Being part of a culture that values academic intelligence also helps. Donaldson (1978) argued that the way we reason depends upon the particular context we are in.

4

'There is strong evidence to suggest that environment plays a great part in intellectual performance' (Cottrell, 2019). Cottrell writes: 'In Japan, the Suzuki Violin Education Programme has trained many children to play the violin to virtuoso level.' She also points out: 'Being part of a culture that values academic intelligence also helps.' Cottrell cites Donaldson (1978), who argued that the way we reason depends upon the particular context we are in.

5

The reasons for appearing 'intelligent' or not may depend upon a complex set of factors, all of which interact (Cottrell, 2019). Butterworth (1992) suggests that we can even believe ourselves to be incapable of a task that is well within our capacities. This can occur simply because we do not recognise the similarity of two tasks when the circumstances appear different. This view is supported by research. It has been demonstrated that students who spend more time early on actively looking for similarities between writing tasks and areas of existing expertise are then more successful at the writing task (Bloggs, 2014). This suggests that academic success may be more a question of good strategy and of building upon experience rather than underlying 'intelligence'.

6

Various psychologists have used experiments on identical twins to argue that intelligence is genetic and 'general'. Others argue that twins' similar physical appearance and cultural upbringing could account for similarities in their performance. Whilst people who do well on one intelligence test do well on other such tests, there is evidence that such performance is also affected by familiarity with the culture and thinking of those who designed the test.

See Answers, page 408.

Making citations and references

Why are references needed?

In academic writing, it is essential to acknowledge, or 'cite' the sources of ideas and information. Such citations allow readers to refer back to the sources for themselves.

There are five main reasons for acknowledging your sources through citations and references.

1 It is a courtesy to the person whose idea or words you have used or referred to.
2 By giving the source you make it clear to the reader that you are not trying to pretend somebody else's work is your own. (You are not 'plagiarising' their work.)
3 It helps your readers to find the original texts or webpages to read themselves, should they wish.
4 If you need to check something later, the reference will help you find it again more easily.
5 People will have more confidence in your assertions if they know where your information comes from. Thoroughness in referencing suggests that you will also have been thorough in checking your facts.

When must you cite your source?

You do this whenever you draw on a source of information:

★ as your inspiration (in general)

★ for a particular theory, argument or viewpoint

★ for specific information, such as statistics, examples, or case studies

★ for direct quotations, reproducing the writer's exact words

★ for texts and information that you paraphrase or allude to rather than quote.

What information do you give?

Imagine that you wished to read for yourself a source used by another author. What information would *you* need to locate that source easily? The information usually provided includes:

★ the surname and initials of the author(s)

★ the title, in full

★ the year of publication

★ for journal articles, the name of the journal and the number of the volume

★ the edition, if relevant

★ the name and location of the publisher

★ relevant page numbers

★ for electronic materials, the URL for the webpage and the date it was downloaded.

Provide extra information if needed. For example, to find a photograph, print or manuscript you may need the name of the library, the collection, and the catalogue number of the item within the collection. The important question to ask is, 'Could somebody else *find* this source from the information I have given?'

Is there a set format for doing this?

Check whether your course requires a particular style such as Harvard, Oxford or Chicago. You might be asked to use the Vancouver style for science subjects, MLA for Modern Languages or APA for Psychology. The basic principles of each are similar:

★ In your text, make it clear whenever you refer to a source or have drawn upon it for ideas or evidence.

★ Provide the full reference, usually in a list at the end or in footnotes (see pages 250–1).

★ Be consistent in your formatting, even in the use of capitals and punctuation.

Reference Management Tools

Free tools available online make the process easier.

Mendeley, Zotero, Endnote, RefMe: help you import references from digital sources, databases and pdfs to produce your list of references in word-processing tools.

CiteULike: useful for storing articles, adding notes, tagging sources you might wish to cite and reference, and producing references in the right style.

Citing your sources: in-text citations

Citations in the body of the text

Whenever you refer to someone else's work for your ideas or arguments, acknowledge this in your work at that point, using the style your course recommends.

Harvard, APA and optional Chicago styles

Provide the author surname and year of publication, usually in brackets unless it flows naturally in the text. If you refer to a specific point or table or use a quotation, provide the page number too. If there are many authors, give the first author at this point followed by 'et al.' (meaning 'and others').

★ ... and as established by Cohen and Smith (2017), there are many ...

★ It was found that this was ineffective 95% of the time (Cohen and Smith, 2017, p. 56). James et al. (2019) also found that ...

★ In 2017, Cohen and Smith found that ...

Vancouver style

Number each item in the order it appears in your work and list it in your references. Whenever you refer to that source in the assignment, use the same number:

★ ... as established by Cohen and Smith (6) and James et al. (11) this is usually ineffective.

★ This is ineffective 95% of the time (6 and 11).

★ Many studies (4, 6, 8, 11 and 12) found ...

Oxford and optional Chicago style

Use a numbered superscript in the text to refer to numbered items provided in full in footnotes. For example:

| In the text: | Personalise your learning.[4] |
| In the footnote: | [4] Stella Cottrell, *The Study Skills Handbook* (London: Red Globe Press, 2019), p. 4. |

In-text citations

There are many ways of citing sources. Here are three examples using the Harvard style.

Short direct quotation – within the text

She argues that 'each of us learns in an individual way' but discourages 'rigid views' about how to learn best (Cottrell, 2019, p. 5).

Paraphrasing

Instead of assuming there is one best approach, you can devise a personalised strategy to fit your circumstances (Cottrell, 2019, p. 5).

Longer direct quotation

A few words, carefully chosen, make the most powerful quotations. Avoid long quotations; they are rarely needed. If the exact wording of a long quotation is essential, indent it and leave space above and below. Incorporate the quotation into your writing with linking sentences and by discussing its relevance.

Cottrell takes a different approach. She argues:

> The best strategies tend to be broad-based, taking into consideration all your needs, including health and well-being, goals and enjoyment (Cottrell, 2019, p. 6).

Here we can see that Cottrell believes study strategies should extend beyond how students engage with course material. Instead, ...

Useful phrases to introduce references

★ As *X* stated/wrote/said/points out/argues ...

★ *X* writes/says/suggests/found that

★ According to *X*, ...

★ To quote from *X*, ' ...'

★ Referring to ..., *X* says that ...

★ In an article entitled *Name of Text*, *X* makes the point that ... / In *Name of Text*, *X* wrote that ...

★ Writing in *Name of Text*, *X* explained that ...

★ In 1926, *X* argued/discovered/found that ...

Bibliographies

A bibliography is a list of everything you read for the assignment, whether or not you referred to it in your writing. Your tutor may require both. Write out using the same conventions as for references.

Writing out your references

At the end of your assignment, provide a full list of the sources you cited in your assignment. A sample reference list is provided below. See also pages 413–20. Note the ways that referencing styles can vary in terms of how items are organised, listed and punctuated. There are specific ways of citing all sources, from newspapers, video, blogs and theses to conference papers. Google university websites for details or use *Cite them right* (Pears and Shields, 2019).

Harvard style

1   List alphabetically, by author's surname. Don't number items.
2   Organise as: Author, date, title, location of publisher, publisher.
3   Use 'single' quotation marks for the title of an article within a journal.

Vancouver style

1   Number in the order items occur in your text.
2   Organise as Author, title, location, publisher, date.
3   For multiple authors, use a comma between authors and a full stop after final set of initials.

For both styles

★ Include every source referred to in your assignment; exclude general reference books such as dictionaries.
★ Don't include items you have not used.
★ For journal items, give details of the specific item and the journal title, volume, number and page numbers.
★ If you use more than one work published in the same year by the same author, label these a, b, c … (Chang, L. 2019a; Chang, L. 2019b) in the text and References.
★ For online items, give the URL and date you accessed it.
★ Italicise titles of books or journals.
★ Use punctuation precisely and consistently.

Sample reference lists		
Harvard style (Alphabetical)	**Source type**	**Vancouver style (Numerical)**
Buetti, S. and Lleras, A. (2016) 'Distractibility is a function of engagement, not task difficulty: Evidence from a new oculomotor capture paradigm'. *Journal of Experimental Psychology: General* 145 (10) 1382–1405.	Journal articles	1 Cottrell S. *The Study Skills Handbook.* 5th edn. London: Red Globe Press; 2019.
Cottrell, S. (2019) *The Study Skills Handbook.* 5th ed. (London: Red Globe Press).	Books	2 Buetti S, Lleras A. Distractibility is a function of engagement, not task difficulty: Evidence from a new oculomotor capture paradigm. *Journal of Experimental Psychology: General.* 2016; 145 (10): 1382–1405.
Miller, E. (2016) 'Here's Why You Shouldn't Multitask, According to an MIT Neuroscientist.' *Tools of the Trade* www.fortune.com (Accessed 17/7/2017).	Electronic reference	3 Miller E. Here's Why You Shouldn't Multitask, According to an MIT Neuroscientist. *Tools of the Trade.* Available from: www.fortune.com 2016 [Accessed 17th July 2017].
Hanh, T. N. (1988) 'The Sun My Heart' (Berkeley: Parallax Press). Cited in S. Cottrell (2018) *Mindfulness for Students* (London: Red Globe Press).	Material cited within another text	4 Wilson M. The search for that elusive sense of belonging, respect and visibility in academia. In Gabriel, D, Tate, SA, eds. *Inside the Ivory Tower.* London: UCL/Trentham Books; 2017. p. 108–23.
Wilson, M. (2017) 'The search for that elusive sense of belonging, respect and visibility in academia'. In D. Gabriel and S. A. Tate (eds.) *Inside the Ivory Tower* (London: UCL/ Trentham Books) pp. 108–23.	Chapters in books	5 Hanh TN. *The Sun My Heart.* Berkeley: Parallax Press; 1988. Cited in Cottrell, S. *Mindfulness for Students.* London: Red Globe Press; 2018.

Review

1 **Gain an overview of the whole process**
Identify the key steps involved in managing information for study and/or for particular tasks and assignments. Consider how these inter-connect, so that you recognise how what you do in one step can help or hinder later steps. Be able to picture the process as a whole, or chart it out.

2 **Define tasks clearly**
Before launching into a task, pause to work out and think through exactly what is required. It will ease your path through the task significantly, as well as saving time, helping avoid errors, and building confidence.

3 **Make full use of library resources**
Be well informed about what is available, especially specialist help and resources. Get to know the librarians, and the best spaces for study.

4 **Develop effective search strategies**
Become more skilled at finding the right material quickly within the vast range of sources available.

5 **Select relevant sources**
Learn to recognise suitable material for your course and assignments. You can't use everything so think carefully about which precise aspects of each source best support the points you want to make.

6 **Use good quality sources**
Find out where to look for good quality sources – don't waste time on poor quality material. Understand conventions such as peer review that help you identify work of suitable quality.

7 **Organise information effectively**
Organise, label, save and store information related to your course so that it is secure and so you can find it and make sense of it again quickly when needed. Keep whittling it down to manageable, useable levels.

8 **Draw upon material appropriately**
Be open, honest and transparent about sources you use for ideas and information. Acknowledge these. Always write in your own words even for your own notes.   Take care to avoid plagiarism, deliberate or accidental.

9 **Cite and reference correctly**
Use a recognised format such as Harvard or Vancouver, or as otherwise advised by your course. Be exacting in applying the format. Ensure your list is comprehensive, consistent and accurate.

Chapter 12

Critical thinking

Why critical thinking matters

Criticality is an ability that we all need and can nurture. It helps us to uncover the ways things work and *why* things occur the way they do. It helps us understand the world around us, to predict more accurately what might happen in future, make wiser decisions, keep things in perspective, act fairly, and resolve problems creatively. Critical thinking can be analytical, reflective and creative. As well as being of personal benefit, it is in high demand with employers, too (Karzunina et al., 2017).

Why critical thinking matters to study

Critical analytical thinking is an essential ability for most courses in Higher Education. In general, the schemes that tutors use to mark or grade student work put a high premium on good critical analysis and on the outcomes of astute critical thinking.

You will be expected to bring a critical approach to every aspect of your study – to what you read, hear, write, say, do, believe and create. You apply criticality for better, or worse, whenever you select what to read, what to include, cite or quote in your work, and in your interpretations of evidence, your acceptance or challenge of other people's reasoning, your decisions on which solutions to apply to problems, which ideas to take forward and which to leave aside.

Throughout your course, you will be expected to examine arguments, evidence and conclusions closely, as well as the links between these. You will evaluate other people's reasoning and evidence, using criteria to guide you. Sometimes those criteria will be provided, but as you advance to higher levels, you will need to become more adept at deciding them for yourself.

Why develop critical thinking abilities?

Our brains have a tendency to look for short cuts and easy answers, and are quite easy to fool unless we use systematic methods to analyse information, situations and even our own thought processes. Throughout life, we learn to recognise that things are not always as they first appear. We have unconscious biases that, by definition, we can't uncover unless we use objective methodologies. We know this and yet it is still easy to omit essential steps and clues that could help us to arrive at the best, most accurate, fairest, and most objective conclusions. That is why we need to be alert, to keep questioning and looking at things with fresh eyes, and from different perspectives.

Things aren't always what they first appear

What characterises critical thinking?

Critical thinking

Critical thinking means putting surface appearances under close scrutiny in order to understand more fully why things are as they are. It requires us to:

★ draw objective conclusions ...

★ based on a sound line of reasoning ...

★ following a balanced, objective, systematic investigation of all, and potentially conflicting, evidence ...

★ keeping our own reasoning process under scrutiny.

(Cottrell, 2017).

The critical process is valued because, at its best, it involves intellectual curiosity and open-minded searching after truth. That can require us to:

★ **exercise impartiality** in the pursuit of accuracy, clarity and deeper understanding

★ **weigh up** opposing points of view in an even-handed way

★ **recognise influences** on our thinking and techniques used to persuade us to a point of view

★ **synthesise** information to create our own position

★ **draw conclusions** with integrity, depending on where the evidence and best reasoning leads.

Edward Glaser (1941) argued that critical thinking entails:

> a persistent effort to examine any belief or supposed form of knowledge in the light of the evidence that supports it and the further conclusions to which it tends.

In other words, it calls for:

★ *persistence*: constant re-examining

★ *use of solid evidence*: evaluating the basis of current beliefs or positions on a given issue

★ *consideration of implications*: pondering where, logically, a viewpoint or conclusion leads and whether that suggests further thinking or evidence is needed.

Critical analytical thinking

Critical analytical thinking involves additional processes:

★ standing back from the information given

★ checking closely whether it is completely accurate

★ examining it in detail from many angles

★ examining material in terms of its component parts and identifying how these relate to each other

★ checking whether each statement follows logically from what went before

★ looking for possible flaws in the reasoning, the evidence, or the way that conclusions are drawn

★ comparing the same issue from the point of view of other theorists or writers

★ being able to see and explain why different people arrived at different conclusions

★ being able to argue why one set of opinions, results or conclusions is preferable to another

★ being on guard for literary or statistical devices that encourage the reader to take questionable statements at face value

★ checking for hidden assumptions.

Critical self-awareness

Self-awareness is essential to good critical thinking. Without this, it is harder to stand back and evaluate objectively whether we have been influenced disproportionately by factors we might not even have noticed consciously. Strong critical analysis benefits from critical reflection, so we become more aware of what we bring to the table, inadvertently, when making judgements, interpreting material, selecting variables, and so on.

Creativity and criticality

To examine issues well, critically and in depth also calls for a range of creative thinking skills. It takes imagination to create alternative mental scenarios, schema and hypotheses that assist criticality. These help to generate appropriate points of comparison which, in turn, help us to identify assumptions and generate relevant questions. It is hard to test out the validity of your position or your critiques if you can't conceive of alternatives and syntheses (page 96).

Develop a detective-like mind

Developing your critical ability is rather like becoming a good detective: hunting out clues, working out whether they are what they appear to be, how they fit together, how they are best interpreted, and what they all mean. As in a good detective novel, when we re-examine the facts, we can arrive at some interesting new conclusions.

Reading

Critical thinking when *reading* involves:
1   identifying the line of reasoning in the text
2   critically evaluating the line of reasoning
3   questioning surface appearances and checking for hidden assumptions, agendas or persuasive devices
4   identifying evidence in the text
5   evaluating the evidence according to valid criteria
6   identifying the writer's conclusions
7   deciding whether the evidence provided supports those conclusions.

Writing

Similarly, critical thinking when *writing* involves:
1   being clear on your position on the issue, including your hypotheses and conclusions
2   constructing a clear line of reasoning – an 'argument' leading to your conclusion
3   presenting evidence to support your reasoning
4   analysing issues from multiple perspectives, weighing up the evidence for each in a balanced way
5   drawing together information and analyses, synthesising these to construct your position on the issues
6   writing in a critical, analytical style, rather than in a descriptive, personal or journalistic style
7   reading your own writing critically, as well as your sources.

Listening

Critical thinking when *listening* involves the same awareness as when reading, plus:
1   checking for consistency in what is said: has the person contradicted what they said earlier? If so, how and why?
2   checking that body language, eye contact, speed and tone of voice are consistent, or 'congruent', with what is being said: does the speaker appear to be telling the truth and to believe what they say?

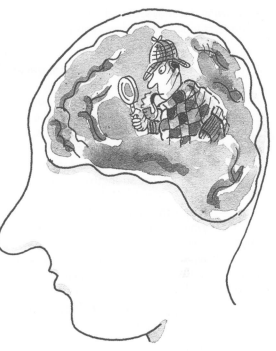

Develop a detective-like mind

Question everything

Turn questions on their head. Imagine if the opposite were true. Test out alternatives mentally: see what questions and ideas these provoke.

Use broad angle questions. Avoid narrow questions that prompt 'yes/no' responses or over-general ones that lack focus: e.g. *'What is your plan to reduce hospital waiting lists?'* rather than *'Do you have a policy to reduce hospital waiting lists'* or *'What are your health policies?'*

Keep questions objective. Don't weight questions to elicit a particular response.

Dig deep. Follow up initial questions with ones that challenge the first answer or probe deeper into some angle of it.

The table on page 256 provides a starting point.

Critical questioning

The following questions, though not exhaustive, offer a useful starting place for digging deeper to develop your understanding of issues you encounter on your course as well as in daily life.

	Critical questions for critical thinking	
What?	What exactly are we talking about here? What do I need to know to make sense of this? What are the most important aspects to consider? What are the arguments for and against? What are the strengths and weaknesses?	What alternative views/perspectives/interpretations/solutions might there be? What else throws light on this? What is the potential? What are we not seeing/hearing/finding?
Why?	Why is this worth thinking about at all? Why does this matter? (Why is it a problem?) Why are we hearing about this now? Why has the issue been framed, phrased or presented in this particular way?	Why did it (or does it) occur? Why does it happen this way? Why does it continue? Why do we need to act now? Why do people believe /trust this?
Who?	Who says so? (What do they know about it?) Who are the experts in this? (What do *they* say?) Who should I ask/read/speak to about it? Whose views or interests are not represented?	Who is (or will be) affected by this? Who benefits if we believe this? (Does that matter?) Who loses out if we accept this?
When?	When does this matter (and when not)? When does this apply (and when not)? When did we find out about this? When was action taken/should action be taken?	When do we need to do what? When this happens, what are the consequences, for whom and why? When do we need to check this next?
Where?	Where exactly did this happen? Where was this discovered? Where is the evidence?	Where are there similar examples? Where can we look for solutions? Where can I find out more?
Which?	Which perspectives have been considered? Which arguments should I weigh into the balance? Which are the most relevant arguments?	Which evidence has been considered so far? (Has it been interpreted correctly?) Which evidence has been ignored, overlooked or not fully considered?
How?	How do we know about this at all? How do I know I can trust the information trail? How might this information have been distorted? How can I check this out?	How could things be (or have been) different? How strong (or weak) is the evidence? How could we think about this differently? How will this affect people for good or ill? How will this pan out into the future? How will we know if it is a success?
How else?	How else could I think about this? How else could this have arisen?	How else could this be interpreted? How else could this be resolved?

Critical thinking when reading

Critical thinking when reading is essential to academic success, as both preparation for class and writing for assignments requires critical analysis of other people's work.

1 Identify the line of reasoning

Most of the texts you are required to read as a student will include an argument. In academic writing, an 'argument' is:

★ a line of reasoning *or*

★ an angle or a point of view *or*

★ a position that is being defended *or*

★ a case that is being made

   * backed up by evidence and examples and

   * leading to conclusions.

When reading, you need to keep asking yourself, 'What are the main things this writer wants me to accept? What reasons does she or he present to encourage me to accept this?' 'Is this really convincing?'

Activity

1 Line of reasoning

Identify the main line of reasoning – the main argument – in Passage 1, 'Rochborough Health'. (See page 409 for feedback.)

2 Critically evaluate the line of reasoning

An argument can be critically evaluated in terms of whether it contains:

★ relevant, contributing and sufficient propositions (reasons)

★ logical progression

★ false premises

★ flawed reasoning.

Each of these is explored below.

Passage 1: Rochborough Health

Outdoor play has beneficial effects for children in terms of both their health and their levels of social interaction. According to clinical trials carried out by Rochborough's Health Council Advisory Body in September this year, children who played outside for over fifty days in the year had a 20% higher lung capacity, and 30% lower incidence of asthma and bronchial conditions than children who played indoors. Children who played outdoors also reported having more friends than those who played indoors. A survey of 30 families by Rochborough Social Amenities Committee found that parents were more likely to let their children play outdoors if they had their own gardens or if there were supervised play areas nearby. Mr Arkash of Milton Road said his children did not feel safe playing on the Children's Meadow on the outskirts of Rochborough as his son had been frightened by a fox there in the past. His little son looked quite tearful as his father spoke. 'He often cries because he has nowhere to play,' said his father. Supervised play areas can be expensive to provide. However, only 18% of homes in Rochborough have gardens. Therefore, to improve the health of all its children, Rochborough needs to provide more supervised outdoor play areas.

Rochborough Playcouncil Newsletter

Relevant, contributing and sufficient propositions

The Rochborough Health passage makes a number of statements or *propositions*. For example:

★ Outdoor play improves levels of social interaction.

★ Only 18% of Rochborough homes have gardens.

These are some of the reasons it gives to support its argument.

When examining the line of reasoning, you need to consider whether the reasons given are relevant and whether they support (that is, contribute to) the overall argument. For example:

★ The reference to the isolated incident of a fox is not very relevant to the argument about health.

★ The reference to the expense of supervised play areas *is* relevant to the argument – however, it weakens or undermines the argument rather than contributing to it, because the piece does not make clear how the expense could be met.

It is important to check that reasons and evidence are both relevant and supportive of the main argument, as this helps you to identify whether the writer's conclusion is valid. Even if the writer has given relevant reasons that contribute to the argument, she or he still might not have given sufficient reasons to prove that the conclusion is the *only* one that could be drawn.

Passage 2: Injuries

There has been a tremendous rise in the rate of industrial injury. This year there were over thirty reports of repetitive strain injury in the factory (Smilex Injury Report 2019). All those injured worked in the fibre department. Ten years ago there were no reported injuries. This shows that our work conditions are taking a more serious toll upon our health than in the past.

Smilex News

The writer of Passage 2 begins from the premise (starting point) that there has been a great rise in industrial injury. The conclusion is that work conditions are having a more serious effect on health than in the past. The writer gives a relevant and contributory reason: the rise in the number of reported injuries. However, the writer does not consider other reasons why the number of reported injuries might have increased – such as whether repetitive strain injury was known about thirty years ago, or whether people were less likely to report accidents in the past.

In addition, the writer has not looked at figures for any other types of injury, or at the health of workers in other departments. He or she makes generalisations based on only one kind of injury

and one part of the factory. The writer might still be *right* about the rise in industrial injury, but has not proved this. He or she has not given sufficient reasons (or evidence) to justify the conclusion.

Logical progression

When we are reading or listening, we tend to assume that there is a logical connection between one thing that is said and the next. Critical analysis helps us identify whether a point does indeed follow logically from another.

A good line of reasoning will:

★ begin from a premise

★ follow in logical stages (*A* leads to *B*; *B* leads to *C*; *C* leads to *D* ...)

★ lead to a conclusion that follows directly from what has gone before (there are relevant reasons, given in a logical order, which build towards the stated conclusion).

The premise in Passage 1 is that outdoor play is good for children's health. The logical progression would be:

★ local evidence supports the health argument (that outdoor play is desirable)

★ parents' attitudes support this argument

★ a lack of facilities prevents outdoor play

★ more outdoor play facilities are needed.

False premises

If there were a reason why outdoor play was *not* good for Rochborough children, the writer of Passage 1 would have started from a 'false premise'. The writer of Passage 2 may indeed have begun from a 'false premise' – believing that industrial injury is on the rise in the Smilex factory. No conclusive evidence of this is given, so it might not be true.

It is useful to be on the lookout for false premises: many arguments are based on weak foundations of this kind.

Flawed reasoning

Here are some examples of 'flawed reasoning'.

Assuming a causal connection

If two things occur at the same time or place, it is easy to assume either that they must be connected or that one must have caused the other. For example:

> I revised really well for that exam and got a low mark, so next time I won't revise and I should get a better mark.

This assumes a connection between revision and failure, without considering other possible reasons for failure. Here is another example:

> The number of cows in Britain has gone down, and the amount of cheese consumed is on the increase. Psychologically, people seem to eat more cheese when they feel that it will run out.

This assumes an increase in cheese consumption is related to the number of British cows, whereas it could be for other reasons such as increased vegetarianism or a rise in cheese imports. The decrease in the cow population might relate only to herds reared for meat – perhaps the number of milking cows is unaltered.

These examples are chosen to highlight the faulty logic, but such flawed reasoning is not always easy to spot.

Drawing general conclusions based on one or few examples

> The woollen jacket caused a serious skin reaction in the three-year-old, so sale of woollen clothing should be banned.

Here a generalised conclusion is made on the basis of a very small sample of experience – just one example. There may have been reasons for the reaction unique to that child. The importance of using an adequate sample is explored further below.

Inappropriate comparisons

In Passage 1 a comparison is drawn between children who play indoors and those who play outdoors. However, it might be that the children who played outdoors were already healthier, and those who played indoors did so because of poor health which might deteriorate further if they play outdoors. For example, asthma sufferers allergic to pollen might have been discouraged from playing outdoors.

3   Question surface appearances

Consider such factors as these:

★ Is the evidence what it appears to be?

★ Might there be other explanations, interpretations or conclusions apart from the most obvious?

★ Has all information been provided? Might you draw different conclusions if you had further details?

★ Are there interested parties who would gain from us believing/concluding this?

★ Are there any hidden assumptions or agendas?

★ Does the evidence come from reliable, disinterested sources?

Activity

2 Vested interests

Look again at the 'Rochborough Health' passage.

➡ What hidden agendas might there be in this piece?

➡ What information might be missing that would lead to a different conclusion?

(See page 409 for feedback.)

---

4   Identify evidence in the text

Identifying evidence in the text is usually fairly straightforward. Look for statistics, examples, case histories, findings from experiments, surveys, questionnaires, case studies and details of events and sources. It could be anecdotal, such as a few people's reports of their experiences.

Activity

3 Types of evidence

What evidence is given in the 'Rochborough Health' passage? (See page 409 for feedback.)

---

5   Evaluate the evidence

It is not enough to write in an essay or report: 'There is evidence on both sides.' Evidence is not all of equal weight. How can we decide which evidence is better? Some basic guidelines are outlined below.

Use valid criteria to evaluate evidence

Critical thinking involves identifying valid criteria against which something can be evaluated.

For example, in declaring that somebody is healthy, doctors take into account certain criteria, such as body temperature, blood measurements, and the absence of known (or common) symptoms of illness. They evaluate whether signs of potential ill health are matters for concern and, on the basis of experience and established medical knowledge, come to a conclusion about whether the evidence points more towards good health than to sickness.

You look healthy to me, as your teeth are not blue.

The following sections give some criteria against which you can evaluate evidence in academic texts and for your own research.

Check the date of the research

Data might be out of date or conclusions based upon them could have been revised. How would your attitude to the 'Rochborough Health' article change if you found out that it was written in 1300, or 1927, or 2019?

Check the source of your information

Articles in academic or professional journals and in recommended textbooks are usually based on in-depth research and are regarded as more reliable than findings recorded in magazines and newspapers. Newspapers and magazines can be useful primary sources for some subjects such as cultural studies, but are not generally regarded as 'authorities' to quote in essays.

Check for bias in your sources

Bias may not be obvious, and it does not necessarily mean that your source was being 'dishonest' or 'prejudiced'. If somebody has a strong interest in the survival of a particular hospital, for example, the evidence they present might be accurate but not the full story. When thinking critically, we need to be continually questioning in our minds whether there are hidden agendas and why evidence appears to point one way rather than another.

It is always worth considering whether political or financial interests might obscure the full picture. Consider also how easy it would be now, or would have been in the past, for diverse views to be printed and circulated. For example, in some societies, such as sixteenth-century Britain, people who spoke, printed or sold certain viewpoints were punished by death or loss of limb.

It is easier for some people, organisations and viewpoints to gain funding and attention to research and promote their views. Others struggle to be heard. This means we just don't hear much about some viewpoints or do so through filters not evident to us. Whilst it is not necessary to write about political, financial or media disparities in every assignment, it is important to be aware of who has access to what kinds of power, resources and information, who does not, and the possible implications.

Beware the allure of numbers and statistics

It is important to check numerical data, and words that *imply* such data, as these are often misused and amounts misrepresented in order to sway the reader.

Most/many

Notice use of words such as 'most' and 'many':

Most people prefer oranges to apples.

'Most' is a very vague amount. If it *mattered* whether this statement were true or false, we would need more details. How many people were asked? How many preferred oranges? Under what circumstances?

Percentages   Notice when percentages are given. Suppose that the statement above read:

> 60% of people prefer oranges; 40% prefer apples.

This looks convincing: numerical quantities are given. But is the difference between 60% and 40% *significant*? Here we would need to know how many people were asked. If 1000 people were asked, of whom 600 preferred oranges, the number would be persuasive. However, if only 10 people were asked, 60% simply means that 6 people preferred oranges: '60%' sounds convincing in a way that '6 out of 10' does not. As a critical reader you need to be on the lookout for percentages being used to make insufficient data look impressive.

Sample size   Notice also that if just 2 more people arrived who preferred apples, there would be 6 of each. A very small increase in the *sample* (the database of people asked) could easily overturn the original percentage, changing it to 50% for apples and 50% for oranges – no difference at all.

The sample size is the number of people, animals or objects used in the research, whether it's an experiment, a survey or whatever. Small samples give very unreliable information. All other things being equal, the larger the sample, the more reliable the data. A thousand participants is often taken as a reasonable number for considering poll statistics to be 'significant'.

Representativeness The sample should be representative of the overall group being studied. If all those asked about fruit preference came from Seville and made their living from oranges, we might not consider them to be either reliable or typical of people in general. Similarly, if all those asked about their preferences were women, or aged ten, or from the south of England, it would not be safe to generalise from them to the rest of the population. To make their sample representative, researchers aim for a good mix of men and women, of different ages, backgrounds and interests.

Conditions of data collection   If you found out that those who said they preferred oranges had received a free orange by the person conducting the survey, you might wonder, reasonably,

whether participants' views had been unfairly swayed, and question the data's validity.

Similarly, if the data were collected in face-to-face interviews by personnel wearing the logo of a company known for its orange juice, participants might be influenced to choose oranges: in surveys and interviews respondents tend to give the answers they think are wanted. It is important to understand the conditions in which data were collected in order to determine how trustworthy they are. Articles in academic journals usually give full details about research conditions.

See also pages 264–5.

Emotive language and persuader words

Certain words can be very persuasive and can promote a position of trust in the reader. Which words they are will vary from subject to subject. For example, for some people the word 'experiment' summons up notions of scientific accuracy and reliability. However, the fact that an experimental approach was used does not in itself mean that the evidence is sound.

Emotive words   The use of words and phrases such as 'cruel', 'unfair', 'abuse', 'natural', 'normal', 'common sense', 'innocent child', 'old', 'little', 'massive', 'unique', 'extremist', 'radical', 'youth', 'new' and even 'final offer' can prompt emotional responses that may lead the reader away from an accurate appraisal of the evidence presented. Images that prompt an emotional response, whether of vulnerable people, cute animals, wedding rings, goals scored or flash cars, can be used in a similar way.

Persuader words Words and phrases such as 'surely', 'clearly', 'obviously', 'it is evident that', 'it is plain to see that', 'naturally' and 'of course' can be used to encourage the reader to assume what is being said is self-evidently true. It is useful to use such words as alerts to pause and apply your critical faculties.

Activity

4 Evaluating the evidence

Evaluate the evidence given in the 'Rochborough Health' passage, using the criteria outlined on pages 260–2. (See page 409 for feedback.)

6 Identify the writer's conclusions

Conclusions generally come at the end of a piece of writing. However, they may also be found at the beginning of the text or even in the middle. They are then harder to find and tend to be less effective.

Often conclusions are 'signposted' by words such as 'therefore', 'so', 'hence' or 'thus'; or by the use of imperatives (words indicating that something *has* to be done) such as 'must', 'should' or 'need to'.

Activity

5 Conclusions

Identify the conclusion in the 'Rochborough Health' passage. (See page 409 for feedback.)

Sometimes, the conclusion might not be stated at all – it might only be implied by the arguments and evidence. There could also be more than one conclusion to draw from a text, with some conclusions stated explicitly and others implicit. For implicit conclusions, you need to consider whether further conclusions are implied by the reasoning and the context. For example:

> In Jonah Holt's new book, *Bad Act*, the characters, plot and setting are compelling, albeit all uncannily familiar to anyone who has read Ida Gold's novels. The twist at the end makes it a good read for those who enjoy crime fiction.

Here, the *explicit* conclusion is that the book is a good read for those who enjoy crime fiction. The reason for this conclusion is given: 'the twist' in the plot. The *implicit* conclusion is that the author plagiarises Ida Gold's work.

Activity

6 Implicit conclusions

For each of the following short texts:

➡ Decide whether there is an explicit conclusion and, if so, say what this is.

➡ Say what you think the implicit conclusions would be.

  1 You want a plant. You like this one and you can afford it.

  2 The election closed very early, but only Happy Party voters had been told this would happen. Happy Party supporters prevented some opposition party voters from voting. Therefore, the election was unfair.

  3 The tree is dangerous. It is leaning over the children's playground. It is heavy, rotten and could break at any time.

(See page 409 for feedback.)

7 Evaluate whether the evidence supports the conclusions

A writer may present evidence which could be considered reliable and based on good research, but then draw conclusions that do not follow logically from it. An exaggerated example illustrates this:

★ Proposition 1 *The karate champion is a woman.* (Verifiable fact.)

★ Proposition 2 *My mother is a woman.* (Verifiable fact.)

★ Conclusion *My mother is a woman, therefore she is a karate champion.* (False conclusion.)

Check for hidden false assumptions

In the above example, the faulty reasoning was based on the false assumption that if *one* woman is a karate champion, then *all* women are karate champions. This false assumption is easy to spot, but it is not always so simple. Researchers might aim at objectivity, but it is difficult to stand completely outside of the common-sense views and ideological context of the society in which one is writing.

Example

Consider the ideas discussed in the student essays about Bowlby's influential studies of the 1950s (pages 331–5). Bowlby's findings (1951, 1969) suggested that infants who were separated from their mothers at an early age had behavioural and emotional difficulties later. This was used to argue the case against mothers working outside the home. The argument for mothers to stay home was no doubt based on genuine concerns for children's well-being, but the conclusion also suited the economic conditions of the time, as there was a shortage of jobs for men who had returned from the Second World War (1939–45).

Later, the conclusion that children were damaged by absent mothers and child care was heavily criticised (Clarke-Stewart, 1988; Tizard, 1991; Benware, 2013). For example, it was argued that Bowlby's data were based on children in very extreme conditions, such as frightened war orphans and sick children in bleak hospitals and institutions of the 1950s. These children were not typical, and needed to be compared with average, healthy children attending friendly, well run nurseries, who saw their mothers every day. However accurate Bowlby's research might have been, his findings didn't justify the conclusions drawn from them. It is quite likely that Bowlby was affected by the dominant belief system of his day, that a woman's place was at home with the children, and that this influenced his interpretation of the data. It is likely that the research of later opponents was influenced by feminism and the increased proportion of women who work.

It is quite typical for research to progress in this way, with later researchers questioning assumptions and ideologies invisible to earlier researchers or challenging the limitations of the sample.

Activity

7 Use of evidence

Do you consider that the evidence in the 'Rochborough Health' passage supports the conclusion drawn? What assumptions are made in the passage? (See page 409 for feedback.)

Critical analytical thinking

Now that you have worked through a passage step by step, analyse Passage 3, 'Children at Play'. This writer covers issues similar to those in Passage 2, so you can compare the passages.

Activity

8 Critical analytical thinking

For Passage 3:

➡ Is the line of reasoning good?

➡ What is the conclusion?

➡ How strong is the evidence?

➡ What are the underlying assumptions?

➡ How well do the reasoning and the evidence support the conclusion?

(See page 410 for feedback.)

Passage 3: Children at Play

Children need to play outdoors and yet it is amazing how few children get that opportunity today. Although Smith (2004) argues that 48% of children prefer to play inside, Jones (1964) found that 98% of children in Britain prefer to play outdoors. I spoke to some parents in Rochborough who said their children missed out by not being able to play down by the river or roam the countryside in safety. Most children are addicted to computer games or their phones. Everybody knows that this is damaging children educationally, and yet nothing is done about it. This is certainly true of Rochborough's children, and the main reason is that they do not have anywhere to play. Hardly anybody in Rochborough has a garden. It would be better for their health if they played outdoors, but parents say they won't let them unless supervised play areas are provided. The parents are worried that they cannot see their children when they are playing. What chance is there for the health of citizens in Rochborough if its children do not get to play outdoors, and end up as screen addicts?

Questioning numbers and statistics?

Can we trust numbers and statistics?

Many people have strong opinions about numbers, especially statistics. It is easy to assume either that numbers 'prove' a case or that all statistics are deceptive. Numbers simply provide information. Their meaning and value lie in your interpretation, in what else you know about the issue and how you use them.

People often quote Benjamin Disraeli's line: 'there are lies, damn lies and statistics'; this is rather unfair on statistics, which are just:

★ methods and techniques used for measuring, organising, interpreting and describing data

★ or specific sets of data produced to measure or make sense of given phenomena.

Are the data relevant?

Data might sound impressive yet be irrelevant to the conclusions being drawn. Whether or not data are relevant depends on the exact point being made. When considering data, ask yourself:

★ Are these relevant to this specific point?

★ Do these provide useful insights or suggest anomalies I should investigate further?

★ How do these affect the way I think about the issue?

Do numbers provide proof?

Numbers may appear to be convincing, but they might not be as reliable as they seem. When using any set of data, be objective and critical. Consider:

★ Do they measure what they purport to measure?

★ Are they likely to be accurate?

★ Could they contain errors or misprints?

★ How were they collected? Might this have led to mistakes or inaccuracies?

★ Who wanted them collected? Why?

★ When were they collected? Are they up to date? If not, does that matter?

★ Are they representative? Or do they refer only to particular sets of people or circumstances?

★ Do they cover exactly what I am looking for – or do I need to find other data?

★ Do they throw any useful light on the issues I am investigating?

What kind of 'sample' was used?

We are often presented with claims about the average number of devices in each home, how the average voter will vote in the next election, or what proportion of pets prefer a particular food. Such figures do not measure every home, every voter or every pet – that would take too long and be too expensive.

The total number of instances of something, such as all the plants in a meadow or the number of people who run marathons, is referred to as a *population*. As it is not usually possible to measure every item in a population, a smaller sample is taken instead.

If the sample is typical of its population, statements that are true for the sample should normally be true for that population as a whole: such a sample is said to be *representative*. If the sample is untypical of the population it purports to represent, it is said to be *unrepresentative, biased or 'weighted' in a particular direction.* If the samples are representative, you can use them to draw inferences about the whole population – these are known as *inferential statistics*.

For the result to be reliable, the sample must be large enough to be a fair representative of the population – if not, claims about proportions or rising or falling trends will be unreliable.

What kind of 'averaging' was used?

Arguments often make use of data based on 'average' instances; the average family, average age, average usage, etc. Check carefully which average is used (mean, median or mode) and whether that is the most suitable for the point being made.

For more about different kinds of averages, see the companion site at www.studyskillshandbook.co.uk.

Are the data based on estimates?

Some data are based not on actual counting but on *estimates*. For example, a newspaper report of the size of a crowd at a public demonstration may be no more than an 'informed' guess. The estimates made by the organisers and by the police might differ – and neither might be correct.

Are the data likely to change?

Estimates may change rapidly or over time. For example, the first estimate of casualties immediately following a disaster will differ from estimates made later when more accurate information becomes available. Data about the overall impact of a disaster change as long-term consequences, such as environmental effects, gradually become apparent.

Are the data still up to date?

Check whether there is an earlier or recent set of data that is more accurate or useful for comparison. For example, if a shop advertised that it won a customer satisfaction survey ten years ago, you might wonder whether current customers are as satisfied. Remember, too, that it takes time to collect, analyse and publish data: some are out of date even before they are published.

What was actually measured?

Historical data need to be treated with caution. During some historical periods, whole sections of populations were simply ignored when making counts. For example, the number of casualties typically cited for the Great Earthquake of San Francisco in 1906 omits the Chinese casualties, even though the

Chinese population at the time was significant. For much of history, the views of only a small segment of populations were counted: we cannot know what 'most people' thought if they were not allowed to vote or to register their opinions.

Good measurements must be accurate: they should measure in full what they say they measure and should not include anything else. Measurements gathered for one purpose might not be suitable to use or cite in other contexts.

What is the context?

As we saw on page 261, to interpret data, you need to understand the context, including the circumstances in which they were collected. Suppose someone won a TV song-writing competition by gaining 56% of the phoned-in votes. Would a music producer be wise to invest in this artiste?

The producer would need to know more. How many people watched the show? What proportion of them phoned in? Were they representative of those who pay for such music?

Perhaps:

★ the winner was supported by people who phoned in more than once

★ the winner was popular with phone voters but not with people who pay for this music

★ the phone lines were not working properly and only 100 people got to vote.

Critical analytical thinking

Use the following checklist to analyse texts for assignments – and to evaluate your own writing critically.

Critical questions	Analysis of the writing
What is the main line of reasoning (the main thesis or argument)?	
Is the line of reasoning clear both in the introduction and in the conclusion?	
What is the key evidence used to support the line of argument? Is the evidence presented in a way that develops the argument and leads clearly to the conclusion?	
When was the evidence produced? Is it up to date? Is it still relevant?	
Is there sufficient evidence to prove the case? Is the evidence relevant? What might be missing?	
What (if any) would have been a better order in which to present the evidence so as to strengthen the line of reasoning?	
Are there any examples of flawed reasoning? Attempts to persuade the reader through an appeal to the emotions? Is evidence interpreted and used correctly?	
Has the writer given sufficient consideration to alternative points of view? Give examples.	

Critical thinking when writing

Critical thinking when *writing* includes most of the elements of critical thinking you would use when *reading*. It can be more difficult to analyse your own work critically, however, and to recognise and admit to your own opinions and bias.

Be clear about your position on the issue, including hypotheses and conclusions

Students' writing is often weakened because their thinking is not clear before they start to write their final draft. Time spent in such critical analysis is equivalent to 'elaborating the problem' – a process which, as we saw in Chapter 4, was one way in which those who achieved well differed from those with poor marks/grades.

Be clear about your conclusions

It is not unusual for students to hand in work which shows that although they have done the necessary reading and even given their work considerable thought, they are not sure of their conclusions. That weakens their argument and undermines their efforts. The whole of a piece of writing should lead to its conclusions: if these are vague, understated or poorly formulated, *all* of the writing loses its force.

As soon as you are given an assignment, write out your initial position on the issue and what you think your conclusion will be: what is the main point that you are trying to argue or prove? Put this where you can see it.

Whenever you discover information or have ideas that require you to revise or fine-tune your conclusion, write out a new one. It may seem paradoxical (or back to front) to write the conclusion first, but it will help focus your work and writing. If you are testing a hypothesis, keep clear records of evidence that either supports or does not support that hypothesis.

Construct a clear line of reasoning

If your conclusions are clear, your argument or line of reasoning is likely to be clear also. The conclusion gives you a goal at which to shoot.

Keep your writing focused, rather than rambling. Bear in mind these four guidelines from Chapter 13:

1 Early drafts help to elaborate and refine thinking. Your final version should state your position clearly.
2 Create a writing plan that sets out reasons, examples and evidence in the most logical order.
3 Consider how best to link up your material, so that your writing is not just a list of facts but an organised, well-developed argument.
4 Keep your argument clear: including too much detail can obscure it. Draw together your best material and ideas, selecting carefully. Shape these to support your argument. Use paragraphing, link words and phrasing to signpost points clearly.

Use evidence to support your reasoning

A large part of your assignment will consist of evaluating and presenting the best evidence to support your case.

Take multiple perspectives

The best answers identify how and why various experts agree or disagree on an issue, and demonstrate how the evidence supports, or does not support, their positions. This means considering strengths, weaknesses, and grey areas. The answer is seldom a straightforward one of right or wrong. Usually there are many contradictory pieces of evidence to weigh up and evaluate against each other. Your final position or conclusions are likely to be a personal synthesis of these.

Analyse your own work critically

Your tutors or examiners will take a critical reading approach when marking your work. Before handing in an assignment, analyse it critically as you would other material you read. Be a fierce critic of your own work so that you can spot weaknesses and address them, and to be clear about the strengths of your own argument. Use the checklist on page 266 to assist your analysis.

Critical analytical writing vs. descriptive writing

Critical writing

In general, students lose more marks for lack of critical analysis than for any other single weakness in their work.

Good critical writing generally makes the difference between getting the highest grades for a degree and getting a lower grade. Typical tutor comments on student writing include:

★ 'More analysis needed.'

★ 'Less description, more critique.'

★ 'Too descriptive.'

★ 'Descriptive rather than analytical.'

★ 'You have told me what the theory is rather than how you evaluate it.'

Finding the balance

Both descriptive and analytical writing have their place. *Descriptive* writing is needed to give essential background information so that the writing makes sense to the reader. However, this should usually be kept to the bare minimum – if you use up most of your word limit on description, you will have fewer words to use for the critical analysis so important to higher grades.

Skilled writers use descriptive writing in the appropriate sections of their writing (see **Writing the report**, pages 365–6), or weave small amounts of descriptive writing *into* their critical writing. Some of the main differences between these two types of writing are outlined in the table below.

Descriptive writing	Critical analytical writing
states what happened	identifies the significance of what happened
states what something is like	evaluates its strengths and weaknesses
gives the story so far	weighs one piece of information against another
outlines the order in which things happened	draws reasoned judgements
instructs how to do something	argues a case according to the evidence
lists the main elements of a theory	clarifies why the theory is relevant/how it applies
outlines how something works	indicates why something will work (best)
notes the method used	draws out its strengths/ weaknesses/appropriateness
states when something occurred	identifies why the timing is of importance
states the different components	weighs up the importance of component parts
states options	gives reasons for selecting each option
lists details	evaluates the relative significance of details
lists in any order	structures information in order of importance
states links between items	draws out the relevance of the links
gives information or reports findings	evaluates information and draws conclusions

Identifying critical and descriptive writing

Descriptive writing: an example

My name is John. I live at 33 Acacia Drive. I have five sisters and brothers. I am good at team games, and enjoy football, cricket, and baseball. Team games were encouraged by both my parents. All of my family took part in sport. Our teachers at Beckfield School were very interested in sports sciences. We were encouraged to drink lots of water to improve our performance. Our team always did well, so it seems to have worked. I also like to go running. I live in the beautiful Welsh borders, so it is a pleasure to take a healthy run each day.

Almost all of this passage consists of statements and descriptions. There is an evaluative comment ('our team always did well') and this is linked to possible reasons (drinking lots of water). However, this link is not *analysed* in depth. The passage overall is descriptive. Compare this with the passage below.

Critical analytical writing: an example

At Beckfield School, teachers took a scientific approach to school sports over a ten-year period. In particular, pupils were encouraged to monitor their intake of liquids. All pupils were required to drink a minimum of eight glasses of tap water a day. The school did consistently well in sports competitions over this period, and the teachers claimed that this was proof of the importance of liquid intake to good performance. However, it is not clear that the school's sports performance can be attributed to water intake. Beckfield School's claims were investigated by an independent researcher, Martinez (2018). Martinez argued that although Beckfield's performance was good, its performance in competitions was consistent with what would be expected of a school of its size. In addition, interviews with pupils showed that most had not followed the school regulations on drinking water. Most pupils stated that they drank less than one glass of tap water a day. Although other research does suggest that water intake benefits performance (Fredo, 2016; Mitsuki, 2016), Beckfield School's claims about the benefits of tap water in its sports success have not been proved.

This is critical analytical writing. There is a clear line of reasoning which takes the reader through what the school claimed and the basis of the school's arguments. The writing then weighs the school's claims against other evidence. It draws upon published evidence rather than personal opinion. The writer considers both sides of the argument, taking account of published evidence that does support the importance of drinking water. This research has been weighed against the facts of the case. The writer draws conclusions: the 'school's claims about the benefits of tap water ... have not been proved'. The conclusion is based upon the evidence from that school.

The passage does contain descriptive writing which gives background detail, such as the first four sentences. Although the passage contains many statements of fact, such as 'most pupils stated that they drank less than one glass of tap water a day', these statements are ordered in such a way that they build up the argument. They are also supported by sentences that take forward the next step in the argument, such as 'However, it is not clear that the school's sports performance can be attributed to water intake.'

Activity

9 Descriptive or critical?

Identify whether the following passages are examples of descriptive or of critical writing. (Feedback is given on page 411.)

Passage 1

In the West, all life forms are divided into one of two categories: plant or animal. Animals move and take in food. Plants are rooted into the earth in some way and lack locomotion. They photosynthesise their food. Zoologists study animals, and botanists study plants. Bacteria were classified as plants because many kinds of bacteria photosynthesise their food. However, they also have locomotion. Recent research has shown that there is an enormous variety of bacteria. Some are able to survive at extreme temperatures and in the absence of oxygen. Most plants cannot usually survive in those conditions. Therefore, even though bacteria photosynthesise, they are not now regarded as plants.

Passage 2

The difficulty in categorising bacteria was partly based on the assumption that all life forms were divided into two main categories, plants and animals. Organisms that photosynthesised and lacked mobility were classified as plants; those that had locomotion and ingested food were classified as animals. Bacteria were traditionally categorised as plants because many forms of bacteria photosynthesised their food like plants. However, bacteria also have locomotion, associated with animal life. Genetic research has now shown that there are at least eleven major divisions of bacteria, all of which are more genetically distinct than plants are from animals (Fuhrman et al., 1992). In addition, the minute organisms formerly described as 'bacteria' are now found to consist of several major kingdoms and domains of unicellular and multicellular life (bacteria, archaea, eucarya) (Woese, 1994). This research is significant as it has shown that the fundamental division of all life forms into 'plant' or 'animal' was an error, and that plants and animals form only a very small part of a much more diverse range of living organisms.

Passage 3

Scientists do not agree about the extent to which creativity can be linked to activity in the right hemisphere of the brain. It is known that the biochemistry of the two hemispheres of the brain is different. For example, there is more of the neurotransmitter, norepinephrine, in the right hemisphere than the left (Oke et al., 1978). Norepinephrine is associated with increased alertness to visual stimuli. It has been suggested by Springer and Deutsch (1981) that this may lead to increased right-hemisphere specialisation for visual and spatial perception. However, this link is not yet proven. It is not yet clear whether one hemisphere of the brain can be responsible for any creative task. Moreover, although it might seem reasonable to assume that responsiveness to visual stimulus may be an important factor of creativity, this has also not yet been proved.

Passage 4

The brain contains millions of neurons. These communicate with each other through electrochemical activity at the synapses found at the end of each neuron. The chemicals that enable this communication to take place are known as neurotransmitters. Each neurotransmitter is associated with different kinds of message. The different messages to the brain influence the way we respond to events that take place in our internal or external world. Some neurotransmitters are associated with mood swings, with depression, with rapid responses, and so forth.

Passage 5

Bowlby's Attachment Theory argues that child development is affected by the closeness of the bond between mother and child. Bowlby claimed that even short spells away from the mother during infancy could have a profound effect upon a person later in life. This became known as 'maternal deprivation theory'. According to this theory, the relationship with the mother during an early 'critical period' gives the developing child an 'internal working model'. This model then forms the foundation of all future relationships.

Critical thinking when listening

When would I do this as a student?

★ In lectures, classes, discussions
★ When using recorded lectures or podcasts
★ When using audio-material online
★ For developing inter-cultural competence.

Listening to audio material

It isn't always possible to go back over what you hear whilst listening, making it harder to notice flawed reasoning. It is also easier to be carried along by the skills and qualities of the speaker.

Prepare in advance. Read or browse a reputable text before listening. If you are already informed about the subject, it is easier to identify flaws in the arguments or evidence.

Identify the thread. Focus on the line of reasoning, or argument, just as you would when reading. This will help avoid being distracted by interesting or emotive details and anecdotes.

Question closely what you hear, even if it sounds plausible or it is your lecturers speaking. Take nothing at face value.

Evaluate the evidence. Identify the evidence used to support the argument. Apply the same critical approaches as when reading.

Check when listening ...

Check whether you are being swayed unduly by such factors as:

★ the speaker's celebrity, role or job
★ impressive verbal fluency or vocabulary
★ clever phrasing or use of humour
★ the passion of the speaker
★ appeals to your emotions
★ use of possibly irrelevant facts or data, used to make the speakers sound more authoritative
★ repetition used to emphasise some points at the expense of others
★ speakers hopping between topics, preventing you from analysing their logic
★ interviewers' use of unfair questioning techniques.

Critical selection of podcasts

The value of podcasts

★ There are podcasts of excellent academic quality, available as open source, giving you access to cutting edge research from around the world.

★ You can listen back over the material, to help you analyse it critically and check the details.

Select good podcasts such as:

★ Podcasts provided by your lecturers – as most likely to be relevant for your course.
★ iTunes: offers podcasts from all kinds of universities and colleges worldwide.
★ Podcasts by known subject experts or produced by academic publishers.
★ TED (www.ted.com): offers free audiovisual sources in a wide range of disciplines.

Content over style

When listening to podcasts created by lecturers, such as on iTunesU, listen for the quality of the content – even if the sound quality and production values are not perfect.

Review

1 **Appreciate the importance of critical thinking**

It has a big impact on grades and affects almost every aspect of study. It is also a skill high in demand by employers. It is an ability that you can develop through practice and through greater awareness of ways that errors, misinterpretations and bias can creep in.

2 **Develop a detective-like mind**

Be open-minded, systematic and honest in pursuit of deeper knowledge and understanding – of the world, issues, events, situations, arts, media – and yourself.

3 **Develop systematic approaches**

Develop questions, approaches and methods that help you dig deeper into the issues in objective ways, and that help protect against unconscious bias, assumptions and other unrecognised influences on your thinking. The seven-step method used in this chapter is a useful starting point.

4 **Use integrity**

Be ready to question your own assumptions, and to recognise flaws in your own position or weaknesses in your data. If your evidence isn't clear, say so or look further.

5 **Keep questioning and re-examining**

Keep considering whether there could be other potential reasons, interpretations, explanations, or angles that haven't yet been thought through in depth. A useful starter checklist is provided (page 256).

6 **Read and listen with criticality**

Become more aware of where you need to slow down, pause and question. Recognise when and why you are more likely to jump to conclusions and make assumptions.

7 **Include critical analysis within your work**

Know what it looks like – and the difference between descriptive writing and critical analysis. Look for opportunities to include strong critical analysis within your assignments and exam answers.

8 **Apply criticality to your own work**

Learn to bring an honest, fair, critical eye to your own writing or other aspects of your course. Set criteria for evaluating your work objectively, so that you can improve it before submitting it, and identify ways of improving your work in future.

9 **Keep developing your critical abilities**

The more advanced your level of study, the more sophisticated you will need to become in the way you engage critically with the debates in your subject. As you progress through your programme, you will be introduced to methods and texts that will refine your criticality.

10 **Find out more**

If you are interested in developing your critical and analytical thinking skills in greater depth, you may find it helpful to look at: Cottrell, S. (2017) *Critical Thinking Skills*. 3rd edn. London: Red Globe Press.

Chapter 13

Writing at university level

Learning outcomes

This chapter offers you opportunities to:

- ✓ **develop your own process as a 'writer'**
- ✓ **become better at managing academic writing tasks from start to finish**
- ✓ **apply a seven-step procedure for writing assignments**
- ✓ **organise and structure material and concepts for academic assignments**
- ✓ **develop strategies for specific aspects of the writing process such as managing writer's block**
- ✓ **approach academic writing tasks at this level with greater confidence.**

Academic writing

Writing a good assignment is both a challenge and one of the most rewarding aspects of study. It offers a great opportunity for focusing your mind and gaining mastery of a new topic, as well as developing a skill useful for life, employment and study. With the right approach, writing assignments can be inspiring, fascinating and enjoyable!

Assignments at this level are meant to stretch you intellectually so they will seem challenging at times. The advantage is that, usually, students find their writing skills develop significantly. This arises from a combination of:

★ enhanced vocabulary and critical awareness gained from reading, writing and discussion on the course

★ the amount of practice they gain in writing notes and assignments

★ working at their writing to improve their grades.

Typically, students have many questions about what is expected of them and what their tutors look for when marking (or grading) written assignments. That sense of 'not knowing' can be unsettling and deter students from starting and persisting with assignments. Chapters 13–16 clarify core conventions and expectations and provide easy to follow procedures for producing a good assignment.

If you find you know some of this already, that is good and should reassure you. If any is new to you, don't worry: it will become very familiar in time.

Writing tasks cannot be separated from other processes such as critical thinking, organisation and research. Before completing a piece of writing, you might find it helpful to look at Chapters 10–12 too.

As your writing skills develop and you become more familiar with what is required for academic tasks, you can become more flexible in your approach. However, creative flexibility usually has to be within the conventions of the subject discipline: be aware of what is acceptable and what is not, for your subject.

Developing your own writing process

10 considerations for developing your own writing process

1. Best way to write?	Every writer approaches it differently: at a set time every day or non-stop for a week; by planning it in detail first or generating ideas and structure through the act of writing. Experiment: find what works.
2. Can't envisage the process?	It is useful to have a mental map of what to do and when (pages 275 and 282–3). This helps you to hold key tasks in mind and manage time. It is likely you will move back and forth to refine and complete a piece of writing.
3. Things don't go to plan?	Be prepared to flex your plan and leave plenty of time to do so. The writing process can be unpredictable: you might find you write for hours when you had planned ten minutes, or take hours to write little.
4. Writing is a messy process?	Yes, it can be. What seemed brilliant when you wrote it might not seem so later. Improving one section can necessitate rewriting others. Clarify your thoughts to help you articulate ideas for your final version.
5. No ideas? Not much to say?	Use lecture material, recommended reading, podcasts and videos to stimulate ideas. Compare and contrast what you discover in these, evaluating their best and weak points. Find details to add. See page 291.
6. Unsure what to write first?	There are no rules. You can start with the parts you find easiest. A draft conclusion provides a useful focus. Introductions can be easier to write once the body of the writing is finished.
7. Can't get started?	Or writer's block? Experiment with tricks and techniques to get something down on paper. See pages 278–80.
8. Can't write well?	Like any skill, writing improves with practice, so don't avoid it: write more! Consider taking a writing course. Keep a blog or journal. Write for yourself as well as your tutors.
9. Not sure what is 'good'?	You don't need to aim at a given written answer for an assignment – there are many ways a piece of writing can excel. Do use academic writing conventions (pages 302–3), marking criteria and feedback (pages 315–16).
10. Writing skills rusty?	If you haven't written much for a while, or want to write something other than assignments, see the companion site for some ideas to get you started and to practise. 🛜 www.studyskillshandbook.co.uk.

Don't get overwhelmed: draw on your existing expertise

Every day you are involved in situations that require you to plan and to make decisions similar to those involved in writing. Choose one activity you completed recently, such as planning a holiday, choosing your course or organising a party. Write down what you did, from start to finish. It probably involved six stages.

In the box opposite, identify ✓ the stages you went through to complete your activity.

Getting organised

- ☐ 1 Deciding in general what to do.
- ☐ 2 Collecting relevant information or materials to complete the task.
- ☐ 3 Planning the order to do things.
- ☐ 4 Carrying out the plan.
- ☐ 5 Checking that you were going about the task in the right way.
- ☐ 6 Reflecting on how you would do it better next time.

Academic writing follows a similar pattern of planning and decision-making. Suppose you were asked to write about 'The influence of theories on cloning animals'. You might know very little about the subject, and you may have no clear opinion. However, you can still approach the writing task much as you did with the activity opposite.

Activity

Approaching a writing task

To plan a piece of writing you would probably take the steps shown in the table, but not in the order given.

➡ Rearrange the steps in the order you would be likely to carry them out.

➡ Consider a second order you could use.

➡ Then look below and compare your responses.

➡ Would your own suggested order suit you better?

Possible sequences

1 9 12 11 10
6 2 13 3 7 8 4 5

1 10 9 11 12
6 2 13 3 8 7 4 5

Steps taken	Order
1 Decide how you would do better next time	
2 Make an outline plan	
3 Put the ideas in order	
4 Research the subject (reading, conducting interviews, experiments, etc.)	
5 Examine the assignment question and decide what is required	
6 Write a rough draft	
7 Take notes from your reading (or interviews, experiments, etc.)	
8 Select the relevant information to include	
9 Write the final draft	
10 Write out the references (books and other sources of information)	
11 Read through the writing, checking for sense and small errors; make corrections	
12 Check if your text is within the word limit	
13 Separate main ideas from supporting detail and examples	

Students' solutions to writing blocks

Here two students describe how they incorporate some of the ideas mentioned in this chapter into their own way of working. How would you adapt their methods to suit you?

Marco

WHAT I USED TO DO

I used to find myself staring at the blank screen, not knowing where to begin. I had done the reading. I knew in my head what I wanted to say, but getting started on a piece of writing seemed harder than climbing Everest. Whatever I wrote seemed wrong. I used to write the first line and delete it twenty or thirty times – maybe more, then leave it, come back, and do the same thing again.

WHAT I DO NOW

I realise now that I used to aim at writing my good draft long before I was ready. My plans were too skimpy to be useful. I was actually trying to develop my ideas, organise information, write a final draft and compose good academic prose all at the same time. No wonder I found it hard.

The first thing I do now is insert an emoticon to smile back at me. It reminds me that this is only a draft – not my final version. That reduces some of the pressure. Next, I look away from the page or screen, and stop writing. I think of a few things I want to include in my writing and jot them down as a list. Once my list gets long, I turn it into a map, chart or diagram to arrange my ideas – I think other people do it the other way round but it seems to work OK for me like this. I push each idea as far as I can take it by asking questions (who? why? always? everywhere? example? how do I know this? etc.). As I read or go through my lecture notes, I add new bits to the chart.

When I have all the information I need on my chart, I check that each piece is where it fits best. I rename themes until I get them right. I number the main themes in the order I'll use them in my writing. I do the same with the topics I will cover under each theme, and any other material – so I know exactly where everything fits. I circle and shade each key theme so it stands out. Sometimes I turn the chart back into a numbered list or plan now, so I am clear what I am doing.

I then start with whatever topic looks easiest and just write the basics – not being too fussy at this stage about whether it sounds good – it's just a starting place. I remind myself that I am free to write any sentence or bits of sentences in any order that I find easiest to do. I can always correct and edit and move things around later. When I have something down in writing, I find it much easier to rewrite it. Ideas and obvious corrections come more easily to me then.

By the time I write my best version, I am already nearly there. By working in stages, there is not that awful moment when writing actually 'begins' – it has developed bit by bit.

Ayeesha

I have revolutionised my writing. I am a 'headings and points' (1, 2, 3) person. I type these out first. This organises everything easily. Then it's like joining up the dots. I write a sentence or two about each point. Everything under one heading is a paragraph. Then I write my conclusion, and the introduction. I keep correcting tiny bits as I go along – I am a perfectionist, I suppose. At the end, if it's an essay, I erase the headings, and find a hundred things to correct – mostly quite small. Then I print it out to read the hard copy, and this usually shows up different things to correct. I might do this many times. I feel like an artist fine-tuning my work until I am happy with it. Well, I am never 100% happy. No piece of writing is perfect. You just have to make a decision at some point that 'that's it', the best you can do for now, and make sure you submit it on time.

Common features of all academic writing

Although assignments differ, most academic writing shares some common characteristics. These require you to do the following.

Draw on good source materials

Do not simply state your personal opinion or what first comes to mind. Draw on good quality material to develop your thinking and to support your case. Use these to provide reasons, evidence, examples and case studies.

Compare and contrast

Most assignments require some element of comparing and contrasting, especially of theories, models or research findings. You would normally evaluate several perspectives, theories or schools of thought, weighing these against each other.

Use criteria to evaluate

It should be clear from your writing which criteria you have used to evaluate evidence. This is often indicated through phrases such as 'the most recent data' (giving dates), or 'data from the largest survey'.

It should be evident that you have really thought about whether the evidence base is convincing, and that you are not over-impressed by material just because it is in print or on the internet. Use Chapter 12 *Critical analytical thinking*.

Show awareness of complexities and nuances

Demonstrate that you are aware that answers are not always clear-cut and that there may be some weaknesses even within an overall strong case. For example, although experts you quote might sound convincing, they may:

★ base their conclusions on a very small number of examples

★ refer to a large survey or database, but not all the data might be directly relevant to the question.

Similarly, be prepared to acknowledge weaknesses in your own arguments, and strengths in potential counter-arguments. State clearly why there are difficulties in coming to a firm conclusion one way or another.

Provide a well-structured argument

In your writing, provide a line of reasoning which gives direction to your writing: each point should follow logically from another. (Use Chapters 12 and 14.)

Make a decision

Don't sit on the fence. Indicate which side of the argument, or which model or theory, you believe is best. Even though the case may be fairly evenly weighted, show that you are able to make a decision on the basis of the evidence.

Synthesise

Look to see if you can draw together the best of several different points of view. Combining these may provide a new overall perspective.

Follow a set structure

There is likely to be a set structure for the type of assignment and a particular style for your subject discipline. (Different styles are considered in the next chapter.) *All* academic writing requires that you group similar points together in one paragraph or section, rather than introducing them in a disorganised way.

Be 'discursive'

Use your writing to discuss the points you make. Link your points so that they feed into sentences and paragraphs, and so each paragraph follows on logically. Every point you make should contribute to a central guiding line of reasoning, as outlined in Chapter 12. All this is different from presenting a random set of points, or a set of headings and bullet points, or stating what others have written.

Be emotionally neutral

Most academic writing apart from experiential writing requires you to stand back and analyse dispassionately, as an objective onlooker.

Analyse the question

Understand the task

However they are worded, all assignment titles contain one or more central questions which have to be answered. Your main task is to apply what you know to a particular problem. It is *not* to show how much you know – however brilliant your piece of writing, if it does not 'answer the question' you may get no marks at all.

You are marked partly on how well you select and organise information to meet the requirements of the question or problem – even in exams. Use the question to guide you in selecting what to read and note.

Analyse the title

Pick the title to bits

It's essential to take the time to understand what is required.

★ Read the title aloud slowly three times.

★ Underline or highlight words which tell you the *approach* to take (page 285).

★ Underline words which guide you on how to select the *subject matter* of the assignment.

★ Write out the title to help you absorb it.

★ How many sections are there to it?

★ Write it out more fully, putting it in your own words. What is the assignment really looking for? What are the central questions?

★ How does the title link to what you have read or heard in lectures?

★ To which topical issues does it refer?

★ Discuss the title with someone else to check for alternative interpretations.

Delve deeper

Write down in your own words exactly what the question requires. It may form a useful part of your introduction later. To help identify the core question(s) you need to address in the assignment title, do this:

★ Note explicit or obvious questions in the title, such as 'Why did this happen?' 'How effective ...?' or 'Which was more successful ...?'

★ Consider why this question was set. Is there some public or academic controversy you should know about? Or a recent publication on the topic? Are there important issues to include?

★ Jot down your initial thoughts about it. What do you already know? Do you have evidence to back up your opinions?

★ What do you not know yet? Where or how can you find out more?

Retain your focus on the title

Put the title where you can see it easily.

Keep checking the exact wording

As you research and write, remind yourself of the *exact wording* of the title. It is easy to forget your focus and drift off on a tangent.

Introductions

In your 'Introduction' (the first paragraphs of your writing), refer directly to the title in order to focus your reader. Indicate how you interpret it, rephrasing it in your own words. (If you misunderstood the question, at least the reader will be aware of what has happened.)

Conclusions

In your conclusion, refer back to the title to demonstrate to your reader that you are still answering the set question. Link your final sentence to the question contained in the title.

Academic keywords used in titles

These words indicate the approach or style expected for the piece of writing.

Account for Give reasons for; explain why something happens.

Analyse Examine in close detail and in terms of component parts; identify important points and chief features.

Assess Evaluate the merits of something, such as an argument, recommendation or application, typically drawing out strengths and weaknesses.

Comment on Identify and write about the main issues, giving your reactions based upon what you have read or heard in lectures. Avoid purely personal opinion.

Compare Draw out the similarities or common features, indicating the relevance or consequences of these similarities.

Consider *As in 'Consider the implications of ...'* *(or similar)* Analyse the key issues, reflecting on the different viewpoints in a balanced way.

Contrast Set two or more items or arguments in opposition so as to draw out differences. Indicate whether the differences are significant. If appropriate, give reasons why one item or argument may be preferable (see Chapter 12).

Critically evaluate Weigh arguments for and against something, assessing the strength of the evidence on both sides. Use criteria to guide your assessment of which opinions, theories, models or items are preferable.

Define Give the exact meaning of. Where relevant, show that you understand why the definition may be problematic.

Describe Give the main characteristics or features of something, or outline the main events.

Discuss Write about the most important aspects of (probably including criticism); give arguments for and against; consider the implications of.

Distinguish Bring out the differences between two (possibly confusable) items.

Evaluate Assess the worth, importance or usefulness of something, using evidence. There will probably be cases to be made both *for* and *against*.

Examine Put the subject 'under the microscope', looking at it in detail. If appropriate, 'Critically evaluate' it as well.

Explain Make clear why something happens, or why something is the way it is.

Illustrate Provide examples or evidence to make a point or clarify a position on an issue.

Interpret Give the meaning and relevance of data or other material presented.

Justify Give reasons, supported by evidence, to support a particular argument, point of view or action; address objections that others might make.

Narrate Concentrate on saying *what* happened, telling it as a story or chronology of events.

Outline Give only the main points, showing the main structure.

Relate Show similarities and connections between two or more things.

State Give the main features, in very clear English (almost like a simple list but written in full sentences).

Summarise Draw out the main points in brief (see 'Outline'), omitting details or examples.

To what extent Consider how far something is true, or contributes to a final outcome. Consider also ways in which the proposition is not true. (The answer is usually somewhere between 'completely' and 'not at all'.)

Trace Follow the order of different stages in an event or process.

Structuring your writing

The structure and organisation of your work is just as important as the content. This helps you to get your point across, and indicates your understanding and clarity of thought.

How do you structure academic writing?

Like a building, a piece of academic writing gains its structure and shape from several elements.

Design: your argument

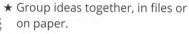

What you are trying to say (your argument) should provide the structure for the whole piece of writing. Your reader should be able to follow your line of reasoning easily: how it moves from *a* to *b* to *c*. (Page 311 and Chapter 14.)

Scaffolding: organising and planning

Organise and plan your work before you start.

★ Group ideas together, in files or on paper.

★ Devise a working plan to guide your research.

★ Make an outline plan for your writing. (Pages 287 and 323.)

Central framework: formal structure

Different formal structures are required for different kinds of assignment, such as essays or reports. (Pages 325–8 and 364.)

Building blocks: paragraphs

Writing is organised into paragraphs, and each paragraph itself has a structure. Clear paragraphing assists the reader. (Pages 293–5.)

Cement: phrasing and linking

Use language to clarify and emphasise points and show the direction of your argument. (Page 296.)

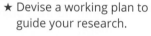

Organising information: grouping things together

First try this ...

For each box, work out:

★ How many circles are there?

★ How many triangles?

★ How many *types* of triangle?

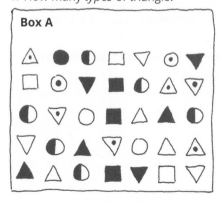

Box A

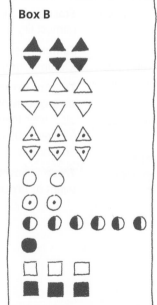

Box B

Comment

You probably found it quicker and easier to find the answers for Box B. If so, why was this the case?

Why group information?

Grouping ideas and points has several advantages.

★ You will be able to find things more easily.

★ You will find it easier to draw up your writing plan and follow it.

★ Your thinking will be clearer.

★ Your readers will be able to follow your argument more easily.

★ You will get in a mess if you don't.

See pages 287 and 289–91.

Organising information: planning your writing

Below are four steps you will need to take in order to organise information for assignments. Each step makes the next one easier. (See also *Reading, recording and using information*, page 245.)

1 Divide the work into topics

When making notes, it may be easiest to use a separate file or sheet for each main point or topic. You could use a large sheet of paper, writing out points so you can see them all clearly.

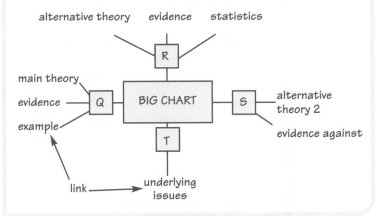

2 Rearrange your notes

★ Either spread out hard copies of notes so that you can see them, or compare on screen.

★ Group related information in one place.

★ Arrange the material in the best order.

notes about Q (red)	notes about R (yellow)
notes about S (green)	notes about T (blue)

3 Write an outline plan

When making notes, it can be easier to use a separate file or sheet for each main point or topic if this helps you to find things faster. You could use a large sheet of paper, writing out points so you can see them all at a glance.

Outline plan

1 Title
2 Introduction
3 Main argument – notes Q (red)
   evidence for – notes Q, p. 3–4
   evidence against: Q, p. 5 (orange)
   evaluation of evidence
4 Alternative theory: notes R (yellow)
   example of application
   evidence for
   evidence against (lemon)
   why not convincing
5 Alternative theory 2: notes S (green)
   evaluation of evidence
   why not convincing
6 Underlying issues – notes T (blue)
7 Conclusions
   a
   b
   c

4 Organise information into paragraphs

Colour-code each set of notes. Give each topic or paragraph a colour; underline the main points using this colour. The plan opposite uses the sequence of colours of the rainbow, to assist memory. Be consistent in using your colour coding on pattern notes, outline plans, and rough drafts. Divide hard copy files of notes using coloured dividers.

Once you start writing, each paragraph should have one main idea – with supporting detail or evidence, and relating to one set (or page) of notes (page 294).

Planning in stages

Develop your outline plan

Drawing up an initial outline plan

Make pattern notes or a structured outline plan showing what you know, what at this stage you think are the main issues, your questions, and a 'To Do' list of things to find out or follow up.

Creating an Action Plan

Convert your 'To Do' list into an action plan with priorities (page 136).

Planning your time

Use *Working backwards from deadlines* (page 140) and your diary or planner to map out when and where you will complete each stage of the writing process. This becomes easier after a few assignments, when you gain a sense of your own pace for working at this level.

What is the *minimum* you can do? What additional research would you *like* to do, if you have time? Depending on how well you proceed, you can adapt your reading and note-making to suit.

Reworking your plan

If necessary, rework your outline plan as you proceed. You may need to rework it several times as you find out more about the subject, controversies and issues, and as your thinking about the topic becomes more sophisticated.

Making a clear final outline plan

Clarify your final plan. Use colour to highlight certain areas, or rewrite untidy parts afresh. Beware of using the excuse of 'neatening' or 'updating' the plan to delay settling down to writing.

For software that helps with this, see the companion site at www.studyskillshandbook.co.uk.

From pattern notes to linear plan

It's essential to be really clear about the structure of your assignment before you start writing your final drafts. Otherwise, your writing and thinking are likely to sound muddled.

Advantages of pattern notes

Pattern notes, or mind maps, illustrate connections and resemble the way the mind organises information in networks, so can be a helpful starting point for generating ideas.

Limitations of pattern notes and 'mind maps'

It can be difficult to write assignments directly from them as they show interconnected webs of ideas as a whole, whereas writing is linear and sequential – one point follows another. They also tend to be less effective for the kinds of analysis, evaluation, comparing and contrasting needed for academic assignments. Consider whether to use charts such as on pages 326–30 instead.

Converting pattern notes into a linear plan

★ *Generate*: Use the pattern notes to brainstorm what you know and to generate ideas.

★ *Find connections*: Use colour, numbers and connecting lines to link related information in the pattern notes.

★ *Group*: Rework the pattern notes, placing together all connected information.

★ *Create a hierarchy*: As a half-way stage between making pattern notes and sequential writing, it helps to organise your ideas hierarchically so that key points stand out from underlying details. (See pages 289–91.)

★ *Create headings and points*: Give each area of your pattern notes a title or heading. Type out a list of the headings, then type a list beneath it of all points that relate to that heading. Use your colour-code as a guide to what belongs in each paragraph.

★ *Relate to the plan*: Position these lists on your spatial plan (page 323).

Concept pyramids organise ideas

What is a concept?

A *concept* is a mental representation of a group of items which are similar in some way. For example, the concept 'cutlery' includes objects as different as a four-pronged fork, a hollowed, round-ended spoon, and a sharp-edged knife. Conceptually, these all share the characteristic of being tools used in eating food. Sometimes the phrase *conceptual category* is used instead of 'concept'.

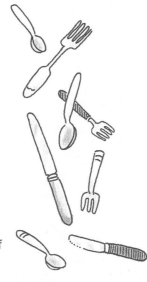

Why concepts are useful

When we come across a new object, the brain matches the main features of the new experience against those of previous experiences. It can then make a good guess at what kind of thing the new object is – its concept category:

'Branches, trunk, leaves, bird's nest: must be a tree'

Once it has identified the category, the brain can second-guess, or infer, other information:

'If it's a tree, it must have roots and sap. It won't leave the area. I don't need to take it for walks. Sorted!'

This ability to identify and share conceptual categories enables us to communicate more easily with other people: we don't need to describe everything in minute detail whenever we speak. In academic writing, if ideas are well organised, the reader can second-guess meaning and other information more easily.

Concept pyramids organise ideas

We can organise concepts into hierarchies – shaped like a triangle or pyramid, as in the simple one for 'tree' below. You don't *have* to use concept pyramids – but they give you an extra analytical tool.

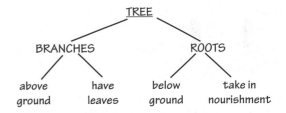

TREE

BRANCHES   ROOTS

above   have   below   take in
ground   leaves   ground   nourishment

The most general information, or the most inclusive heading, is placed at the top of the pyramid. Aspects of the tree are placed below. Details of those aspects are placed below again – and so on.

Each level of the pyramid shows information of a different category. There are technical names for different category levels, but everyday terms work just as well.

Technical term	Everyday term
Superordinate category	Upper level (*tree*)
Intermediate or basic category	Intermediate level (*oak tree*)
Subordinate category	Lower level (*red oak tree*)
Exemplar	Example (*this red oak tree*)

On another pyramid, *plant* might be the upper-level concept, and *tree* would then be at the intermediate level.

Concept pyramid example: Contrast birds and mammals

The example below is of a more detailed concept pyramid, showing how different levels of information about animals can be arranged.

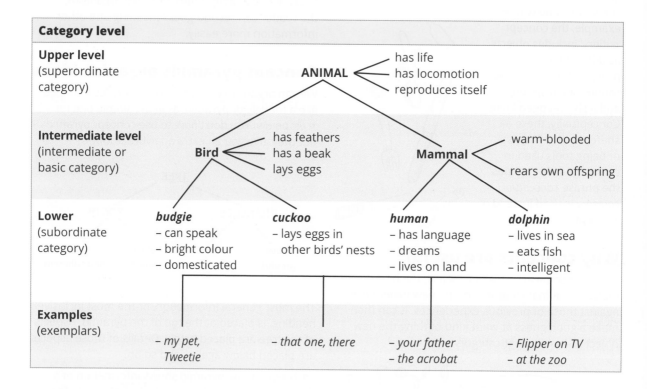

Category level				
Upper level (superordinate category)		ANIMAL — has life / has locomotion / reproduces itself		
Intermediate level (intermediate or basic category)	Bird — has feathers / has a beak / lays eggs		Mammal — warm-blooded / rears own offspring	
Lower (subordinate category)	*budgie* – can speak – bright colour – domesticated	*cuckoo* – lays eggs in other birds' nests	*human* – has language – dreams – lives on land	*dolphin* – lives in sea – eats fish – intelligent
Examples (exemplars)	– *my pet, Tweetie*	– *that one, there*	– *your father* – *the acrobat*	– *Flipper on TV* – *at the zoo*

Examples at different levels

If the upper level were *painting*, an intermediate level could be the style, *Impressionism*. A lower level would be painters, such as *Monet*, and examples could be Monet's paintings *Water Lilies*, *Wisteria*, and *Poplars*. You might have separate hierarchies of details of the paintings – with *size*, *colour*, *design*, or *brushwork* as category headings.

If the upper level were *instrument*, an intermediate level could be *drum*, and a lower level might be a *timpani drum* or *African drum*. Specific examples would be *that drum on the table*, or *Gino's new drum-set*.

Using pyramids when planning essays

For using pyramids when planning essays, see Chapter 15, page 324.

Use pyramids to plan assignments

Use pyramid questions

Ask yourself key questions, to search for or organise the information at each level.

Upper level

★ How many major schools of thought or key theoretical perspectives do I need to consider for this question?

★ Which are the most relevant for my assignment? (If unsure, go down to the intermediate level and check who said or wrote what.)

Intermediate level

★ Which theorist (or judge, writer, or similar) said what, when?

★ How can I sum that up briefly?

Lower level

★ Overall, how good is the general evidence to support this position or theory?

★ What are the general implications of the position or theory?

★ What are the general applications of the position or theory?

★ What is the general evidence against the position or theory?

Exemplar level

★ Do I need to include specific examples of applications, implications or evidence? If so, which are the best examples?

★ Given the word limit and the time available, how much detail should I include? For instance, have I space only to mention the name and date and one line about this example of research? Or am I short of words so far in this assignment? If so, can I give more details?

Use pyramids to help with word limits

Having mapped your information as a pyramid, do you have the right amount for the word limit?

Too much information?

You need to decide what to include and to leave out.

★ If you have several examples at any one level, select just one or two examples of them. Do the same with the other levels.

★ If you would exceed the word limit by going into detail, it might be sufficient just to refer to specific examples in passing (just naming them). If more is needed, you would need to edit your writing elsewhere. It depends on what works best.

Too little information?

Generate more material to meet the word requirements.

★ Add further middle or lower level examples.

★ Provide further details of specific examples.

★ Critically evaluate the significance of your examples to your overall argument.

Balancing the pyramid

Usually, it is more important to explore ideas and analysis at middle and lower levels rather than including much detail for specific examples. (See also page 402.)

Drafting and re-drafting your writing

The art of writing is in the craft of redrafting

Professional writers redraft many times before they are happy: writing rarely flows 'all at once' into its final version. You would expect to write several drafts of an assignment to shape and fine-tune it.

Drafting stage 1: Lay words down

Use your plan. Don't worry about style or good English at this stage – just get started.

Focus on the assignment question. Write out your interpretation of the title.

Clarify your core points. Write out your central ideas, hypotheses, conclusions or the main direction of your line of reasoning.

Write headings and subheadings. Use your plan (or the pyramid you have created) to identify these. You can retain these headings and sub-headings in most reports and some dissertations, but leave these out of the final draft of an essay. This provides your structure.

Add in supporting details below each heading.

Link it up. Write your headings and points into sentences. Connect your sentences (page 296).

Stick to your plan. Check back to it after writing each paragraph. Go back to the assignment title and its central questions: check that you haven't gone off on a tangent. If so, put a line through anything irrelevant. Be a harsh critic and strong editor of your own work.

Drafting stage 2: Fine-tune the structure

Re-read to check information is grouped, ordered and paragraphed well (page 293). If not, re-organise it.

Check that your line of reasoning (Chapter 12) takes the reader smoothly from one paragraph to the next. If needed, add phrases or sentences to link ideas better. Check whether you could summarise any sections to release words for use elsewhere in the assignment. Rewrite.

Drafting stage 3: Meaning and style

Read what you have written aloud. How does it sound? If you are stumbling as you read, this may indicate poor flow or missing words. Check whether you can improve continuity, links, sentence lengths and overall style. Add sentences or phrases to clarify points. If you have a screen-reader, you could use this to read your text aloud. Listen for meaning, and for punctuation pauses.

Drafting stage 4: Fine-tuning

Aim to leave at least a night between drafts – this makes it easier to detect errors and areas that need rephrasing. See **Editing your draft**, page 297.

Saving your drafts

★ Save each draft as a separate file (draft 1, draft 2, etc.). Name and date each in the footer.

★ Alternatively, use a tool such as Google Docs that enables you to return to revised edits (page 246).

Check using a hard copy

It is easier to identify some errors on hard copy. Print out final drafts and read carefully for errors.

Writing strong paragraphs

The role of paragraphs

Paragraphs are the building blocks of your writing. They should organise material so it is easier for readers to understand, whilst also dividing the page into shorter sections that are easier on the eye.

Successive paragraphs should follow on logically, taking the reader from *a* to *b* to *c*. Phrases within them should link material with earlier or later paragraphs.

Paragraph structure

Paragraphs are, typically, several sentences long. They organise material around a central theme or key point.

A paragraph's opening sentence ...

★ is usually the 'topic sentence' that introduces the subject of the paragraph (such as through a summative statement, argument, question or recommendation)

★ can indicate whether the paragraph reinforces the argument or takes a new direction.

A paragraph's following sentences:

★ develop the theme of its 'topic sentence'

★ offer evidence and examples to clarify and support the key point

★ follow each other in a logical order, taking the argument forward.

Activity

1 Analysing paragraphs

Choose two or three pages from one text.

➡ Read the topic sentences – the ones that sum up the main theme of each paragraph. These are often, but not always, the opening sentences.

➡ How well do the topic sentences sum up the main ideas of those paragraphs?

➡ How are the paragraphs linked?

➡ If paragraphs lacked a clear topic sentence, were they more difficult to read?

A paragraph's final sentence:

★ sums up the paragraph and/or indicates a change of direction for the next paragraph.

Activity

2 Paragraphs and sentences

Separate this passage into paragraphs and sentences with correct capital letters and punctuation.

A Life of Adventure

mary seacole was born in 1805 in kingston jamaica her mother practised as a 'doctress' using medical knowledge which women had brought from africa and developed in the tropics from her mother mary inherited her medical skills as well as her ability to run a boarding house from her father a scottish military man she inherited her fascination with army life marys own medical reputation was established during a series of cholera and yellow fever epidemics she made her own medicines and emphasised high standards of hygiene as well as enforcing strict quarantine on victims by these methods she saved many lives on the outbreak of the crimean war mary volunteered her services to the british army although she had worked for the army before at its own request this time she was turned down undaunted mary made her own way to the war zone once in the crimea she not only nursed the soldiers but also ran a hotel and sold food wine and medicines after the war mary was treated as a celebrity she was decorated by the governments of four countries in england a poem in her honour was published in punch and even the royal family requested her company and medical expertise

Activity

3 Identify the theme

★ Re-read the paragraphs for Activity 2.

★ Decide the main theme of each paragraph and sum it up in 1–4 words.

See page 294 for answers.

Planning your paragraphs

Writing paragraphs

If you have difficulties with paragraphing, this can help.

★ Divide a page into three columns:

1 Arguments	2 Main information	3 Supporting detail

★ In column 1, jot down the ideas, theories, opinions and line of reasoning that you want to include in your writing.

★ In column 2, jot down the main examples and types of evidence that support your line of reasoning.

★ In column 3, write down lesser details, facts, names, statistics, dates and examples that support your main argument.

★ Each paragraph should have:

* one item from column 1

* one, two or three items from column 2

* several items from column 3.

★ Items selected for each paragraph should all help to make the same point.

Alternatively, using a concept pyramid:

★ Each paragraph is likely to need one item at the intermediate level, at least one at the lower level, examples, and a few details.

Suggested answer (for page 293)

Activity: Answer

3 Identifying the theme

The main themes of the paragraphs are:
1. general information: birth and background
2. early medical reputation
3. the Crimean War
4. after the War.

Activity: Answer

2 Paragraphs and sentences

A Life of Adventure

Mary Seacole was born in 1805 in Kingston, Jamaica. Her mother practised as a 'doctress', using medical knowledge which women had brought from Africa and developed in the Tropics. From her mother, Mary inherited her medical skills as well as her ability to run a boarding house. From her father, a Scottish military man, she inherited her fascination with army life.

Mary's own medical reputation was established during a series of cholera and yellow fever epidemics. She made her own medicines and emphasised high standards of hygiene as well as enforcing strict quarantine on victims. By these methods she saved many lives.

On the outbreak of the Crimean War, Mary volunteered her services to the British Army. Although she had worked for the army before, at its own request, this time she was turned down. Undaunted, Mary made her own way to the war zone. Once in the Crimea, she not only nursed the soldiers, but also ran a hotel and sold food, wine and medicines.

After the war, Mary was treated as a celebrity. She was decorated by the governments of four countries. In England, a poem in her honour was published in *Punch* and even the Royal Family requested her company and medical expertise.

Reflection

The value of paragraphing and punctuation

Did you find it easier to read the text for Activity 2 once it had been punctuated? If so, did this increase your appreciation of the value of good paragraphing and punctuation?

Did you have difficulty adding in the punctuation? If so, you could ask your tutors whether any additional support is available.

Checking your paragraphs

If paragraphing isn't your strong point, then when you have finished your early drafts, you can check your paragraphing by doing the following exercise.

1 Read each paragraph

Read each of your paragraphs in turn. Decide what is the main topic of each.

2 Sum up the topic

Sum up that topic in about 1–4 words.

3 Give the topic a name and colour

Write the topic in the margin. Give it a colour.

4 Which is the topic sentence?

Is it evident which sentence is the 'topic' sentence – that sums up the topic of the paragraph? Highlight it. Is it at the beginning of the paragraph? If not, would it be more powerful there?

5 Is everything relevant?

Check whether everything in each paragraph relates to its topic sentence. If you're unsure about something, underline it and check whether it would be better placed in a different paragraph. Is anything superfluous? If so, cross it out.

Make time for relaxation and exercise – you can go on thinking about your assignment!

6 Is everything in the right place?

Once you have assigned a different colour to each topic (see 3 above), search for each topic in turn throughout your writing to see whether any material on that topic has wandered into other paragraphs. If so:

★ highlight it in the topic colour – using colour will show up whether your material is well organised or scattered

★ cut separated items of the same colour and then paste them together into one paragraph

★ rewrite the paragraph, integrating the segments you have moved, so that the paragraph flows well.

7 Are sentences in the best order?

In each paragraph, are the sentences in the best order? Is it clear how each sentence leads on to the next?

8 Is the line of argument clear?

Is it clear to the reader how the topic sentences of each paragraph relate to each other?

Is it clear how the material in each paragraph builds on that in previous paragraphs in order to establish an argument with a clear direction?

9 Are paragraphs well-linked?

Is it clear how each paragraph leads on to the next, such as through phrases that link the ideas in one paragraph to ones that precede or follow on from it? (Pages 294 and 296.)

10 Is every paragraph relevant?

Is every paragraph relevant to the title? Are they all needed in order to make the argument?

Linking ideas together

Certain words are used to link ideas and to signpost to the reader the direction your line of reasoning is about to take, such as re-emphasising the direction of the argument or introducing an alternative viewpoint. Below is a selection of words used to link ideas, depending on the direction of your argument.

Adding to points made already

★ also; moreover; furthermore; again; further; what is more; then; in addition

★ besides; above all; too; as well (as)

★ either; neither … nor; not only … but also; similarly; correspondingly; in the same way; indeed

★ in fact; really; in reality, it is found that …

★ as for; as to; with respect to; regarding

Writing in lists

★ first(ly); second(ly); third(ly)

★ another; yet another; in addition; finally

★ to begin with; in the second place

★ moreover; additionally; also

★ next; then; and to conclude; lastly; finally

Putting the same idea in a different way

★ in other words; rather; or; better; in that case

★ to put it (more) simply

★ in view of this; with this in mind

★ to look at this another way

Introducing examples

★ such as; for instance; namely; as follows;

★ an example of this is; including, for example; as in the following examples;

★ especially; particularly; in particular; notably; chiefly; mainly; mostly

★ this is evident in …; this can be seen in; we can see this in …

Introducing an alternative viewpoint

★ however; by contrast; another way of viewing this is; alternatively; again; rather; one alternative is; another possibility is

★ on the one hand … on the other hand

★ conversely; in comparison; on the contrary; in fact; though; although

Returning to emphasise your earlier viewpoint

★ however; nonetheless; in the final analysis; despite x; notwithstanding x; in spite of x

★ while x may be true, nonetheless

★ although; though; after all; at the same time; on the other hand; all the same; even if x is true; although x may have a good point

Showing the results of something

★ therefore; accordingly; as a result

★ so, (then,) it can be seen that

★ the result is; the consequence is

★ resulting from this; consequently; now

★ we can see, then, that; it is evident that

★ because of this; thus; hence; for this reason; owing to x; this suggests that; it follows that

★ in other words; otherwise; in that case; that implies

Summing up or concluding

★ therefore; so, my conclusion is

★ in short; in conclusion; to conclude; in all; on the whole

★ to summarise; to sum up briefly; in brief; altogether; overall; thus; thus we can see that

Activity

Check for linking words

How are these words used in the sample essays on pages 331–5 and 337–43?

Editing and proof-reading your drafts

'Editing' is working on your draft in order to improve it. When you edit, you can ...

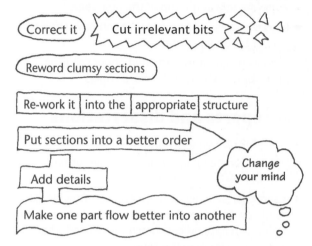

Correct it

Cut irrelevant bits

Reword clumsy sections

Re-work it | into the | appropriate | structure

Put sections into a better order

Add details

Make one part flow better into another

Change your mind

Different kinds of editing

Typically, you would need to go through your work several times, with a different focus each time.

1 Meaning

★ Does it make sense? Read it aloud slowly.

2 Organisation and structure

★ Have you used the appropriate structure?
★ Is connected information grouped together?
★ Is information presented in the best order?
★ Is the work well paragraphed? (Pages 293–5.)

3 Evidence

★ Have you backed your argument with evidence, examples, details, and adequate research?

4 References

★ Is the source of your information clear?
★ Are your quotations accurate?
★ Are citations and references written correctly? (Pages 249–51.)

5 Style

★ Is the text easy to read?
★ Is it too chatty? Or long-winded? Or pompous?
★ Are any sections confused?

★ Is it precise and succinct? (Page 304.)
★ Is the style appropriate? (Chapter 14.)

6 Presentation

★ Is the text formatted consistently?
★ Does it look neat and well presented?
★ Does it follow any presentation guidelines you were given?

Reflection

Editing and proof-reading your drafts

Which aspects of editing and proof-reading do you need to spend most time on?

Proof-reading

Edit your draft until you are happy with it. Then do final proof-reading using hard copy.

★ Read it once again aloud – does it make sense?
★ Look for typing, spelling and punctuation errors. Check you have written in sentences.
★ Look up doubtful spellings. If you used a spellchecker, look for words that are not misspelt but are not those you want, such as homophones (e.g. 'there' and 'their').
★ When proof-reading for grammar and punctuation, it can help to read sentence by sentence from the end of your work backwards (and word by word for spelling), to avoid drifting into skim-reading.
★ Everyone has their own pattern of errors. If there are certain mistakes you make repeatedly, note these down and be particularly careful in checking for them.

Resources to help strengthen and edit drafts

★ Checking the quality of your essay (page 317). This can be used for assignments too.
★ Project report or dissertation: checklist (page 369).

Presenting your writing in assignments

For all assignments

Typically, students are required to submit their work electronically. Software is used to check that it is all their own work. Make sure nobody can copy your work before tutors have returned it marked or graded.

Submit complete, well-organised work

★ If you saved several drafts, make sure you submit the right one.

★ Complete and attach cover pages, if required. These may include a confirmation that the work is all your own.

★ If you have collated references in dedicated software, include these within your assignment.

★ Number your pages.

★ Remove all colour coding, underlining, inserted comments, links and tracked changes that you used to help the process of writing your work.

★ Leave space to one side or between lines for your tutor to add comments and feedback easily.

Anonymity and confidentiality

★ If work must be submitted anonymously, take care not to include your own name anywhere.

★ Include your student number on every page.

★ Write the assignment's short title in the footer, as well as any assignment code number.

★ Check that any confidential material is removed. This includes avoiding giving thanks and acknowledgements to individuals and organisations at the start or end of the material or in citations or references if they provided material to use confidentially.

Hard copy

★ If you are required to submit in hard copy, your final text should be neatly presented.

★ Print on one side of the page only.

★ Occasional minor corrections made neatly by hand are acceptable, otherwise type corrections and print a good copy.

For essays

★ Write the title at the top of the first page.

★ Remove any sub-headings that you have used to help organise your work.

★ Follow any guidance provided about securing pages or using folders for hard copies.

For reports and dissertations

★ Write the title on a cover page.

★ Use section headings, all in the same format. Number sections and paragraphs.

★ Insert charts, tables and appendices. Provide clear headings. Check that headings and numbering for material in appendices match those used when referring to them in the report.

★ Remove any unnecessary appendices – such as anything not referred to within your report.

★ Follow any instructions about binding projects.

Format

Adapt to purpose

Use legible fonts. You may wish to work in a larger font then reduce this and double space text for submission.

For your final copy

★ Use only one type size for your main text.

★ Use one clear, simple font for your final draft – not script designed to look like handwriting.

★ Vary font size for headings and sub-headings. Be consistent in the way you use them.

Check lecturers' preferences

Find out whether your lecturers have preferences and requirements for aspects such as sub-headings, numbering, double spacing, margins, active or passive voice, referencing style and so on. If you wish, you can use the chart opposite to record and keep track of these.

The chart on page 299 is also available on the companion site.

Presenting work to meet course requirements

Note any special requirements for presenting your work. Then check these carefully for each assignment before submitting it.

This is also available for use on the companion site at www.studyskillshandbook.co.uk.

Tutor	Subject/module:
Aspect	**Requirements**
Electronic submission only or is hard copy also required?	
If a hard copy is required, print on one side or both?	
Begin each section of a report on a fresh page?	
Use sub-headings (or not)?	
Number sections and/or paragraphs? In which format?	
Leave a wide margin for tutor comments? (Left or right?)	
Give my student number on each page?	
Write the assignment title and/or code on each page?	
Write as 'one', 'I' or 'we'? (Address the reader as 'you'?)	
Use passive or active voice? (Passive: 'The essay was written'. Active: 'I wrote the essay'.)	
Is a cover sheet required? What information should it contain? Where can I download this?	
Which software is used for checking for plagiarism and copying? Where can I see this? Can I try it out?	
Which style should be used for references? Any special layout needed for references?	
Bibliography needed? Any special layout?	
Anything else? (E.g. Use of diagrams, charts, graphs? Standard keys on maps? Use of colour in diagrams? Is annotation needed? Any instructions on number, size, location or labelling of appendices?) Any requirements for binding the work?	

Review

1 **Aim to enjoy the process**
You can gain great satisfaction and enjoyment from writing assignments: mastering the subject, developing ideas, arguing your position, honing skills. Take pride in finishing a piece of work.

2 **Be braced for the challenge**
Writing can be tough at times. Even talented writers can face writer's block, procrastinate or struggle to find the right words to express themselves. Accept it and gain from the challenge.

3 **Practise: develop your talent**
You can benefit from making *any* kind of writing a regular activity. You can build speed, become better able to think and write simultaneously and learn to improve a piece of writing.

4 **Develop your own process**
Find a system that works for you. Use tricks and triggers to get you through the writing assignment, if needed.

5 **Keep it manageable**
Approach academic writing as a task with sets of manageable steps you can follow, given conventions you can adopt, and requirements you can meet.

6 **Write to the brief**
Analyse the title closely. Use that and any course guidance to shape your writing. Check you have not drifted from the subject.

7 **Clarify, plan, organise**
Academic writing is only partly about content: it involves clarity about the task, and strong organisation, planning and structure.

8 **Clarify your thinking**
Confused thinking leads to confused writing. Clarify your thoughts before you write, or through writing your first drafts. Be able to state, argue and explain your position aloud.

9 **Review, redraft, edit**
Don't expect to complete everything in one go. Keep working up your initial draft, rephrasing, improving and correcting until it is the best it can be. Leave enough time to do this well.

10 **Proof-read**
Always check carefully for grammar, spelling, punctuation and other errors. These create a poor impression, can reduce the sense of what you write, and affect your grade.

11 **Evaluate your own writing**
Use the self-evaluation (page 274) and checklists (pages 266, 317 and 369) to develop a strong sense of what to look for in your writing. Be systematic in using criteria and lists to check your work until you do so automatically.

12 **Language skills matter**
It is difficult to gain high grades if grammar, punctuation and phrasing let you down. It is worth investigating language workshops or courses at your institution, local college or online.

Chapter 14

Developing your academic writing

Learning outcomes

This chapter offers you opportunities to:

- ✓ consider further requirements of academic writing including stylistic conventions, precision, and distinguishing fact and argument from opinion
- ✓ become aware of how different approaches to research impact upon academic writing
- ✓ understand the influence of the 'scientific model' on academic writing, including for non-science subjects
- ✓ understand better what is meant by terms such as 'subjectivity' and 'objectivity', 'quantitative' and 'qualitative'
- ✓ learn when and how to use four of the main writing styles used for academic work: descriptive, argumentative, evaluative/analytical, and reflective/experiential
- ✓ understand what gains good marks for an assignment and how to use tutor feedback constructively
- ✓ evaluate your own work for yourself.

Writing improves through practice and informed reflection. As you progress through a course of Higher Education, your tutors will expect your writing style to continue to improve. In particular, your writing should demonstrate that you are aware of academic conventions and when to use them.

You will also be required to move flexibly between different writing styles, moving from precise descriptive summaries to critical analysis or evaluation, depending on the task. It is important to achieve the right balance between, on the one hand, description and summary, which are important but more superficial, and writing that involves criticality, evaluation, insight, judgement and decision-making. Writing that involves deeper thought tends to contribute more towards higher grades.

This chapter helps you to build awareness of what is expected in academic writing. If possible, browse through it at least once before completing your first assignment. Return to it in more detail, along with Chapters 12, 13, 15 and 16, before writing up your assignments.

Stylistic conventions for academic writing

Would that more of the youthful populace were so moved as to indulge in the daily pursuit of informative literary input such as might raise the accuracy of their perceptions regarding their health.

Studies by World Youth (2019) reveal that young people benefit from reading about their health.

So basically, you need to go read more, man!

There is no single style that can be used in all academic writing. Each academic discipline has developed its own particular styles, and in some subject areas you may find that even various branches of the discipline use quite distinct writing styles.

The following conventions apply to *most* academic writing. Nevertheless, if your tutors offer specific guidance, follow their directions.

Use formal English

Academic English is more formal than the language used in everyday conversation, emails, social media or magazines. It shouldn't sound 'chatty'. It also avoids slang and colloquialisms such as these:

★ 'The writer is *out of order to* suggest ...'

★ 'As an artist, she is the *GOAT*.'

★ 'These findings need to be *taken with a pinch of salt*.'

★ 'The argument was *a bit over the top*.'

Aim for clarity

Write so that your reader can easily follow what you are trying to say. Do not use long words and technical jargon simply in order to sound impressive. Check whether your sentences are so long and complicated that they are hard to follow. Avoid antiquated language, convoluted sentences or

mannerisms – as well as using up your word limit and obscuring your argument, these could be off-putting to your readers.

Learn how to use specialist terminology

It is important to learn the specialist styles and technical terms used for your subject, and to extend your vocabulary.

★ If you are not familiar with specialist terms, look for explanations of these in introductory textbooks or glossaries.

★ Pay attention to how such terms are introduced in books and articles – note the different forms used, such as noun and verb forms, and past tenses.

★ Do not litter your writing with terms that you yourself do not understand – it is better to write in your own words than to sound as though you do not understand what you are saying.

Reflection

Browse through several articles for your own subject, looking just at the writing style.

★ What features do each of the pieces share?

★ Are these features of your own writing?

Avoid abbreviations and contractions

For assignments, write words out in full:

★ 'dept.' as 'department'

★ 'e.g.' as 'for example'

★ 'didn't' as 'did not'

★ 'they're' as 'they are'

★ 'isn't' as 'is not'

Be impersonal

Most courses prefer you to avoid personal pronouns such as 'I'/'we' and 'you'. Instead, sentences begin in impersonal ways such as:

★ It can be seen that …

★ There are a number of …

★ It has been found that …

Be cautious

Academic writing generally sounds cautious. Writers indicate that they are aware that nothing is completely certain as further research could challenge what is currently understood. They use words that express this lack of certainty, such as:

★ appears to; seems to; tends to; may; might; possibly; probably; apparently; generally; seemingly.

They use phrases such as:

★ in some cases, this …

★ the evidence suggests that …

Avoid misplaced conjunctions

Except in creative writing, the following words are not used at the start of sentences: *or*, *and*, *but*, *yet*.

Numbers

Numbers below a hundred are usually written in full in non-scientific writing:

★ thirty-one per cent

★ nineteen members.

However, figures are retained in statistical and scientific work:

★ 31 per cent

★ 15°C

★ 7.3 newtons.

★ 0.54 mg

Be objective

Academic writing avoids subjective judgements so also avoids words such as 'nice', 'wonderful', 'worthwhile', 'usual', 'normal' or 'natural' if used in a potentially subjective or culturally specific way.

Avoid apologies

Don't apologise to the reader for any weaknesses you think there might be in your work, such as that you found the subject difficult or had no time to write a conclusion. Write with confidence – even if you don't feel it!

I'm afraid this is a complicated subject and I was only able to read …

Sorry, sorry,

Sorry again!

Addressing the reader

Avoid asking readers questions and telling them what to think or do. Don't use rhetorical questions.

Shouldn't we all be more aware of this? We should all take action now!

Be concise

Delete unnecessary words:

~~A man called~~ Jay Singh invented …

~~In a book called~~ *Scottish Pathways*, …

Use continuous prose

Write in full sentences, grouped together into paragraphs (see page 293). For essays and dissertations, avoid lists of points: incorporate the points into sentences. Lists and headings may be acceptable in reports and projects.

Being precise

Example of a vague sentence

> Some people did not like the idea at the time and made the politicians stop it but then he attacked him publicly.

Why is it vague?

★ 'some people' – who exactly?

★ 'the idea' – which idea?

★ 'at the time' – when? date?

★ 'the politicians' – all politicians? or a certain group? or a political party?

★ 'made the politicians' – how did they 'make' them?

★ 'stop it' – stop what? how was it stopped?

★ 'people did not like the idea' – why not?

★ 'he' and 'him' – who exactly?

It can be confusing to have more than one pronoun (such as 'he', 'she', 'it', 'this' or 'that') in a sentence.

Activity

Which of the following is most precise?

1 A woman ruled the country.
2 Mrs Thatcher served as Prime Minister in Britain between 1979 and 1991.
3 A woman ruled Britain during 1979–1991.
4 Mrs Thatcher ruled Britain for several years and introduced many policies which affected various aspects of people's lives.

Answer

Response 2 – the others all contain vague information.

> ... rather than sort of not saying quite what you mean, if you know what I mean ...

Using facts, opinions or arguments

> I think there should be fewer adverts on TV.

Opinions

Opinions are personal beliefs. These are not always based on good evidence and may even run *contrary* to the evidence.

What is considered 'natural' or 'normal', for example, is generally a matter of opinion. Even if most people agree with you, it is still opinion, unless you can give *evidence* that proves the case.

Facts

Facts can usually be checked against evidence. Facts used in academic writing are generally those gathered and recorded in some formal way, such as in journals or official records.

> There were an average of 35 adverts an hour on channel X, on 25th July 2019.

SURVEY

> Adverts for toys should not be shown on TV because research by Dr Meehan (2019) suggests that they ...

Arguments

Arguments are *reasons* (which can include facts) given to support a point of view.

As you write, question what you write

As you write, keep checking for precision. Ask yourself questions, such as 'when exactly?', 'why exactly?' or 'who?' Check that you have given your readers enough detail for them to know exactly what you are talking about.

Writing for different subjects

Different approaches

Each academic subject has a slightly different approach regarding:

★ *research methodology* – how to conduct research

★ *evidence* – what is regarded as appropriate and sufficient

★ *writing genre* – the preferred writing styles and conventions

★ *objectivity* – how far your approach should be objective or subjective, quantitative or qualitative, scientific or personal.

As a student, you will need to identify the approaches taken by your subject and produce work appropriate to that subject. You will need to be particularly aware of this if you take a 'joint' or 'combined' honours degree, but even *within* a subject, approaches can vary depending on the area of study.

The influence of the 'scientific' model

Academic writing has been heavily influenced by the notion of being 'scientific' – even when the subject is not obviously about science. Although this view is changing, the approach you are expected to take is likely to be affected by some of the principles of the scientific model, so it is helpful to know what it involves.

The main features of the scientific model are:

★ objectivity

★ a testable hypothesis

★ replicated results

★ controlling for variables

★ quantitative analysis

★ accurate description

★ qualitative analysis.

Objectivity

The scientific model values objectivity. This means that instead of relying on personal opinion or common sense, scientists test possible explanations against the available evidence. If data is objective, two people undertaking the same research in the same way should arrive at the same results and conclusions.

A testable hypothesis

A hypothesis is a possible explanation of why or how something occurs, consistent with available evidence. The hypothesis is formulated in a way that can be tested.

A hypothesis cannot be proved true, but it can be proved *wrong*. If a hypothesis survives many attempts to prove it wrong, increasingly it may be considered reliable and trusted as a 'theory'.

Replicated results

For a piece of scientific research to be taken seriously, another researcher needs to have repeated the research with similar results.

This 'replication' indicates that the first results were reliable, and not just a 'one-off' or due to individual opinion or bias. (However, it is still important to think hard about whether bias might be built into the research method itself.)

'Scientific' approaches

Controlling for variables

Scientists need to know that what they *think* they are testing is what they are *actually* testing. They need to make sure that 'variables' – all the things that can change, such as the weather, or the time of day, the people involved or the materials used – have not influenced the results unexpectedly.

Usually, research experiments are run many times to check the effects of different variables. The researcher tries to change only one variable at a time, keeping everything else constant. This is known as 'controlling for variables'.

For example, researchers comparing the effect of blue light or red light on plant growth would check that everything *apart* from the colour of the light was identical. For each light colour they would use the same type and size of plant, the same amount of water, the same levels of nutrients, the same temperature, and the same air source.

Quantitative analysis

Scientific research relies heavily on quantitative data. This means it focuses on changes or differences that can be *measured*. Standardised measurements are used – such as number, time, weight and length – so that results are easy to compare objectively. Thus, experiments might investigate:

★ whether the height (measurable) to which a particular kind of plant grows depends on the temperature of the environment (measurable)

★ whether fruit yield (measurable) depends on the amount of light (measurable)

★ whether how many words somebody can read in a given amount of time (measurable) depends on the size of print (measurable) or the age of the person (measurable).

The approach is: 'If *this* changes while everything else stays the same, does it have an effect on *that*?' This could also be stated as: 'If X changes while A, B and C stay the same, does it have an effect on Y?' Quantitative analysis involves analysing the relationship between changes in one variable and changes in another.

When changes in X exactly match changes in Y, the changes are said to be 'correlated'. It is important to understand, however, that correlation does not prove that changes in X *cause* changes in Y, or vice versa. Correlation could be due to chance, or both X and Y might be affected by a third variable, Z.

Accurate description

When writing up research, scientists describe their methodology, research conditions and results exactly, so that anyone who wishes to replicate their research can set up near-identical conditions. You will be expected to write accurate descriptions in the same way, such that someone else could replicate your research.

Descriptive writing for reports is very precise: no unnecessary words are used. (See pages 310 and 267–70.)

Qualitative analysis

In qualitative research, the data used are not easily measurable. The experiment is not completely objective: some judgement and interpretation are involved. It is acknowledged also that the researcher is in some way part of the experiment itself and could influence its results unintentionally – such as in the phrasing of survey questions.

Scientists use qualitative analysis in the 'Discussion' part of a report, where they make sense of their results and offer possible reasons for why things did not go as expected. Here they evaluate strengths and weaknesses, such as in the way they designed the experiment or worded the experimental hypothesis.

Nevertheless, science generally regards subjectivity as a 'problem', and often uses language which makes it sound as if no scientists were involved – as if the experiment just happened on its own:

> The experimental design could have been improved by ...

rather than:

> I could have improved the design by ...

Alternatives to the scientific model

Most academic disciplines are influenced by the scientific model. However, subjects vary in how far they value the different aspects of the model. The main differences are in varying attitudes to subjectivity and to qualitative data.

Subjectivity and objectivity

Subjectivity simply means bringing yourself, your own views, opinions, experiences or value judgements into your research or writing. In counselling or fine art, a high value is placed upon subjectivity – that is, upon personal emotions, feelings, intuitions and experiences. It is the opposite of *objectivity*, the aim of the traditional scientific model.

In many subjects, however, you need to combine the two: to analyse both objective criteria, such as the results of independent surveys, market research or case studies, and your subjective response – your feelings, tastes, interests or intuitions.

(See also **Reflective Writing**, pages 314–15.)

Quantitative approaches in non-science subjects

Science subjects tend to avoid research where it is difficult to control for variables or to quantify results. For example, issues such as gender, romance or childhood change over time, but as these changes are not easily measurable they would not usually be studied by scientists.

Non-science subjects often find ingenious ways of categorising such information, however, so that it can be roughly standardised according to set criteria. This enables a wider range of issues to be studied in relatively objective ways.

Example: attitudes to children

Researchers interested in how attitudes to childhood changed over time would look for an objective way of analysing data rather than simply relying on their opinions. They might choose to focus on how often popular magazines referred to themes of 'childhood innocence' and 'goodness' compared with themes on 'disciplining bad children'. One approach could then be to count how often a popular magazine included each theme, and compare data over ten-year intervals to see whether the number of references changed significantly over time. This would give quantitative data.

The researcher here would also have to classify information carefully to be clear what type of material should be included under chosen themes ('innocence' and 'discipline'). Classification of words and themes involves some subjectivity, as people mean different things by the same words. For example, someone quoted in a magazine as saying 'A good child does as his mother says' might have meant that the child obeyed from being disciplined, or because of inherent virtue – or something else entirely.

Qualitative analysis

It is not always easy to draw a line between what is quantitative and what is qualitative – as you can see from the example above of attitudes to childhood. In that instance, the researcher needed to make subjective judgements about what was *meant* by innocence or discipline. Usually social science researchers acknowledge their subjective role in the experiment as interpreters of the evidence. Social science and arts subjects may aim at objectivity and quantification where this is possible, but are also interested in the subjective – how decisions and interpretations are arrived at. They are more accepting of blurred edges between objectivity and subjectivity.

As a student, you may be asked to make qualitative evaluations about project evidence, about decisions made during work placements, or about art or literature. Your lecturers will look for:

★ the relevance of the detail you select

★ the criteria you use in making decisions

★ the aptness of your interpretations.

Polar opposites in academic approaches

For each of the aspects numbered below, find out whether it is the convention in your subject area to be nearer the North or the South Pole. This may vary depending on the type of assignment.

Consider how far each dimension is important for your assignment. Indicate this ✓ along each dotted line.

North Pole

1 Every attempt is made to control the conditions under which the research takes place, so that the researcher can decide which variables to manipulate and measure

2 Results can be generalised – that is, they would hold true if the research were repeated

3 Numbers and standardised measurements make it easier to generalise results

4 Objective views are formed, based on evidence and facts rather than personal opinion

5 The role of the scientist in the research is minimised and rarely discussed

6 Individual differences are not important – generalised findings are valued

7 Personal experience is regarded as individual and irrelevant: it is not referred to

8 The language is clinical, neutral, impersonal and dispassionate, even if the researcher is passionate about the subject

South Pole

1 Every attempt is made to keep the research true to real life – that is, to give it 'ecological validity'

2 The unique is considered worthy of study – results may be impossible to repeat exactly

3 Creative interpretation is highly valued

4 Subjective responses, feelings, intuition and creativity are regarded as valuable resources

5 The role of the researcher is made explicit – it is considered useful to discuss how the researcher's presence influenced the results

6 Individual instances, and opportunities for detailed interpretation, are valued

7 Personal experience is highly valued as giving insight and a deeper understanding

8 The language used allows the personality and feelings of the writer to shine through

Developing your academic writing

Different writing styles

Compare the following two styles of writing. The first is conversational:

> Mount Pepé is going up – it's going to take everything with it when it goes. And I mean everything – villages, farms, trees, the lot. It's frightening to think of how powerful a volcano can be. Think of the damage they cause! Remember Pompeii and Mount Etna!

The second is in a general academic style:

> In order to assess whether it is necessary to evacuate the villages on Mount Pepé, three main factors need to be taken into consideration. The first, and most important, of these is the element of safety. According to seismic experts currently working on the volcano, there is likely to be a major eruption within the next ten years (Achebe, 2018). According to Achebe, the eruption is likely to destroy villages over a radius of 120 miles (Achebe, 2019, p. 7).

Notice the differences between the two examples. For each piece, consider questions such as these.

★ Does it use full sentences?

★ How formal does it sound? (What is the writer's 'voice'?)

★ How is emotion expressed?

★ Is personal opinion expressed? If so, how?

★ How are other people's views included?

★ Is the sequence logical?

★ Does the piece observe the conventions listed on pages 281 and 301–7?

Styles of academic writing

Although academic writing is distinct from other kinds of writing, it isn't all the same. There are different styles *within* academic writing, including:

★ descriptive

★ argumentative/analytical

★ evaluative/analytical

★ reflective, drawing on personal experience.

These are explored in more detail below.

Finding the appropriate style

When writing an assignment, it is important to choose the appropriate writing style. Look at the two examples below, of draft introductions to an essay in response to the questions, 'What problems faced Henri IV on his accession to the throne? How successfully did he solve them?' The first follows the guidance for introductions given on page 284, and analyses the problem set. The second uses descriptive writing, giving background details not relevant to the question.

The first example is of a good introduction:

> In 1598, Henri IV was anointed king of a war-torn France, the country having been split by religious and political wars since the death of Henri II almost half a century earlier. The problems Henri IV faced were essentially threefold. He needed to resolve Catholic–Protestant divisions within the country; to curb the power of the Guise, Montmorenci and Bourbon factions which threatened to subvert royal power; and he needed to restore the French economy. This essay will look at the three areas in turn, but will also show how they were interrelated. It will demonstrate how Henri IV tackled each, and argue that ultimately he was extremely successful in solving what had seemed intractable problems.

The second is an example of interesting but irrelevant description (for a *history* essay):

> Henri was brought up by his grandfather in the mountains of Navarre. His grandfather was a very religious man and brought his grandson up as a Protestant. Because of his religion, he wanted Henri to appreciate the simple things in life – the fields, the flowers, good wholesome food such as bread and local cheese, and the beauty of the natural surroundings. Henri was allowed a great deal of freedom, and was allowed to roam barefoot in the mountains, and to play with animals …

★ Compare each example with the conventions listed on page 281.

★ Which writer might find it easier to write a good observation case study (page 310)?

Descriptive writing style

You are likely to include descriptive writing in most assignments. In some ways it is the easiest style, as we are used to describing things in everyday life. On the other hand, it is easy to give too much detail and forget its underlying purpose.

Purpose

In Higher Education, there will be a specific purpose for including description, such as to:

★ *state precisely* the methods used in an experiment

★ *provide essential background* for readers

★ *outline what occurred* such as results of lab experiments or key events in history, or critical incidents for reflective essays

★ *give precise observations* – such as of animal or people behaviours

★ *describe main features or functions*, such as of bodily organs in a biology essay

★ *summarise briefly the main points* – such as when reviewing a book or referring in an essay to expert theories, research findings, or recommendations.

Typical mistakes

★ Writing too much description: summarise instead

★ Overgeneralising: be specific

★ Providing only *description* of core theories or the work of main figures: spend more time on evaluative critique of these than description.

Examples of descriptive writing

Note the differences between the two following types of descriptive writing. The first is from a cognitive psychology report.

METHODOLOGY

Participants

There were twenty English first-language speakers in each condition, forty subjects in all. These were matched for age and gender across conditions.

Procedure

(See Appendix 1 for instructions.) Each participant was tested separately. They were asked to indicate whether each string of five letters (such as *yongt*) presented on the screen was a real word. For real words they were to press the 'y' key on the keyboard; otherwise they pressed the 'n' key …

The second example is from an observation case study from the social sciences.

The man did not appear to be interacting with the child. The train entered Ely station, and he looked to the pushchair, perhaps to see if it was obstructing the exit. He looked out of the window. The child pointed to the door, and leaned towards him; he instantly leaned towards her to listen.

She said, 'Get off soon?'

He replied, 'Not now. In five minutes we're getting off.' The child still leaned towards him, but he didn't say anything else, and looked away. The child turned away and put the teddy on the seat. The man leaned across her, picked up the teddy, and returned it to her lap, saying 'Hold it.' They looked at each other for a moment. The child half-smiled, and they both looked away, so they were looking in opposite directions.

From this you will see how descriptive writing can vary depending on the subject. Look carefully at journal articles and other examples from your subject area to become familiar with the appropriate style for your work. (See also pages 366 and 267–70.)

Argumentative style

Strong assignments normally include excellent critical analysis and argument. Chapter 12 looks in more detail at argument as part of critical analytical thinking.

Tutors usually expect assignments to be 'discursive': to debate diverse perspectives on the issues using clear reasoning.

Reflection

Find the 'Editorial' section in two quality newspapers. How do the writers try to persuade you to their points of view?

What makes good argumentative writing?

To argue a point of view effectively, you need to do the following.

★ State your position clearly.

★ Provide good reasons to support your position presented as a compelling 'argument'.

★ Give evidence or examples to support your argument.

★ Show where the evidence comes from, and that it is relevant and reliable.

★ Consider, and address, facts and arguments that appear to contradict, undermine or could challenge your case.

★ Demonstrate convincingly that your argument or position stands up to scrutiny. (Why do you think you are right?)

Your case will not be convincing if you merely argue, 'Well, that's my opinion' or 'That's my experience' and fail to consider any alternatives seriously.

Writing the argument

1   State your position

★ Sum up your argument in one brief, clear sentence.

★ Don't be tempted to sit on the fence. You can sound cautious, and show that there are strong arguments on more than one side, but indicate which side *you* find most convincing.

2   Support your argument

★ Show why your position is a good one.

★ For each main point, give evidence (dates, names, statistics, examples, opinions from other sources).

Here is the evidence, my Lord …

★ Consider: 'Would the evidence stand up in court?' Is it really convincing?

3   Consider the opposition

Assume that your reader disagrees with you: you have to convince the reader with good evidence and examples.

★ What could your opponents argue?

★ What evidence might they have?

★ How could you persuade a neutral party that your case and your evidence are better?

Activity

Develop an argument

➡ Choose a subject about which you feel strongly.

➡ What is the debate? Engage in it.

➡ What is your own case or position?

➡ List your reasons for taking that position.

➡ List possible arguments *against* it.

➡ How could you reply to each counter-argument?

➡ Use the planner on page 326 to write out your argument.

Evaluative/comparative style

Comparative evaluation is most obvious in 'compare and contrast' essays. However, most assignments involve an element of evaluation, even if this is not obvious from the title. You might need to evaluate:

★ two or more schools of thought

★ two or more theories or theorists

★ which of several items, models or ideas is best for a specific purpose

★ how well two authors debate an issue.

Features of evaluative writing

Evaluative writing involves the following:

Comparing

Find the points of similarity. Show that you are aware of subtle differences despite similarities.

Contrasting

Set items in opposition, in order to bring out the points of difference.

Evaluating significance

Evaluate the *significance* of any similarities or differences. Do they matter? Do they have important implications for decision-making or for probable outcomes (which animal is likely to survive, which treatment should be offered, which model or recommendations to use, and so on?)

Making a judgement

Indicate which theory or side is preferable. Give the reasons for your judgement, based on an analysis of the evidence.

Showing your criteria

Refer to the criteria you used in arriving at your decision, such as the scale or currency of the data or quality of research evidence you used.

Synthesis

Draw out potential ways of combining the strengths of different approaches so as to arrive at an alternative way of looking at the issue.

Get the balance right

In evaluative writing such as in 'compare and contrast' assignments, it is important to be balanced in the amount and kind of information you use and to compare 'like with like'.

'Compare and contrast' at the same category level

Suppose you are asked to compare and contrast two animals in terms of habitat. First, compare them at the basic category level, making it clear you are comparing, for example, birds with mammals (see page 289). You can then compare examples of these, such as cuckoos and dolphins, at the next category level. You should not compare cuckoos with mammals, as these are not equivalent concepts – they are at different conceptual levels on the pyramid.

Balance

If you go into detail about one theory, drawing on its best examples, then you should balance this by a similarly detailed exploration of alternative perspectives, drawing on their best examples too.

Check your content for balance

When you have completed a draft, map out what you have actually written using a concept pyramid (page 289). Compare how you allocate words at each conceptual level. You may find you have focused on some items at a basic category level but referred to other items only in terms of exemplars (such as writing in depth about birds as a general category, but about mammals only with respect to dolphins).

This would not balance like with like. Use your pattern notes (page 228) or pyramid (page 291) to plan your work, allocating similar attention to each conceptual level.

For **Compare and contrast essays**, see page 328.

Reflective Writing: Using personal experience

For all assignments

Academic writing requires thought and reflection. For most assignments, it is expected that your personal reflections are implicit: you don't refer to them but you aim to demonstrate good critical reflection through the way you discuss, debate and present issues in your assignments.

And then I thought that as I had been living in the same address for two years it was time for a change. So, in 1967 I moved down to Essex. I lived in Barr Road, but I soon moved to Small Street ...

For experiential assignments

Drawing on personal experience and reflection is an important feature of some courses: to explore your creative process in the arts, your responses and interactions in clinical or counselling work, or your process of personal improvement in business and work-based roles. Find out whether your course expects you to draw on experience.

Two phased approach

Typically, you address the reflective aspects of assignments in two phases (Cottrell, 2015).

Phase 1: Generating raw content

Maintain a blog, journal or notebook of events, thoughts and emotions, as a stream of initial thoughts. See **Reflective journals**, pages 99 and 101.

Phase 2: Analysis and synthesis

In Phase 2, stand back from your initial reflections, considering them in a more detached, analytical, questioning way.

Activity

Question your reflection

➡ What have you learnt? How can you or others apply these lessons?

➡ How is this relevant to the course (or work)?

➡ Is it legitimate to generalise from it?

➡ How does it link to theories you study? How does your experience support or contradict what is published about such issues?

➡ If your experience or conclusions differ from those published, why might this be the case? Is it atypical? Does it suggest areas for further research?

Decide what to use in assignments

Use short, highly relevant, examples of your reflection to introduce or illustrate your points.

★ Be highly selective – you can't include it all.

★ Look for relevance to the assignment brief.

★ Is it useful, rather than only of passing or personal interest?

★ Choose and summarise the best examples.

★ Edit out unnecessary words (with dots ...).

Draw on reflection critically

Bring a critical, selective eye to your reflections, using these as relevant examples within a structured assignment.

★ Keep any description short. Avoid long lists and detailed accounts of events.

★ Use examples as a starting point, from which to draw out wider points, linked to your reading and relevant to the course.

★ Consider how typical your experience is. Refer to reports or articles that suggest your experience is typical or atypical.

★ Be careful to maintain confidentiality, erasing all names or information that could identify persons or organisations.

Reflective writing

Tutors look for evidence of ...

Thought: that you think deeply about the issues, relating reflection to course material, reading and, if relevant, workplace application.

Critical selection: that you know what is relevant and suitable, avoiding repetition, irrelevance, and confidential or sensitive material; that you draw reasonable conclusions from material included.

Relating theory to experience: that you draw on relevant research findings and theories to help elucidate and make sense of your experience.

Implications and application: that you can use reflection to draw out lessons learnt for personal or professional change or future research.

Self-awareness: that you demonstrate:

★ personal awareness of how your action (or inaction) has consequences, influencing the outcome of a situation directly or indirectly

★ that you take personal responsibility rather than allocating blame for things that go wrong

★ that you can deal with uncomfortable feelings

★ that you know when to ask for advice or help.

Awareness of others: such as other people's needs, interests, roles, sensitivities; the value of diverse personal qualities and contributions to different situations; your understanding of group dynamics and intercultural sensitivities.

Assignment awareness, such as that you:

★ interpret the task correctly

★ are aware of what to include for your audience

★ respect matters of confidentiality if you refer to others or to workplaces, etc.

★ draw on reflections in an academic way, with relevant reading and references.

See also: **What gets good grades?** (page 315.)

Reflective writing styles

In an academic context, reflective experiential writing combines various styles (pages 306–12):

★ *Descriptive*: you describe, briefly and succinctly, events, issues, objects, etc.

★ *Analytical*: you select and account for key aspects of the event, issue, object, outcome, etc.

★ *Evaluative*: typically, you would include some evaluation of your own role in events.

★ *Critical*: you include academically informed reasoning on the significance or meaning of your experience and its relation to theory or professional practice.

Example: Drawing on experience

Suppose you wrote about your own experience, saying:

> Working this way, I found that I was less stressed and my work improved.

You could provisionally generalise this:

> It would appear that the absence of stress can produce more effective results.

You would then need to ask questions such as:

★ How valid is this generalisation?

★ Do other people feel the same way as you?

★ Are there any research studies about this?

★ Are there circumstances where stress can produce *better* work?

Example: Implications and applications

★ If a similar situation arose again, I would take a different course of action. I would do X ....

★ It would be useful if future research looked at why this occurs in situation X but not in Y ....

★ The experience suggests that there are new data security issues that are of particular relevance to this profession.

For *Reflective essays*, see pages 329–30.

What gets good grades for written assignments?

To get good marks or grades, you do not necessarily have to work longer hours. You *do* need to:

★ identify the task correctly

★ discover the underlying issues

★ find out exactly what is expected.

Although all subject areas have their own assessment criteria, the following general requirements provide a good guideline as to how marks are allocated.

Level descriptors

Find out whether your university or your college provides details of the characteristics of each level of study. These may be outlined in your course handbook or on the department website. If so, make sure that you understand what they mean, as they indicate what tutors expect of students for your level or year of study.

★ What do the descriptors for your level/year mean for your current assignment?

★ What is expected at the next level up – are you working towards that level yet?

Marking criteria

★ If your course provides marking criteria, check these before you start your assignment, and refer to them as you work.

★ Go through drafts of your assignments, checking them against the marking criteria.

See also: *50 Ways to Boost Your Grades*. Stella Cottrell, 2019.

Lowest marks or grades

These are awarded for work which:

★ has weak structure

★ shows little research, thought or reflection

★ is mostly descriptive, with little analysis, synthesis or argument

★ considers issues from only one perspective.

Tutors' or examiners' comments may resemble these:

'You have just written out my lecture notes and paraphrased a few lines from books, without considering why this is such an important issue.'

'The student seems to have written out everything he knows about the subject, in any order, with lots of mistakes, and has not answered the question.'

Better marks or grades

These are awarded for work which:

★ meets the set criteria and follows appropriate conventions

★ shows understanding of the key issues

★ is focused on answering the question

★ is well structured and organised

★ demonstrates good background reading

★ develops a strong argument and presents a clear position on the issue

★ uses evidence and examples to support arguments, points and conclusions

★ indicates the relationship between issues or concepts within the subject area

★ reveals some thought and reflection

★ is succinct, well-expressed, correctly referenced and error-free.

Highest marks or grades

These are awarded for work which is strong in all the features required for 'better marks' and, in addition:

★ engages actively with subject-related debates in a thought-provoking way

★ demonstrates a deeper and more subtle understanding of the significance of the issues and evidence, drawing out complexities or nuances

★ synthesises material well.

Using feedback from tutors

'What if my work gets bad grades …?'

Although a grade or mark of 'B' or '64%' can indicate how well you are doing, the *comments* you receive are more important. You may feel discouraged or inclined to throw your work in the bin if it is returned covered with your tutor's comments, but do read them – they are likely to be your passport to better results.

It can be distressing if tutors seem insensitive in their comments. It is best not to take criticism personally. Focus instead on the issues behind the words: what lessons can you learn and apply to future work? Look for underlying issues that you could apply even to different kinds of assignments.

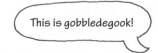

It is natural to have strong feelings about your grades. As these are based on set standards and criteria rather than effort, it can feel frustrating if they don't seem to reflect your hard work. You might feel angry or disappointed.

Don't give up. Wait a day or two, then start an action plan.

Action plan for using tutor feedback

Read through your work and the tutor's comments. Be constructive. Keep asking yourself, 'How can this help me to improve my work?'

1 After each comment, check whether you understand why the tutor wrote it. Highlight any comments that could be useful for future pieces of work.

2 Create a table or divide a page into sections to show:

   * major issues in the feedback, such as not answering the question, lack of evidence, poor argument, weak structure (aspects that impact most on grades)

   * minor errors: spelling, punctuation, grammar.

3 Go through your tutors' comments, listing them under 'Major issues' or 'Minor errors'.

4 Compare this with lists made for any previous work. Are there any mistakes you keep making?

5 Number the items in order of priority (with '1' for the most urgent matter to work on). See page 136.

Action plan	
Major issues	**Minor errors**
2 paragraphing	① spelling authors' names
3 referencing	3 commas
① structure	2 '-ed' endings for past tense

Making improvements

1 Select one, two or three priority issues from each list to work on in your next piece of work. Set yourself realistic targets.

2 Consider how you will deal with each item on your list. Don't panic! Think constructively.

3 Make sure you understand *why* you received that feedback.

4 Re-read any relevant sections in this guide.

5 If there are comments you do not understand, or if you do not know how to improve in your 'priority areas', ask your tutor for advice.

6 Find out what gets good marks – *ask*!

7 Ask your tutors for examples of the kind of work they would *like* you to produce.

Reflection

Using advice and feedback

★ How well do you use your tutors' feedback?

★ Apart from comments on your work, is any feedback provided to the whole class or on the department website?

★ How could you make better use of the totality of advice and feedback provided by tutors and other students?

Evaluate written assignments for yourself

Learn to evaluate your work accurately and fairly. You can use this checklist to evaluate whether your assignments need further work before you submit them.

This is also available on the companion site at www.studyskillshandbook.co.uk.

Content and relevance

- ☐ It adheres to the assignment brief
- ☐ It answers the question(s) posed by the title
- ☐ Sufficient space is allocated to the most important points
- ☐ It demonstrates wide reading
- ☐ It demonstrates thought and reflection
- ☐ I have an interesting angle on the issues
- ☐ It is all relevant to the set question/title.

Argument and critical analysis

- ☐ I engage well with relevant debates
- ☐ My own position comes across clearly
- ☐ I make a strong case to defend my position
- ☐ I include much strong critical analysis of arguments, theories, evidence, etc.
- ☐ My line of reasoning is clear and logical
- ☐ I weigh evidence fairly for diverse viewpoints
- ☐ I provide sufficient examples and evidence to support my position and points I make
- ☐ I synthesise material/arguments well
- ☐ The conclusion is concise and follows logically from the case I have made.

Structure and grouping

- ☐ It has a strong overall structure
- ☐ Ideas are grouped and suitably linked
- ☐ Points are presented in the right order
- ☐ Each paragraph is well structured
- ☐ Each paragraph follows logically from others.

Clarity, writing style and readability

- ☐ It adheres to academic conventions
- ☐ The writing styles are appropriate for my course and the assignment content
- ☐ The language is clear and straightforward
- ☐ It is obvious which sentence in my introduction summarises my position
- ☐ The introduction is clear and to the point
- ☐ I have followed through on what I said I would do/cover in my Introduction
- ☐ It avoids lengthy description
- ☐ The text is not chatty or flippant
- ☐ It is free of slang and colloquialisms
- ☐ It is succinct, making best use of the word allocation
- ☐ Sentences are of reasonable length
- ☐ It avoids repetition
- ☐ It flows well and easily when read aloud.

General

- ☐ It is all in my own words, free of plagiarism
- ☐ It is presented as required
- ☐ Grammar and punctuation are correct
- ☐ Every source I have used is correctly cited
- ☐ My list of references includes every source that I have cited in my writing
- ☐ Citations and references are accurate
- ☐ I have taken account of feedback I received for earlier work (page 316).

Review

1 **Recognise the distinctiveness of academic writing**
It has its own traditions and conventions. These have developed over time, usually to bring accuracy, precision and clarity to specialist areas.

2 **Apply the right conventions**
Learn and apply the stylistic conventions relevant to academic work in general, and especially those used in your subject discipline.

3 **Appreciate the impact of 'scientific' approaches**
Most academic writing uses or has been strongly influenced by the scientific model, which values objectivity and quantitative data. Knowing this can help you understand the approach taken by your course and can help your own writing.

4 **Identify the right 'polar' position**
Depending on the subject discipline, the correct stylistic aspects can be 'polar opposites'. Know which apply in your discipline.

5 **Recognise the main styles of academic writing**
Be aware that there are different styles. Get a sense of what these are like and when they are used in your subject discipline.

6 **Include strong critical analysis**
Almost all assignments require you to include critical analysis. Engage with the key debates for your subject, weighing these up rather than describing them.

7 **Compare and evaluate**
Almost all writing involves some elements of comparative evaluation and synthesis. Understand how to evaluate fairly and at the right conceptual level.

8 **Use reflection and experience appropriately**
All subjects require you to reflect and call upon experience, but only some require this to be included within an assignment. Use reflective writing in an academic way, to make a well-supported point. Avoid waffle.

9 **Use description judiciously**
Generally, for academic writing, use description sparingly, selectively and for a specific purpose.

10 **Understand how your writing is graded**
This will not only help you gain good grades, it is a good guide for producing strong writing to meet a brief, whether as a student or in other contexts.

11 **Use tutor feedback constructively**
Welcome all criticism and use it to strengthen your work. Remember that tutors' comments are there to help you succeed.

12 **Be able to judge your work for yourself**
Learn to critique and evaluate your own work in depth, fairly and accurately. You can use checklists in this *Study Skills Handbook* to help you develop this ability.

Chapter 15

Writing Essays

Essays

You benefit if you can master the process of writing essays*, as these are a significant aspect of many courses. They can have a great impact on your grades if they form part of your assessment.

Essays can sound daunting as they are not typical of the kind of writing we undertake as part of our everyday lives. There are broad rules or conventions to apply. However, once you know what to expect and have a process for writing them, they can become a valuable way of exploring a topic in depth and developing your own perspectives on core issues in your subject.

Why write essays?

Essays help you to elaborate, structure and present ideas on a given subject, and to develop generic written communication skills. Writing them can sharpen your thinking as well as improve your writing.

As you progress through your course, you would be expected to raise the quality of your essay-writing so that you can cover

more complex topics in different styles for diverse audiences. You learn to write with greater precision, clarity and professionalism, and this benefits you when writing in both academic and work-related contexts.

Marita was determined to finish this essay

*In some countries, these are referred to as 'papers'.

What is an essay?

Essay-based assignments are designed to focus your reading and thinking on a key aspect of the course. While working on an essay, you should engage with the debates and issues, decide your own position, and communicate this in a compelling argument. Essays follow a broad set of conventions. The diagram below answers typical student questions.

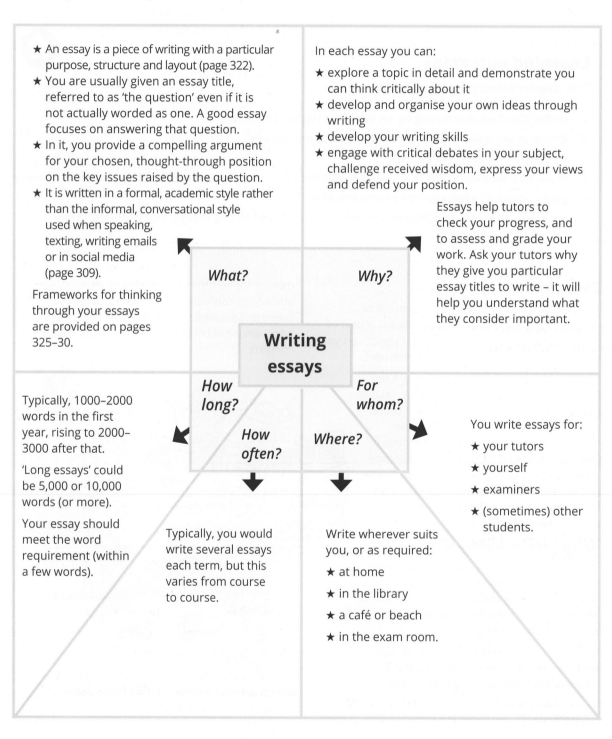

★ An essay is a piece of writing with a particular purpose, structure and layout (page 322).
★ You are usually given an essay title, referred to as 'the question' even if it is not actually worded as one. A good essay focuses on answering that question.
★ In it, you provide a compelling argument for your chosen, thought-through position on the key issues raised by the question.
★ It is written in a formal, academic style rather than the informal, conversational style used when speaking, texting, writing emails or in social media (page 309).

Frameworks for thinking through your essays are provided on pages 325–30.

In each essay you can:

★ explore a topic in detail and demonstrate you can think critically about it
★ develop and organise your own ideas through writing
★ develop your writing skills
★ engage with critical debates in your subject, challenge received wisdom, express your views and defend your position.

Essays help tutors to check your progress, and to assess and grade your work. Ask your tutors why they give you particular essay titles to write – it will help you understand what they consider important.

What?

Why?

Writing essays

How long?

For whom?

How often?

Where?

Typically, 1000–2000 words in the first year, rising to 2000–3000 after that.

'Long essays' could be 5,000 or 10,000 words (or more).

Your essay should meet the word requirement (within a few words).

Typically, you would write several essays each term, but this varies from course to course.

Write wherever suits you, or as required:

★ at home
★ in the library
★ a café or beach
★ in the exam room.

You write essays for:

★ your tutors
★ yourself
★ examiners
★ (sometimes) other students.

Devising your own essay title

A short history of the world in five succinct paragraphs

Some programmes will require you to devise your own essay titles. There is an art to this, as a good title can help you to produce a forceful piece of work. In choosing your title, consider each of the following elements.

Core questions

Good essay titles usually contain one or two key questions which the assignment should answer. The title may contain a question, such as:

> To what extent are interest rates affected by consumer spending?

However, the question is not always obvious. For example:

> Compare and contrast the effects of consumer spending and stock market variations on changes in interest rates.

Although the wording is different, the core questions in both cases are 'What affects interest rates the most? What else affects interest rates to some extent?'

In addressing each title, you would be expected to compare and contrast the effects of different factors on changes in interest rates, and to include similar material in each essay.

Factors to contrast

Choose a title that allows you the opportunity to analyse, compare, contrast, evaluate, challenge and debate alternative perspectives, research findings and/or theories. That helps you to produce a strongly structured argument and an essay that is interesting to read.

Aim for clarity

★ Avoid long, complicated titles.

★ Avoid using several questions within the title.

★ If you use a quotation, keep this short and follow it with a typical assignment question.

★ To check whether your title is clear, ask a non-expert whether she or he understands it.

Research evidence

Ensure that you can:

★ find published research to support the topic

★ access this material easily

★ collect easily any new data you need.

Scale: keep it manageable

Ensure that the title:

★ is narrowly defined – select a specific topic, issue or timescale rather than trying to cover everything on the subject

★ can be researched within the time limits

★ can be discussed in reasonable detail within the word limit.

Issues for debate

Select an area where there are hotly debated issues or differences of opinion relevant to your subject. Devise a title that allows you to discuss these: it will help you to develop a good argument and line of reasoning (Chapter 12).

Activity

Essay titles

Read the following titles. What do you think are the weaknesses in each?

1 Reptiles

2 'The world is a safer place today than it has ever been.' J. K. Moody (2018). Is this really true?

3 What were the main changes in the use of technology within the British home during the twentieth century? What was the incentive behind innovation? Who promoted change? Did these affect women differently from men? What forces have hindered change?

4 The negative effects of violence on TV

5 Describe how placebos work

For a discussion of these titles, see page 411. For guidance on devising titles for projects and dissertations, see page 354.

Structuring your essay

1 Title/question

As stated on page 284, every essay title contains an actual or implied question. The whole of your essay must focus on the title and address that question.

2 Introduction

Length: about one-tenth of the essay.

In your introduction, explain what the essay is going to do.

★ Explain how you interpret the question and summarise your argument and conclusion.

★ Define any key terms (if necessary).

★ Identify the key points, controversies or angles that you are going to cover, without going into detail.

★ Give a brief outline of how you will approach the question.

3 Main body: Develop your argument or line of reasoning

Length: Around 75–85% of your essay.

Paragraph 1 of main body

★ This paragraph covers the first issue your introduction said you would address.

★ The first sentence (the topic sentence) introduces the main idea of the paragraph.

★ Other sentences develop the argument of the paragraph. Include relevant examples, details, evidence, quotations, references.

★ Lead up to the next paragraph.

Paragraph 2 and other paragraphs

★ The first sentence (the topic sentence) links the paragraph to previous paragraphs, then introduces the main idea of the paragraph.

★ Other sentences develop the paragraph's topic.

(For more about paragraphs, see pages 293–5.)

4 Conclusion

Length: about one-tenth of your essay.

The conclusion contains no *new* material.

★ Summarise your overall argument and main reasons that support it.

★ Bring out the most important point(s).

★ State your general conclusions; clarify why they are significant.

★ In the final sentence, sum up your argument, linking it to the title.

5 References and/ or bibliography

List all the books, articles and other materials you referred to in the essay (page 251). If a bibliography is required, list relevant texts, including those you read but did not refer to in the essay.

This outline structure of Introduction, Body and Conclusion is good for many types of writing. For structuring different types of essay, see pages 325–30.

Planning your essay spatially

It can sometimes be difficult to gain a sense of what the word requirement means in terms of how much you will actually write.

Before beginning any work on an assignment:

1 Work out roughly how many words you type on one page of A4 paper – typically about 300 words.
2 Check the overall word limit for your assignment. (This could be 1200 words.)
3 How many pages of your writing or typing will your essay occupy? (For instance, 1200 words at 300 words per page is four pages.)
4 Take that many pieces of paper. Draw out in pencil how much space you will give to each section, item or topic, as in the sample essay below. How many words can you allocate to each section? Or to each topic or example?

5 It may take a few attempts to get the balance right. Note how little or how much physical space you have on the page for each topic or example – that indicates how much (or little) you can write on each.
6 If you wish, continue to plan out your essay, point by point, on these sheets. Notice how much space each item can take.

With this spatial plan, can you now see:

★ how many pages of your writing your assignment will take?

★ where sections or topics will be on the page?

★ how your word limit divides up?

★ how little or how much you need to research, read and note for each item?

An outline plan for the essay on pages 331–3 (1000 words)

Page 1

Introduction (c. 100 words)
★ definitions
★ what the essay will cover and the order

paragraph 2 (c. 150 words)
★ maternal deprivation theory – early bonding essential
★ later: 'secure base' + 'exploration' behaviours
★ opposes childcare as harmful

Page 2

paragraph 3 (c. 150 words)
★ why Bowlby's ideas appealed
  * social reasons
  * research evidence, then – e.g. Goldfarb (1947) Robertson (1967–73)

paragraph 4 (c. 150 words)
★ later evidence undermined earlier research e.g. Tizard (1970s)
★ Bowlby seemed less convincing
★ childcare did not seem so bad

Page 3

paragraph 5 (c. 200 words)
★ Ainsworth (1975) – Strange Situation criticised as culturally specific (e.g. Mesman 2016)
★ fathers play bigger role than previously thought (Benware, 2013)

paragraph 6 (c. 100 words)
★ impact of theory on childcare
★ teachers as 'safe base' for students
★ attachment patterns can be passed on between generations (Main 1996)

Page 4

conclusion (c. 100 words)
★ sum up
★ theory has been modified
★ quality of care is more important than quantity

References

Frameworks for *'compare and contrast'* essays

One easy way of organising information for 'compare and contrast' essays is by making a simple grid and writing information in the appropriate columns.

★ Use one column for each of the key items you are comparing (e.g. theory, reports, policies, etc.).

★ Group similarities together.

★ Group differences together.

★ At the end, jot the main points in the boxes for the introduction and conclusion.

Introduction:
Main themes:

Areas to be compared and contrasted	A Birds	B Fish
Similarities 1 group behaviours 2 3 4 5	flocks	shoals
Differences 1 respiration 2 locomotion 3 4 5	flies (wings)	swims (fins)

Significance of similarities or differences. (How did I decide whether something was significant?)

Conclusion. (Draw the reader's attention to the main points.)

Three ways of writing out the essay are given below. Whichever one you use, be consistent with it for that essay. Before you begin writing from the grid, it is a good idea to map out your points spatially (see page 323).

Method 1

This method is straightforward, but tends to take more words than the others.

★ Work down the chart.

★ Write out all your points for column *A*.

★ Write your points for column *B*, in the same order as for column *A*. Highlight the point of similarity or contrast.

★ Do the same for any other columns you add.

★ Draw together the significance of the similarities and differences.

Method 2

★ Work across the chart.

★ Select one item from column *A* and 'compare and contrast' it with column *B* (and any other columns).

★ Go on to the next item in column *A* and compare that with column *B* (and any others). Continue until all points are covered.

★ Draw together the significance of the similarities and differences.

Method 3

If the similarities are so strong as to make the items almost identical, state in the introduction that you will look at similarities together, and then at points of contrast separately.

★ Describe one way in which *A* and *B* are similar.

★ Continue until all points of similarity are covered.

★ Continue with points of contrast as for either method 1 or method 2 above (depending on which is clearest to read).

★ Draw together the significance of the similarities and differences.

A blank outline is available on the companion site at www.studyskillshandbook.co.uk, if you wish to use this to organise information.

Reflective essays

Reflective essays are different from other kinds of essay as they start with thinking about your own experience. Depending on the course, this could be:

★ A life-transforming moment or critical event

★ An aspect of professional practice

★ Personal experience of material covered in class

★ A person, place, art or work that inspired you

★ The consequences of your actions.

Choosing a strong topic

The choice of material, your experience, is especially important for reflective essays. Such essays are personal – but you are still engaged in an academic process. It is easy to choose experience of personal interest but that doesn't lend itself to a strong academic piece of writing. Select experience that:

1 **Requires you to think**. It could be something you found challenging or confusing at first. Discuss how you tried to make sense of the confusion or difficulty.

2 **Is open to interpretation** – something that can be considered and written about from multiple vantage points so there is plenty to write about.

3 **Relates to theory covered on the course**. You can then write about how you drew on this to make sense of your experience. This brings in the academic dimension.

4 **Taught you something relevant**. The purpose of reflective essays is to demonstrate that you can learn from experience. Ideally, this should be relevant to the topic you are studying, such as your clinical practice, creative process, study habits or inter-personal skills.

5 **Engages you emotionally and intellectually**, so that it inspires or moves you, but not so much that you can't stand back and consider it critically. That helps create a strong essay.

The place for emotion

Although there is space to explore, analyse and account for your emotional responses in reflective writing, it is not usually the place for emotional outpourings. Your personal diary or journal is a good place for that. If relevant, draw on it in a critically reflective way within your essay.

Structure

As with other essays, include an introduction and conclusion. See page 323.

Writing style and process

The reflective writing style can be challenging, although it does not need to be once you become familiar with it. Part of the challenge is in combining personal subjective experience, which engages your feelings, with critical distance that enables you to analyse it with some dispassion. You bring different aspects of yourself to the writing process. For that reason, it is usually easier to complete it at different times, depending on where you are in your feeling and thinking.

For more about reflective writing style and process, see Chapter 14, pages 313–14.

The silver lining of my disastrous day at work is… great material for my reflective essay!

Framework for a reflective essay

Reflective essays vary depending on the topic. The framework on page 330 is one way of integrating experience and theory.

Adapt the blank template on the companion site at www.studyskillshandbook.co.uk to suit your title.

Framework: Reflective essays

Title	In your experience, is what X writes about Y accurate?		**The inner commentary**
Define the limits of the question	Define what X says about Y; consider if that is true for me. Draw out implications/lessons.	←	★ What exactly do I need to know about Y and what X thinks about it? ★ What exactly do I need to cover? What is not relevant here?
Options for my position on this	Somewhere between 'always (very) accurate' in my experience to 'never/not at all'.		
My experience	Forgetting to do Y at work.	←	What are the best experiences to choose from to do justice to this question? What seems tempting but could take too long to explain? Is that likely to bring up too much emotion for me just now? What had most impact on me at the time – or later on?
My position (Thesis)	X is partially but not wholly accurate about Y, from my own experience of …	←	What, in a few words, is my position on the question?
Background	Brief description of Y, what X says about it, why it (or what X says) is important.	←	Set the scene by clarifying exactly what X said on this topic. Emphasise what he said about C and D as these are relevant to my experience, and G and H as these were not.
The event ★ Consequences ★ How I felt ★ Any later outcomes	★ Outline of my experience: what happened? ★ What were the outcomes? ★ My initial and later responses ★ Longer-term effects.	←	State briefly what happened at the time, the outcomes, and how I felt.
What I learnt	Things I take away from the experience. What I would do differently in a similar situation.	←	Give some thought to the meaning of this: how did it affect me, the way I think, feel and do things? Is that useful or not? Are there things I am still coming to terms with? Or habits, behaviours or responses I still need to change?
Relate the experience to specific theories: what X said …	X was partly correct … But	←	How far does my experience compare with what X's theory suggested would occur? What did I experience or learn that X did not cover? Why might X be only partly accurate: what was different about my circumstances compared with those covered by X?
Relate to the broader field	Relevance of any other theories or writing on the topic	↗	
Any broader lessons?	e.g. Lessons for the profession? For students? For fine-tuning the theory? Etc.	↗	Is there any other school of thought or writer (etc.) that I find more useful in trying to understand my issues?
Synthesis / Conclusions / Ultimate position			Taking a wider view, are there bigger issues or questions to consider or lessons to learn?
What I learnt from the experience. Whether this is typical or generally applicable, given the theory. What I learnt from thinking about the experience in the light of X's theories (and others' theories if relevant). What is the broader significance (if any)? What my experience says about whether X is accurate about Y.		←	How and when does my experience show X to be accurate – or not – about Y?

Adapt the blank template on the companion site to suit your title.

What is an essay like?

Essay 1

Below is a sample first-year essay for an assignment of 1000 words.

1 **Read it**.
Gain an overall sense of the essay.

2 **Evaluate it.**
Use the criteria in **Evaluate written assignments for yourself** (page 317) or **What gets good grades?** (page 315). Essays should be addressed to an 'intelligent reader' who does not know much about the subject, so it should not matter if you do not know much about the topic. Put yourself in the role of a tutor marking it. This will give you a better sense of what your tutors look for in *your* essays.

3 **Comment**.
Add your comments down the side of the essay or in your journal.

4 **Compare**
Compare your own comments with those on pages 333–4. Check whether these suggest that you can identify the right points when evaluating your own essays.

The question set: How has Bowlby's Attachment Theory been modified over time? How relevant is Attachment Theory to how we work with children today?

Page 1

Paragraph 1   Attachment theory originated in the work of Bowlby (1907–90). The theory was that an infant's ability to form emotional attachments to its mother was essential to its survival and later development. This raises important questions about what circumstances could affect the mother–child bond, and the effects on the child of different kinds of separation. This essay looks in particular at Bowlby's work on maternal deprivation, and at how early research and the later work of Mary Ainsworth seem to support Bowlby's Attachment Theory. It also looks at later challenges to that evidence, which suggest that short spells of separation may not have negative effects upon attachment nor on the child's development. The impact of these theories on childcare practice will be explored throughout the essay and brought together towards the conclusion.

Paragraph 2   Bowlby's Attachment Theory originally claimed that if bonding was to occur between a child and its carer, there must be continuous loving care from the same carer – the mother or 'permanent mother substitute'. Without this, he argued, chances of bonding were lost forever, and the child was likely to become delinquent. Originally this was formulated as a theory of 'maternal deprivation'. Later Bowlby focused more specifically on the first year of life, which he called the 'critical period'. During this time, he believed, the child organises its behaviours to balance two complementary predispositions. These predispositions are firstly 'proximity-promoting behaviours', which establish the mother as a secure base, and secondly 'exploration', away from the mother. Bowlby argued that the infant develops 'internal working models' of its relationship with the mother, which become the basis of later relationships. He argued that the mother should be at home with the child for these behaviours to develop, and that even brief separation was harmful.

Paragraph 3   Bowlby's ideas were popular with governments at the time, as there was a shortage of jobs for men returning from the Second World War: day care during the war had enabled many women to work outside the home. There was also other evidence that appeared to support Bowlby. Goldfarb (1947) compared children who had experienced continuous foster care from nine months onwards with those reared in institutions. He found that the foster children were less likely to suffer intellectual, social and emotional difficulties. Similarly, children who stayed in hospital showed distress and little affection to parents when reunited with them (Robertson, 1967–73). Bowlby's own research into adolescent delinquency indicated childhood maternal deprivation as a recurring factor.

Paragraph 4   Much of this research evidence has since been revised. Bowlby's adolescent research was based on evacuees in the post-war years, a time of unusual trauma and disruption. With respect to Goldfarb's research, the Tizards (1970s) found that although children's homes could have a negative effect on development, this could be because of unstimulating environments and the high turnover of carers. Some four-year-olds in children's homes had more than fifty carers. The majority of children's homes are now much smaller than in the past and there is a recognition of the role staff continuity and relationships play in children's well-being and development.

Paragraph 5   Although Bowlby's theory of maternal deprivation has been largely discredited, Mary Ainsworth (1978) built on Bowlby's ideas about exploratory bases and separation anxiety in her now widely used 'Strange Situation' experiment. Findings based on the Strange Situation would appear to support Bowlby and the idea that care outside the family is undesirable. However, criticisms were made of the conclusions drawn from the Strange Situation, such as that it didn't take into consideration how accustomed the child was to being separated from the mother (Clarke-Stewart). Others argued that the conclusions were too culturally specific, and that cultures such as Japan's and the USA's vary in how much they valued childhood independence and so would interpret the results differently (Mesman et al., 2016). The theory traditionally focused on interactions between children and a primary caregiver. It has been further modified by those who argue that multiple attachment figures determine children's attachment patterns. Benware (2013) emphasised the role played by fathers whilst Van Ijzendoorn (2005), amongst others, proposes a 'social network' model of attachments in which infants have multiple simultaneous attachments to both family and non-family caregivers. In this model, the quality of the multiple attachments determines the infant's overall pattern of attachment.

Paragraph 6   Attachment theory can enhance our understanding of other areas of child development. For example, studies conclude that pre-school teachers can act as a 'safe base' for children and enable them to develop secure attachment patterns. The same is true for other childcare professionals. There is good evidence to suggest that good attachment relationships lead to children being better able to adjust to school life and form relationships with peers. Main and colleagues (1996) explored how attachment patterns may be passed on between generations, creating potential interventions for those parents with insecure attachments as children.

Paragraph 7   Bowlby's original Attachment Theory has been modified; there is now less emphasis on the 'critical period', on the irreversibility of early weak bonding, and on the necessity of exclusive, continuous maternal care. Separation and reunion behaviours are still regarded as useful indicators of later difficulties, although it is now recognised that many other factors, such as marital discord, have to be taken into consideration. In general, there has been greater recognition that it is the quality of care, rather than the quantity, that is important. Subsequent modifications in the theory have accompanied changes in childcare, hospital and nursery environments. Although there is still popular belief in maternal deprivation, many professionals now agree that studying how we form and maintain attachments can tell us a great deal about child and adult development and behaviour.

References

Benware, J. (2013). 'Predictors of Father-Child and Mother-Child Attachment in Two-Parent Families'. All Graduate Theses and Dissertations. 1734. https://digitalcommons.usu.edu/etd/1734.

Burman, E. (1994). *Deconstructing Developmental Psychology*. London: Routledge.

Cassidy, J., Jones, J. and Shaver, P. (2013). 'Contributions of attachment theory and research: A framework for future research, translation, and policy'. *Development and Psychopathology, 25(4)*, 1415–1434.

Clarke-Stewart

George, C., Kaplan, N. and Main, M. (1996). 'The Adult Attachment Interview'. http://library.allanschore.com/docs/AAIProtocol.pdf (downloaded 21.04.18).

Van Ijzendoorn, M. H. (2005). 'Attachment in social networks: Toward an evolutionary social network model'. *Human Development*, 48, 85–88.

Main et al. (1996)

Mesman, J., van Ijzendoorn, M. H., Sagi-Schwartz, A. (2016). Cross Cultural Patterns of Attachment. www.academia.edu (accessed 07.04.18).

Comments

Overall this is a reasonable essay. Good points include:

★ the style is very clear and precise, few words are wasted and it meets the word requirements

★ there is evidence of broad reading and consideration of research into different perspectives

★ the clear line of reasoning – on the whole, the essay follows the introduction, and evidence is used well to support the arguments made

★ it is well structured: ideas are well ordered and generally well paragraphed, although paragraph 5 could be split into two

★ the research evidence has been evaluated in terms of its strengths and weaknesses

★ the writer's point of view (the general disagreement with Bowlby) is clear, and evidence is used to support this.

The essay could be improved, however, to achieve a higher mark. For example:

★ *Fulfilling undertakings made in the introduction*   In the introduction, the writer says she will bring together ideas on childcare practice at the end of the essay, but she has not done so.

★ *Balance* The author does not include much about 'working with children' today compared with discussion of the theories.

★ *The author's position*   An indication of the author's position and/or conclusions could come across more clearly in the introduction. This would have helped her to identify that the childcare aspect was weak, and would have been a stronger opening than stating that all would be 'brought together at the end'. It is best to avoid an 'all will be revealed' approach.

★ *Answering the question*   Discussion of theory is relatively strong. Unfortunately, as the author neglected the second part of the question, she could not gain marks for this; and that would bring down the overall grade.

★ *Citations in the text*   Although the essay cites sources reasonably well overall, paragraph 6 makes several statements without saying where the evidence or idea comes from. Some citations, such as in paragraph 5, omit the date.

★ *References at the end*   Not all citations given in the text have been included in the list of references, and some have not been written out in full. The references list includes items not obviously cited.

Essay 2

Now compare Essay 1 with a second essay on the same subject.

How has Bowlby's Attachment Theory been modified over time? How relevant is attachment theory to how we work with children today?

1   The world of psychology contains many theories about children, some more useful than others. One such theory is that of 'attachment', which was the idea of a psychologist called Edward John Mostyn Bowlby, son of Major Sir Antony Bowlby. What are the main elements of Bowlby's theory? Well, first there is his early work about attachment. Second, there are his adaptations of

5   his theory into his later ideas about maternal deprivation. There was a lot of research to support Bowlby at the time, and his ideas were very useful to society so it is not surprising that he had a big following in his day. Later, some of his ideas were discredited but some of his ideas were picked up by Mary Ainsworth. She developed something called the 'Strange Situation' which has been used by many people interested in the welfare of children.

10   Bowlby actually believed that it was a tragedy for the child if the mother was not with him throughout his early childhood. He was very opposed to the idea of mothers going out to work. During the war, a lot of mothers had left their children in special nurseries set up by the Government. These nurseries enabled women to work in factories making armaments or to go out to grow food and any other jobs formerly filled by men. Many women enjoyed this

15   new-found freedom and learning new skills like building bridges, driving buses and being radar operators. Bowlby argued that the women's gains were at the expense of the child. He used examples of children that had been abandoned in the war to show that a lack of good mothering had led these children into delinquency and other serious life-long problems. Later Bowlby argued that it might be acceptable for the mother to be absent if there was

20   a suitable kind of carer who was always present so that the child got continuity. He felt that it was from this carer or the mother that the baby was able to learn how to form any relationships. So basically, if the baby did not have its mother, it did not have a sense of how

to form a relationship, so then it was not able to have the building blocks of any relationship which made relationships in general always difficult. He was actually influenced by the ideas of
25 Lorenz who found that ducklings who lacked their mother at a critical age adopted other objects such as toys to be their mother instead. Bowlby said that human babies also had a critical period for bonding with their mothers – actually up to nine months old. Harlow found that monkeys were also disturbed and when they grew up were not able to look after their babies.

    Mary Ainsworth found that if babies were put in a situation with a stranger, they behaved
30 differently depending on whether they had a good relationship with their mother. She said that how babies behaved with a stranger and then afterwards with their mother for leaving them alone with the stranger let you predict whether the baby would be a delinquent later. She said her experiments using the Strange Situation showed that babies who were in day care were more likely to grow up delinquent. But is this really the case? Not every psychologist thinks so
35 and it is important to consider other views. What about the role that fathers play? Many would think it entirely unreasonable to dismiss the contribution that they make to a child's upbringing and it is sexist to blame mothers only when things go wrong. Grossman and colleagues say that fathers play a major role in their children's attachment. Research suggests that children, in fact, have multiple attachments to family members and even those outside of the immediate family.
40   Some people think day care may actually be good for children. Studies have shown that day care can, in fact, make children more intelligent and better able to get on with other children. Not all mothers feel fulfilled staying at home with their children and some might end up developing mental illnesses like depression, where they feel very low and may even be suicidal. Drug treatments and counselling can help women recover and depression is a very treatable
45 condition. It is surely better for a child to be in good day care, rather than staying at home with a mother who is depressed?

    So, there are some strong arguments for and against attachment theory. Bowlby makes some very interesting points about the importance of mothers and the need children have for good care. His research does seem to indicate that poor care leads to children becoming delinquents.
50 On the other hand, there are times when mothers would do better for their children by being out of the home so you cannot assume that it is always best for the child to be with its mother. Looking at society today, we are seeing more and more children with problems. The rise of delinquency in children today is a fascinating subject that requires greater consideration by researchers to work out what the causes are.

References

Psychology by Richard Gross, published in paperback by Hodder Arnold in 2015
John Bowlby – *Attachment Theory*

Activity

Evaluating Essay 2

Using the checklists on either page 297 or 315:

1. Underline sections which you think could be improved.

2. Write comments in the margin as if you were a tutor giving the student advice.

3. Identify reasons why Essay 1 would receive a higher mark than Essay 2.

When you have finished, compare your comments with those below.

Feedback on the Activity

Introduction   This lacks focus. The first sentence, in particular, is too general and adds nothing to the essay.

Length and conciseness   This essay is 851 words long, which is too short. It should be 950–1050 words for a 1000-word essay (Essay 1 is 960 words long). Overall, too many words are used to say too little. This means that the writer will not cover as much relevant information in the essay as someone who writes in a more concise style, and will therefore lose marks. (See especially lines 2–4, 14–16 and 42–4.)

Line of argument   It is not clear from the introduction what the writer's line of reasoning or main argument will be. This is also the case in the conclusion, which does not identify a clear point of view.

Addressing the question   The first half of the essay does not address how Bowlby's theories were modified by research findings. The second half does not consider the impact of attachment theory on childcare.

Structure   The early comments about the usefulness of Bowlby's ideas could be omitted as the essay looks at this later (lines 5–7).

Detail   The writer goes into too much unnecessary detail at various points of the essay, for example about women's work during the war and about treatment for depression. Neither is strictly relevant to this essay, and such details waste valuable words.

Paragraphing   Paragraph 2 is far too long, and its central point is not clear.

Referencing   No dates are given for the references cited, for example for the work of Lorenz (line 25), Harlow (line 27) or Grossman (line 37). Few of the references cited within the text are listed at the end of the essay. The two texts listed at the end are not referenced correctly.

Precision   Some of the research evidence cited is rather vague. Essay 1 makes it clear that there were two stages to Bowlby's research, but this is not clear in Essay 2.

Vocabulary   Words such as 'actually' and 'basically' are not generally used in this colloquial way in academic writing (lines 10, 22, 24, 27 and 40).

Clarity   Some sections (such as lines 19–20 and 30–2) could be written more clearly.

Critical comparison of two essays

Two further essays are provided below: the first essay is a final draft, and the second could be considered an earlier draft of this. These enable you to see how you can work up early drafts to develop a stronger answer – and to develop your awareness of the difference between stronger and weaker essays. Although these are on stem cell research, you do not need a science background to be able to compare and analyse them using the broad criteria provided on page 315: **What gets good grades?** The word limit is 1500 words.

Analyse Essay 3 below, drawing out what you consider to be the strengths and positive features. Compare these with the comments provided on page 340.

Essay 3: Final draft

The ethical implications of stem cell research outweigh the benefits – discuss.

Paragraph 1   Corrigan et al. (2006) describe stem cell research as 'something of a political, ethical, social and legal minefield'. In this essay I shall explore this 'minefield', examining key arguments for and against stem cell research from the perspective of both the perceived benefits and the ethics of such research. I shall argue that whilst the *potential* benefits, as opposed to the *actual* benefits, of stem cell research are great enough to justify its continuance, great care must be taken to address more subtle social ethical implications such as access to stem cell therapies and unrealistic expectations of what stem cell research can achieve.

Paragraph 2   Stem cells are cells from mammalian organisms which have the potential to replace themselves and to develop into specialised cell types. Initially, stem cells were thought to only be found in mammalian embryos around 5–7 days after the egg has been fertilised. These cells are 'pluripotent' – they have the ability to become any type of cell in the organism. This allows them to repair or replace absent or damaged tissues, potentially opening up new avenues for medical treatment. Later, pluripotent cells were also found in a number of other sources such as amniotic fluid and adipose tissue (King and Perrin 2014).

Paragraph 3   Contrasting 'ethical considerations' to 'benefits' seems to suggest that there are no ethical *imperatives* for undertaking stem cell research. Stem cells are the only cells that we know of to date with adaptive capacity of this magnitude. This gives them enormous potential for improving health and well-being, for humans and also for animals. Research on stem cells enables scientists to study how organisms develop or respond to conditions such as illness or different medications. In turn, this can lead to stem cell therapy, where stem cells are used to repair the damage caused by injuries such as spinal cord injury or illnesses such as Parkinson's Disease. Stem cell therapy can also be used for therapeutic cloning, where genetic material is used to stop transplanted tissues being rejected by the recipient.

Paragraph 4   Leventhal et al. (2012) argue strongly for the benefits of stem cell research. There have, indeed, been a number of studies which have demonstrated successful use of stem cell therapies. Trounson and McDonald (2015) cite several small studies that show stem cells have a favourable effect on reversing Age-related Macular Degeneration. Sun and Tan (2017) reviewed studies of the use of stem cells in the treatment of Parkinson's Disease and concluded that there was encouraging evidence to suggest that some methods could enable recovery of motor abilities. In addition, results sometimes occurred even two to three years after surgery. This has led to media articles claiming stem cell therapies to be the new 'great hope'.

Paragraph 5   Given these potential benefits, the question arises of why anybody would object to stem cell research. One key ethical concern is whether any benefit, actual or potential, could outweigh damage to human life. One argument is that stem cell research has relied on cells taken from human embryos and that this is always wrong. Ethical concerns from this perspective range from the 'right to life' of cells considered to be embryos, to the risk of wastage of human cells when such cell groups, or embryos, are created but not used. Jensen (2008) explores the moral arguments of using embryos for stem cells versus embryos being destroyed in abortions. McLaren (2007) refers to these as 'personal and research ethics'.

Paragraph 6   Conversely, evidence presented to the UK House of Lords Science and Technology Select Committee in 2002 suggested that many people believe that human life and personhood are not created at the point of conception when, in effect, there is just a mass of undifferentiated cells. Fourteen days is the threshold where the first cell specialisation can be seen such that it becomes reasonable to refer to an 'embryo' forming; this could be regarded as the start of 'human life' and personhood. Research on pre-embryos, that is, cell groups of less than 14 days old, has generally attracted less controversy. Using 'pre-embryos' would largely overcome this particular ethical consideration. However, this argument has potentially been eclipsed by the availability of stem cells from less controversial sources.

Paragraph 7   Whilst there is encouraging research which indicates the potential for the use of stem cells, the amount of evidence about the efficacy of stem cell therapy, gathered through high quality clinical trials, is limited to date. The hope that stem cells could be used to 'cure' conditions which were previously thought of as incurable has attracted a great amount of attention from scientists, the media and the general population. However, small-scale findings have been heralded by the media as 'breakthroughs' in treatment, resulting in what has come to be known as 'stem cell tourism'. Here, individuals with specific conditions travel to countries where stem cell therapies are readily available in the belief that therapies branded as 'innovative treatments' can cure them. Bowman et al. (2016) note the rise of patients with incurable neurological conditions travelling huge distances to seek stem cell therapies. They call for greater regulation of stem cell therapies.

Paragraph 8   Therapeutic misconceptions can also lead to the creation of 'false hope' for those taking part in clinical trials. Corrigan et al. (2006) discuss the difficulties in designing high quality clinical trials where a 'double blind' study of the impact of stem cells on neurological conditions could result in those in the control group undergoing procedures such as having holes drilled into their heads to mimic real treatment. They suggest that where there are no other recognised treatments for conditions, experimental stem cell therapies might be considered. However, it would be feasible to focus experimental treatments on terminal conditions such as end-stage Parkinson's Disease or Alzheimer's, mostly experienced by those in later life, who might be considered to have 'less to lose'.

Paragraph 9   If and when stem cell therapies are demonstrated to be clinically effective there will be further ethical considerations regarding access to treatments. Stem cell therapies are currently expensive and likely to remain so for many years. However, demand for them is already high and likely to rise if their efficacy is more effectively demonstrated. For state-funded health care systems like the UK National Health Service, giving access to stem cell therapies for all those in need will have major financial implications. However, failure to fund treatments would result in them only being available to those wealthy enough to afford them.

Paragraph 10 Although there is a wide range of ethical implications to take on board when considering stem cell research and therapies there is evidence to suggest that actions can be taken to mitigate some of these. Overall, a balance needs to be found between managing expectations of treatment and encouraging more high quality research to enable treatments to be developed more quickly, and deterring people from seeking treatments that have not yet been proven to be effective. This could be achieved, in part, through legislation, such as in the UK, where the world's first 'stem cell bank' was established in 2004 to regulate and provide stem cells for use in clinical research. Only cells which have been 'deposited' in the bank can be used in clinical research. The International Society for Stem Cell Research, formed in 2002, can play a significant role in managing the hype around stem cell therapy through issuing guidelines for research and development. Even controversial areas such as stem cell tourism may have ethical benefits. Petersen et al. (2017) suggest that patients might benefit from being able to travel to undertake 'innovative' treatments which have not yet been approved in their own country, as long as they received the right information and support.

Paragraph 11 This essay has examined some of the key ethical issues relevant to the use of human stem cells in research. In considering the benefits of stem cell therapy, it indicates that the evidence for clinical efficacy is still rather limited. Moreover, the hope that stem cells will lead to cures for serious illness and injury has led to unrealistic reporting of achievements, which in turn has led some people to seek experimental treatments with little evidence that they will be successful. There is agreement between many key figures that stem cell therapy holds great potential to benefit human well-being. When this potential is aligned with good regulation that supports high quality clinical research and helps to manage expectations, then the benefits of stem cell research could be said to outweigh the negative ethical implications.

References

Bowman, M., Racke, M., Kissel, J., Imitola, J. (2015). 'Responsibilities of Health Care Professionals in Counseling and Educating Patients With Incurable Neurological Diseases Regarding "Stem Cell Tourism"', *AMA Neurology*, 72(11):1342–1345.

Corrigan, O., Liddell, K., McMillan, J., Stewart, A., Wallace, S. (2006). *'Ethical, legal and social issues in stem cell research and therapy'*, A briefing paper from Cambridge Genetics Knowledge Park. Available at: www.eescn.org.uk/pdfs/elsi_ed2.pdf (accessed 12th September 2010).

Great Britain. Parliament. House of Lords (2002). *Stem Cell Research*. Report of the Science and Technology Select Committee. London: The Stationery Office (HL 2001–02 (83)).

Jensen, D. A. (2008). 'Abortion, embryonic stem cell research and waste', *Theoretical Biomedical Ethics*, 29(1): 27–41.

King, N. M. P. and Perrin, J. (2014). 'Ethical issues in stem cell research and therapy', *Stem Cell Research and Therapy*, 5(4): 85.

Lindvall, O. and Hyun, I. (2009). 'Medical innovation versus stem cell tourism', *Science,* 324(5935): 1664–1665.

McLaren, A. (2007). 'A scientist's view of the ethics of human embryonic stem cell research', *Cell Stem Cell,* July (Online). Available at: www.cell.com/cell-stem-cell/archive?year=2007 (accessed 8th September 2010).

Petersen, A., Munsie, M., Tanner, C., McGregor, C., Brophy, J. (2017). 'Re-framing "Stem Cell Tourism"'. In: *Stem Cell Tourism and the Political Economy of Hope. Health, Technology and Society*. London: Palgrave Macmillan.

Sun, A. X. and Tan, E. K. (2017). 'Towards better cellular replacement therapies in Parkinson disease', *Journal of Neuroscience Research*, 96(2): 219–221.

Trounson, A. and McDonald, C. (2015). 'Stem cell therapies in clinical trials: Progress and challenges', *Cell Stem Cell Review*. Available at: http://dx.doi.org/10.1016/j.stem.2015.06.007 (accessed 07.04.18).

Comments for Essay 3

Strengths

Overall   This is a good essay. It is succinct, using the word limit to full advantage. It flows well, uses language clearly and accurately, and has been closely proof-read to remove errors.

Introduction   It has a strong introduction. Though brief, it signals a great deal to the reader, including that the essay is likely to be well-written and closely argued. The reader knows in broad terms what the content and argument of the essay will be without this being laboured. The author's own position comes across clearly, and the reader knows from the outset that the writer's position is more nuanced than simply taking one side or the other. The opening sentence draws the reader in by reference to a potential 'minefield', creating a strong image and suggesting that interesting issues will be examined, albeit in the context of the set title.

The second and third paragraphs provide explanations of technical terms, and background to the issues. This is useful as a 'general reader' might not be clear what stem cells are and why they are so significant for research. This is done briefly, without excessive background description.

Use of sources and evidence   The essay demonstrates a good grasp of the issues, and engages well with debates. This is based on evidence drawn from authoritative sources. The writer uses sources well, referring to them briefly as evidence to support the points being made, but without becoming weighed down in lengthy descriptions of what they are about.

References and citations   Sources are cited correctly throughout the essay and referenced comprehensively and correctly at the end.

Critical analysis, argument and synthesis   There is excellent use of critical analysis. The writer evaluates different perspectives in an objective way, indicating how experts with different views arrived logically at their own conclusions, but without being drawn into agreement with all of them. In particular, the writer argues that the title, itself, is contentious, and drawing a potentially false dichotomy between 'ethics' and 'benefits'. This makes it easier for the writer to synthesise material from different sides of the debate to create his or her own position on the issue. It also indicates that they are not likely to take any statement on face value – even if in an essay title. The essay develops the argument that it is the unrealistic expectations of stem cell therapy that are problematic, rather than the research itself.

Structure   The essay is well organised and structured. Paragraphs follow each other logically, each focusing on a particular perspective. This helps to develop the argument towards its conclusions.

For example:

★ Paragraph 4 clarifies the arguments in support of stem cell research.

★ Paragraph 5 introduces an opposing argument.

★ Paragraph 6 refutes the arguments given in paragraph 5.

★ Paragraph 10, having considered counter-arguments, provides a strong focus for the author's argument that negative ethical implications of stem cell research can be mitigated.

Conclusion   In the conclusion, the author summarises the arguments. The author's own position is reaffirmed in the closing sentence, which ensures that it cannot be missed by the reader.

Introducing Essay 4

Essay 3 did not arrive at this point through a single draft. 'Essay 4', below, is an earlier draft for comparison. Using ***What gets good grades?*** (page 315), draw out what you consider to be errors and weaknesses of Essay 4 at this stage. Assume that the writer has undertaken the same background research and reading as for Essay 3. Compare your points with those made on page 343 – or by referring back to the previous essay:

The ethical implications of stem cell research outweigh the benefits – discuss.

Essay 4 (Draft version)

Paragraph 1   Stem cell research is an emotional issue, which leaves audiences divided. Is it something that might save countless human beings or an immoral activity, responsible for the deaths of thousands of babies? There are strong arguments on both sides, as this essay will show.

Paragraph 2   Stem cells are pluripotent cells. They have the potential to replace themselves and to develop into specialised cell types. Stem cells can be found in mammalian embryos around 5-7 days after the egg has been fertilised. Stem cells can also be found in the blood of the umbilical cord and in the adult organism, where they support the development and renewal of specific tissues such as in the nervous system. Tutter et al. refer to stem cells as 'a great hope for a new era of medicine'.

Paragraph 3   Much of the contention surrounding stem cells comes from the fact that the cells have to be taken from human embryos, which causes great distress to many religious people. They believe that human life begins at the minute when sperm meets egg. Therefore, even if stem cell research uses embryos young enough not to look like babies, they believe that a life is being taken. Doerflinger (1999) believe that at the moment of fertilization a new human life is created with the same moral rights as an adult human. There is also the issue that some of the stem cells cultivated for use in research might not be used and could go to waste. Consequently, it is wrong to destroy or make use of a human embryo of any age. Evidence presented to the UK House of Lords Science and Technology Select Committee in 2002 suggested that many people viewed life and personhood as developing over the course of gestation from conception to birth. In 1985 the term 'pre-embryo' was introduced to refer to embryos less than 14 days old – a threshold where the first cell specialization can be seen. Research on pre-embryos has generally attracted less controversy but is not accepted by everyone.

Paragraph 4   Up until now, there have been some studies which have suggested that using stem cells might have a therapeutic benefit. Bang et al. (2005) found that when stroke patients were given stem cell transplants they tended to make more progress over a twelve month period.. Vidaltymayo et al. (2010) reviewed studies of the use of stem cells in the treatment of Parkison's Disease. They state that there is some encouraging evidence to suggest that some patients are better able to move after stem cell transplants. However, results did not always become clear quickly and in some cases took up to two to three years after surgery to appear. This raises the question of whether the effects were actually to do with the stem cell treatment at all or might be down to other factors.

Paragraph 5   Stem cells have a range of potential uses. Research on stem cells allows for the study of how organisms develop or respond to conditions such as illness or different medications. Stem cell therapy involves the use of stem cells to repair the damage caused by injuries such as spinal cord injury or illnesses such as Parkinson's disease. It can also involve altering a cell's genetic material to stop transplanted tissues being rejected by the recipient. This is known as 'therapeutic cloning'.

Paragraph 6   Although there is some quite encouraging research about the benefits of stem cells, there have not yet been enough clinical trials to prove that stem cell therapy is beneficial. This has proved to be quite problematic. Every time that a trial is conducted and hints at a benefit for using stem cells it is blown out of all proportion by the media. A study might only show that a person getting stem cell treatment makes slightly better progress than a person getting other treatments but often this is reported in the media as if a cure has been found for the disease. This is clearly unhelpful as it makes people with incurable diseases believe that they could get better if they only had access to stem cell treatments. Cohen and Cohen (2010) warn us that there are already a number of stem cell tourists who travel to different countries in the hope of getting access to stem cell treatments. The Cohen's say that there should be laws in place to stop this from happening. The media should also be banned from reporting on stem cell research unless a cure for a fatal disease has actually been found.

Paragraph 7   Therapeutic misconceptions lead to the creation of 'false hope, for those taking part in clinical trials. As Corrigan et al. (2006) point out, it can be very difficult to design clinical trials where the effect of stem cell treatment is compared to patients who have required no treatment at all. For example, if the trial was looking at treatments for a neurological condition and required holes being drilled into the skull a person in the control group would have to go through this procedure without getting any treatment and would not know if they were in the treatment group or not. This would not generally be acceptable. However, it is possible that patients with incurable, terminal conditions such as end-stage Alzheimer's disease might be willing to volunteer for such trials as they might feel that they have nothing less to lose. Although this might offer a solution, it should be born in mind that patients with late-stage neurological conditions might not be considered in the best possible position to offer informed consent to take part in these trials.

Paragraph 8   If and when stem cell therapies are shown to have clinical benefits to patients there will be a further range of ethical issues which must be considered. As noted previously, demand for these treatments will be high and it will be vital to ensure that access is carefully controlled. For countries with publically-funded health care, the cost of stem cell therapies will be particular issue and it will be important to ensure that therapies are truly effective before public funds are committed to them. However, at the same time, if funding is not allocated to these treatments it is likely that they would only be available to those who have the money to buy them privately. This will result in a situation where the rich can afford treatment and the poor are left to die. As can be seen, there is a wide range of ethical implications to take on board when considering stem cell research and therapies. If therapies are to be used effectively, expectations of their success need to be carefully managed. This will involve a mixture of more high quality trials and better control over media reporting of trials.

Paragraph 9   Even with this, care will need to be taken to ensure that people cannot access treatments with limited or unproven benefits and that money is not the main factor in deciding who does or does not get treatment. This could be achieved through legislation, such as in the UK, where the world's first 'stem cell bank' was established in 2004 to regulate and provide stem cells for use in clinical research. Only cells which have been 'deposited' in the bank can be used in clinical research and treatments. This ensures quality control.. If this was repeated around the world then it is possible that stem cell tourism might start to be seen as something desirable rather than as a problem. Lindvall and Hyun (2009) suggest that terminally ill patients might benefit from being able to travel to undertake 'innovative' treatments, which have not yet been approved in their own country. After all, matters of life and death should not be decided by a postcode lottery.

Paragraph 10   In this essay, I have shown that the subject of stem cell research and treatment is an 'ethical minefield'. There are ways of making this less dangerous but it would appear that the field cannot entirely be cleared of mines. Furthermore, the role of faith in the lives of human beings cannot be underestimated. Even though, according to National Centre for British Social Attitudes (2016) in the UK, only y% of people go to church on a regular basis, over x% of the population identifies as being a Christian. This suggests that there will be a high percentage of the population for whom stem cell research is never going to be acceptable, whatever checks and balances are put in place. However, stem cell therapies still show great potential to improve the lives of humans and this should not be ignored. If actions can be taken to address some of the ethical concerns raised in this essay then stem cell therapies could yet prove to be the great hope for a new era of medicine" (Tutter 2006 p. 1).

References

Bang, O.Y., Lee, J.S., Lee, P.H., Lee, G. (2005) 'Autologous mesenchymal stem cell transplantation in stroke patients', *Annals of Neurology* 57(6), pp. 874-882.

Cohen, C.B. and Cohen, P.J. (2010) 'International Stem Cell Tourism and the Need for Effective Regulation: Part I: Stem Cell Tourism in Russia and India: Clinical Research, Innovative Treatment, or Unproven Hype?, *Kennedy Institute of Ethics Journal* 20(1), pp. 27–49.

Corrigan, O., Liddell, K., McMillan, J., Stewart, A., Wallace, S. (2006) *'Ethical, legal and social in stem cell research and therapy'*, A briefing paper from Cambridge Genetics Knowledge Park. Available at: www.eescn.org.uk/pdfs/elsi_ed2.pdf (Accessed 12th September 2010).

Doerflinger, R.M. (1999) 'The Ethics of Funding Embryonic Stem Cell Research: A Catholic Viewpoint', *Kennedy Institute of Ethics Journal* 9(2), pp. 137-150.

Great Britain. Parliament. House of Lords (2002) *Stem Cell Research*: report of the Science and Technology Select Committee. London: The Stationery Office (HL 2001-02 (83)).

Lindvall, O. and Hyun, I. (2009) 'Medical Innovation Versus Stem Cell Tourism', *Science* 324(5935), pp. 1664-1665.

Tutter, A.V., Baltus, G.A. and Kadam, S. (2006) 'Embryonic stem cells: a great hope for a new era of medicine', *Current Opinion in Drug Discovery and Development* 9(2), pp. 169–75.

Comments for Essay 4

Overall   This draft is less economical in its use of language, repeating points or providing too much explanatory detail. For example, in paragraph 3, it cites Doerflinger simply to repeat the preceding statement about life beginning at the moment of fertilisation. Such wordiness means fewer words remain to allow breadth or depth on some key issues. The essay could be better organised in parts, and many minor errors remain so it requires further proof-reading.

Introduction   This is overly brief, makes no direct reference to the title, and does not give the reader a sense of the author's position, content or line of reasoning. The questioning style used here is best avoided, not least as it creates confusion about what is meant by 'both sides': this could refer to 'benefits versus ethics' or 'saving countless lives versus an immoral act'.

The essay lacks clear definitions and background explanations. In paragraph 2, 'pluripotent' is a technical term that a general reader might not know. Without a definition, the usefulness of stem cells, and their benefits, is less clear.

Critical analysis   Rather than maintaining an objective position, the author uses emotive comments ('deaths of thousands of babies'.) In paragraph 6, the author is not objective about the role of the media and the unhelpful advice to advocate press censorship weakens the essay. In paragraph 7, the argument is conveyed through wordy and emotive detail (drilling through skulls).

Argument   The line of argument is weak and hard to follow. The negative stance taken in paragraph 3, the emotive content and general argument suggest the author is strongly opposed to stem cell research on ethical grounds. However, the conclusion argues that its potential should not be ignored; that is confusing. It is also unclear what evidence is being used to support such a position. Although paragraph 9 had considered ways of reducing negative ethical implications, it was not made clear how that material influenced the writer's argument.

Use of sources and evidence   Whilst it is evident the writer has carried out background research, many of the sources used are considerably less recent than in Essay 3. This is not always problematic in essays but is not ideal in essays on a 'cutting edge' topic.

Not all items are cited in the text or list of references. Some, such as Tutter's study (paragraph 2), are not correctly referenced. Evidence and language are used with less precision in Essay 4 than in Essay 3. In paragraph 2, little evidence is given for why stem cell use is contentious. The author uses vague terms such as 'many' and 'they'. In paragraph 4, the citation of the Bang study does not indicate the comparison group against which progress was measured in the experimental group. In paragraph 6, a number of unsubstantiated claims are made about the role of the media in increasing demand for stem cell therapies. Paragraph 8 states that demand for treatment will be high. As this is not yet known, it would be better to use a phrase such as 'it is likely that ...' or 'demand could be high'.

Structure   The essay is poorly organised. Material in paragraph 5 interrupts the logical order of the argument; it would fit better near the beginning as background information. Paragraph 6 fits most logically after paragraph 4 as it continues to outline doubts about the potential benefits of stem cell research.

Conclusion   The conclusion is weak. The argument, mid-paragraph, that 'stem cells show great potential', is important but poorly located and the author hasn't provided evidence to support it. New material is introduced about religious perspectives. Religion appears to be equated with being Christian. The author makes an unsubstantiated assumption that a high proportion of Christians would oppose stem cell research. Also, the conclusion states that the essay has shown that the subject is an ethical minefield: that is not the task set by the essay title. Similarly, the final sentence does not bring the reader's focus back to the subject of the essay, as specified in the title.

Editing   The essay hasn't been proof-read so there are many minor errors that need tidying up:

★ Paragraph 10: Add missing details of percentages.

★ References are not formatted consistently.

★ The author needs to ensure that all sources cited in the text are added to the list of references.

★ Typing, punctuation and spelling errors (e.g. 'Cohens' rather than 'Cohen's' in paragraph 6, 'Parkinson' not 'Parkison's' in paragraph 4 and 'borne' not 'born' in paragraph 7).

Review

1 **Familiarise yourself with essays**
Get to know what essays are for and the skills they develop. Read and critique essays to gain a feel for strong and weak essays.

2 **Find the debate**
Recognise the potential for critical debate in titles set by your tutors. Provide yourself with a strong debating position if creating your own titles.

3 **Devise strong titles**
If choosing your own title, style it so that the essay can be well-informed, interesting and manageable. Select one that enables you to develop a compelling argument.

4 **Take a position**
Know where you stand on the issues: make sure this comes across clearly in the essay. Show that your position is based on a sound consideration of at least two contrasting perspectives.

5 **Use a strong structure**
Create an outline, and group information logically within this so that your essay is easy to read and flows logically.

6 **Shape your thinking**
Consider using the frameworks and templates to help organise your thought process and material. Create a useful internal dialogue to guide your writing.

7 **Plan your essay**
Find a style of planning that helps you allocate your time and word allowance efficiently. A good plan ensures you know what to write about next.

8 **Provide a clear introduction**
Let your reader know what to expect. Follow through on what your introduction promises. Check that your conclusion and introduction relate to each other logically.

9 **Conclude forcefully**
Sum up your position bringing out your best arguments. Link back to the title explicitly so that the reader is left in no doubt that you have answered the question.

10 **Critique writing**
Use your experience of evaluating pieces of writing in this chapter to critique other writing. Decide how well their structure supports their argument.

11 **Think like your tutor**
Use set criteria to evaluate essays: gain a sense of what your tutor is looking for.

12 **Connect it all up**
Use chapters on researching your work, critical thinking and developing your writing, to raise the quality of your writing.

Chapter 16

Managing assignments

Research projects, reports, case studies and dissertations

Learning outcomes

This chapter offers you opportunities to:

- ✓ **understand what is required for completing research-based assignments**
- ✓ **understand the process for undertaking larger-scale assignments such as final year projects, long essays, case studies and dissertations**
- ✓ **recognise factors to consider when choosing an appropriate topic and title and developing your research proposal**
- ✓ **consider different research strategies to use for your assignment**
- ✓ **produce the content for each section of your assignment and write this up in the appropriate style.**

Almost all courses set tasks which require you to undertake some kind of primary research for yourself. This might consist of many smaller projects for which you write short reports, or larger-scale assignments such as a final year project, in-depth case study, long essay or dissertation.

Students often find such assignments daunting, especially if it is the first time they select a topic for themselves or their first large-scale assignment. However, they generally enjoy them because:

- ★ they find the assignments interesting
- ★ typically, such assignments are set at a point in the course where you have already had practice in the underlying academic skills
- ★ the course provides in-depth training in the more specialist skills needed.

Arguably, the most challenging and important aspects of such assignments are in:

- ★ understanding what is required in terms of the brief and the process
- ★ choosing a manageable topic

- ★ planning and managing the task as a project.

This chapter looks at:

- ★ what is required of you
- ★ how to approach the task and manage the process
- ★ and how to write up your assignment.

Understanding and defining the task

Chapters 10 and 11 looked at core research skills that you would call upon for assignments. They highlighted the importance of starting out by defining the task as closely as you can. Chapter 4 (page 70) showed that good problem-solving (and grades) benefit from time spent initially in defining, or 'elaborating', what is involved in the task.

Defining the task: starter questions

★ What is the purpose? Why are such assignments set at all?

★ What is the assignment brief?

★ What are the end-point or 'outputs'?

★ What do I know already?

★ Broadly, how will I approach this?

What is the purpose?

An 'apprenticeship' in your field

Research is core to academic life. These kinds of assignments acquaint you with the techniques for managing research within your field.

Understanding your discipline

Undertaking a research project helps you to understand your subject better. It gives you hands-on experience of working with raw materials typical of the discipline. You gain insights into how knowledge is constructed and advanced within your field, the difficulties that are encountered, and the issues that need to be addressed.

To give you choice and independence

Research tasks provide opportunities for you to investigate topics that are meaningful, relevant or interesting to you or your workplace.

Varied skills and employability

To accomplish such assignments successfully, you use and develop skills relevant to employment:

★ project management – the tasks call for advanced organisational skills

★ time management, so that different aspects are completed on schedule

★ self-management – to keep yourself motivated and focused over longer periods.

What is the assignment brief?

If your course provides an assignment brief, this is your starting place. It can cover:

★ the topic – or the choices open to you

★ the title, or a selection of titles from which to choose

★ the word limit

★ criteria used to grade your work

★ useful source materials as starting places

★ details of any methods, approaches, techniques, equipment or software you must use

★ guidelines on presenting your work

★ deadlines for submitting your work.

Use the brief and marking criteria

★ Read these many times; underline key words.

★ Summarise them in your own words.

★ Highlight requirements you must meet.

★ Highlight in a different colour the aspects over which you have some choice.

★ Keep referring to the criteria. Display them where you can see them. Keep using them to check your work is on track.

What is the end-point?

Clarify what you have to produce. Is it an essay, report, dissertation, or some other kind of output? Do you have choice?

Find out what a good report, dissertation or whatever you need to produce is like in your subject and whether examples are available through your library or department. Check what they are like to read. Note titles used in previous years and the kinds of data or material students use. Gain a good overall sense of what you need to produce.

Defining the task: what is a project?

Characteristics of projects

Projects share the following characteristics.
1 *Unique* Each has a specific purpose, brief or angle.
2 *Informed* They are based on research.
3 *Focused* They focus on one topic in depth.
4 *Set apart, yet relevant* They are usually outside of the usual patterns of study or work.
5 *Time-bound* They must be completed within a given time frame.
6 *Managed* They require excellent organisation, preparation, planning and scheduling.

1   Unique

In each project, there will be some aspect – the subject matter, the client group, the data or the finished product – that makes it different from everybody else's. Your tutors will be looking to see that your work is *original*. This does not mean making major discoveries, but you should bring some new angle. This might be that you:

★ test out other people's findings for yourself

★ conduct a questionnaire or survey so that you can draw conclusions from your own data

★ apply existing research to a new area such as by using a different demographic, sample or focus.

2   Informed

Although your project will be 'unique' in the ways described above, your tutors want to see that you have used previous research to inform your own project. Your project report should be explicit about how you drew upon previously published materials and well-tried methods in shaping your own project.

3   Focused

In elaborating the task, take care to ensure your choice of topic and the scale of work are manageable. Choose a topic that can be researched and completed to a high standard within the set time and word limits. If necessary, narrow the focus so that the workload is realistic. Avoid large subjects that can only be covered in a superficial way within the time and word limits.

Identify central questions to answer through your research, so that you have a clear focus. Avoid collecting and including material that, though interesting, is not directly related to the project focus. Your tutors will want to see that you can design a manageable, focused project, using an appropriate methodology.

4   Set apart, yet relevant

Projects are usually one-off pieces of work, relevant to the course but covering ground chosen by the student. Make clear to your tutor how the subject you have chosen is relevant to the course and its learning outcomes.

5   Time-bound

Typically, projects are larger pieces of work than standard essays, with higher word limits and more complexity. The time allocations for projects therefore tend to be greater than for essays. It is important not to let that create complacency: as there is more work to do, it must be carefully planned and managed to avoid problems along the line.

6   Managed

Projects usually require you to think and plan ahead. Pay careful attention to small details. For example, you might need to book rooms or resources well in advance, ensure that participants are available, co-ordinate schedules with others, design materials and deal with setbacks. These tasks are not necessarily difficult, but take time, thought and good organisation.

Typically, research-based assignments require you to:

★ break the project down into manageable tasks or steps

★ make a good choice of subject

★ identify appropriate methods, including ways of collating, recording and analysing source materials and data

★ produce a report

★ complete the project on time.

Dissertations and final year research projects

These larger-scale assignments enable you to:

★ undertake a substantial piece of independent work with a high degree of choice in the topic

★ pursue in depth a topic that interests you

★ put your personal stamp on a piece of work.

Differences from earlier assignments

Scale Dissertations and final year projects are larger-scale assignments based on broader reading and research, resulting in an extended piece of writing.

Timing These are usually set towards the *end* of your programme as the culmination of your study, and when you will have developed the right skills through working on earlier assignments.

Independence and personal involvement You have more control over the nature and scope of your assignments. They require strong commitment. Students tend to become highly engaged in investigating their specialist topic and take pride in the end product. As these assignments are time-consuming, it is important to choose a topic that really absorbs you.

Time As this is a major piece of writing, all of your study time may become dedicated to managing, researching and writing it up.

Background research You will read specialist material and use original documents or data. You will find that you read far more than for other assignments. This makes it all the more important to maintain accurate, well organised records to help you find information when needed.

Self-management and motivation Independent study on this scale can leave students feeling isolated or adrift. Devise strategies to keep yourself motivated and on schedule even when working alone for extended periods on a topic that only you are researching in that depth.

Skills Such large-scale assignments provide opportunities for you to refine and extend a wide range of skills, from collecting, analysing and communicating information, to decision-making, project management and problem-solving.

Similarities between dissertations/final year projects and earlier assignments

Essays	Project work	Reports
Like an essay, a dissertation or final year project:	As with other projects, a dissertation or final year project:	As with other project reports, a dissertation or final year project report:
★ follows the basic procedure for writing assignments (Chapters 13–15)	★ requires strategy and management	★ includes an abstract (page 367)
★ adheres to academic conventions (pages 302–3)	★ requires a systematic methodology	★ has many of the features of a report (page 363)
★ involves research skills (Chapters 10–11)	★ uses data you have collected yourself	★ is structured in sections (page 364).
★ includes continuous prose within most sections	★ is unique – nobody else will have covered exactly the same ground or be using the same data	
★ requires analytical and critical reading and writing skills (Chapter 12).	★ is a one-off, time-bound task	
	★ uses new material or approaches that you have devised, to test out theories, hypotheses or methodologies from your subject discipline.	

Projects and dissertations: clarifying your process

As careful planning is essential, an important first step is to map out your process from start to finish so that you can conceptualise it. Adapt the chart below, if necessary, to outline your own process.

Preparation

1 Organisation and planning
Using your project brief and this process chart as guidelines:

★ List everything you need to do up to the end of the process.

★ Draw up an action plan and prioritise (page 136).

★ Schedule each step into your diary.

★ Agree how you will work with your supervisor.

★ Plan in support from peers.

★ Book facilities for binding your work, if required.

2 Prepare the groundwork to help select a topic

★ Literature search: survey the field for ideas and background reading.

★ Brainstorm potential topics.

★ Focus your reading on likely topics.

★ Check potential topics for feasibility.

★ Consider ethical implications of each.

★ Narrow your list of topics.

3 Decide on a topic, title and research strategy

★ Decide on a topic.

★ Clarify exactly what you are setting out to investigate and demonstrate.

★ Specify your research question or title precisely.

★ Write a project hypothesis/thesis statement as required.

★ Decide your research strategy and methodology.

4 Draw up and agree your proposal

★ Draw up a specific proposal or outline, as required.

★ Check with your tutor/supervisor that the project is suitable.

★ Gain Ethics Committee permission, if needed.

★ Revise the proposal if/as advised.

5 Undertake a literature review

★ Read and take notes on key literature on your chosen topic.

★ Keep details of all works that you cite, to include in your references.

★ Select the most relevant items for your project.

★ Write the review, demonstrating the relevance to your work of each item you mention.

Research

6 Implement your research design

★ Fine-tune your methodology, scaling the project to the brief.

★ Identify participants and/or equipment.

★ Design materials (if needed).

★ Develop forms or databases to gather and record data.

★ Collect data or analyse your source materials, keeping accurate records of what you find.

★ Write up your methodology section.

7 Present and discuss results (for experimental research)

★ Collate data, drawing up tables and graphs if relevant.

★ Summarise your results and their significance.

★ Identify whether your findings support the research hypothesis.

8 Discuss your findings and draw conclusions

★ Write the discussion section, bringing critical analysis to your methods and findings.

★ Identify the significance of your research and ways that the topic could be further researched.

★ Draw conclusions and/or make recommendations based on your findings and analysis.

Analysis

9 Rework your drafts

★ Go back over each section, checking that the argument and the details are consistent and that you meet the brief.

★ Check whether earlier sections need rewriting in the light of what you have written in later sections.

10 Write the abstract and references

★ Write your abstract or summary (if required).

★ List all references carefully.

Writing up

11 Prepare for handing in

★ Check that you meet presentation requirements in the brief.

★ Check heading levels and page numbering.

★ Add appendices, numbering these as you did in the report.

★ Fine-tune the phrasing.

★ Edit and proof-read several times.

Fine-tuning

Projects and dissertations: managing the process

Manage the scale

Scale each aspect of the project in terms of the word limit, deadline and assignment brief. This means:

★ choose a topic and title which have challenge but which are feasible

★ scale your reading to fit the task – don't read lots more material than you can use

★ choose methods, sample sizes or source materials that give you significant results – with a reasonable workload

★ scale your writing of each section of the report/dissertation to match its word limit.

Manage the focus

Decide on a topic and title/research question:

★ that meet the assignment brief and criteria

★ that enable you to be specific about what you are looking for

★ that enable you to bring an individual 'angle'

★ that enable you to envisage what your results or conclusions would look like.

Manage your time

★ Start early – don't wait to get started.

★ Consider your options, but aim to narrow your focus early, so that you can start to conduct your more detailed research in good time.

★ Once you have chosen a topic, stay with it. Organise and plan your work, scheduling your time in detail (see Chapter 6). You need a clear sense of:

* the range of tasks to be undertaken

* the order in which you will do them

* how much time to put aside for each.

Draw on skills already acquired

★ Research skills (Chapters 10–11)

★ Maintaining high motivation (Chapter 5)

★ Analysing material critically (Chapter 12)

★ Writing and referencing (Chapters 13–15).

Manage your supervision

Time spent with project tutors and dissertation supervisors can be invaluable. As the time available for each student is limited, plan how you will use it.

★ Don't wait for your tutor or supervisor to contact you: make contact at agreed, regular intervals.

★ Do as much as you can before contacting your supervisor.

★ Prepare a list of questions in advance. Put these in order of priority.

★ If you get into difficulties, ask for help. Experiment with ways of solving the problem before contacting your supervisor. Be prepared to talk through your attempted solutions and their limitations.

Maintain contact; use support

★ Maintain contact with other students to share experiences and gain different perspectives.

★ Organise a support group (page 183).

★ If feasible, attend lectures in related subjects to gain background information or to fire your interest and imagination.

It can feel isolating when working on your own projects

Developing your research proposal

What kind of proposal?

Find out what kind of proposal you need to submit: the timing and contents of this vary. You may have to submit:

★ just the title

★ and/or a rationale and outline plan

★ and/or a full or partial literature review

★ or a pilot of your methods and results.

Scoping the field

Your proposal needs to show that you have a good background knowledge of the subject. You scope the field in several stages.

★ Browse widely to see what is written.

★ Dip into materials to look for ideas.

★ Select items to read in greater depth to build your knowledge.

★ Read more about areas that might provide fertile ground for a project.

★ Investigate a few selected topics in depth, to find a specific project area.

★ Continue to narrow your focus towards a title and hypothesis (pages 354–5).

★ Check that there is sufficient literature on your chosen topic to draw upon for your literature review (page 356).

★ Browse previous student dissertations to develop a feel for suitable projects.

Clarify your purpose or rationale

Once you have chosen a title, clarify your rationale for choosing it, so that you can put it into your proposal or talk it through with your supervisor/tutor. What lends it importance? For example, you might be:

★ looking at documents in the light of a newly developed approach in the field

★ testing out a theory or previous findings

★ addressing a known gap in the data

★ conducting a project for an employer

★ adding data on a new population, such as fellow students or local people.

Decide on a method

Aim to draw on methods that have been covered as part of your course. Think through the practicalities. Avoid complex methods that are difficult to complete or that allow errors to creep in. Think through how your methods will provide the information or data you need. See pages 357–61.

Consider the ethical implications

In deciding on a project, consider how your methods would be viewed by your department's ethical committee. Address all potential issues to avoid your proposal being rejected or sent back for amendment. Ensure you can demonstrate the following.

★ No one will be harmed.

★ Legal requirements are met, such as data security, child protection, health and safety.

★ Participants will understand what they will be required to do, and be well informed about the project's aims and the use that will be made of the results, and how confidentiality will be maintained.

★ You will gain the signed consent of participants to use their data.

★ You adhere to the general spirit of ethical enquiry as well as your institution's rules and regulations.

Use supervisor guidance effectively

Supervisors and project tutors know the field and are there to guide you. Check with them that you are on the right track. Follow up on their guidance on such matters as:

★ the project topic and title

★ the theoretical background

★ reading and source materials

★ methods to use and ethical considerations

★ software for analysing data

★ scale and challenge: is your project over ambitious? Too challenging? Too basic? Too easy? Ethically dubious? Too time-consuming? Not suitable for meeting the learning outcomes of the course?

Choosing a topic

Choosing the *subject* is the most important aspect of project and dissertation management.

Advancing knowledge and understanding

Reports and dissertations are expected to advance, in some small way, knowledge and understanding of an issue, methodology or application. As you look for a topic and title, consider how you would answer the question: 'In what way will this research add to what is known about this subject?' It takes time, thought, and research to identify a new angle.

Build on what has gone before

Select a topic:

★ that is already well researched

★ in which your lecturers have expertise

★ in which there are well-established research methodologies and techniques

★ to which you can bring something new (for example, where you might replicate a piece of research using a new client group, in a related area, or with a small modification)

★ with few ethical and financial considerations.

Look for your own angle, much as you would when developing a new thread on a discussion board.

Develop a long list of potential topics

★ Jot down many possible options: be imaginative initially so that you have a good set of angles to pursue.

★ Browse journals, book reviews, other dissertations, and podcasts for ideas on what is topical in the subject.

Small is beautiful

Typical difficulties arise from topics that:

★ are too broad and would take too long to complete well

★ lack a research basis so that it is hard to find a theoretical base, established methods to draw on, or material to write about in the literature review

★ are too ambitious in attempting new ground. You need to be realistic: a topic is still 'original' even if it is a replication of previous research or varies in just one small aspect.

Start early on a list of potential topics

Narrow your list

Eliminate items that are likely to:

★ be too complicated for this level of study

★ raise ethical questions too difficult to address

★ take too long to research

★ require you to exceed the word limit when you came to write them up

★ bore you easily

★ be covered by other students.

Identify your niche

Aim to select a topic:

★ that will engage your interest, and …

★ for which there are some gaps in the research (indicated by lecturers or your own reading)

★ that relates to your town, background, year group or some other area you know well or can access easily: build on what you know

★ that is relevant to your workplace or your employer, or that will be advantageous to your own academic or career prospects

★ that you might like to explore in more depth if you progress to post-graduate study.

Specifying your title and thesis statement

Specify your research questions

As soon as you can, narrow your focus until you settle on a title. Be clear which question(s) you are setting out to address. Jot these down.

Wording the title

Although the aim of the title is to address one or more well-defined questions, for reports and dissertations this may be worded more like a statement than a question. For example:

★ 'The effects of local flooding on small businesses in Smalltown'

★ 'The application of ABC techniques to stimulate nitrogen fixation in leguminous plants'

★ 'Using XYZ software to improve athletic performance'.

Check for feasibility

At every stage, check whether what you are setting out to do is feasible in terms of scale, time, methods, ethics, participants and resources needed. The exact wording of your title has a bearing on these considerations. Check that it is sufficiently specific.

You may find it helpful to add a subtitle that provides greater specificity. For example:

★ 'The effects of local flooding on small businesses: A comparative case study of two engineering SMEs in Smalltown one year after the 2018–19 floods'.

Thesis/position statements

A thesis statement or position statement sums up your central message. It should:

★ form part of your introduction

★ be succinctly written: usually only one or two sentences long

★ demonstrate clearly and unambiguously your position or perspective on the issue

★ be the point to which you return continually, to focus your readers

★ give shape to the flow of your argument

★ be reinforced within your conclusion.

The value of thesis statements

Clarity Summing up your position in this way helps you to distil and clarify your thinking.

Focus It helps to focus your thinking before you start to gather the information and write your report. It prevents you from wasting time accumulating lots of material that you won't use, and from going off on interesting tangents.

Structure, relevance and organisation It provides a clear reference point to which you should return, continually, as you consider whether material is relevant to include and where it fits in your overall argument.

Formulating your statement

Be well informed Read, think, write exploratory thoughts, map these out, discuss them, until you are clear about your position on the issue.

Be specific Be precise and clear about what you are looking for and what your position is.

Check your evidence base Make sure there will be sufficient evidence to provide a strong basis for the position you take.

Interest and conviction Choose a position that allows you to debate the issue in a forceful, interesting way, where you can sound convincing and draw on different angles and perspectives.

Example: Thesis statement

Although it may appear to be common sense that infants suffer if mothers go out to work, this report argues that the stay-at-home mother is an abstract ideal and does not represent the lived circumstances of mothers over the last 60 years. It demonstrates that it is not beneficial to either the infant or the family unit as a whole if mothers are pressurised into a particular position on whether to stay at home or go to work.

Formulating your hypothesis

Most reports, especially in science subjects, include a **hypothesis**.

What is a hypothesis?

The hypothesis is formulated *before* you start the research, and states what you *expect* will happen – or what you are likely to find to be the case. For example:

★ that there is a link between two factors

★ how people will behave in certain circumstances

★ what the outcome would be if two substances combined

★ that x causes y.

This is a theoretical assumption and should be a logical assumption based on your knowledge of the subject. Your research tests your hypothesis to see whether it can be supported by the evidence. You design your research to ensure that you test your hypothesis in an objective way.

The nature of a hypothesis

You can't 'prove' a hypothesis. You can:

Disprove it – if your evidence doesn't support it. That can be a useful thing to do and adds to knowledge of the topic, so don't be discouraged if your results do not support your hypothesis.

Provide evidence to support it – the information or data you collect can provide evidence that supports the hypothesis under the particular conditions of your own research and on that occasion. You or others might look to replicate your research and gain different results that do not support the hypothesis on that occasion.

Using your hypothesis

Your hypothesis provides a clear focus on what exactly to read, research, measure and discuss. You refer back to it in sections of your report.

★ Results section: you state clearly whether the data support or do not support the research hypotheses.

★ Discussion section: you analyse why the results do or do not support the hypothesis. Might the hypothesis have been supported under different conditions?

★ Abstract: this focuses on your hypothesis and whether the results support it to any significant extent.

Writing the research hypothesis

The hypothesis must be worded very clearly and precisely. It usually states that something will or will not happen.

> ### Example: Research hypothesis
>
> The research hypothesis was that adults would show a preference for savoury food coloured blue over savoury food coloured with food dyes simulating natural colourings. The second hypothesis was that there would be no significant difference in the preferences of men and women.

> ### Activity
> ### Formulating hypotheses
>
> Decide whether the following are well-worded hypotheses.
>
> **Hypothesis 01** The research hypothesis was that physical activity reduces depression.
>
> **Hypothesis 02** The research hypothesis was to find out whether physical activity reduces depression.
>
> **Hypothesis 03** The research hypothesis was that 20 minutes of brisk walking a day for 8 weeks would reduce sleep disturbance as a symptom of clinical depression in women aged 30–40.
>
> *Answers are given on page 411.*

Conducting a literature review

Once you have chosen your title, you can conduct a more in-depth search of the literature, focused on what you now know will be relevant to your project.

Be selective in what you read

You will be faced with a large amount of relevant material. As you won't be able to read and use it all, you need to make good choices about what to use and what to leave out. Do this in ways that will enable you to demonstrate in your literature review that you have:

★ a breadth of understanding of the field

★ a depth of understanding of your specialist topic

★ a good grasp of what is the most significant material, and what is less so.

Know your field

★ Undertake a preliminary survey of the material, tracing research in your topic back to its origins.

★ Read the abstracts of a range of journal articles. Identify those most relevant, to read in full.

★ Note recurrent key themes and issues.

★ Note how issues relevant to your project are treated by key schools of thought in your subject.

★ Identify the leading figures relevant to your selected topic – those whose primary research, theories or writings are regarded by academics as essential to know about – even if you do not read their work in detail. What did each contribute? What did others find to be the limitations of that research? What did they do to improve upon it?

★ Investigate and chart the variety of perspectives on the core issues held by experts in the field: in what ways, and why, do they agree or disagree?

★ Read specialist material, such as articles in more specialist journals, or monograms, or expert texts.

Read critically; note selectively

★ Make brief notes of materials that look relevant.

★ Evaluate what you read for its relevance and significance to your own selected title, thesis statement or hypothesis.

★ Look for 'chains': consider how each piece of research or set of ideas influenced others. Trace briefly how the understanding of this topic has developed through successive theories and research findings.

★ Make a list of at least 5–10 key pieces of research or developments in theory that have had most influence on the subject. Chart briefly how each influenced others in the chain.

★ Identify how your project or dissertation will follow on from what has gone before.

Write your literature review

Write up your review of the literature when:

★ your research proposal is agreed (unless you need to submit it as part of the proposal)

★ you are clear on your research design

★ and you know, therefore, which material will be the most relevant.

See page 365.

Newton's Mechanics   Einstein's Theory of Relativity   Chien-Shiung Wu Conservation of Parity

Research design and methods

The term 'research design' refers to the way in which you will conduct your research. This includes matters such as:

★ the source materials or data you need

★ the exact methods for collecting these

★ if relevant, the number and type of people you want to interview or to take part

★ what, exactly, you want participants to do

★ how you will design questions to achieve only the exact data you need

★ designing forms to record and collate data.

Deciding on your raw material

Most projects and dissertations use data that you have generated or collected yourself. This may be through observation, experiment, questionnaires or similar. Alternatively, in your subject, you may select texts, artefacts, parliamentary papers, philosophical tracts, historical documents or published data and consider these from a new perspective.

Each subject has its own conventions about acceptable material and research methods. Your supervisor or tutors will give you details of these. Journal articles provide a good feel for how material and data are generated and analysed in your subject. However, basic principles – of being accurate, being as objective as possible, and avoiding distortion – are common to most subjects (page 281 and Chapter 14).

Precise thinking and methods

When designing your research strategy, you need to think in very precise ways. Look for conditions, or variables, that may affect your results in ways that you had not intended or that leave it open to doubt what might have given rise to your results. If there are flaws in your research design, your results will not be valid. Keep returning to the question:

★ Will this method, or this wording, yield exactly what I need?

Research useful methods

When conducting your literature search:

★ Look for ideas on methods to adapt.

★ Look for research that employed similar methods to those you are planning to use. What insights do these provide into how you might fine-tune your own methods?

Collecting, collating and analysing data

Plan to collect enough data to achieve convincing and reliable results. Collecting and analysing data is time-consuming, however, so take advice on what is the acceptable minimum for your subject. Having too much information is not helpful for student projects: it simply means that time is wasted in collecting, sorting and selecting material that you cannot use.

Design forms to collect information in a way that helps you collate it quickly (pages 358–9). Once you have collected your information, organise it into charts or tables so that you can interpret it. Look for patterns and trends. Make relevant comparisons.

Your tutors will be looking to see how well you make sense of your findings.

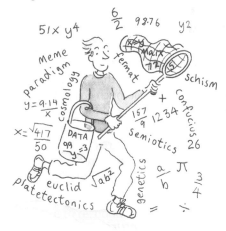

Pilot your methods

It is good practice to test out your methods in a trial run. Examine the process and the results in detail to see where you could make improvements. If you use a pilot, mention this in the methods section of your report, and include the materials in your appendices.

Checklist for evaluating your questionnaire

Use this checklist to think through whether your questionnaire will be manageable and will work in the way you want. Check off each aspect ✓ once you have considered it.

Does it take a reasonable time to complete?

☐ 1 How long will it take to complete?

☐ 2 Is that time reasonable?

☐ 3 Is every question necessary (or do any waste time)?

☐ 4 Is the time required for completing the questionnaire spelt out clearly to the participant?

Will the questions yield the information I need?

☐ 5 Have I used closed questions to elicit precise answers when needed?

☐ 6 Are there sufficient options to enable people to make accurate responses?

☐ 7 Are any back-up questions needed in order to clarify responses?

☐ 8 Will the questions yield the precise data that I need?

☐ 9 Are there any leading questions (which would invalidate my results)?

Is it clear to participants what they have to do?

☐ 10 Are the instructions clear?

☐ 11 Are examples provided?

☐ 12 If participants are asked to select from a range of responses (such as between 1 and 5), is the range used in a consistent way from one question to the next?

☐ 13 Will it be obvious to participants how to use the rating system?

☐ 14 Is it clear how to submit the survey if online?

Are questions easy to answer?

☐ 15 Is every question a single question?

☐ 16 Will people understand the questions?

☐ 17 Could any question be interpreted in a way other than the one I intended?

Does the questionnaire encourage participants to complete it?

☐ 18 Does it look as if it will be quick and easy to complete?

☐ 19 Do questions flow in a logical order?

☐ 20 Are any questions too personal for people to feel comfortable answering?

☐ 21 Do any questions assume that participants would have specialist information or background knowledge that they might not have?

Is the questionnaire manageable for me to use as a researcher?

☐ 22 Will responses be easy to record?

☐ 23 Will responses be easy to collate?

☐ 24 Will responses be easy to analyse?

How do I know it will work the way I want it to?

☐ 25 What issues were raised by the pilot?

☐ 26 Have I addressed these fully?

Interview techniques

Prepare for the interview

Good preparation helps to ensure that you remain in control of the interview, keeping it focused and limited to a reasonable length.

★ Prepare questions in advance.

★ Consider how to introduce yourself and the project – briefly. Be clear that it is a student project. If any company is involved, provide details.

★ You must tell participants what happens to the data and how you will ensure confidentiality.

★ If responses are to be held on an electronic database, participants must know this and agree to it.

★ Decide how you will close the interview.

Consistency

If you are interviewing more than one person, it is important that you carry out all of your interviews in near-identical conditions, to ensure consistency.

★ Prior to the interview, make a list of questions, with possible prompts for each.

★ If there is more than one interviewer, agree questions, prompts and any other words in advance. Practise so that you phrase questions and record responses in the same way.

★ Conduct the interview just as you practised it. Interview each person in the same way.

Conducting the interview

★ Give participants your full attention (avoid answering your phone, checking messages, etc.).

★ Know your questions well so that you do not have to read them and can engage participants better.

★ Sit at right angles to the interviewee.

★ Use eye contact, and smile occasionally.

★ Be confident but polite.

★ Keep it short: don't impose on people's time.

★ Thank people for participating.

Pilot the process

★ Practise the whole interview. Check that it will work in the way you want.

  ★ Check that you can record responses easily. If not, is this because the questions are too complex, or do you need a better chart to record responses?

  ★ Analyse the answers from the pilot. Are they yielding the kind of data you want? If not, design new questions.

  ★ Following the pilot, adapt your interview so that it is easy to conduct.

Ground rules and boundaries

Where there are a number of interviews with a single person, such as for a case study, the interviewer might become too involved. Take steps to ensure that you remain interested but detached.

★ Be clear with participants what you expect.

★ Explain what will happen during and after the interview, and how long it will take.

★ Specify your requirements for interview space or privacy. Negotiate acceptable alternatives. If there are any risks to you, do not proceed.

★ Do not make promises.

★ Do not get drawn into sharing personal experiences, as this can lead to unforeseen consequences. It can also distort the kind of information you receive in answer to your questions.

After long interviews

★ Write up your notes as soon as possible.

★ If you are required to transcribe the interview, write down exactly what was said, indicating pauses, coughs, 'ums' and 'ahs', and so on.

★ Go through your notes with coloured pens or pencils, marking all sections that refer to similar themes.

★ Write a list of the themes, and where you can find these in your notes.

Presenting and analysing the data

Presenting your results

Decide which method of presentation will show your results most clearly. You may wish to use a table, chart, or graph.

Tables

Add up responses for each question. If you segment responses, such as by age, gender, location, job or similar, state this clearly in the title of the table.

Table 1: Preferences for samples of font style, by gender

	Women	Men	Totals
Sample 1	8	15	23
Sample 2	13	5	18
No preference	9	10	19
Totals	**30**	**30**	**60**

Tables are useful for setting out information in clear categories. For example, Table 2 indicates preferences (three options) by gender (two options) and occupation (two options).

Table 2: Preferences for samples of font style, by gender and occupation

	Sample 1	Sample 2	No pref.	Totals
Male staff	13	2	0	15
Female staff	4	6	5	15
Male students	2	3	10	15
Female students	4	7	4	15
Totals	**23**	**18**	**19**	**60**

Bar charts

Bar charts provide a visual representation of the numerical value of a chosen variable. Label the horizontal line (axis) with your chosen variable: in the example below, this axis refers to preferences for each of the font style samples. Label the vertical axis with the numerical value of your variable. In this example, that is the number of people who prefer each sample.

Figure 1: Preferences for samples of font style, by sample

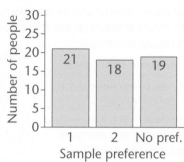

Pie charts

Pie charts are useful for presenting information in a way that the eye can take in at a glance.

Figure 2: Preferences for samples of font style, by occupation

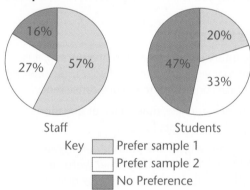

Staff   Students

Key: Prefer sample 1 / Prefer sample 2 / No Preference

Analyse the data

It is easier to look for patterns and to draw conclusions when you have organised your data according to categories, as in the charts and tables above. It is important to organise results in different ways and to compare the results.

★ Analyse your data. What do they tell you? Is this what you expected? Do the data support your research hypothesis?

★ How do your findings compare with those in the research literature?

★ What questions are you not able to answer because of the way you designed your research? Could the design be improved?

★ What questions are raised by your research?

Characteristics of reports

What is a report?

A report is the formal method of communicating the results of a project or research assignment. It may cover a laboratory experiment, survey, questionnaire or case study. Dissertations using those research methods require similar, though extended, reports. Reports are structured in broadly similar ways so that readers can find information quickly. They differ from essays.

Reports ...	Essays ...
1 originate from outside an educational context: they are typical of writing required in professional work settings	1 originate in academic settings: they are rarely used anywhere else
2 present research data and findings that you have collected yourself	2 debate or critique theories and ideas, usually in the form of a structured argument; they seldom present your own data or new research
3 are structured as on page 364	3 are structured as on page 322
4 are divided into distinct numbered sections, each with a clear descriptive heading. (See the diagram on page 368.)	4 do not have distinct 'sections'; they flow as a continuous piece of paragraphed text. Paragraphs should not have headings or numbering. (If these are used during drafting, remove them before handing in the essay.)
5 contain tables, charts, and appendices	5 do not include tables or appendices
6 utilise several writing styles, depending on the section (see pages 365–7). They are written concisely and give precise details.	6 use a consistent writing style throughout
7 include descriptions of the research methodologies used	7 do not refer to the methodologies you used (unless these are the topic of the essay)
8 include a discussion section that identifies how the research design or methodologies could have been improved and areas for further research	8 are not usually reflective about the process of researching and writing the essay itself
9 may include recommendations for action	9 do not include recommendations

Different goals

The style and content of your report should be appropriate to the readers for whom you write.

★ If you make recommendations for action, evaluate different options.

★ For business reports, include details of costs, losses and potential profits for each option.

★ For a report based on an experiment, describe the experiment and the conditions under which it took place.

★ If you are writing for a client (such as a work placement employer), tailor your report to the client's own requirements.

Reports and dissertations: structure and content

Check your course requirements. Typically, you would include some or all of the following sections.

Title Write this in the centre of the first page, with the course title, and the date.

Acknowledgements Thank people for help or for permissions to use their material.

Abstract Give a succinct summary of your project report or dissertation, clarifying why the subject is significant or worthy of study, and your conclusions. For experimental reports, state your research proposal or hypotheses, the methods used to test these, the results, whether these were significant, and whether they supported the hypotheses.

Abstracts may be reproduced and read separately from the rest of the report, so repeat information included in other sections.

Contents List the main sections and the page on which each begins (including appendices).

Tables and illustrations List any illustrations, charts, maps and so on, giving the page number for each.

Introduction Briefly discuss what the research is about – why is it important or significant? State your proposals or hypotheses briefly: what are you going to show or test through your research?

Review of the literature Discuss the most important writings on the subject, highlighting the key contribution of their findings or perspectives to the development of this line of enquiry within your field. Focus on how previous research leads up to your research. Introduce your experimental hypothesis, if you have one.

Method How did you conduct your research? What methods did you use? Did you replicate methods used by other researchers?

Exactly what were the conditions of the experiment? How many people or items were included? How did you select them? What instructions did you give to participants?

Measurement criteria Discuss the kinds of data you gathered. How did you analyse them? How reliable or accurate were your data?

Results Present your main findings briefly, using headings for clarity. Give results in the order in which you conducted any experiments, or start with the most important. Be honest about your results: do not assume these are 'poor' if they don't prove your hypothesis. The integrity of your results and reporting are more important.

Discussion This is a longer section. Analyse and explain your findings. Were they what you had expected? Were they consistent with your hypothesis? How are they significant? Did they support or challenge existing theories?

Demonstrate that you understand your results and findings: what had an impact on them? How could your research design, methods or sources be improved, refined or extended – such as by using new variables, sources or data?

Conclusions If a conclusion is required, summarise your key points and show why your hypothesis was supported or should be rejected.

Recommendations In subjects such as social policy, business or health, you may be asked to give a numbered list of suggestions for action.

References List the sources you cited in your report or dissertation. Use the format required on your course. See pages 249–51.

Bibliography If required, list relevant further reading.

Appendices Include essential items only, such as instructions given to participants, materials developed for your research, tables and graphs. Include only items mentioned (and numbered) in your report.

Writing the report: the opening sections

Writing it all up

If you write up sections of the assignment as you complete each set of related tasks, you will find it easier once you come to draw your report or dissertation together. Different sections of reports require different writing styles – further details are given on pages 265–7.

Introduction

Your introduction provides a succinct summary of your research. It includes your rationale for the research (page 346) and the thesis statement. For science reports, state the research hypothesis (page 355). Summarise what you did, the results, whether the hypothesis was supported or not, and whether the results were statistically significant. For shorter reports, the introduction may also incorporate the literature review. Write succinctly, fitting in as much key information as you can in as few words as possible.

Other types of introduction

If your report was commissioned by a business or agency, the introduction should state:

★ who commissioned the report
★ why the report was commissioned
★ the scope of the report: what it will cover
★ definitions of any terms
★ the methodology
★ a summary of findings and recommendations.

The literature review

For larger projects and dissertations, this forms a separate section. Avoid describing the content of previous literature. Focus instead on what each item you mention contributes to the line of enquiry, such as its use of new sources, data, populations, how it led to a refining of theory, changes in method, or opened up new avenues for enquiry.

Reports or dissertations with longer word limits require reference to a greater number of items, but would not usually include more information about each unless some were highly significant. In the example below, note how few words would be devoted to any one piece of previous research cited. The final paragraph shows how the student's project will build on previous research.

Example: The literature review

It has been argued (Ayer 2010; Bea 2012) that diet can be affected by the colour of food. For example, Bea found that 15% of participants in a series of six experiments showed strong aversions to certain food colour combinations. People were less likely to eat food if they disliked the colour combination. Dee (2013) found that food colour preferences are affected by age, with green being the least popular food colouring amongst children. However, Dee's results have been challenged: Evans (2014, 2016) found children's preferences for colour only applied to certain types of food. For sweet foods, for example, children showed a strong preference for red products, but chose green as frequently as other colour options.

Jay extended this area of research to non-natural food colours. Early indications (Jay 2018a) suggest children are likely to select blue coloured food even though blue foods do not often occur naturally. This research was replicated by Kai (2019). Similar results were also found for adults (Jay 2018b). However, Jay's research included only sugar-based products. As Evans has shown that there are different colour preferences for sweet and savoury produce, Jay and Kai's findings may not hold true across all food products, especially for savoury foods.

Jay's research (2018b) indicated strong adult preferences for sweet food coloured blue; Jay argued this was probably due to its 'novelty value'. The aim of the current research was to see whether adults showed the same preferences for blue food colouring when presented with savoury food options. The research hypotheses were that ... [see page 355]. It was assumed that the 'novelty effect' would hold true for savoury products.

Writing the report: the body of the report

The main body of a project report details your research design, your methods, your results, and an analysis of these.

Methodology or 'research design'

This section details how you gained your data and analysed it, so that readers can decide whether your results or conclusions are reliable. It also enables others to replicate your research to test your findings. The writing is descriptive, and lists actions in the order undertaken: 'First this was done, then that was done ...'.

Example: Methodology

Participants

The research participants were 32 adult students, all aged over 25. There were equal numbers of men and women.

Materials

Four types of food were prepared (potato salad, chapati, rice, couscous) and each was divided into 4. Four different food dyes were used; three were dyes used in the food trade designed to look like a 'natural' food colour; the fourth dye was pale blue. A quarter of each of the four food types was dyed a different colour so that all foods were available in each colour, to give 16 possible options.

Method

Firstly, participants were told that all of the food was coloured using artificial dyes. Each person was then allowed to choose three items to eat. This meant they could not select one of each colour. A record was kept of the colours selected by each person. The results were then calculated according to food colour preference overall, and preferences by gender.

Results

The results section simply presents the data: it does not discuss them. Keep this section short; include only relevant and representative data. State whether your results support the research hypotheses. Often they do not: this is neither 'good' nor 'bad'.

Normally you would present results both in a brief paragraph, and in tables or charts which summarise the data. You may be asked to present your data as appendices only.

Example: Results

24 of the 32 participants (75%) did not select a blue food item. The findings do not support the first research hypothesis. However, 7 of the 8 participants who did select a blue option were women; 44% of women chose a blue option compared with 6.25% of men. This does not support the second research hypothesis.

Discussion

This section makes a critical analysis of the data. It draws out interesting findings such as:

★ the significance of your results and whether they support or differ from previous research

★ your conclusions, and the evidence for these

★ if relevant, your reasons why the research hypothesis was not supported

★ suggestions of how improvements or variants to the research could yield different outcomes or further useful research

★ how your results could be applied elsewhere.

For the research above, the discussion might analyse:

★ *The sample* Was it representative? Could the ethnic mix or age range, or asking students only, have made a difference?

★ *The method* Could this have been improved? Did the blue food look unpleasant rather than simply 'unnatural'? Would there have been a different response to an unnatural-looking green?

★ *Future research* What research is needed to clarify these results further? For example, do colour preferences apply to all foods or only to some? How long does the 'novelty factor' last?

Example: Part of the Discussion section

The research indicated that even when participants were told that all food options were artificially coloured, they still chose savoury food that looked 'natural' rather than food dyed blue. This suggests that adults have a preference for natural colours in savoury food. However, the blue dye was streaky; this might have distorted the results.

Writing the report: conclusions, recommendations and abstracts

Conclusions

Conclusions sum up your research, setting out its significance and your findings. No new information or references are included. The conclusions are also included in the abstract, the introduction, and the discussion.

For the research above, the conclusions might include:

★ a note that your research findings are not consistent with previous research findings

★ a brief summary of *why* your results may be different (for instance, adult participants rather than children, and savoury food rather than sweet)

★ notes of any shortcomings of the research (the streakiness of the blue colouring might have affected responses and distorted results).

Example: Conclusions

The research suggests that adults do not select savoury foods dyed blue, if given the choice of other options of dyed food. The 'novelty effect' of blue products, suggested by previous research, did not hold true for savoury foods. The research suggests that people choose savoury food on a different basis from sweet food. However, this hypothesis would need to be tested further by researching the choices made for sweet and savoury products by a single group of participants (etc.).

Recommendations

The purpose of recommendations is to suggest ways forward. They might propose how to improve current ways of working, or action that needs to be taken. They are numbered. For example, if you were undertaking research for an agency, your recommendations might be:

1 Undertake further research using a larger sample.
2 Avoid use of blue food dyes in the manufacture of savoury food products for adults.

Research undertaken from an academic or scientific perspective rather than, for example, a marketing one, does not usually include recommendations.

Abstracts

Although the abstract is presented at the start of the report, before the contents page, it is more efficient to write this last. Leave plenty of time for this: it can take a number of drafts to rephrase it in order to fit everything in. The abstract sums up your aims, your research hypothesis, your methodology, your findings and your conclusions. You may be set a tight word limit, such as 50–100 words. An abstract needs to be both brief and concise.

Example 1: Abstract (50-word limit)

This report suggests that research into truancy has neglected the critical role of school play-time. In-depth interviews with 6 former truants, now students, highlight the pivotal role of group dynamics within the playground. The interviews suggest that 'feeling like an outsider' at play-time encourages initial acts of truancy.

Example 2: Abstract (100-word limit)

This report presents an analysis of adults' responses to dyed savoury foodstuffs. The initial hypotheses, based on Jay's research (2018b), were that adults would show a preference for food dyed blue over natural-looking foods, and there would be no gender differences. This project replicated Jay's methods, substituting savoury for sweet foods. 32 adults aged over 25 were asked to select three items from a selection of 16 choices. Neither hypothesis was supported, as 75% did not select a blue option, and 44% of women selected a blue item compared with 6.25% of men. However, only the first result was statistically significant.

Summaries

Some subjects require a summary rather than an abstract. This is usually longer than an abstract, but still no more than a page. The summary contains the aims and objectives, a brief outline of the research problem, the methodology, the key findings, the conclusions and the main recommendations.

Writing the report: layout, presentation and style

Style and presentation vary depending on your discipline and assignment: a case study requires a more qualitative, text-based report whilst a scientific report will focus on the presentation and analysis of quantitative data. In scientific reports, sections will generally be numbered, whereas sub-headings are generally used for reports in arts, humanities and social sciences.

Headings for sections

Give each main section of your report a heading to indicate what it covers (see page 364). Use brief section headings to break up your report and to introduce different kinds of subject matter within each section. For reports on experimental research, number each section in a logical way, as below.

9 Results

9.1 Results of experiment A

9.1.1 In experiment A, none of the participants completed ...

9.1.2 On the second attempt, 4% of participants completed ...

9.1.3 On the third attempt, 17% of participants completed the ...

9.2 Results of experiment B

9.2.1 In experiment B, 33% of the participants completed ...

9.2.2 On the second attempt, 64% of participants completed ...

9.2.3 On the third attempt, 97% of participants completed the ...

Levels of heading

Headings are organised into levels: 'A', 'B', 'C', 'D'. To avoid confusion, be consistent in your usage throughout your report and avoid using more than four levels. An example would be:

A   Main heading: the title, in large print.

B   Section headings: in a slightly larger font than the text, and in bold type.

C   Sub-headings: may be in italics or bold.

D   Other lesser headings: should stand out clearly.

Presenting the text

★ Number the pages in order. On the contents page, give the page number for each section.

★ Use fonts that are easy to read.

★ Leave clear margins at each side.

★ Avoid fancy graphics, unless specified.

★ Use a clear layout. Include only essential tables and diagrams in the body of the report. Place others as appendices at the end.

Writing style

All writing in a report or dissertation is:

★ *formal* – avoid slang and abbreviations

★ *focused* – address only the project brief

★ *concise* – avoid tangents and unnecessary examples

★ *subject-specific* – follow the style appropriate to your subject.

Writing for a purpose

The content will depend on the purpose of the report. For example, the report on pages 365–7 is written about research undertaken on campus. However, if you undertook similar research for a company wanting to launch a range of picnic food, the research and the report would reflect those different purposes. For example:

★ The introduction would state briefly what the company wanted the research to achieve.

★ The sample would be bigger, focusing on members of the public rather than students.

★ If the sample were bigger, the method should be simpler. For example, you could offer a choice of only two food items, one dyed and one not, followed by fewer questions.

★ The discussion would focus on the implications of the results for the proposed range of new foods.

★ You would probably make a recommendation – in this case, not to use blue colouring.

Project or dissertation report: checklist

This checklist can help you identify whether there is further work to do on your report before submitting it. Check off each item ✓ once you are satisfied it is completed correctly.

Done ✓	Item
	1 The whole report/dissertation meets the assignment brief and marking criteria
	2 The assignment is true to the agreed proposal (if relevant)
	3 The title is precisely worded and makes clear what the report is about
	4 The abstract or summary is succinct and meets any word limits
	5 All required sections are included
	6 All material is in the right sections
	7 The Contents page is complete, accurate and includes page numbers
	8 The thesis (or position) statement, or hypothesis, is precisely worded
	9 The rationale or purpose of the work comes across clearly
	10 The Introduction is succinct and covers all sections in brief
	11 The literature review demonstrates the breadth, depth and relevance of previous research
	12 The research methodology is accurately written, with full details written precisely and succinctly
	13 The results or findings are presented clearly, accurately and truthfully
	14 It is clearly stated whether the results support the hypothesis and are significant or not
	15 The Discussion analyses, critically, the results or findings in the light of previous research, and critiques the research design and methodology used
	16 Conclusions and/or recommendations are included, if required
	17 All the information is relevant
	18 The writing style is correct in each section
	19 It is clear and easy to read
	20 All sections are clearly headed and numbered
	21 It meets the word requirements
	22 Citations and references are complete and accurate
	23 All necessary appendices are there, and include only relevant material
	24 Appendices are named and numbered exactly as mentioned in the report
	25 Pages are numbered
	26 It has been carefully proof-read to remove errors, typos, etc.
	27 It is neat, presented as required by the course, and bound if necessary
	28 Any necessary cover sheets such as integrity statements are completed.

Review

1 **Define your task**

The larger the project, the more important it is to start it off well. Before settling on a topic, give thought to exactly what is required.

2 **Conceptualise the process**

Map out the stages and distinct steps to take from start to finish – to help you to plan, time and schedule tasks and give you confidence that you know what to expect.

3 **Draw on your expertise**

Use the skills and habits you developed for essays and smaller scale projects. The practice you gained with these will make larger-scale assignments much more manageable tasks.

4 **Find a topic you will enjoy**

Choose carefully. Select a topic that will sustain your interest and dedication for the duration. Look for something that fascinates or really matters to you. Bring your own angle or touch of originality. Take pride in creating a report that is unique.

5 **Scale and focus it well**

Make sure it can be managed within the time, word constraints, resources and project brief. Working within such constraints is part of the brief. The project objectives may seem minor compared with published work but that is to be expected for a student assignment.

6 **Plan! Plan! Plan!**

Larger assignments involve more decisions, more complex sets of processes, more reading, larger data sets, more thought, and greater word limits – requiring great planning and scheduling.

7 **Research the literature**

Read widely on your selected topic, so you know who has done what, and how, in this area before. Draw on this to find your own angle on the topic.

8 **Decide the research design**

Decide a methodology and work out exactly what you will do. Draw on tried and tested methods. Test and pilot your methods first to check the research will provide the material you need.

9 **Act with integrity**

Be transparent about your methods. Stick closely to your protocols. Present your results accurately and honestly. Whether or not things go to plan, use your report to describe precisely what happened and to examine the results impartially, so lessons can be learnt for the future.

10 **Know your audience**

Design your research and present your findings in the styles expected for your audience, whether your tutor, potential readers in your subject area and/or a client such as a business or employer.

11 **Enjoy your specialism**

Very few people will know as much as you do about the topic you research for a project. Enjoy that feeling of being an expert, even if in a small, defined area.

12 **Find out more**

See Cottrell (2014) for a more detailed step-by-step approach to writing reports and dissertations.

Chapter 17

Devising your revision and exam strategy

Learning outcomes

This chapter offers you opportunities to:

✓ take charge of your exam experience and gain a greater feeling of control
✓ devise your strategy for exam preparation to optimise your results
✓ develop a constructive mindset towards revision and exams
✓ consider common pitfalls that lead to students under-performing – and how to avoid these
✓ develop strategies and techniques to use during the exam itself.

Doing well in exams at this level involves drawing on a wide range of skills and qualities, from good decision-making, critical thinking, memory and writing skills to managing time, regulating stress, keeping things in perspective and exercising a high degree of self-efficacy. As you can see, if you develop skills and strategies covered in earlier chapters, you will already have strong personal resources to call upon for exam success.

Take back control

Knowing you have exams to take can feel as if power is being taken away from you: usually, you don't know the questions in advance, the ways of examiners might seem mysterious, and you don't know what you will remember or what it will be like on the day. However, through devising a good strategy, you can take charge of many aspects of the exam process so that, when revising, you can feel more in charge. When you enter the exam room, you can feel more confident and assured that you have put yourself in the best possible position to perform well.

Make peace with exams

There is no need to regard exams as a battle. You can feel much better about them if you can find potential benefit in them and understand their

purpose. It is possible to approach them with a cool head, especially if you have in place strategies for retaining and regaining calm (Chapter 7).

Strategy and technique

One useful first step is to decide on a strategy to plan and prepare towards your exam. Shape this so that it is realistic and suits you and your circumstances. Prepare well: don't leave things to chance.

Whilst not every aspect of exam success is about strategy, preparation, practice and technique, these go a long way. This chapter looks at ways of approaching exams across the length of your course, and at tactics to draw upon to enhance your chances of success.

Brain full

Planning and preparing your exams strategy

More than just 'revision'

Whilst good revision is essential, a good exam strategy involves more than just revising. It is usually broad-based, taking into account many factors that impact on exam success, from well-being and stress-management to paced overlearning, enjoyable social learning and more. These are not last-minute tactics but ways of learning and being that are built up over time.

When to devise your strategy

Start straight away – now, or when your course begins. This will give you a wider set of choices when devising your strategy. For example, you can start to integrate exam preparation into the way you tackle other aspects of your course, such as your reading and note-making, reducing work-load and pressure later on.

Get exam-organised

As with many other aspects of study, exams benefit from excellent organisation, and suffer if there isn't a methodical approach.

★ Be well-informed about your exams: find out about these early in the course (see below).

★ Think through the tactics to use as part of your preparation: see pages 376–7.

★ Organise a schedule across the course: decide when you will tackle different aspects of your preparation.

Get into your diary ...

★ Dates and times of exams (and re-sits)

★ Actions that contribute to your preparation

★ Dates for mock exams offered through the course

★ Dates of any revision and other exam preparation sessions offered through your course or institution

★ Dates of stress-busting or similar support offered through your course or institution

★ Dates that exam results are published.

Be exam-informed

★ How many exams will you have to sit?

★ What kinds of exams are these? (Essays? Open book exams? Multiple choice? Short answer? Practicals? Oral exams? Presentations? Performance? Etc.)

★ What does each entail? How many questions will you have to answer? How much time will you have for each? How are marks or grades allocated? How will they be assessed?

★ What support, if any, is provided to help you prepare? Are any mock exams provided?

★ Where can you get past papers?

Organise your material

The process of sorting, distilling and organising notes and making decisions reminds you of material covered during the year and helps to reinforce memory of it.

1 *Select*. Think through how much material you can use realistically in the exam, and when and how you would use it. Remove material you won't use.
2 *Choose a few key citations* (in exams, the name and date will usually suffice).
3 *Distil*. Make one set of reduced notes or flash cards to use for quick reference.
4 *Make it memorable*. Organise and work creatively with material you selected, so that it is attractive to work with and easier to remember (see Chapters 8 and 18).
5 *Cross reference material*. Consider where segments of information would be useful for several different kinds of exam questions. Flag that in your notes.
6 *Add to notes*. Keep your thinking fresh and lively: add information or ideas that arise from revising material.

Take stock of your process

Once you start your preparation, give yourself credit for that: you don't need to be one of those students who keeps putting off exam preparation then panics as the exam looms. From time to time, pause to check whether your preparation is working, and adapt it as needed.

Revising for exams

What is revision?

Exam revision is a process of learning material ready to use to answer diverse exam questions. It involves:

★ checking you have covered the syllabus in sufficient breadth and depth to answer questions well

★ reminding yourself of what you have learnt

★ checking your understanding and recall

★ devising mnemonics to help recall in the exam.

Good revision helps you draw together various strands of your study and recognise areas that need more work.

Draw up a timetable

Work out exactly how much time you have to revise, given potential 'emergencies', and time to relax.

★ If they carry equal marks, divide the time equally between the subjects you are studying, and then between the selected topics.

★ Set aside time for practising past papers.

★ Apply time management skills (Chapter 6).

Take care of your well-being

The pressure of exams often leads to neglect of essential components for exam success, even the everyday basics of taking good care of yourself. This is counter-productive.

★ Sleep, relax and take plenty of breaks.

★ Eat nutritious food.

★ Take care of your physical health.

★ Build in some physical exercise – it stimulates the brain and releases stress too!

★ Avoid social isolation – gain some companionship.

(See Chapter 7).

Select what to revise

The revision process is especially one of selection.

★ Select which topics you are going to revise. If you will need to answer three exam questions, revise at least five topics.

★ Work out answers to a range of possible exam questions for each topic so that you feel able to deal with almost any question that might be set on the topics you have chosen.

★ Select the most important theories, references and evidence for each topic. It is much easier to do this before the exam than during it.

Keep it lively and effective!

When revising, it is easy to drift into reading through notes without a clear focus. This leads to boredom, poor recall and stress.

Watch out for such drift! Change tactics if you become bored or lose concentration. (See pages 376–7.)

Build up writing speed

Quality and relevance are more important than quantity. Concise answers can gain high marks. However, if you type most of your work, your hand-writing speed might diminish. Practise writing anything at speed daily to build muscles needed for hand-writing at speed.

New reading just before the exam

Opinion varies on whether you should read new material just before exams. It can keep your thinking fresh and bring your work into perspective. If it confuses you, then focus on material you have already.

Tactics to use in your exam prep strategy

Devise an exam strategy that you can make work effectively for you. That might take some trial and error during revision sessions and before early exams.

★ Select ✓ from the options below to help decide your tactics.

★ Work these into an **Action Plan** (page 381).

☐ Work on your exam psyche

Getting into the right frame of mind makes a huge difference to exam preparation and success on the day. It is wise to consider it an essential part of your strategy.

☐ Be more aware of thought patterns and feelings that undermine your confidence, especially if these distract you from study.

☐ Replace negative thoughts with ones that help you prepare more constructively and make you feel better about exams.

You can do this!

Work on your exam psyche

☐ Acknowledge if this is difficult to do on your own. Be open to speaking to a study counsellor or tutor – or join a study group.

☐ Regard difficulties as challenges for which you can devise a strategy. Then put time aside to work out what that strategy will be.

☐ Get the 'virtuous circle' going

If you don't feel the motivation, it is harder to settle into study. Self-awareness is key.

☐ Work on it. Be aware of what it takes to get you started and what will not work. Improve your attitude towards exams.

☐ Action boosts motivation. Do some exam prep to boost motivation: set a virtuous circle in train.

☐ Look for the positives

Exams can bring positive benefits! Identify some to help generate a more positive attitude. For example:

★ Preparing for them can energise you and sharpen your focus. That enables intense learning that is rare under any other conditions.

★ Typically, you include less information in an exam answer than in coursework – so you can be more selective in what you read, revise and learn.

★ Compared with continual assessment, there is less pressure on you throughout the year.

☐ Use exam-friendly study habits

☐ Make exam-friendly notes throughout the year: inviting, clear, visual, colourful, dynamic and memorable. Leave lots of space to annotate and add information and mnemonics.

☐ Don't wait until just before the exam to condense notes/ make flash cards: build your set as you go along (page 400).

That would be a good point to include in an exam answer if I am asked about …

Use exam friendly study habits

☐ When you write an essay or report, reflect on which sections you would include and which you would need to condense or omit in an exam.

☐ Review material across the course so you build familiarity and give the brain time to absorb it.

☐ Consider the exam questions you would set on each topic and draw up an outline for these.

☐ Listen out in class for clues that lecturers provide about what is essential to understand or learn.

☐ Use time carefully

☐ Draw up a revision timetable you can stick to.

☐ Start revision early: less pressure, better recall.

☐ Draw up a **Priority organiser** with a revision focus (page 136).

☐ Make a **Time circle** for revision (pages 133–5).

See **Time management** (Chapter 6).

☐ Use past exam papers

☐ Become familiar with these, including instructions for conduct during exams, the look of exam papers, and the way questions are phrased.

Use past exam papers

☐ Each question links to one or more course topics. Find those links. Consider which issues the question is directing you towards.

☐ Check which questions come up regularly.

☐ Look for patterns in the types of questions asked – consider what these involve.

☐ Brainstorm answers to past questions.

☐ Make outline plans for these.

☐ Time yourself writing *some* of these, to build writing speed and for general practice.

☐ Consider in advance what detail needs to be *left out* of exam answers.

☐ Questions might seem vague so as not to 'give away the answer'. Get used to working out what is really being asked.

☐ Consider potential ways that exam questions could combine your 'best' topic(s) with others. Revise material enough to answer such questions.

☐ Prepare with others

☐ Arrange study sessions with 2 or 3 classmates.

☐ Ask each other questions.

☐ Debate the issues.

☐ Devise outline exam answers together.

☐ Test and quiz each other.

☐ Encourage and motivate each other (Chapter 8).

☐ Use support

☐ Ask tutors how exam and course essays differ.

☐ Attend advice sessions and 'mocks'.

☐ Work your material!

☐ Work with the material interactively so the brain registers it.

☐ Devise mnemonics (Chapter 18).

☐ Return to the same material several times, spaced over time, to lay down and reinforce recall.

☐ Revise by ear

☐ Record yourself answering questions – listening to your own voice can help you remember the material.

☐ Avoid 'pitfalls'

☐ Recognise 'revision pitfalls' that apply to you (pages 378–9). Decide approaches to address these and plan them into your exam strategy.

☐ Recognise exam day pitfalls (page 386). Plan out how you will avoid these.

Revision pitfalls – and how to avoid them

Ten common pitfalls in revision …	… and how to avoid them
1 Leaving revision until the last minute.	Revision is a means of reinforcing your knowledge and understanding of course material, for everyday use or preparation for an exam. This is often neglected until an exam is looming, but is much more effective if paced throughout the course.
	★ **'Spare titles'** When planning and reading a topic, jot down potential essay titles typical of those for exams on your course. Jot brief notes, or page references to material, under each title, to build on for revision later.
	★ **Want-to-look-at notes**. Make your own notes readable, attractive and visually compelling, so you want to return to them. Working on them helps recall.
	★ **Paced 'over-learning'**. Start early in learning names, dates, formulae, set sequences of information, steps in a process, key points, etc. (page 400).
	★ **Build intensity** over several weeks before exams. Read pages 382–7 well before the exam. See also Cottrell (2012) for a 'peak performance' approach.
2 Reading through notes over and over again.	★ **Engage the brain**. Use creative and interactive strategies (see Chapters 4 and 8). This keeps your mind alert and helps to integrate information.
	★ **Read to a question**. Read with a focus on which material to include or omit for varied exam answers on the same topic. Ask in the library for past exam papers and also devise stretching questions of your own.
	★ **Discuss reading and past exam questions** with others. Social learning adds interest and you may remember the conversations.
	★ **Check the gaps**. Time yourself writing exam answers without looking at your notes. Follow up by reviewing areas you couldn't recall (it also increases your ability to think and write at speed and under pressure).
3 Writing or typing notes out over and over again without much thought.	★ **By hand**. Writing and/or drawing by hand helps the brain remember material.
	★ **Work it mindfully!** As with reading (2 above), engage the brain when writing.
	★ **Visual recall?** Check whether rewriting notes helps or hinders your visual recall of where material lies in your notes.
	★ **Distil**. Condensing notes into shorter sets of points or flashcards forces you to think about what to include and why, aiding recall.
4 Writing out essays and learning them or course assignments by rote to regurgitate in the exam.	★ **Recognise the problem**. It's time-consuming and counter-productive. It is unlikely that the identical question will be set, and exam answers are usually much shorter than course-work assignments.
	★ **Build flexibility**. Reflect on, plan and practise a wide range of answers, familiarising yourself with sets of organised material so you can select just what you need for the exact title set. Don't learn precise wording by rote.

Ten common pitfalls in revision ...	... and how to avoid them
5 'Tomorrow syndrome' – constantly finding other things to do instead.	★ **Get to the root**. Why are you putting it off? Address those reasons. ★ **Schedule**. Make a revision timetable and stick to your plan. ★ See *Tricks for getting started* (page 279) and ***Managing your time*** (Chapter 6). ★ **Social learning**. You may be missing company. Have a go at revising with other students. Involve others in your revision: explain a subject to them. Ask them to test you on your memory triggers, or to ask you questions from your notes.
6 'I can't force myself back to study.'	★ **Carrot rather than stick?** Rather than 'forcing' yourself, *encourage* and *entice* yourself to study through making it more enjoyable, setting short-term goals, challenges, adding a creative angle, studying with others. ★ **Re-connect to the purpose**. Rekindle your motivation (Chapter 5). ★ **Breaks**. Check that your revision timetable has sufficient breaks for rest.
7 'I start to panic and feel I can't do it!'	★ **Manage the overwhelm**. Break tasks into smaller steps you know you can manage (page 119). Focus on these and tasks completed rather than still to do. ★ **Environment**. Work with calm and positive-minded people. ★ **Create a routine**. Devise and stick to a plan so you feel more in control. ★ **Talk it through**. If the problem continues, speak to a tutor or professional counsellor. ★ See also Chapters 7 (on dealing with stress) and 18 (on memory).
8 'I can't cope with the boredom of it. I start to daydream or wonder why I'm bothering.'	★ **Work in many shorter spells**. Don't give yourself time to get bored. ★ **Create interest**. Boredom suggests that you are not using a variety of interactive techniques in a lively way. Make it enjoyable (Chapters 4, 5 and 8). ★ **Add variety**. Don't keep doing the same old things in your study sessions. ★ **Look for unusual angles**. Think of ways in which seemingly unrelated material could be linked. Make up quiz questions. Design memorable images. ★ **Set greater challenges**. Achieve more in the time. Read a more advanced text. Consider how you could weave advanced material into your exam answers.
9 'I have too many responsibilities to find time to revise.'	★ **Make use of short spells of time** – on buses, during tea breaks, and the like. ★ **Divide** your material into short sections. Always carry some with you. ★ **Carry an exam question** in your head; jot down ideas as they occur. ★ **Value your goals**. Your education matters and isn't forever, so make time.
10 Stopping revision before the process of over-learning is complete.	★ **Keep testing yourself**. Checking your recall also strengthens it for next time. ★ **Manipulate the information**. Don't just know the facts, understand what they are for and how you would use them in answering different kinds of question. ★ **Don't give up**. If the material hasn't stuck, keep working at it.

Revision and exam preparation

Preparing for exams: checklist

- [ ] 1 I can find something positive for me in taking these exams
- [ ] 2 I can develop the right frame of mind for these exams
- [ ] 3 I know exactly when the exams are
- [ ] 4 I am aware how many questions are required for each exam
- [ ] 5 I have read the course or module details carefully to check what I am expected to know about the subject
- [ ] 6 I have organised my notes so that the material is easy to learn
- [ ] 7 I have worked out how many topics I need to revise for each exam
- [ ] 8 I am aware of the range of questions that can come up for each topic
- [ ] 9 I have made a realistic revision timetable, with clear priorities
- [ ] 10 I know how to work on exam answers using past papers
- [ ] 11 I have started to practise writing out answers at speed
- [ ] 12 I am aware of the memory strategies I can use for revision
- [ ] 13 I know how the marks are weighted for each question
- [ ] 14 I am aware of how to use time most effectively in the exam
- [ ] 15 I am aware of how to avoid common revision pitfalls
- [ ] 16 I am aware of how to avoid common pitfalls in exams
- [ ] 17 I know the differences between exam answers and coursework
- [ ] 18 I know how to manage stress and use it effectively.

If you spotted any gaps, follow up on these straight away. Decide how you will approach them drawing on material in this book. Consider any help and support you might need from others. Build these into your Action Plan (page 381).

Reflection

Improving revision strategies

In what ways have your past revision strategies and your approach to exams helped or hindered your exam success? What can you change or improve for your next set of exams?

Revision: seven-point action plan

1 **Positive state of mind** (e.g. maintaining motivation; giving myself positive messages; regulating stress; accepting the challenge, keeping exams in perspective). *Things I will do:*

2 **Time** (e.g. going over my work from early in the year in different ways; organising and using time effectively (Chapter 6); dealing with my excuses; using spare moments, etc.). *I will:*

3 **Variety** (e.g. working in many short spells; using varied and interesting ways of going over my material). *I will:*

4 **Over-learning** (e.g. rewriting notes, flash cards, new essay plans, memory triggers). *I will:*

5 **Practice** (e.g. doing past questions; working under exam conditions; having a trial run) *I will:*

6 **People** (e.g. revising with others; using available support; asking for help, etc.). *I will:*

7 **Selection** (What topics will I revise? What level of detail can I really use under exam conditions?) *I will:*

Countdown towards the exams

Plan towards 'peak performance'

Prepare towards exams so that you are most likely to 'peak' on the day of the exam. Just as athletes train so that they are 'in the zone' on the day, you can prepare for exams so that you increase your chance of optimal performance in the exam itself. If this interests you, it is explored in more detail in Cottrell (2012) *The Exam Skills Handbook: Achieving Peak Performance*.

Use the whole course

Make use of time, resources and support across the whole of your course to prepare you for the exam. Avoid seeing an exam as an 'added extra' to struggle through at the end: consider it an integral part of the course. See page 376.

Practise – as a 'dress rehearsal'

Like most things, exam performance improves with practice. Attend mock exams if provided, even if you feel you're not ready – the experience is important. If none are provided, devise one for yourself (or with course mates). Ideally, do at least two mocks, to practise applying what you learn from first attempts.

★ Choose a past paper or devise your own.

★ Set up your mock so that it is a good dress rehearsal for the real exam. Avoid behaviours that would not be permitted in the real exam – such as peeking at the answers, communicating with others, taking a meal or phone break.

★ If doing this with others, arrange seating so you can't see each other's answers.

★ Write your answers within a set time limit – work alone, in silence.

★ Afterwards, go through your answers. Identify ways of strengthening them.

The week before

★ Drink plenty of water – avoid dehydration.

★ Build in movement and exercise to work off excess adrenalin.

★ Work daily on relaxation, so that your thinking remains clear and focused. You will still feel some nervous energy, which is useful for exams.

★ Test recall and understanding using notes, quizzes, flash cards or explaining aloud.

★ Organise cover for domestic or work responsibilities. Plan for emergencies.

★ Avoid people who make you feel unsure of yourself, the super-confident or super-anxious.

★ Visit the exam room and get the feel of it.

Find out the exam 'instructions'

If possible, familiarise yourself with the instructions, or 'rubric', on exam papers: these can be difficult to understand if you read them for the first time under the stress of the exam itself.

Plan out exam time in advance

For each paper, work out the times that you will start and finish each question. Commit these times to memory; in the exam room, jot them down and keep sight of them.

The night before

★ Check over any exam details you have.

★ Prepare what you will need: pens, ruler, water, snack, exam room number, identity card, warm jumper, etc.

★ Let go of stress: take a walk or get exercise. Use your mindfulness or relaxation techniques.

★ Eat a proper meal. Have a snack and relaxing bath before bed. Leave plenty of time for sleep.

The day of the exam

★ Eat well beforehand to maintain stamina. Include slow-releasing carbohydrates such as bread and cereals, avoiding processed sugar.

★ If you practise mindfulness, plan in time for this before leaving home and for a few moments once in the exam room. (See Cottrell, *Mindfulness for Students*, 2018.)

★ Leave plenty of time in case of travel delays.

★ Plan to arrive at the exam room as it opens: it may take time to find your seat and settle in.

Exam details

A blank template is also available on the companion site.

Subject area:	**Exam title:**
Date:	**Day:** **Time:**
Campus/Site:	**Building:**
Length of exam:	**Room:**

Number of questions I have to answer (in each section, where applicable):

Preparation: time needed for reading through questions; choosing questions; planning answers.
Final check: time needed to check for sense, for errors, that questions are correctly numbered, neatening the script, and so on.

Total preparation and final check time needed:

Time left for writing answers (total time *minus* preparation and final check time):

Total marks available for each question	Length of time to spend on each question	Time to start each new answer
1		
2		
3		
4		
5		

Any unusual features of the paper or exam conditions?

Which aids – dictionaries, calculators, etc. – are permissible for this paper?

What must I take to the exam room? Identity card? Pens? Coloured pencils? Any special equipment? A jumper? Water? Snacks, to be eaten quietly? Glucose tablets?

In the exam

First things

★ Orientate yourself.

★ Find a positive, calm, focused state of mind.

★ Check that you have been given the right exam paper. (Mistakes *do* happen!)

★ Read the instructions slowly, at least twice, taking in what is required.

★ Fill out personal details exactly as required.

★ Take a look at the whole paper. Always check both sides, even if you think one side is blank.

★ Divide your time equally among questions that carry the same marks. Jot down the times you will begin each question.

Selecting exam questions

1 **Read twice**. Read each question at least twice, so you really absorb what is written.
2 **Elaboration**. Work out what is expected, in general, for each question. Which part of the course does it refer to? Towards which issues is the question directing you?
3 **Identify 'possibles'**. Tick all questions you could attempt. Tick twice the ones you could answer best. Don't rush this – it's vital that you choose the questions that will do you justice.
4 **Double-check**. For the questions you select, highlight key words in the title. Notice how many parts there are to the question. Read questions through phrase by phrase to make sure you have not misread or misinterpreted them. At this stage you may realise that a question is not what you thought, and may need to select a different one.
5 **'False friends'**. If a question sounds like one you have done before, check the wording very carefully before you select it. A slight difference in wording might require a very different answer.
6 **Decide**. Decide which questions you will answer and in which order. It can be useful to start with a question you can answer well to warm up, then go on to your best question.
7 **Jot down emergent ideas and material**. At any time, jot down quickly ideas that arise about any of your selected questions, using a separate sheet. Note the question number beside each idea. It can help build answers as you go.

'What if I go blank?'

★ Have a go at recalling your memory triggers or 'hooks' – images or mnemonics or places you were when you revised the material.

★ Don't try to force the memory. Leave a space so you can come back to it: it might come back later.

★ You might be too tense – use a relaxation exercise you have used before (page 167).

★ Use a 'getting started' trick: see page 279.

★ Keep writing. On spare paper, jot down words that have anything to do with the question. These can start to prompt memory and ideas.

★ Ask yourself questions, starting with the most basic – who? when? what? how? – until you become more focused.

Writing exam essays

Follow a similar procedure to that used when writing any other essay. Argue a strong case. Use structure, organisation, evidence and a clear line of reasoning – without these, you will get few marks for content. Exam essays can be *easier* to write because:

★ you need less evidence and fewer examples than for coursework

★ you can write less about each point

★ you can miss out some background detail

★ you don't need to give a bibliography or to write out references in full

★ examiners are generally more sympathetic about weak presentation, minor grammatical errors, spellings, and forgotten details than for coursework.

Use pyramid questions to guide you

Learn the pyramid questions (page 291) as a song, a list, chant or rap: find a rhythm or beat to help recall. Use these to guide your essay planning in the exam room. This is especially useful if you find it hard to organise and structure information at speed, or if you go blank in exams.

Top tips for different kinds of exam

Multiple choice questions (MCQs)

1 **Revise to recognise**. The answers are contained in the MCQ: you just need to be able to recognise the right answer when you see it.

2 **Check the precise wording** of each question. In MCQ exams, most marks are lost through misreading questions.

3 **Check carefully for qualifiers** or absolutes that can catch you out, such as 'always' or 'never'.

4 **Rephrase questions** that have complex wording so they make more sense to you (retaining the core question).

5 **Come up with your own answer** before checking the options – then look to see if it matches an option.

6 **Make it 'true' or 'false'**. If the answer isn't obvious to you, check whether you can turn the question into a statement with a true/false answer. Consider each of the choices as 'true' or 'false'.

7 **Answer easy questions first**. The answers to others might come to mind later on.

8 **Don't make risky guesses**, on the basis of whether you have used an option (such as 'C' or 'true') a lot or not at all.

9 **Use reasoning**. If you don't know the answer, pause to see if you can work out which options to eliminate on the basis of what you do know: reduce the odds of an incorrect response.

10 **Keep going. Stay focused.** When there are many questions, losing a few seconds between each can mean lost time mounts up.

Short answer questions (SAQs)

1 **Revise for depth and breadth**. Use numbered lists and Question and Answer formats to test yourself on a wide range of potential topics.

2 **Prepare examples** to illustrate key concepts or issues.

3 **Count the parts**. There is often a set number of points or steps to cover in SAQs. Make a numbered list to ensure you learn and include them all.

4 **Be precise**. State just what is needed, with accuracy. Avoid waffle and long responses: these won't gain additional marks.

5 **Allocate time wisely** to match the weighting of the questions and so that you answer all required questions.

6 **Make each point stand out**. Don't lose out just because it isn't clear whether you have covered all required points or steps.

7 **Think logically**. If you don't recall an answer at once, think calmly through discussions, formulae, experiments or conventions covered in class.

Orals and presentations

1 **Practise aloud, confidently** before the exam so that this feels familiar. Be aware of when you are mumbling or gabbling.

2 **Don't rush your answers**. Take your time to think through your answers and speak them at a pace others can follow easily.

3 **Repeat the question aloud** – or rephrase it. It gives you more time to think and if you have misinterpreted the question, the examiner might point this out, or you might be able to tell from their response and adjust your answer accordingly.

4 **Don't repeat yourself** – once you have made a statement in a talk or given your answer to questions, don't go over these in different words. Let the examiners absorb what you say, in quiet.

5 **Look like you enjoy it**. Even if you don't, act 'as if' you do. It helps put your examiners or listeners at ease. Stay professional in your approach and retain your concentration.

6 **Decide your message**. If you have a choice, select a topic about which you can make three or more interesting points.

7 **Research the topic well** – don't expect to 'wing it' just because it isn't a written exam.

8 **For presentations**, see Chapter 8.

Doing well in exams

Common pitfalls in examinations ...	... and how to avoid them
1 Doing silly things Silly things can fail exam candidates or lose marks or the examiner's goodwill.	Well before the exam, find out what is required. Make sure you turn up at the right exam centre on the right day. Check that you have been given the right exam paper. Be sure to write your name or exam number on the answer paper and on any additional sheets. Read the questions. Check the back of the exam paper. Answer the right number of questions. Put time aside to check such details carefully.
2 Mystifying the exam The examiner won't pore over your script for hours, nor see through your answer to what you don't know. There is no 'magical ingredient' you have to deliver.	Examiners have a large pile of scripts. They want to get through these as quickly as they can, with just a few minutes for each. They may check your introduction and conclusion for the gist of your argument, skim the answer to evaluate your line of reasoning, check that you are using material from the course to support your answers, and consider what grade the work is worth, using similar criteria to those on page 315. They are unlikely to mark it as closely as tutors mark coursework. Often a second examiner goes through the same process: if the two disagree, a third person (the external examiner) will consider the answer. Only excessively bad grammar, spelling errors or handwriting are likely to stand out.
3 Using exam time poorly and answering too few questions Use all the time available – and wisely!	Give equal time to questions that carry equal marks – and more time to any that carry extra marks. The law of diminishing returns applies to the amount of time spent on any one question: if you spend twice as long on one question, you are very unlikely to gain twice as many marks. You are more likely to pass if you give reasonable answers to the set number of questions than if you spend all your time writing some brilliant essays, but miss one altogether. If you run out of time to complete a question, leave a space – you might save time later so you can return to it at the end.
4 Writing everything you know about a topic There is no value in simply writing down all you know to 'prove' you've learnt it.	The examiner is not interested in how much you know – indeed, you may get no marks at all for simply listing a lot of information. Just as for coursework, marks are given for showing you can make sense of the question, relate it to course issues, debate the issues, develop a line of critical reasoning, evaluate opposing viewpoints, be selective in an intelligent way, and offer relevant supporting evidence.
5 Abandoning structure and the usual essay writing techniques	Because of the speed at which exam markers work, they appreciate answers with clear, well-organised structures, good introductions and conclusions, correctly numbered questions, and clearly labelled scripts which are easy to read. You lose goodwill if your script is messy, illegible or confusing to read.

Exam day strategy: checklist

Do I ...	Yes	No	Things to do, or to watch out for
1 read the whole exam paper carefully?	☐	☐	
2 follow all instructions?	☐	☐	
3 answer the correct number of questions in full?	☐	☐	
4 plan time well, so that I can check through my answers?	☐	☐	
5 know exactly how long I have for each question?	☐	☐	
6 share out time according to the marks available?	☐	☐	
7 use all of the available time?	☐	☐	
8 read each question at least twice?	☐	☐	
9 spend time working out what all the questions mean?	☐	☐	
10 ask myself what the examiner is looking for?	☐	☐	
11 spend enough time considering the best questions for me?	☐	☐	
12 feel confident about what I am expected to do?	☐	☐	
13 find questions that are similar to ones I have practised?	☐	☐	
14 find I have revised enough topics?	☐	☐	
15 know what a 'good' answer looks like?	☐	☐	
16 know which writing style is appropriate?	☐	☐	
17 know the correct format or layout?	☐	☐	
18 plan my answers (on paper or in my head)?	☐	☐	
19 develop a clear argument (where appropriate)?	☐	☐	
20 use examples from the course materials?	☐	☐	
21 keep strictly to answering the question set?	☐	☐	
22 avoid irrelevant detail and going off at tangents?	☐	☐	
23 get to the point quickly?	☐	☐	
24 avoid flowery language and vague introductions?	☐	☐	
25 include an introduction and a conclusion?	☐	☐	
26 keep focused on the exam during the exam?	☐	☐	
27 check my answers carefully for mistakes?	☐	☐	
28 read and correct answers so they make sense?	☐	☐	

If you answered 'yes' to most of these questions, then your chance of exam success is high.

If not, then this gives you some pointers for adapting your strategy. Look through the relevant sections of this *Study Skills Handbook* for guidance on what to practise. If you are still uncertain, consult with your tutor.

Memorisation techniques

Below are tried and tested methods to help remember material you want to recall as needed.

Spaced repetition or 'over-learning'

Repeat the information at least three times. Then check back at spaced intervals over at least several days. Check often, for short periods, rather than longer on fewer occasions.

Test your recall

Testing and quizzing yourself on the information are amongst the most effective memorisation methods.

Sleep on it

The brain needs sleep to lay down memories. Review material, sleep, then check what you can recall.

Association

Link what you need to remember with something you already know. See **Active learning** (pages 110–12).

Mnemonics

Any trick to help you remember is a mnemonic (pronounced *nem-on-ic*). A typical trick is to use the first letter of each keyword or set of items you want to remember to form a single word that prompts memory of the whole – just as 'C·R·E·A·M' for Chapter 5.

Make a memorable listening experience

Discuss what you're trying to learn with friends. Listen to your voice saying or reading it. Record yourself. Use accents. Exaggerate. Be dramatic. Sing it! Rap it!

Write it down

In your own words, write things out over and over again.

Personalise its significance

Relate what you learn to yourself. (How does it *affect* you? Who or where does it remind you of? Why does it matter to you or people you know?)

Playful enjoyment of the material

Think in a playful way that relaxes your brain and helps it enjoy learning the material. Look for the fun, humour, oddities, puzzles, etc.

Draw on advertising techniques

Advertising agencies deliberately set out to make us remember their advertisements. The 'tricks' and 'devices' they employ to prompt our memory can also be used to help us to remember what we study.

Reflection

What makes it memorable?

Think of three adverts (from TV, magazines, hoardings, etc.). What makes these three memorable for you? How could you apply similar devices to help recall course material?

Devices used by advertisers

Which of these devices work best for you?

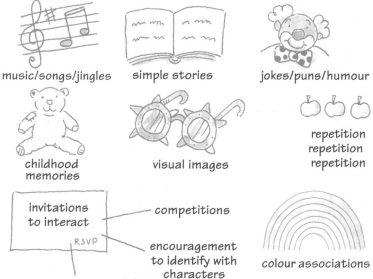

music/songs/jingles simple stories jokes/puns/humour

childhood memories visual images repetition repetition repetition

invitations to interact — competitions

RSVP

encouragement to telephone in

encouragement to identify with characters

colour associations

Help your brain to remember

Talk to your brain

Although it might sound odd, but you can tell your brain what you want it to do and if it can, it responds. Talking to it helps it (you) to pay more attention to what you are doing. Tell it what you want to remember. Ask it to 'go fetch' specific pieces of information, then do something else whilst it searches.

Where did I store that piece of info?

Get your brain to pause

The brain likes to move on to new stimulus quickly, without taking in much of what it considers at speed. Help your brain to linger on material you need to learn so it can absorb more of the details.

★ Tell it to pause.

★ Create spaces when reading, writing or revising to stop and reflect upon what you have just covered. Consider when and how you might make use of it.

★ Use strategies that force the brain to slow down and engage more deeply with the material, such as those in the C·R·E·A·M strategy (pages 89–123).

★ Map out in a diagram, chart or information board how the material connects up: making links helps the brain to pause, make stronger neural connections and integrate information.

Locate the information in the brain

Make an experiment. While trying to visualise or recall information, first look up and to the left; then do the same but looking up and to the right. Also try looking left, then right, and then down to each side.

Which direction worked best? Does this hold true for different kinds of information? When you need to recall something, look first in the direction that is appropriate for you for that specific kind of information.

Work with your brain

Don't fight your brain or give it a hard time remembering. Help it along by giving it what it needs to help you. Unsurprisingly, the starting points are those things you need to survive, learn and thrive, as outlined for 'optimal learning' (pages 76–7). That includes these basics:

Sleep	Breaks	Being hydrated
Food	Good nutrition	Feeling safe

Other ways to enhance the natural working of your brain to improve memory and recall are covered on the following pages. They include:

★ Understanding the basic working of the 'triune' brain

★ Enhancing each stage in the memory process

★ Strengthening your brain's encoding of information

★ Organising information in ways that the brain prefers.

What do we remember?

Flanagan (1997) argues that we remember:

★ 20% of what we read

★ 30% of what we hear

★ 40% of what we see

★ 50% of what we say

★ 60% of what we do

★ 90% of what we read, hear, see, say *and* do.

Is that true of you?

The triune brain

The brain has three main functional areas.

1. The neo-cortex

This is what people think of when they imagine a brain or 'grey matter'. It controls intellectual processes such as language, thinking and handling numbers.

2. The mammalian brain (or limbic system)

This consists of various organs that control functions such as emotions, pleasure, romance, moods, and immunity to disease. It affects our attitude to learning and can draw resources away from our grey matter.

3. The reptile brain

In evolutionary terms, this is the oldest part of the brain. It manages basic instinctual and survival responses. It interprets excess stress or anxiety as a 'danger' to our survival, then tries to help us 'escape' by drawing resources to the large muscles. It produces extra adrenalin, putting us in a heightened, alert state, ready to flee. This takes resources away from parts of the brain used for thinking and logical argument. Being in 'survival mode' is not helpful to study – if we don't use up the adrenalin, we can feel tense, over-alert, easily distracted and unable to think clearly and concentrate.

Learning

Learning involves interaction between these three aspects of the brain, which are linked through the limbic system. As a result, some psychologists believe emotions are the strongest stimulus to memory. The Accelerated Learning Movement uses music, images and other associations to create unconscious emotional arousal that speeds learning.

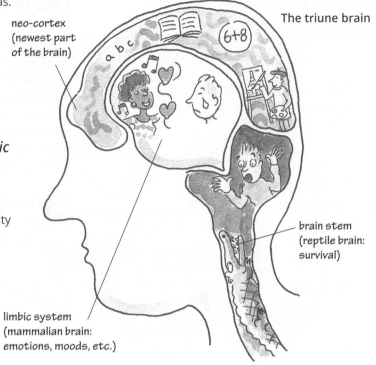

The triune brain

neo-cortex (newest part of the brain)

brain stem (reptile brain: survival)

limbic system (mammalian brain: emotions, moods, etc.)

A state of 'relaxed alertness' helps the imagination, and increases suggestibility and openness to new information (Rose, 1985).

Optimising study with the triune brain

Get relaxed: to help exit 'survival mode'. If you feel tense, use up excess adrenalin: go for a walk, stamp your feet, exercise or move around as you learn.

Adapt your mindset: take a positive emotional outlook on each task; persuade yourself it is easy, enjoyable, exciting, fun, interesting, full of surprises.

Engage your emotions. Set yourself targets that engage your competitiveness; make it personal. Make your notes pleasant and appealing. See pages 227–8 and 393.

Listen to music which has an expressive and recognisable melody played on string instruments, and has a steady bass rhythm of about 60 beats per minute. Possibilities include classical Baroque music (such as Bach or Vivaldi), classical Indian music, and New Age healing tapes.

Work with the memory process

Another way of helping your brain to improve recall is to enhance the operation of distinct stages of the memory process.

Stages in the memory process

1 *Taking in information* – noticing or attending to new stimulus (information) and absorbing it.
2 *Retaining it* – in short-term memory.
3 *Encoding it* – interacting with the information in working memory so that the brain can store it in long-term memory.
4 *Maintaining it* – reducing loss through disuse or interference.
5 *Recalling it* – retrieving or remembering information, whether on purpose, by accident, or in dreams. Recall can seem accurate even when it is not.
6 *Refreshing* – relearning after forgetting.

Stage 1: Taking in information

What we already know and have a name for affects how we direct our attention, what we notice, and therefore what goes into memory. We need to maintain our attention in order to remember.

If you study on 'automatic pilot', little attention is involved so you will remember less. You will remember more if you:

★ direct your attention consciously and purposefully

★ focus in a relaxed way – not with hard concentration

★ take breaks and make changes in what you are doing, so as to maintain relaxed attention – a few minutes moving around or doing something different is sufficient

★ link information to what you know

★ give names and labels to information so that the brain can grasp hold of it more easily

★ deliberately arrange or adapt information so that it is structured and yet stands out as odd, distinct, different or more interesting – so that it grabs your attention.

Stage 2: Retaining information long enough to remember it

Rehearsing new information in short-term memory helps the brain to hold onto it. Repeating it gives the brain time to call up stored memories to help you make sense of the information and encode it for storage.

Rehearsal must start within a few seconds, as information fades quickly. It is a useful strategy for holding onto names, dates, numbers, formulae and instructions for long enough to write them down. You can then employ other memory strategies to remember the information long-term.

Stage 3: Encoding information – the key to memory?

The brain encodes new information so that it can be represented in the memory. Coding mechanisms vary, and include oral, auditory, tactile, verbal, semantic (related to meaning), visual, emotional, or motor (using a muscle sequence), or relate to stories, events and other connections.

For example, when you tell a story, the brain encodes the pattern of fine-muscle movements you used to speak and stores them. It can also encode and store the sound of your speech on your own ear; the images and emotions that the story brought to mind; the look of the text; and details such as who was in the room, or the buzzing of a neon light. The brain links information it has encoded – so any one aspect could trigger streams of memory later. The more facets of an experience the brain has encoded, the more triggers there are to help rich recall.

It follows that you can assist your memory by *choosing* to encode information in several ways. Some are suggested below, but you can devise your own too.

Use multiple encoding to reinforce memory

Use your environment

★ Use a different room for each topic.

★ Notice aspects of the environment such as the light or feel of the room – how do you feel in that place?

★ Attach your notes to the furniture. Notice their location.

★ Associate a different location with each subject. Associate furniture, windows, plants and ornaments with particular topics.

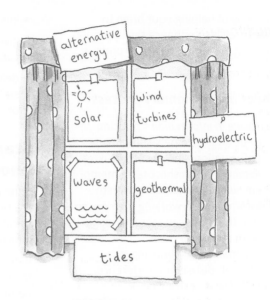

Use your clothes

★ Associate items of clothing with topics in your learning – a shoe could represent one aspect of foreign policy; each button on a shirt could represent a quotation. Clothes with patterns, pockets and buttons are especially useful.

★ Wear these clothes into the exam room as a memory trigger.

Use the parts of your body

Parts of your body are especially helpful as triggers to memory, as your body will be there in the exam room!

For example, each hand could represent an essay plan – each finger one major topic; each segment of each finger a principal reference you would use. The fingernails could represent counter-arguments; the knuckles could be associated with relevant quotations.

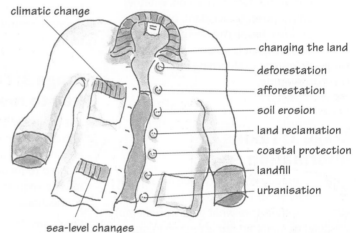

Use motor memory

★ Study on the move. If you exercise, associate each movement with something you wish to remember. To refresh the memory, go through the exercise in your mind.

★ Writing, drawing and speaking also use motor memory: the fine-muscle sequence is recorded by the brain.

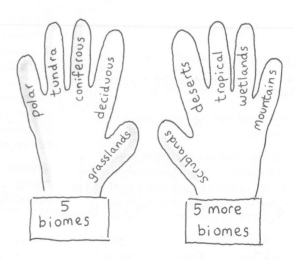

Use multiple encoding to reinforce memory

Use auditory memory

★ Using a digital recorder, record yourself and then play this recording back.

★ Sing an essay plan for a possible exam essay to a well-known tune. Make a list of which tunes go with each subject.

★ Go over a topic with a real or imaginary friend, or your cat.

★ Read notes aloud in peculiar voices. Over-dramatise to make the notes memorable.

♫ The Coriolis Effect is the deflection of winds by the Earth's rotation

I knew that

Use visual memory

★ Make page layouts clear and attractive.

★ Turn your material into a film sequence that you can watch in your mind's eye.

★ Assign to a topic an object such as a car, and label different bits of the object with the things you need to remember: the steering wheel with your main point; the four wheels with four main theorists; the doors with examples of practical applications of the theory; items in the boot could remind you of background information or historical development; and parts of the engine or objects on the front seat could indicate future developments.

★ To remember complex lists and formulae, such as accountancy balance sheets, use a sequence of images, linked by a story.

★ Use scale (size) and visually distinct images to separate out similar or confusing material, such as information about similar theories. Arrange these in a visual hierarchy.

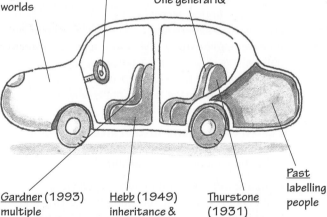

There are many views of intelligence

Futures
how individuals represent their worlds

Spearman (1927)
One general IQ

Gardner (1993)
multiple intelligences

Hebb (1949)
inheritance & environment

Thurstone (1931)
6 types of intelligence

Past
labelling people

bad solution

OK solution

good solution

excellent solution

best solution

Use multiple encoding to reinforce memory

Use colour

★ Assign each subject area a different combination of colours.

★ You may find it useful to use a given colour for references or for formulae throughout your notes, so that you can spot these easily.

★ Give each theme a different colour. As each theme appears, highlight it in the colour you allocated to it. You can then see at a glance which pages cover what, and which combinations of themes come up together. This makes reading more interactive and finding information faster.

★ Use colour on pattern notes (page 228) or in concept pyramids (page 291) to indicate information of similar types or levels. Organising your information clearly in this way can aid recall (see page 402). You may also find that you remember different colour combinations easily.

★ To help you recall sequences of information, use colour combinations that are familiar to you, such as the rainbow, traffic lights, or national flags.

Use verbal memory

★ Reduce information to keywords.

★ Organise information into hierarchies under headings (see **Concept pyramids**, page 291).

★ Write out your information in the fewest words possible – this process promotes focus, interaction with the material and rehearsal, as well as providing 'at a glance' reminders – all of which help with recall.

Use semantic memory

★ Spend time considering the *implications* of what you have found out. For example, who is affected? What would it mean for the future? What changes might arise? Which theories could this information overturn? Are there legal or ethical consequences?

★ Think of a different way of saying what you have already written.

★ Decide which are the three most important aspects of the subject, or the most important theories or ideas. Then decide which is the *one* most important.

★ Consider all the ways in which one area of a subject is similar to another.

Stage 4: Maintaining it

Reducing loss from disuse

If we don't use material, we lose it. Most information is lost in the first 24 hours: if you can hold onto it for a day, you are more likely to remember it forever. We forget material fast in the first few minutes, then less so as time goes by. Memories that require or incorporate muscle movement fade less quickly. We can reduce how much we forget – by drawing upon it in passing, when making sense of further new material, or by incorporating it into our knowledge base and values.

Reducing loss from 'interference'

Quick forgetting occurs mainly because of the vast range of interference the brain encounters, such as lapses in attention, everyday distractions, emotions, stresses, new experience, as well as from the next thing we read or study. If we cover a great deal of material in a short time, each new piece is likely to replace those we have just learnt or else interfere with the next thing we learn. That is why, as a student, it is useful to:

★ **Learn to focus and sustain attention**: some people use mindfulness as outlined in Cottrell, (2018) to enhance these abilities.

★ **Engage actively** with material, organising, clarifying, explaining, reflecting, reinforcing and encoding it as outlined above and in Chapter 5.

★ **Alternate tasks**. Avoid learning two similar kinds of information in quick succession: the more similar the material or task, the greater the interference.

★ **Vary activity**. Intersperse academic tasks with those that cause less interference such as music, dance, exercise, relaxation and sleep.

Stages of the memory process

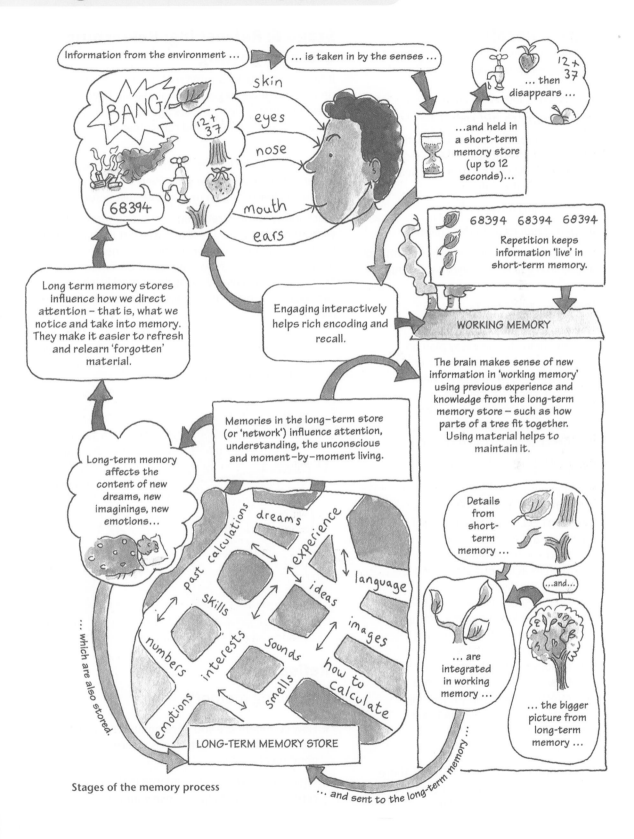

Information from the environment ...

... is taken in by the senses ...

... then disappears ...

skin
eyes
nose
mouth
ears

BANG

12 + 37

68394

...and held in a short-term memory store (up to 12 seconds)...

68394   68394   68394

Repetition keeps information 'live' in short-term memory.

Long term memory stores influence how we direct attention – that is, what we notice and take into memory. They make it easier to refresh and relearn 'forgotten' material.

Engaging interactively helps rich encoding and recall.

WORKING MEMORY

The brain makes sense of new information in 'working memory' using previous experience and knowledge from the long-term memory store – such as how parts of a tree fit together. Using material helps to maintain it.

Memories in the long–term store (or 'network') influence attention, understanding, the unconscious and moment–by–moment living.

Long-term memory affects the content of new dreams, new imaginings, new emotions...

Details from short-term memory ...

dreams
experience
past calculations
language
skills
ideas
numbers
interests
sounds
images
emotions
smells
how to calculate

... and ...

... are integrated in working memory ...

... the bigger picture from long-term memory ...

LONG-TERM MEMORY STORE

... which are also stored.

Stages of the memory process

... and sent to the long-term memory ...

Work with the memory process

Stage 5: Recall

Good recall is linked to how much attention and awareness you bring to processes of taking in material and encoding it.

Over-learning to aid recall

If you want to recall information at will, such as for exams or for complicated sequences that you use regularly, you can use 'over-learning'. This is a combination of:

★ active learning (Chapter 5)

★ using techniques from this chapter

★ checking over what you have learnt, multiple times, until you know it without prompts.

Strategy for over-learning

1. Make a set of pattern notes or an outline for an essay plan on a large index card or on paper, so that you have an overview.
2. Write names, dates and keywords for the references for each topic on index cards. Check that you can recite or reproduce the information on the card from memory.
3. If you can't, put the prompt card into a plastic folder (so it won't get smudged) and carry it around with you. Glance at it briefly in spare moments, such as at the bus stop or while doing the dishes.
4. Do this several times over a few days. Just looking at the prompt from time to time, or running the information through your head, will keep the memory fresh. Little and often is more effective than simply repeating the information over and over on one occasion.

If you still find material hard to recall, there is probably a way of encoding it that suits you better: experiment to find it.

Stage 6: Refreshing: Relearning after forgetting

It takes less time to commit material to memory a second time round. If we forget material that we have revised, or even information learnt years ago such as at school or for a quiz, we learn it faster and remember it better when we return to it.

This indicates why it pays to interact, learn and review material from early in the year. Even if you forget most of it, you can learn it again much faster just before the exam.

Much information is retained in our long-term stores without our being aware of it. If we start to think about the topic, snippets of information can emerge that we might not even realise we had learnt or remembered. That it is why it is useful to jot down quickly what you can recall of a topic – it can stimulate release of stored memories.

Great! It's all coming back to me now!

When refreshing memory, it helps if you learn correctly the first time around!

Reflection

Improving memory

★ How confident are you of remembering information for exams and other situations where you need good recall?

★ Which of the strategies explored in this chapter could you use to help improve your recall?

Memory thrives on organisation

Activity

Organisation and memory

1 Read List A for 15 seconds, then cover it.
2 Recite a nursery rhyme (to prevent rehearsal).
3 Write down the words you remember.
4 Check List A and jot down your score.

List A

plum	elbow	giraffe	caravan
puppy	banana	foot	apple
pony	cherry	barge	bungalow

Now do the same with List B, including the underlined words. Even if you did not do well with the first list, have a go.

List B

Fruit	Animal	Home	Body
plum	giraffe	house	foot
banana	puppy	apartment	knee
apple	donkey	bungalow	elbow
cherry	pony	caravan	hand

You probably remembered many more items from List B. List B is more memorable because:

★ grouping similar items together helps recall

★ using group headings helps recall

★ being able to see that there are only four types of information gives the task manageable boundaries

★ many of the items on List B were also in List A – and going over information again helps recall.

Organising information into pyramids

Concept pyramids (see pages 289–91) organise associated information into hierarchies. They are excellent memory aids.

In an experiment in 1969, Bower and other psychologists asked a group of people to learn 112 words. The words were grouped and linked meaningfully, as in List B above, and organised into four pyramids. People remembered 100% of the words by the third attempt.

By contrast, a second group of people were given the same words, also arranged into pyramid shapes, but this time with the words randomly assigned to each pyramid – they were not meaningfully (or semantically) linked. The second group remembered only 47% of the words by the third attempt.

This suggests the importance of both:

★ linking information meaningfully, *and*

★ organising ideas into hierarchies or concept pyramids.

Review

1 **Find your method**

Memory is an active process. There are innumerable ways of enhancing it: if one doesn't work, try another that suits you or the material better.

2 **Rehearse and self-test**

Repeat at least three times. Check or test your recall at least three times.

3 **Focus your attention**

Give material full attention at least once, so your brain knows what it is meant to be taking in.

4 **Space it out**

Space out the times you revise material and test recall over several days, so your brain has time to work on it between each occasion.

5 **Create mnemonics**

Use memory joggers and have fun inventing your own. Go over these until you can't forget them.

6 **Use the power of sleep**

Once you have actively worked with material to aid recall, let the brain lay down memory of it whilst you sleep.

7 **Optimise brain power**

Enhance your memory by working with your brain so it can do its job. Feed it, hydrate it, rest it, stimulate it, entertain it.

8 **Manage brain resources**

Work on reducing stress and anxiety so that the brain doesn't divert the resources needed for thought and recall into 'survival' responses.

9 **Chunk and organise**

The brain likes information sorted, chunked, organised, layered, labelled, numbered, linked – so it can retrieve material more quickly and easily.

10 **Cover all bases**

Work to your strengths – and address thought processes that you tend to neglect. If you think with pictures, number and sequence these. If you use lists, sing or colour them. If you enjoy detail, ensure you have the whole picture and work out how everything fits together. If you like the 'big picture', attend to sequence, order and levels of significance.

11 **Shock, horror, drama, funny, moving, weird!**

Make the brain sit up and take notice! Work with your material and use mnemonics in ways that the brain finds hard to forget.

12 **Use multiple encoding: combine methods**

look at it	repeat it with rhythm	write it	summarise it
sing it	break it up	draw it	organise it into lists
colour it	give it headings	number it	give it a shape
act it	turn it into a diagram	repeat it	make it bizarre
say it aloud	sleep on it	add humour to it	look for patterns in it

Appendix: Further resources

Below is a list of general sources useful for students, also available on the companion site at www.studyskillshandbook.co.uk for easy access to links.

Also recommended: you might also find it useful to see *The Macmillan Student Planner* which is updated annually and lists a wide range of useful websites, contacts, apps and other resources for students.

Maintaining calm; managing stress

www.mind.org.uk/information-support/tips-for-everyday-living/student-life/#.W_BNCKd0eYV – how to cope with student life. A range of downloadable resources from the mental health charity Mind.

www.studentminds.org.uk/informationhub.html – information hub. Information and resources from student mental health charity Student Minds.

www.nhs.uk/conditions/stress-anxiety-depression/understanding-stress – how to deal with stress. Free National Health Service website with lots of information about managing stress.

Cottrell, S. M. (2018). *Mindfulness for Students.* London: Red Globe Press. Companion site with guided meditations and links to resources: https://macmillanihe.com/resources/pages/mindfulness-for-students.

Cottrell, S. M. (2019). *50 Ways to Manage Stress*. London: Red Globe Press.

Well-being

www.studenthealth.co.uk – health advice for students, written by doctors

www.studentrecipes.com – simple recipes aimed at students

Most major supermarkets and media providers host a wide range of recipes on their websites, e.g. www.bbcgoodfood.com

Employability and personal development

www.prospects.ac.uk – information about graduate employment

www.milkround.com – career guidance for students

www.companieshouse.gov.uk – lists all UK public companies

https://ise.org.uk – useful publications on graduate and employer trends

http://vault.com – what it is like to work for named companies

www.ratemyplacement.co.uk – opportunities for work placements and internships

www.gov.uk/set-up-business – advice on setting up your own business

Cottrell, S. M. (2017). *Skills for Success: Personal Development Planning and Employability*. 3rd edn. London: Red Globe Press.

Cottrell, S. M. (2019). *50 Ways to Boost Your Employability.* London: Red Globe Press.

Useful study apps

GoConqr (iOS and Android) – create slides, flashcards and mind maps from your notes. The app allows you to collaborate with other students.

Inspiration (iOS) – mind mapping app. Also available as a PC version from www.inspiration.com.

RefMe (iOS and Android) – turns webpages or scanned book bar codes into references in a variety of formats. Also includes a plagiarism checker.

MyStudyLife (iOS, Android and Windows) – synchs your timetable and exams across all devices. The app will give reminders.

Hold (iOS and Android) – block access to distractions such as social media and earn points for doing so. Points can be exchanged for a variety of rewards such as free cinema tickets or coffee.

10 Relating your studies to real life. *Effective. This can help to make your studies more relevant, interesting and meaningful, making it easier to understand the material and to remain motivated.*

Chapter 8 Being fair to everyone in the group (page 182)

★ Does everybody get a chance to contribute, or do some people (or groups) dominate?

★ If people have accents, or dialects, or stutters, are they treated with the same respect when they speak?

★ Is everybody's experience and background included in the way subjects are discussed? Are there assumptions that everybody is married, in a relationship, or wants to be? Or shares the same cultural background and assumptions? Or is able to get about easily?

★ When people make comments or ask questions, are they sensitive to the feelings of others – or aware of issues that might cause distress?

★ Where does the group meet? Can everybody get there, even in a wheelchair or using a stick?

★ Do you know when somebody is trying to lip-read? What could group members do to make this easier? Examples include keeping their hands and writing materials away from their faces, and not sitting in silhouette against the source of light.

★ What might cause interference or pain for someone using a hearing-aid?

★ What words or behaviour might other people find offensive?

★ Are there people who look left out, or uncomfortable, or angry? Why is this happening?

Chapter 11 Advanced online searches (page 241)

1 False. 'AND' excludes references that do not contain both words, so there are likely to be fewer references. (Page 240.)

2 True. (Page 240.)

3 *A*. (Page 240.)

4 *C* – the search will find only matches of the exact phrase. (Page 240.)

5 **design*** would find **design**, **designers** and **designs**, but would also find irrelevant entries such as **designate**.

6 *A*. A suitable search string would be: **nurs* AND method*.** This would find additional references such as pages that mention **nursing**, **nurses**, **method**, **methodology** or **methodologies**.

B. A suitable search string would be: **monopoly? as a trend? in world? trade?** You might then retrieve an item such as *Monopolies as a developing pattern in the global market*.

7 *B* – this focuses on relevant items but looks for relevant alternatives such as **world**, **designers** and **designs**. *A* might narrow your search too far, and *C* might include many irrelevant items such as **global warming**, **globalisation**, or **local design**, yet omit reference to **designers**.

Chapter 11 Detecting plagiarism and copying (page 248)

Text 1 This is plagiarism (see page 70, section 9). Although a few words have been changed, this is copied out almost entirely word for word, and there are no references. It is not acceptable.

Text 2 This is not an example of plagiarism because it summarises the original text (pages 65–70) in the writer's own words. The quality of the text could be strengthened by including some references. However, the summary is sufficiently general to mean that references are not essential in order to avoid plagiarism. It is acceptable.

Text 3 This plagiarises the original text (pages 65–8). It copies, almost word for word, a sentence or bullet point from each of these pages. Tutors refer to this as 'cut and paste' or 'scissors and paste' writing. It is not acceptable.

Text 4 Text 4 is almost identical to text 3, but is properly referenced. However, tutors would not be pleased to see so little in the student's own words. If this continued throughout the essay, it would receive a very low mark. It would simply be well-referenced copying – which is not acceptable.

Text 5 This text is in the student's own words. The student has made his or her own connections between different parts of the original text in a meaningful way, rather than simply 'cutting and pasting'. The student has read other material on the subject and included this. There is proper referencing both of the source of ideas and of individual pieces of research. This is acceptable work.

Text 6   This student simply paraphrases the source text (pages 65–6). This might be acceptable for writing a summary or a journalistic type of article. However, there are no references and little evidence of any independent thinking or 'working' with the material. This may not be deemed to be plagiarism or copying, but for an essay or report it would receive a low mark.

Chapter 12   Critical thinking when reading (pages 257–63)

Passage 1: Rochborough Health

Activity 1: Line of reasoning

'Outdoor play is good for children's health, so Rochborough needs better facilities for it.'

Activity 2: Vested interests

The article was published by the Playcouncil, who are likely to have a vested interest in arguing for more supervised play spaces.

Activity 3: Types of evidence used

The main evidence is of two kinds: surveys and anecdotes. The detail about the Arkash family is anecdotal (it is just one person's experience). There is also a statistic about garden ownership.

Activity 4: Evaluating the evidence

The evidence about health and parental attitudes comes from official sources which could be considered relatively good 'authorities' and thus reliable. This evidence is relevant and contributes to the argument.

On the other hand, the writer generalises from only one set of health factors (those related to the lungs). It is possible that children who play outdoors have *different* health problems – such as skin complaints or broken ankles. Alternatively, it is possible that the children who played indoors did so because they were more prone to sickness already (such as asthma and pollen allergies). Sickness may have been the *cause* of their playing indoors, rather than the *effect*.

We don't know how representative the children in the survey were of all Rochborough children.

The anecdotal details about the Arkash child and the fox are emotive, and not really relevant to the main argument. The anecdote provides human interest for journalistic writing, but would be unacceptable in most academic writing.

No source is given for the figure of 18% garden ownership: we can't judge whether it is reliable.

The writer twice mentions the effects of outdoor play on social interaction, but gives no evidence or details. She or he could link this in more to the main argument.

Activity 5: Conclusions

The conclusion is that Rochborough should provide more supervised outdoor play areas.

Activity 6: Implicit conclusions

1   There is no explicit conclusion. The implicit conclusion is that you should buy this plant.

2   The explicit conclusion is that the election was unfair. The implicit conclusions are that the election results shouldn't count and that the election should be held again.

3   The explicit conclusion is that the tree is dangerous. The implicit conclusion is that it should be made safe or removed.

Activity 7: Use of evidence

The writer makes a reasonable case and gives supporting evidence. However, there is insufficient evidence to support the conclusion that 'in order to improve the health of its children, Rochborough needs to provide more supervised outdoor play areas'. We don't know what it is about playing outdoors that led to the health improvements. For example, it may be that children ran about more when they were outdoors, and that an indoor running area would have the same effect.

Underlying assumptions

The passage assumes:

1   That playing outdoors is better for all children's health. This may not be the case.

2   That the health of children who play indoors at present would necessarily improve by playing outdoors. This may not be true.

3   That playing outside decreases the incidence of asthma and bronchial conditions.

4   That beneficial effects are available only from outdoor play areas. In fact, it may have been other factors about the outdoor play, such

as space to run or things to climb, that led to improved health indicators.

5   That there are not enough supervised play areas already for Rochborough children. No figures are quoted for existing supervised play areas so we do not know whether more spaces are needed. The sources the writer quoted don't mention a need for more play spaces. We do not know what percentage of children already play outdoors. All these gaps mean that the writer has not given sufficient evidence to support the conclusion.

Activity 8: Critical analytical thinking

Below, is passage 3 again, set out with reference numbers added to help you locate points raised in the analysis that follows.

Passage 3: Children at Play

Children need to play outdoors (1) and yet it is amazing how few children (2) get that opportunity today. Although Smith (2004) argues that 48% of children prefer to play inside, Jones (1964) found that 98% of children in Britain prefer to play outdoors (2b). I spoke to some parents in Rochborough (2) who said their children missed out by not being able to play down by the river or roam the countryside in safety (3). Most children are now television addicts or, worse, are addicted to computer games (4). Everybody knows that this is damaging children educationally (5), and yet nothing is done about it. This is certainly true of Rochborough's children (4), and the main reason is that they do not have anywhere to play (6). Hardly anybody in Rochborough has a garden (2). It would be better for their health if they played outdoors (7), but parents say they won't let them unless supervised play areas are provided (2). The parents are worried that they cannot see their children when they are playing. What chance is there for the health of citizens in Rochborough if its children do not get to play outdoors, and end up as TV addicts? (8)

Analysis
Logical progression: the line of reasoning

This kind of writing is likely to receive a comment such as 'What is your point?' It is difficult to identify

the thread running through the passage: the line of reasoning is weak. The writer hops backwards and forwards between different types of information, as at (8), having already mentioned these points earlier. The final sentence does not add to what has been stated earlier, at (4).

The conclusion

The conclusion is not clear. The nearest approximation to a conclusion is at (1), 'Children need to play outdoors', as this largely sums up the passage. The writing does not draw its information towards a final conclusion, and the final lines of the passage don't lead anywhere. Compare this with the 'Rochborough Health' passage, which leads to a clear conclusion.

The evidence

The evidence is weak, with insufficient detail. The places marked (2) all require further evaluation of the evidence: 'How many children? How many parents? How representative are they of Rochborough parents as a whole? What other views were expressed? How many exactly have gardens? How do we know this?'

A tutor might also comment that the writer has not analysed the sources. At (2b), although the writer uses statistics, these are not recent. She or he offers no possible explanations for why Smith's and Jones' research had different findings – such as that they were looking at two different generations of children. The evidence cited confuses the argument rather than supporting it.

Offering evidence to support reasoning

At (7) and (5), issues about health or education could be developed into interesting points, but no evidence or details are given so the reasoning is weak. Compare (7) with the same point in the 'Rochborough Health' passage, which is more convincing.

The evidence: emotive language

At (3) the writer appeals to a 'golden age' when childhood was safer or better. Referring to children as 'addicts' is also very emotive.

The evidence: sources of information

The assertions at (4) may or may not be true. No reliable sources are quoted, so these may be just speculation.

Underlying assumptions

That 'Everybody knows' (5) is an assumption on the part of the writer. How does he or she know what 'Everybody knows'? Our own experience might suggest to us that most children are not 'addicts'.

Does the reasoning support the conclusion?

The main conclusion, that children need to play outdoors, is poorly supported by the reasoning. Although some reasons are given, these are in a jumbled order, without supporting evidence, and are mixed in with irrelevancies such as computer addiction. It is not clear whether an argument is being made on grounds of children's health.

Activity 9: Descriptive or critical? (page 268)

Passage 1

This is mainly descriptive writing. The writer describes the way that the living world is divided between animals and plants, and gives information about recent research. The passage consists mostly of statements. The statements are not linked and ordered in such a way that they build up clearly towards the conclusion. There is little weighing of the evidence in the build-up to the conclusion. The significance of the conclusion itself is not very clear.

Passage 2

This writing is more critical than the previous writing as it gives a reasoned account for the difficulties in classifying bacteria. It draws on research to show why the difficulties existed, and evaluates the significance of the research for the wider question of classifying life forms.

Passage 3

This is critical, analytical writing. The writing evaluates the evidence for the theory that the right brain is associated with creativity. The writer draws out aspects about current findings that may prove to be significant in the long term. The writer questions 'reasonable assumptions', making clear what has and has not been proved at the time of writing.

Passage 4

This is descriptive writing. It describes one aspect of how the brain works.

Passage 5

This is descriptive writing. It describes Bowlby's theories but does not critically evaluate them. Compare this with the critical analytical writing on pages 337–40.

Chapter 15 Devising your own essay title (page 321)

1 The title is far too general. Compare this with a stronger title such as: 'To what extent have reptiles been more successful than amphibians in adapting to environmental challenges?'

2 The title is too general. You could give more focus by adding: 'Discuss with reference to ...', and add a specific region, timescale and field of enquiry. For example: 'Discuss with reference to the control of nuclear waste in Europe and the Pacific Rim' or 'Discuss with reference to the impact of mobile phones on personal safety'.

3 This title is too long and contains too many questions. An alternative question for this topic could be: 'Domestic technology since 1970: labour-saving or labour-creating?'

4 The title is biased towards one (negative) point of view, and contains no obvious question.

5 Descriptive essays are unlikely to give opportunities for the critical, analytical reasoning that gains good marks. Contrast this with: 'How effective have placebos been in testing medical interventions for children?'

Chapter 16 Formulating your hypothesis (page 355)

Hypothesis 01: This hypothesis is worded clearly but is not precise. It states that physical activity would reduce depression but it does not give any details about what kind of activity and how much of it would have what kind of impact upon whom.

Hypothesis 02: This is not worded as a hypothesis because it does not state what the research is expected to reveal.

Hypothesis 03: This is clear, precise and states exactly what amount and kind of exercise over what timescales would have what sort of impact for which population.

international students'. *Journal of Counseling Psychology* **59**(1), 97–106.

Wilkinson, G. (1997). *Understanding Stress*. Family Doctor Series. London: British Medical Association.

Wilson, M. (2017). 'The search for that elusive sense of belonging, respect and visibility in academia'. In Gabriel, C. and Tate, S. A. (eds.) *Inside the Ivory Tower*. London: UCL/Trentham Books. pp. 108–23.

Wilson, P. (1997). *Calm at Work*. London: Penguin.

Wilson, T. D., Reinhard, D. A., Westgate, E. C., Gilbert, D. T., Ellerbeck, N., Hahn, C., Brown, C. I. and Shaked, A. (2014). 'Just think: The challenges of the disengaged mind'. *Science*, 4 July, **345**(6192), 75–7.

Woese, C. R. (1994). 'There must be a prokaryote somewhere: Microbiology's search for itself'. *Microbiological Reviews*, **58**, 1–9.

Wood, E., Zivcakova, L., Gentile, P., Archer, K., De Pasquale, D. and Nosko, A. (2012). 'Examining the impact of off-task multi-tasking with technology on real-time classroom learning'. *Computers and Education*, **58**, 365–74.

Wright, K. P. Jr., Hull, J. T., Hughes, R. J., Ronda, J. M. and Czeisler, C. A. (2006). 'Sleep and wakefulness out of phase with internal biological time impairs learning in humans'. *Journal of Cognitive Neuroscience*, **18**, 508–21. DOI: 10.1162/jocn.2006.18.4.508.

Yoder, J. D. and Hochevar, C. M. (2005). 'Encouraging active learning can improve students' performance on examinations'. *Teaching of Psychology*, **32**(2), 91–5.

YouGov (2016). 'One in four students suffer from mental health problems', 9 August 2016. Available at: https://yougov.co.uk/news/2016/08/09/quarter-britains-students-are-afflicted-mentalhea/ (accessed 18 November 2018).

YouthSight (2013). 'Psychological distress in the UK student population: Prevalence, timing and accessing support. Final research findings'. Available at: www.nightline.ac.uk/wpcontent/uploads/2014/08/Psychological-distress-prevalence-timings-accessingsupport-Aug-2014.pdf (accessed 18 November 2018).

Index

abbreviations   102, 229, 303

abilities   66, 69–70

abilities, spatial   66

abstracts
  in journal articles   238, 243
  published   238
  for reports   367

academic careers   12, 50, 60

academic conventions   14, 281, 302–3, 306–8
  features of academic writing   281, 302–3

academic discipline   22

academic integrity   22, 247–8

academic performance   2, 21

academic skills   14, 22, 169
  see also APT-S; study skills

academic success   vii, 1, 6, 7, 9, 11, 12, 24, 30, 59, 66–8, 119, 169
  see also golden rules

action learning groups   183

action plans   27
  for revision   381
  study skills   27

active learning   5, 89, 110–12, 122, 215–18, 220, 221
  active reading   215–223

agency   15, 21, 32–3, 76–7
  see also control; engagement; self-efficacy

ambiguity   17

analysis, qualitative and quantitative   44, 256–65, 409–11

analytical thinking   253, 254, 255, 263, 317

analytical writing   267–70

annotating   221–3

anxieties   15, 64, 115, 151, 152–3; 164–7
  see also stress management

applying knowledge   16, 43, 44, 75, 103, 314, 407

apps   36, 84, 147, 159, 278

APT-S study skills   20–3, 169

argument   304, 311, 312, 317, 321, 326
  clarity of   281, 302

see also critical thinking, reasoning, line of

articles in journals *see* journals

assessment   14, 33
  see also assignments; grades; marking criteria

assignments   35, 104, 105, 133, 137, 140, 157, 273, 282–3
  see also essays; writing
  assignment brief   23, 188, 236, 284–5, 300, 345, 346, 349, 351

assignments, managing   319–44, 345–72

assistive technologies   41, 82

assumptions making   202
  identifying assumptions   262, 409

attendance   30, 31, 32, 39, 40, 105, 156

attention   43, 72, 84, 217, 221, 224, 407

attitude   5, 78

attributing sources   245, 247, 249–51

'audience-awareness'   191, 368

auditory learning strategies   68, 217, 225, 390, 391, 392–9

autonomy   21

averaging   264

bar charts   362

barriers to learning   19, 154

'belonging', sense of   33, 34, 36, 152, 183

bibliographic databases   234, 238

bibliographies   250

blogs   99, 101

Boolean operators   235;   240

boredom, managing   102, 104, 114, 141, 148, 379, 388

brain   69, 151, 393, 394
  and better learning   42, 77, 393, 395–400, 401–3, 404
  plasticity/adaptability   5, 69
  triune   394

understanding your brain   69, 99, 141, 151, 393

breaks when learning   77, 141, 165

calm, finding   166, 167, 168, 384, 388

capped marks   30

career planning   10, 11, 12, 15, 44, 50–1, 55–7, 58, 59, 60, 62, 101, 159, 201
  see also personal development planning

case studies   93   370–1

causality   258–9

categorising   289–91

challenge, taking on   2, 4, 7, 9, 119, 155, 300

challenging others' ideas   36

charts, bar and pie charts   362

cheating   30, 159, 184, 235
  see also plagiarism

checklists, using   139

choices, wise choices as a student   7, 10, 11, 12, 15, 19, 49, 50, 114, 154

citing sources *see* referencing

'coasting'   6

classes, scheduled   13, 32, 34–39
  follow-up   40

collaborative learning   15, 18, 23, 41, 57, 159, 171–196

commitment, making a   154, 168

commitment required   15, 55

communication skills   22, 177–81, 183, 196
  e-communications for study   18, 41
  group projects   41, 185–88, 192–5

community, learning   34
  see also learning community

companion site   2

compare and contrast   44, 281, 285, 312, 321, 325, 328

completing your course   12, 154–8, 160–1

Notes

Notes

Notes